A History of Britain in 100 Objects

Paul Chrystal

DestinWorld
publishing

First Edition 2022

ISBN 978 1 8380086 5 9

British Library Cataloguing-in-Publication Data
A catalogue record for this book is available from the British Library.

Published by Destinworld Publishing Ltd.
www.destinworld.com

Cover design by Ken Leeder

A History of Britain in 100 Objects
Paul Chrystal

About the author

Paul Chrystal was educated at the universities of Hull and Southampton, where he took degrees in Classics. For the past 35 years he has worked in medical publishing, much of the time as an international sales director for one market or another and creating medical education programmes for global pharmaceutical companies.

More recently he has been history advisor to Yorkshire visitor attractions, writing features for national newspapers, and broadcasting on talkRADIO, History Hack, BBC local radio, on Radio 4's PM programme and on the BBC World Service.

He is contributor to a number of history and archaeology magazines and the author of over 130 books published since 2010 on a wide range of subjects including classical and social history, the BAOR, the 'Troubles', pandemics (including COVID-19) and epidemics, and many local histories.

He is a regular reviewer for and contributor to *Classics for All*. He has contributed to a six-part series for BBC2 'celebrating the history of some of Britain's most iconic craft industries'. He is an editorial advisor for the Yale University Press classics list and a contributor to the classics section of *Bibliographies on Line* published by Oxford University Press.

He is past editor of *York History*, journal of the York Archaeological & Architectural Society; in 2019 he took over the history editorship of *Yorkshire Archaeological Journal*. Also in 2019, he was guest speaker for Vassar College New York's London Programme in association with Goldsmith University. In 2021 he assisted in the research for an episode of *Who Do You Think You Are?* aired in 2021. In 2022 he was commissioned by Mars Confectionery to produce a piece celebrating 90 years of Mars in the UK.

Paul is married with three children and lives near York.

By the same author

A History of the World in 100 Pandemics, Epidemics & Plagues (2021)

A History of Sweets (2021)

War in Greek Myth (2020)

The Romans in the North of England (2019)

A Historical Guide to Roman York (2021)

The Cold War: the British Army of the Rhine (2018)

The Troubles (2018)

Factory Girls (in press 2022)

Acknowledgements

Images on pages 94-95 courtesy of Dorset County Council and Oxford Archaeology. Thanks too to Patrick Brennan for permission to use the Bolckow, Vaughan & Co Munitionettes team photograph, published in his *The Munitionettes: A History of Women's Football in North East England During the Great War*. And to Geoff Cook, Rheolwr Cynadleddau a Digwyddiadau – Conference & Events Manager, Neuadd Y Ddinas – City Hall, Caerdydd – Cardiff for the image of the wonderful statue of Boudica.

Contents

Introduction

There are many ways by which the history of a nation can be described: places, people, its laws, politics, economics or culture. Significant objects are another defining factor and it is objects which this book uses to tell a history of Britain from prehistoric times to the modern age.

One hundred historically significant objects speak out as emblems of a specific event in Britain's history – from the building of Stonehenge to the development of a vaccine for coronavirus, from a lock of hair preserved from Roman York to the cracking of the Enigma code in World War Two. This fascinating book depicts and describes some of the significant and enduring objects that have shaped, influenced or defined Britain on a unique journey from prehistory to 2022. Some were invented and developed in Britain; many are quintessentially British. Others the British simply embraced and allowed to forge a place for themselves in the story of our nation.

Selection in a book of this kind is always problematic: what do you include and what do you leave out? Nevertheless, I have relished the challenge, the enjoyable task of choosing 100 objects from the magnificent panoply of British history, of selecting some of the 100 most 'iconic' objects. My plan has been to illuminate both the less obvious and the more unusual, to describe and depict objects which may surprise readers with their historical significance and enduring importance. To make you readers say to yourselves 'well, I never realised that'…

CHAPTER 1

PREHISTORY

1

The crocodile fossil
Teleosaurus chapmani

*The crocodile fossil Teleosaurus chapmani in Whitby Museum –
over 201 million years old.*

Dinosaurs, or at least their fossils, are cropping up all the time, it seems. In September 2021 two new species of carnivorous dinosaurs were discovered on the Isle of Wight. Named 'riverbank hunter' and the 'hell heron', both were a type of dinosaur known as spinosaurids which are thought to have roamed around the island some 129 million years ago.

That same year, a new species of dinosaur with an extremely protrusive nose, *Brighstoneus simmondsi,* was identified by a retired GP who whiled away his COVID-19 lockdown rummaging through boxes of ancient bones as part of his PhD studies.

It is nearly 100 years since our first object came to light. Discovered in 1824, our magnificent specimen was unearthed in the alum shale of Saltwick near Whitby at a time when teams of quarrymen were at work extracting alum from the alum shale there – one of Britain's first chemical industries. The first reported marine reptile discovery hereabouts, however, was that of a crocodile as reported in the *Gentleman's Magazine* of 1759: 'Skeleton of an Allegator found in the Allom Rock near Whitby, January 3, 1758'. It was described by John Wooler in the *Philosophical Transactions of the Royal Society*. The specimen, later named *Teleosaurus chapmani Konig*, was donated to the British Museum in 1781.

The alum quarrymen had little concern for palaeontology but saw the skeletons as a way of supplementing their meagre wages and duly sold them as curiosities for the best price. The Rev George Young and others became concerned that such specimens were being 'lost' to Whitby, which led them to form the Whitby Literary & Philosophical Society in 1823 and establish a museum to house those fossils.

One of the major early attractions was another skeleton of the fossil crocodile *Teleosaurus chapmani* (or *Steneosaurus Bollensis*), our skeleton, purchased for £7 in 1824. The collector, Brown Marshall, a carpenter from Whitby, spotted the snout sticking out of the cliff and excavated the skull and the bulk of the skeleton by perilously hanging from the top of the cliff on ropes. Part of the tail was taken out three years later. This amazing discovery is the most intact fossil of *Teleosaurus Chapman* in the world, with only sections of both forelimbs and a majority of the rostrum (a beak-like projection) missing. It is an extinct genus of *teleosaund crocodyliform* from the early Jurassic to middle Jurassic (201.3 Ma million years ago to 174.1 Ma). The average size of this long-lost beast would be 2.5–3.5 metres long. Over the next few years, thanks to the Rev Young, the museum gained a world reputation for its rich fossil collection, particularly the beautiful and gigantic

marine reptiles held there. To learn more about the fascinating story behind many of these large fossils, read *The Floating Egg* by Roger Osborne, geology curator at Whitby Museum.

The coastline at Whitby and Staithes today is a superb destination of great interest to both the amateur and professional geologist. This section of the British coastline is known as the 'Dinosaur Coast'.

Further information at:

https://whitbymuseum.org.uk/whats here/collections/fossils/
The History of Fossil Crocodiles 1. Nature 33, 331 (1886).
Roger Osborne, *The Floating Egg: Episodes in the Making of Geology*, London, 1999.

2

The stone tools and footprints probably left by *Homo antecessor*

Above and next: The stone tools and footprints from 900,000 years ago found at Happisburgh on the Norfolk coast, probably left by Homo antecessor.

We hear a lot about footprints these days – carbon footprints mainly, which are what we all leave behind us when we get in the car, fly away on holiday or eat roast beef, for example. One man who can probably claim to have left no carbon footprint was the *homo antecessor* (Pioneer man), who made what seemed to be his indelible mark on Britain some 900,000 years ago. *Homo antecessor* was smaller-brained than us but walked upright and was fully bipedal. His footprints as pictured here were a set of fossilised hominid prints from the early Pleistocene Age, over 800,000 years ago, and discovered, purely by chance, in May 2013 in a freshly uncovered sediment layer of the Cromer Forest Bed at low tide on the foreshore at Happisburgh. They were scrupulously photographed in 3D before being destroyed by the tide two weeks later. Talk about good timing: just in time archaeology.

Less than a year later, they were hailed as the oldest-known hominid footprints to be found outside Africa. The prints were discovered by Nicholas Ashton, curator at the British Museum, and Martin Bates from the University of Wales Trinity St David's, who were carrying out research as part of the Pathways to Ancient Britain (PAB) project. There were about 50 prints found in an area measuring 430sqft; 12 were mainly complete and showed heels, arches and, in one case, toes.

From a forensic reconstruction it has been hypothesized that a group of five or so individuals, both adults and children, with the tallest about 5ft 9in tall, were walking south (upstream) along mudflats in the estuary of an early path of the River Thames that flowed into the sea much

farther north than it does today, and when southeast Britain was joined to the European continent. Archaeologists have speculated that the group was scouring the mudflats for seafood such as lugworms, shellfish, crabs, and seaweed. The group might have lived on an island in the estuary that provided safety from predators and were travelling from their island base to the shore at low tide.

Objects discovered at Happisburgh since 1820 make it one of the most significant places in prehistorical Britain, while the multitude of objects revealed tell us a massive deal about everyday life in those ancient days. The shoreline here is prone to severe coastal erosion, constantly exposing new material, as when in 1820 fishermen trawling oyster beds found a rich harvest in their nets: not fish but teeth, bones, horns, and antlers from elephants, rhinos, giant deer, and other extinct species. An exceptionally high tide in February 1825 exposed more prehistoric remains when it swept away sediment that had buried an ancient landscape of fossilised tree stumps, animal bones, and fir cones. When, in January 1877, a great storm hurled huge ironstone slabs from the sea bed onto Happisburgh beach, the slabs gave us preserved impressions of leaves from oaks, elms, beeches, birches, and willows that were growing all those years ago. Pleistocene bison bones, exposed in the 1870s, give us our first evidence of early human activity, particularly when in 1999 we found that they were scored with cut marks, indicating that the animals had been butchered by humans with stone tools.

A palaeolithic black flint handaxe was found on the beach in 2000. Between 2005 and 2010, 80 palaeolithic flint tools were excavated and are believed to have been fashioned by *Homo antecessor*, the same people thought to have left the footprints, and are the earliest artefacts to have been found not just in Britain but in northern Europe.

The National Trust reveals that 'The beautiful Sefton Coast at National Trust Formby also contains a tantalising glimpse into the lives of our ancient, hunter-gatherer ancestors. From 6000BC the footprints of the humans that lived on the coast and the animals that sustained them were preserved. The sediment beds that contain the footprints are exposed by tidal erosion and offer a unique insight into the prehistoric life of the area'.

Further information at:

Ashton N, *et al*, *Hominin Footprints from Early Pleistocene Deposits at Happisburgh, UK*, PLoS ONE 9(2): e88329, 2014.
What do microfossils tell us about the first humans in Britain? Section 3, Happisburgh about 840,000–950,000 years ago, Natural History Museum, London.
https://www.nationaltrust.org.uk/formby/features/prehistoric-footprints-at-formby

3

The oldest human fossils around 500,000 years old, of Homo heidelbergensis found at Boxgrove in West Sussex

The first thing to say is that what is commonly known as 'Boxgrove Man' is quite possibly a woman; whatever, it is a fossil belonging to either a female or male *Homo heidelbergensis*, an extinct relative of us modern humans (*Homo sapiens*), and about half a million years old. The fossil was discovered in Eartham Pit, Boxgrove, by Andrew Woodcock and Roy Shephard-Thorn in 1974. They recorded the geological sequence, *in-situ* artefacts and fossil mammal remains. Between 1982 and 1993 Mark Roberts and his team at the Institute of Archaeology at University College London extended the excavations at the site.

Findings were scanty: only the shinbone and two teeth from another individual were found, so little can be learnt about the characteristics of the human to whom the fossil belonged. We do know, however, that the species was good at adapting to the cold, and that our Boxgrove Man or Woman was about 40 years old; the tibia is very sturdy, indicating that it belonged to a strongly built adult, 5ft 11in, so tall, and weighed roughly 14 stone. It is quite possibly the oldest human fossil ever discovered in Britain; indeed, it is the only postcranial element of *Homo Heidelbergensis* to have been found in northern Europe (postcranial means bones from anywhere other than the skull). Boxgrove is also one of the oldest sites in Britain and indeed Europe that furnishes evidence of hunting and butchering by early humans.

Archaeology suggests that these were hunters using stone tools since the team discovered hundreds of flint tools at the site. Also uncovered

Tibia from Boxgrove (Homo heidelbergensis) discovered in Boxgrove, West Sussex, 1993. (photographer, Locutus Borg: (José-Manuel Benito Álvarez)).

at the site were the remains of now extinct species of rhinoceros, lions, bears, frogs, various birds and voles, presumably hunted down by *H. heidelbergensis* with his or her stone tools. These beasts were butchered maybe by our subject, or else he or she simply scavenged them. Both ends of the tibia show signs of gnawing, possibly by a wolf, suggesting that Boxgrove hominids were scavenged by other animals. In 1995 two incisor teeth from another individual hominid were found showing severe periodontal disease and tool cut marks, which are thought to have been caused by use of flint tools near the mouth rather than by cannibalism.

A number of the animal bones unearthed at Boxgrove are the oldest found specimens of their species, such as the wing bone of the great auk discovered in 1989. The combination of bones, stone artifacts, and the geology of the landscape gives a very complete picture of this part of the British coastal plain as it was half a million years ago. In August 2020 archaeologists said they had discovered the earliest bone tools ever found in Europe at the site. They added that it provides further evidence that early human populations at Boxgrove were cognitively, socially, and culturally sophisticated:

'Boxgrove is simply one of the great Early Palaeolithic/Middle Pleistocene sites in the world … the quality of preservation, the range and depth of its myriad lines of multidisciplinary evidence are beyond nearly all other sites.'
– Mark Roberts (2011)

To learn more:
Pitts, Michael and Roberts, Mark, *Fairweather Eden: Life in Britain half a million years ago as revealed by the excavations at Boxgrove*, London, 1998.
English Heritage, *Boxgrove: A Middle Pleistocene hominid site at Eartham Quarry, Boxgrove, West Sussex*, Archaeology Data Service.

4

The Amesbury Archer

Sadly, the Amesbury Archer was not really from Amesbury (although he was, of course, found nearby) and it is unlikely that he was an archer. Oxygen isotope analysis in the Archer's tooth enamel reveals that the 'archer' was a 35 to 45-year-old male and that he grew up outside Britain, probably somewhere near the Alps. He was strongly built; he had an abscess on his jaw and had suffered an accident a few years before his death that had ripped his left knee cap off, causing a nagging painful infection and a pronounced limp. Despite his name, he won't have been doing much hunting; moreover, there is no evidence that he sported the strong upper body muscles needed for firing a bow.

His grave, found three miles south-east of Stonehenge, has yielded a large number of grave goods, indicating that he was a man of some wealth; they include five beakers, 18 arrowheads, two bracers (archer's wrist guards), four boars' tusks, 122 flint tools, three copper knives, a pair of gold hair ornaments and a cushion stone (an anvil for metalworking). Many of the finds have continental provenance.

The 18 barbed arrowheads scattered around his waist and legs were never made to be fired and were simply part of the funerary ceremony. Any bow would have rotted away. The Amesbury Archer is important in the history of Britain for a number of reasons:

- With 100 or so items, his grave is the richest of any found from the Early Bronze Age.
- This was a time when the first metals were brought to Britain: the Archer was buried with two gold hair tresses which is the oldest securely dated gold ever found in Britain (dated to around 2400 BC).

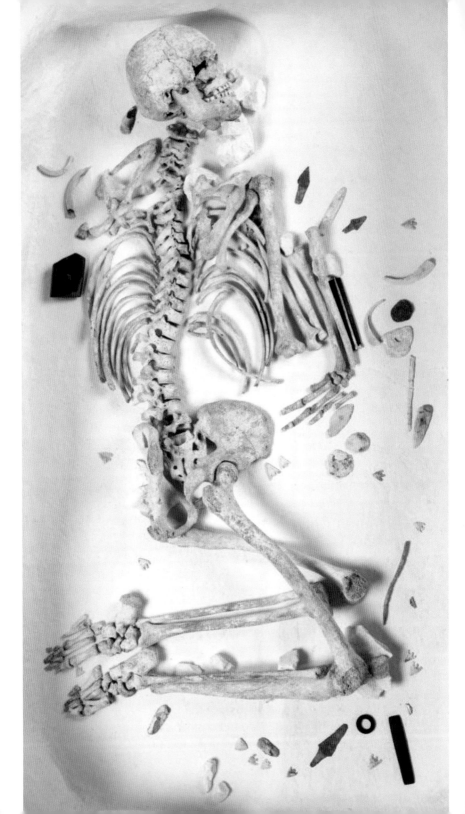

- The archer was buried three miles from Stonehenge just when the massive stones were being brought to Salisbury Plain in Wiltshire to form the world-famous monument.
- The Archer was from the Alps region; the distinctive Beaker pottery and other artefacts which began appearing in Britain around the time of the Archer were from Europe. At first it was thought that this was as a result of mass migration or invasion, but it is more likely to be attributable to trade and cultural links. The Archer is therefore an example of people from abroad bringing the Beaker culture from the continent to Britain. He would have been one of the first people in Britain to have been able to fashion gold.
- Together with the cushion stone, the opulent grave goods suggest that this man was in fact a wealthy metalworker.

His skeleton is now on display at the Salisbury Museum.

A male skeleton, sometimes called the Archer's Companion, found nearby is believed to be that of a younger man related to the Archer, as they shared a rare hereditary anomaly, calcaneonavicular coalition, fusing of the calcaneus and of the navicular tarsal (foot bones). The graves were not far from those of the Boscombe Bowmen.

Further reading:

Fitzpatrick, A.P., 'The Amesbury Archer,' *Current Archaeology*, 184, pp. 146–52, 2003.

Stone, R., 'Mystery Man of Stonehenge', *Smithsonian*, pp. 62–7, August 2005.

Opposite: The skeletal remains of the Amesbury Archer.

5

The Ringlemere Cup
found in Kent, 1700–1500 BC

The Rillaton Cup
found in Cornwall, 1700-1500 BC

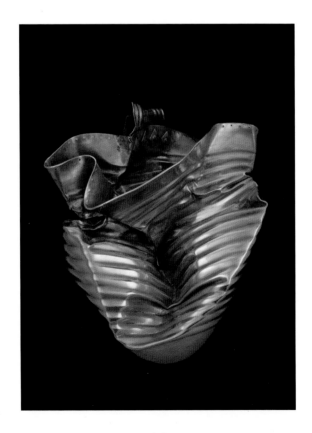

This magnificent Bronze Age vessel was found in the Ringlemere barrow near Sandwich in 2001. The body of the cup was created by hammering a single piece of gold, with the handle cut from a flat strip of gold and attached by rivets. Recent plough damage explains the unfortunate mangled condition, but we know that it was 14cm high with corrugated sides. The cup, more likely a votive offering than a grave good, resembles a late Neolithic ceramic beaker with Corded Ware decoration, but it is much later.

Only seven similar gold 'unstable handled cups' (unstable because of the round bottom) have been found in Europe, all dating to the period between 1700 and 1500 BC. The Ringlemere cup is most similar to that other British example, the Rillaton gold cup unearthed in Cornwall in 1837 (see below). The other examples are two from Germany, two from Switzerland, one now lost from Brittany, and an unprovenanced, perhaps German, example. Two other silver cups and, from Britain, two amber and some shale cups, all share the same basic shapes. The British finds are from around the Wessex area; those on the continent are from near the Rhine or the Channel coast, suggesting that the vessels related to a specific cross-channel trading zone.

The cup was discovered by metal detectorist Cliff Bradshaw in 2001. Through the Portable Antiquities Scheme and the Treasure Act 1996, the cup was declared to be treasure in 2002. It was bought by the British Museum for £270,000, with the money paid split between Bradshaw and the Smith family, owners of Ringlemere Farm. It resides in the prehistory galleries at the British Museum.

Further information at:
Needham, Stuart (ed.), *The Ringlemere Cup: Precious Cups and the Beginning of the Channel Bronze Age*, British Museum Research Publication, 163, 2006.

It was during the Bronze Age (c.2500 BC–c.800 BC) that communities in Britain and Ireland first learned how to work metal, leading to the extensive production of not only gold but also copper and bronze items. Gold artefacts

Opposite: The Ringlemere Cup.
The Portable Antiquities Scheme, Daniel Pett.

in particular were, of course, prestige items used to designate the high status of those individuals who wore or were buried with them.

Around 1,500 gold objects dating to the Bronze Age survive in collections, around 1,000 of them from Ireland and the other 500 from Britain. Bronze Age gold artefacts had begun to be 'discovered' by the 18th century but unfortunately their historic importance was rarely appreciated and countless thousands were sacrilegiously melted down or lost. The archaeologist George Eogan noted that investigation of Bronze Age gold artefacts revealed not only 'the work of craftsmen and technicians' from that period, but also aided our understanding of 'broader aspects of society such as social stratification, trade, commerce and ritual.'

The Early Bronze Age in the British Isles was distinguished by the adoption of the 'Beaker culture', which had arrived from continental Europe. Eogan noted that the 'evidence from archaeology is that Beaker-using communities were the earliest metallurgists in Britain and Ireland', with their produce including 'copper artefacts such as tanged daggers but also gold objects as well as the use of gold for embellishment.'

Further information at:

Barrett, John C., F*ragments from Antiquity: An Archaeology of Social Life in Britain, 2900–1200 BC*, Oxford, 1994.

Eogan, George, *The Accomplished Art: Gold and Gold-Working in Britain and Ireland during the Bronze Age*, Oxford, 1994.

The Rillaton Cup

This gem is early Bronze Age, 1700–1500 BC, and was found in Rillaton, Cornwall.

'A Bronze Age gold cup, formed from one sheet of gold and decorated with horizontal concentric corrugations, which continue downwards from the middle in a convex manner and upwards in a concave manner, terminating at the bottom around a central boss and flattening out at the top to create a rim.'
– Royal Collection Trust

The Royal Collection goes on to tell us that it was excavated in 1837 along with a bronze dagger; human remains were found along with beads, pottery, glass and other items from a stone cist beneath a cairn of stones. The cup was in a ceramic vessel which no doubt helped to keep it intact. The land where it was excavated belongs to the Duchy of Cornwall, so the cup and dagger were presented to William IV as Treasure Trove

The Rillaton Cup

shortly before he died. Queen Victoria and Prince Albert displayed the items at their private museum in Osborne House. After Queen Victoria's death, the cup was moved to Marlborough House and then eventually to Buckingham Palace, where it was placed in a cabinet of gold items in King George V's Audience Room. After the King's death in 1936, Queen Mary advised her son Edward VIII to transfer the cup to the British Museum on long-term loan. And that's where it is today. A replica of the cup is in the Royal Cornwall Museum at Truro.

Some have it that Rillaton is haunted by the spirit of a druid priest, who offers travellers a drink from an inexhaustible cup. One night a traveller hurled the cup's contents at the ghost; he was later found dead in a ravine.

The Mold Cape

A stunning solid sheet-gold object dating from about 1900–1600 BC in the European Bronze Age. It was found at Mold in Flintshire in 1833 and is thought to have formed part of a ceremonial dress.

The cape was in a Bronze Age burial mound in a field named Bryn yr Ellyllon, the Fairies' or Goblins' Hill. The gold cape had been placed on the body of a person who was interred in a rough cist within a burial mound.

Mold cape on display at the British Museum (photographer: Mark Ramsay).

The preserved remains of the skeleton were fragmentary, and the cape was badly crushed. An estimated 200 to 300 amber beads, in rows, were originally on the cape, but only one bead survives at the British Museum. Remains of coarse cloth and 16 fragments of sheet bronze, which are likely to have been the backing for the gold, were also found: in places the gold was riveted onto the bronze sheeting with bronze rivets. Two gold 'straps' were also found, as well as an urn with large quantities of burnt bone and ash.

Further information at:

Clarke, D. V., *Symbols of power at the time of Stonehenge*, National Museum of Antiquities of Scotland, 1985.
Powell, T. G. E., "'The gold ornament from Mold, Flintshire, North Wales,' *Proceedings of the Prehistoric Society*, 19, pp. 161–79, 1953.

6

The Wandsworth Shield

300 BC

The Wandsworth Shield, Iron Age shield boss in La Tène style, British Museum, Room 50 (photographer: Johnbod).

The Wandsworth Shield is a circular bronze Iron Age shield boss decorated in La Tène style which was recovered from the Thames at Wandsworth sometime before 1849. It was found along with another incomplete bronze shield mount: the Wandsworth Mask Shield; both are in the British Museum. The Wandsworth Shield is characterised by its bold repoussé decoration comprising two mirrored birds with outstretched wings and long trailing tail feathers; this has led Barry Cunliffe to say he considers the shield to be 'among the masterpieces of British Celtic art'.

The Wandsworth Shield is dated to the second century BC while the mask shield is dated to the later third century BC.

Further information at:

Brailsford, J. W., *Early Celtic Masterpieces from Britain in the British Museum,* London, 1975.

Cunliffe, Barry, *Iron Age Communities in Britain: an account of England, Scotland and Wales from the seventh century BC until the Roman conquest,* London, 2005.

The Battersea Shield

Like the Wandsworth Shield, the mid fourth-century Battersea Shield is one of the most significant pieces of ancient Celtic art found in Britain. It comprises a sheet bronze covering of a (now lost) wooden shield also decorated in La Tène style. The shield is on display in the British Museum while a replica is housed in the Museum of London.

It was dredged from the Thames in 1857, during excavations for the predecessor of Chelsea Bridge; in the same area workers found large quantities of Roman and Celtic weapons and skeletons in the riverbed, leading many historians to conclude that the area was the site of Julius Caesar's crossing of the Thames during the 54 BC invasion of Britain, although it is now thought that the shield was a votive offering, which, of course, predates the invasion.

The decoration is typically Celtic La Tène style, consisting of circles and spirals. There are 27 small round compartments in raised bronze with red cloisonné enamel; the bronze within the compartment forms a kind of swastika, which was associated with good luck and 'solar energy'. This symbol was known as the whirling sun in ancient days.

The shield was almost certainly made in Britain because of its specifically British form of central circular shield boss.

Further information at:

Green, Miranda (Miranda Aldhouse-Green), *Celtic Art, Reading the Messa*ges, London, 1996.
Stead, Ian Mathieson, *The Battersea Shield*, London, 1985.

The Battersea Shield
(photographer: BabelStone).

7

The Stanwick Horse Mask

AD 40–AD 80

Stanwick was one of the most important settlements in Brigantia during the early stages of the Roman occupation of Britain. The territory of Brigantia covered most of the land between the Rivers Tyne and Humber and the Mersey estuary in the west, forming the largest Brythonic Kingdom in ancient Britain. The Brigantes posed the biggest and most persistent threat to the Roman occupation of Britain.

Stanwick Iron-Age Fortifications ('Stanwick Camp') is a massive Iron-Age hill fort, an *oppidum*, comprising over 5.6 miles of ditches and ramparts. Rising to a height of almost 16ft in places, the ramparts completely surround the village of Stanwick St John and form one of the largest Iron Age settlements in Britain, in extent if not in population. It may well have been the stronghold of Venutius or Cartimandua, two of the early leaders of the tribe, or of both, for a time before their acrimonious split some time after AD 51. Mortimer Wheeler has argued that Stanwick was where Venutius rallied his anti-Roman tribesmen and allies for his revolt against the Romans.

In 1845 a hoard of 140 metal artefacts known as the Stanwick Hoard, which included four sets of horse harnesses for chariots and a bronze horse head 'bucket attachment', were found, by accident, at Melsonby. These are now in the British Museum, which also has the Meyrick Helmet that may have been part of the hoard or at least made at Stanwick. In these troublesome times it was by no means unusual for such hoards to be buried as part of a religious ceremony.

Opposite: The Stanwick Horse Mask.

This is how the British Museum describes the horse helmet:

'Copper alloy sheet metal mount in the form of a stylised horse's head. Sub-rectangular in outline, convex in section, with features executed in low relief and two lateral tabs for attachment. Made to be attached to a wooden object, possibly a bucket.'

Research has shown that many pieces of the hoard are made from brass rather than bronze. Brass was not used to make objects in Britain until the Romans invaded in AD 43.

Further information at:
Chrystal, Paul, *The Romans in the North of England*, Darlington, 2019.
MacGregor, M., 'The Early Iron Age Metalwork Hoard from Stanwick,' N.R. Yorks, *Proceedings of the Prehistoric Society*, 28, pp. 17-57, 1962.
Spratling, M. G., Metalworking At The Stanwick Oppidum: Some New Evidence, *Yorkshire Archaeological Journal*, 53: 14, 1981.

The Meyrick Helmet.

The Meyrick Helmet

This superb helmet is an Iron Age bronze, peaked helmet, decorated in a fusion of the Roman and the La Tène style, on display at the British Museum. It is one of only four Iron Age helmets to have been discovered in Britain, the other three being the Waterloo Helmet, the Canterbury Helmet and the North Bersted Warrior helmet. Unlike the Waterloo Helmet, which bears two cone-shaped horns, the Meyrick Helmet is hornless and is probably based on a Roman model. Vincent Megaw at the University of Leicester suggests that the helmet may have belonged to a British auxiliary attached to the Roman army during the campaigns against the Brigantes in AD 71–74.

Whatever, it is probably part of the Stanwick hoard. The helmet is first recorded as part of the collection of arms and armour accumulated by Sir Samuel Rush Meyrick (1783–1848), and so must have been discovered some time before 1848.

Further information at:
Jackson, Ralph, 'The Meyrick Helmet: A New Interpretation of its Decoration', in Raftery, Barry (ed.), *Sites and Sights of the Iron Age: Essays on Fieldwork and Museum Research,* Presented to Ian Mathieson Stead, Oxford: pp. 67–73, 1995.

CHAPTER 2

ROMAN BRITAIN

Emperor Claudius's invasion in AD 43 was followed by over 350 years of Roman rule which saw our islands shaped and constantly reshaped in its role as Roman Britain's second city, playing a key role in the wider Empire, despite, or maybe because of, its position at the north-western extremity of that empire. Roman Britain has left a rich legacy replete with treasures: what follows is a mere handful of the significant objects which the Romans and their subjects have left behind.

8

Gelt Woods Graffiti

Brampton, near Carlisle

Fascinating graffiti at Gelt Woods.

Man and woman have been scribbling, scratching and scarring graffiti onto walls, trees and anything else they could since the dawn of time. Who knows, you yourself may have left your mark somewhere at some time. Just look at the myriad examples in Basra, Pompeii, the Mirror Wall at Sigiriyainin modern-day Sri Lanka or the walls of the Reichstag from 1945 Berlin daubed by victorious Russian troops.

The famous good luck phallus.

The Roman soldiers toiling away repairing Hadrian's Wall in second century AD-northern Britain were no different; they were just as prolific.

The sheer cliff face of a sandstone quarry near Brampton, two miles south of Hadrian's Wall, is the site of some revealing Roman graffiti being excavated by archaeologists from the University of Newcastle-upon-Tyne ince February 2019. To access the 'written rock of Gelt' as the find is now called, the archaeologists have to abseil 30ft down the quarry face in a project funded by Historic England. The graffiti includes a phallus which would have been meant as a good luck sign for the soldiers who were presumably digging for stone with which to repair Hadrian's Wall. To the Romans, the phallus held none of the repressed sexual overtones it has in our society. The 'dig' is a race against time so that the findings, first discovered in the 18th century, can be recorded before they are lost forever as a result of erosion of the sandstone in which they were inscribed.

Other carvings include a caricature of the senior officer in charge of the quarrying and an inscription dating to AD 207, a time when Hadrian's Wall was subject to a major repair and a renewal programme. The caricature shows two eyes and a mouth, which archaeologists believe is a humorous cartoon of the commanding officer. 'It is very rough. Classical sculpture it is definitely not,' said Mike Collins, inspector of ancient monuments for

This smiley face was surely a cartoon lampooning the workers' commanding officer (photograph courtesy of Historic England).

Hadrian's Wall at Historic England, adding that after a hard day in the quarry with a demanding boss it is easy to imagine the circumstances in which it was done.

A shallow relief of a left-facing bust, new writing and lettering which was thought to have been lost to erosion have also been uncovered. The information gleaned is very important because it gives the names of men, and in some cases their rank and military unit. One inscription, which refers to the consulate of Aper and Maximus, can be dated to AD 207:

APRO ET MAXIMO CONSVLIBVS OFICINA MERCATI – which translates as 'In the consulship of Aper and Maximus'.

Another inscription reads VEX LI EG II AVG OF APR SVB AGRICOLA OPTIONE, which translates as 'a detachment of the Second Legion Augusta, the working face of Apr... optio under Agricola.

The archaeologists work with rock climbing specialists to gain access to the graffiti on a system of ropes and pulleys. They are using an imaging technique known as structure-from-motion (SfM) photogrammetry to produce a 3D record of the writings for the public to view on the 3D content sharing platform Sketchfab.

Mike Collins said, 'These inscriptions at Gelt Forest are probably the most important on the Hadrian's Wall frontier. 'They provide insight into the organisation of the vast construction project that Hadrian's Wall was, as well as some very human and personal touches, such as the caricature of their commanding officer inscribed by one group of soldiers.' Ian Haynes, professor of archaeology at Newcastle University, added, 'These inscriptions are very vulnerable to further gradual decay. This is a great opportunity to record them as they were in 2019, using the best modern technology to safeguard the ability to study them into the future.'

Another find shows a relief of a man's head and shoulders, the name Gaius and an arrow pointing downwards. Tragic story of a comrade falling off the quarry cliff? Or is it an illustration showing workers how to extract the stones from the cliff?

More information can be found at:

https://archaeology.co.uk/tag/written-rock-of-gelt

9

Hair-do and headpot

found in York

A Roman lady's hair piece.

Some museum pieces succeed in bringing to dramatic life the times from when they originate. The next two objects do just that, giving us a glimpse into the real world of Roman Britain – you can almost touch the everyday life and times of York during the Roman occupation with this head of hair and the head pot.

Twenty five lead coffins have been excavated in York – some lined with wood, some enclosed in wood, one as the lining to a stone coffin. One discovered in 1875 under the railway station booking office contained the skeleton of a teenage girl whose preserved head of auburn hair was fashioned into a bun with two jet pins with cantharus shaped heads; it is now resplendent in the Yorkshire Museum, York.

Jet is significant in that it was all the rage in Roman York since extensive deposits of it were mined by the Romans on the coast around Whitby. The wealthier women of Rome were sometimes buried adorned with their jewellery and the finest jet items from around Whitby – bracelets, rings, hair pins, medallions with figures in relief – have been found in York burials.

Further information at:
Chrystal, P., *Roman Women*, Stroud, 2014.

Head pots were also very fashionable in the early part of the third century; parts of up to 50 different head pots have been excavated in York. They may have been *à la mode* during the reign of Septimius Severus and were first made here by military potters from North Africa around AD 211. This marvellous – and (unusually) intact – example shows a woman with the hairstyle and facial features modelled on Severus's Syrian wife, Julia Domna, who resided in York with him.

In 1984 Gillian Braithwaite declared in a paper that head and face pots are among the most attractive and least documented products of the Romano-British pottery industries. Face pots, with their crude, barbaric, comical features stuck unclassically and incongruously on a Roman jar, 'are quite unlike any other type of Roman pottery, where free-hand figurative decoration is practically unknown.' Head pots, with their contrived hair styles, are more what we expect from the Roman world and fit more into what we consider 'Roman' and classical-looking. 'Yet they seem to be a purely insular development, found only in the remote province of Britain and with no obvious close counterparts anywhere else in the Roman Empire except perhaps in North Africa.'

(Images courtesy of York Museums Trust)

Further information at:

Braithwaite, G., 'Romano-British Face Pots and Head Pots,' *Britannia*, 15, pp. 99-131, 1984.

Chrystal, P., *The Romans in the North of England*, Darlington, 2019.

Chrystal, P., *A Historical Guide to Roman York*, Barnsley, 2021.

Chrystal, P., *Roman York*, 2022.

A complete female head pot.

10

Gladiators found dead in York

The gladiator graves.

There has been much publicity surrounding 96 burials found in part of the sprawling extra-mural Roman cemetery around York's Mount and in Driffield Terrace in particular (SE59324510 and SE59285095). Evidence is pointing to the conclusion that these were gladiators who had been decapitated. Here is a summary of that evidence, most of which relies heavily on a report by the York Archaeological Trust (YAT 2015) –https://www.yorkarchaeology.co.uk/resources/finding-the-future/resilience-year-2-3/gladiators-year-2/. The burials took place over the second and third centuries AD, maybe extending into the fourth.

It all started in 2004 when 82 inhumations and 14 cremated burials were excavated; all were young male adults and cuts to the neck bones of 40 individuals suggested they had been decapitated. Twenty-five of the decapitations exhibited a single cut to the neck. Multiple cut marks on some of the skeletons suggested that the victim was relatively still at the time of assault and the majority of blows were delivered from behind, soon after death. As well as the decapitations, there were three cases of unhealed blade injuries, two to the backs of the hands and one to the femur. Three individuals had cuts to the neck. There was also evidence of large carnivore bite marks on one individual, from a bear, lion or tiger. Kurt Hunter-Mann reveals that most of the deceased seem to have taken a savage beating or to have been tortured before death:

'Nearly a third of the adults had one or more fractured teeth, mostly upper front teeth and molars (back teeth). The majority of the upper tooth fractures were on the left side, indicating a blow from a right-handed opponent wielding a blunt object. The back tooth fractures were more evenly distributed and can be attributed to blows delivered to the chin or to teeth clenching. Thirteen individuals had healed cranial trauma, and there were a couple of cases of possible peri-mortem blunt force injuries to the cranium. Trauma to the rest of the body included a fractured scapula blade; several fractures of vertebral processes; a healed blade cut to the left thigh; two fibula fractures; and five metacarpal fractures, all in the right hand. There was also a high prevalence of broken ribs. Fractured clavicles, wrists, ulnas and a vertebra suggest injuries due to falls, whereas fractures and soft tissue injuries evident in the feet and ankles indicate twisted ankles. Stress injuries indicative of an active lifestyle were also common.'

Further information at:

Hunter-Mann, K., 'Romans Lose their Heads in York,' *York Historian*, 23, pp. 2–7, 2006.

https://www.yorkarchaeology.co.uk/wp-content/uploads/2015/08/Driffield-Terrace.pdf

Opposite: Roman writing boards, found under the Bloomberg building, London, from the first century AD, on display in the Museum of the London Mithraeum.

11

The Bloomberg tablets

Many of us are familiar with the marvellous Vindolanda Tablets – and rightly so. They give to the world a vivid and fascinating account of life at the very edge of empire. Apart from providing copious and invaluable information relating to provincial military life and administration, the tablets give us a fascinating insight on literacy among officers and their wives, rank and file soldiers, and civilian contractors.

Excavations on a three-acre site between 2010 and 2013 before the construction there of the Bloomberg LP building on Queen Victoria Street unearthed a treasure trove of thousands of preserved personal artifacts, from leather boots and good luck charms, from an amber gladiator amulet to a hoard of 405 preserved wooden tablets dating from AD 50–80, buried 40ft beneath the street. They were soon acclaimed as the earliest handwritten documents to be found in Roman Britain, pre-dating the Vindolanda Tablets by up to half a century. The Bloomberg site was well-known as the site of the Temple of Mithras, partially excavated in the 1950s; when the Bucklersbury building was demolished in 2010, archaeologists had another chance to dig. Numerous artifacts were discovered, including the Bloomberg Tablets. We have the subterranean River Walbrook to thank for their astonishing preservation: wood usually rots away over time but the diptych tablets were preserved by the thick, wet mud of the river, which reduced exposure of the tablets to oxygen.

Decipherment of the tablets, written in Roman cursive style, is ongoing but the 88 legible writing tablets, which have been translated, yield personal correspondence, loan notes, bills of sale, and the oldest intrinsically dated financial document to emerge from the City of London, dated to 8 January AD 57, legal documents, including the appointment of a judge to hear a case between two litigants, Litugenus and Magunus, on 9 November AD 78, and educational material. One tablet depicts part of the alphabet (ΛBCDIIΓGI IIKLMNOPQRST), suggesting the presence of Britain's first school. That unique financial document tablet mentioned above reads:

'In the consulship of Nero Claudius Caesar Augustus Germanicus for the second time and of Lucius Calpurnius Piso, on the 6th day before the Ides of January [8 January 57 AD] I, Tibullus the freedman of Venustus, have written and say that I owe Gratus the freedman of Spurius 105 denarii from the price of the merchandise which has been sold and delivered. This money I am due to repay him or the person whom the matter will concern ...'

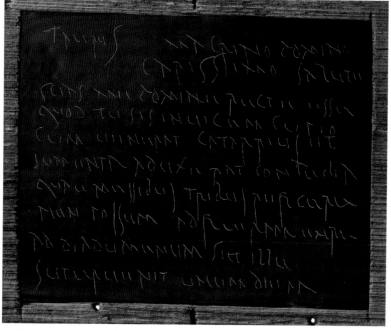

Reconstructed text from Bloomberg Tablet WT29 as it may have originally appeared. It reads: 'Taurus to Macrinus. [My] dearest Lord, greetings. I hope you are in good health … Catarrius [took my] beasts of burden away – investments that I cannot replace for [the next] three months'.

The tablets provide us with a veritable goldmine – an amazing record of London life – for the identification of occupations and professions with over 100 names of people of all different walks of life who lived in London then: slaves, merchants, soldiers, and politicians. Notably, Julius Classicus is there: he was a Roman auxiliary commander, later known as a leader of the Batavian revolt and the prefect of the Sixth Cohort of Nervians in the first decades of Roman London.

The first-known mention of the name of the city of London now supersedes the previously earliest reference in Tacitus's *Annals*. Dated somewhere between AD 65 and 80, it reads, '*Londinio Mogontio*', which translates to 'In London, to Mogontius' (a Celtic personal name), some 50 years before Tacitus. There is also reference to the reprovisioning of London after it was sacked around AD 61 by Boudica; this tablet is a contract dated 22 October AD 62, and details the transportation of 20 loads of provisions from Verulamium (St Alban's which was also sacked) to London.

Roger Tomlin has deciphered and translated the tablets; he commented:

'[These tablets] provide some very personal glimpses into the lives of the first Londoners ... These include an urgent appeal ("I ask you by bread and salt") by a man named Atticus who beseeches his correspondent to make payments totalling 36 denarii as quickly as possible, as well as the woes of a financier named Titus whose ill-judged loan has made him a laughing stock in the market ("they are boasting through the whole market that you have lent them money," his correspondent writes. "Therefore I ask you in your own interest not to appear shabby ... you will not thus favour your own affairs").'

For more information, see:
Chrystal, Paul, *Roman Record Keeping and Communications*, Stroud, 2018.
Tomlin, Roger, S.O., *Roman London's first voices: writing tablets from the Bloomberg excavations*, 2010–14 (Mola Monographs 72), London, 2016.
'*Earliest written reference to London found*,' *Current Archaeology*, 1 June 2016.

12

The hand of god

Vindolanda

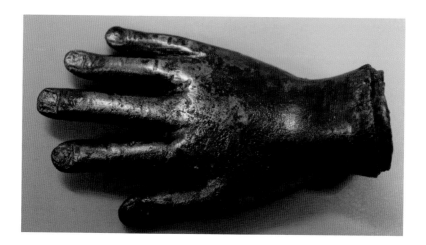

ven by Vindolanda's and Bloomberg's impressive archaeological and
historical standards, one day in 2018 saw a huge archaeological event
when the ground yielded a magnificently preserved sculpture of a
child-sized hand, made of over 2kg of solid bronze. Vindolanda's archaeologists found the hand 5ft below ground level in a ditch fill from the Severan
period (ca. AD 208-212).

When conservators cleaned off the centuries of dirt, they found a
high-quality hand, finely crafted and very realistic, especially on the palm
side. They also saw that the hand originally had an attachment (now lost) in
the palm. A socket at the base of the hand suggests it was not, as so often,
broken off a statue, but rather it was a grand standalone piece originally
fixed to a pole.

The find site is close to the remains of the shrine to Jupiter Dolichenus found in the northern wall of the third-century fort during a 2009 excavation. Archaeologists believe the hand was associated with the temple, serving a votive function in the worship of Jupiter Dolichenus, a god and mystery cult that flourished in the Roman Empire from the early second to mid-third centuries AD. Votive hands have been found at or near other Jupiter Dolichenus temples; they were bigger, however, and several had inscriptions referring to the deity which clarified their votive role.

Dr Andrew Birley, CEO and director of excavations at the Vindolanda Trust commented, 'We did not expect to find such a beautifully preserved and rare cult artefact so soon after the start of the 2018 excavation season. When we excavated the nearby temple to Dolichenus in 2009 it was clear that the temple treasures had been removed in Roman times. However, this find being made in a nearby area reminds us that the life of the temple and the practices associated with the worship of Dolichenus had clearly stretched beyond the confines of its stone walls.'

Our hand may well have been awarded to the military garrison at the Wall for delivering victory in the largest military combat operation ever carried out in Britain, before or since, namely the Roman invasion of Scotland in AD 209–10. It involved a 50,000-strong Roman invasion force, elements of which penetrated as far north as modern Aberdeenshire. Thousands of tribespeople, mainly from the Caledonian and Maeatae tribal confederations, were killed.

The Romans claimed that the native chieftains had reneged on a peace agreement – and were therefore rebels, not just ordinary enemies. The 50,000-strong invasion was led by the emperor himself – Septimius Severus – whose military and political credibility was therefore very much at stake.

Founded in Doliche, modern-day Dülük, Turkey, the mystery religion of Jupiter Dolichenus spread throughout the Roman Empire in the early second century, largely thanks to its popularity with the highly mobile army. It was supported by all the Severan emperors, which is why its popularity plummeted in the mid-third century when the last of the Severans, Alexander Severus, was assassinated by the army in AD 235 and Maximinus Thrax was elected his successor by those same assassins. Thrax rose from humble origins and was extremely suspicious that people were out to topple him (they were), so he took action against anything and anyone associated with his predecessors. The worship of Jupiter Dolichenus was one of the casualties.

Cleaned and conserved, the bronze hand is on display at the Vindolanda Museum in the same gallery as the stone altar.

Further reading:

Beard, Mary, *The Religions of Rome*, I, Cambridge, 1998.
Chrystal, Paul, *The Romans in the North*, Darlington, 2020.
Keys, David, '*Ancient Roman "hand of god" discovered near Hadrian's Wall sheds light on biggest combat operation ever in UK*,' *Independent*, 27 June 2018.

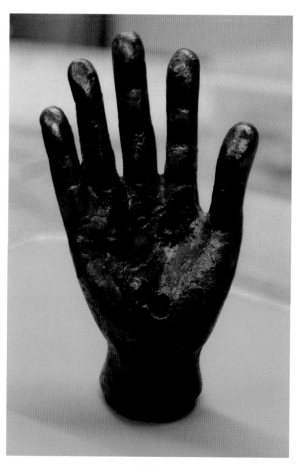

13

The Portland Vase

Above and next: The Portland Vase and details.

The Portland Vase is a glorious example of a Roman cameo glass vase from between AD 1 and AD 25. It is the best-known piece of Roman cameo glass and has served as an inspiration to many glass and porcelain makers from the early 18th century onwards. It is first recorded in Rome in 1600–01, and since 1810 has been in the British Museum in London. It was bought by the museum in 1945.

The vase is about 9.8in high, is made of violet-blue glass and is surrounded by a single continuous white glass cameo, making two distinct scenes, depicting seven human figures plus a large snake and two bearded and horned heads below the handles. The meaning of the images on the vase continues to baffle and speculation falls into two main groups: mythological and historical. Historical interpretations focus on Augustus, his family and his rivals, especially given the quality and expense of the object.

The Wedgwood Museum, in Barlaston, near Stoke-on-Trent, contains a display describing the challenges of replicating the vase, and several examples of the early experiments are shown.

At 3:45pm, on 7 February 1845, things literally fell apart: the vase was shattered by William Lloyd (William Mulcahy), who, after an all-week drinking session, hurled a nearby sculpture at the case, smashing both it and the vase. He was arrested and charged with wilful damage. When his lawyer pointed out an error in the wording of the act which seemed to limit its application to the destruction of objects worth no more than £5, he was convicted instead of the destruction of the glass case and was ordered

to pay a fine of £3 (about £375 in 2022) or languish for two months in prison. Lloyd remained incarcerated until an anonymous benefactor paid his fine. The owner of the vase declined to bring a civil action against William Mulcahy because he did not want his family to suffer for 'an act of folly or madness which they could not control'.

Further information at:

Brooks, Robin, *The Portland Vase: The Extraordinary Odyssey of a Mysterious Roman Treasure*, New York, 2004.

Painter, Kenneth, 'The History of the Portland Vase,' *Journal of Glass Studies*, Corning Museum of Glass, 32: pp. 24–84, 1990.

Walker, Susan, *The Portland Vase*, London, 2004.

The Staffordshire Moorlands Pan, mid-second century AD

The Staffordshire Moorlands Pan, known also as the Ilam Pan, is an enamelled bronze *trulla* with an inscription referencing four of the forts of Hadrian's Wall. It was found in June 2003 in Ilam, Staffordshire, by metal-detectorists, and, in 2005, was bought jointly by the Tullie House Museum in Carlisle, the Potteries Museum in Stoke-on-Trent and London's British Museum, with the help of a grant of £112,200 from the Heritage Lottery Fund. It is a find of great national and international significance.

This special bronze pan is inscribed with the name Aelius Draco and four forts on Hadrian's Wall, MAIS (Bowness-on-Solway), COGGABATA (Drumburgh) VXELODVNVM (Stanwix), and CAMMOGLANNA (Castlesteads). It was used for cooking and serving food, decorated in a Celtic style, weighing 132.5g, and 47mm high in height with a maximum diameter of 94mm.

The decoration consists of 'eight roundels, with eight pairs of intervening hollow-sided triangles. Each roundel encloses a swirling six-armed whirligig centred on a three-petalled device inlaid with red, blue, turquoise and yellow-coloured enamel.'

The Staffordshire Moorlands Pan, found in a very well-preserved condition with intact enamel inlays (photograph by Dominic Coyne, Young Graduates for Museums and Galleries programme, August 2007).

The British Museum suggests that Aelius Draco (or Dracon) may have been a soldier or junior officer, of Greek origin, who was granted his citizenship under Hadrian, and who had the pan made as a souvenir of his military service on the Wall.

Apart from the forts, we have RIGORE VALI AELI DRACONIS, which refers to the wall, VALI, and probably that soldier DRACO. AELI may be part of his name, but it was also Hadrian's family name, so may agree with VALI, telling us that the Romans called the wall the 'Aelian Wall'.

Further information at:

Chrystal, Paul, *A Historical Guide to Roman York*, Barnsley, 2021.
Jackson, Ralph, 'The Ilam pan,' in Breeze, David J. (ed.), *The first souvenirs: enamelled vessels from Hadrian's Wall*, *CWAAS extra series*, no.37. Carlisle, pp.41–60, 2012.

14

Fourth-century Chi-Rho fresco

from Lullingstone Roman Villa, Kent

Chi-Rho fresco from Lullingstone Villa, which features the only known Christian paintings from the Roman era in Britain.

Lullingstone Roman Villa was built in first-century AD Roman Britain in Lullingstone near the village of Eynsford, Kent. It gives us a fascinating glimpse of the Roman-British villa with its wealth of treasures, including the beautiful mosaics.

The dining room (*triclinium*) was highly decorated with a pair of large mosaics on the floor dating from the mid-fourth century. One depicts the abduction of the princess Europa by Jupiter or Zeus, who is disguised as a bull, whilst the other depicts Bellerophon slaying the Chimera, surrounded by four sea creatures, including dolphins. In each of the four corners of the Bellerophon mosaic there is a bust of the seasons personified, including winter, spring, summer and autumn. Surrounding these mosaics were smaller images depicting hearts, crosses and swastikas, possibly designed to ward off the Evil Eye.

The star of the show, however, is what is termed the Pagan shrine and (later) Christian chapel – one of the earliest in Britain. The original pagan shrine room was dedicated to local water deities, and a wall painting depicting three water nymphs dating from this period can still be seen in a niche in the room. In the fourth century the room above the pagan shrine was converted to Christian use, with painted plaster on the walls, including a row of figures of standing worshipers (*orans*), and this stunning Christian Chi-rho symbol which is in the British Museum.

The evidence of the Christian house-church is a unique discovery for Roman Britain and the wall paintings are of international importance. Not only do they provide some of the earliest evidence for Christianity in Britain, they are almost unique – the closest parallels come from a house-church in Dura Europus, Syria.

The emperor Constantine died in York in AD 337 – he was the first emperor to adopt the Christian faith, beginning the end of the persecution of Christians in the Roman Empire in what was known as the Triumph of the Church. The decisive battle of the Milvian Bridge took place between Constantine I and Maxentius in 312. It takes its name from the Milvian Bridge, an important strategic crossing over the Tiber, north of Rome. Constantine was victorious: the battle enabled him to become the sole ruler of the Roman Empire. Maxentius, however, drowned in the Tiber during the battle; his body was later fished out and decapitated, his head was paraded through the streets of Rome the day after the battle and, for good measure, carried to Carthage as a warning to the Carthaginians to keep the corn supply coming to Rome.

Constantine's army came to the battle with strange symbols depicted on their standards and their shields. Lactantius states that, on the eve of the battle, Constantine was told in a dream to 'depict the heavenly sign on the shields of his soldiers'. So, 'he marked on their shields the letter X, with a perpendicular line drawn through it and turned round thus at the top, being the cipher of Christ'. This was the 'heavenly divine symbol' (*coeleste signum dei*). Eusebius of Caesarea (d.AD 339) says that Constantine was marching somewhere when he looked up to the sun and saw a cross of light above it, and with it the Greek words Ἐν Τούτῳ Νίκα. The Latin translation is '*in hoc signo vinces*' – literally 'In this sign, you will conquer' or 'By this, conquer!' (I. AD 28-32).

At first Constantine was baffled, unsure of the meaning of the apparition, but the following night he had a dream in which Christ explained to him that he should use the sign (the *labarum*) against his enemies.

The *labarum* (λάβαρον) was a *vexillum* or military standard that displayed the 'Chi-Rho' symbol ☧, a christogram formed from the first two Greek letters of the word 'Christ' (ΧΡΙΣΤΟΣ, or Χριστός) – Chi (χ) and Rho (ρ). Since the vexillum consisted of a flag suspended from the crossbar of a cross, it was ideally suited to symbolize the crucifixion of Christ.

Further information at:

Chrystal, Paul, *A Historical Guide to Roman York*, Barnsley, 2021.
Fulford, Michael, *Lullingstone Roman Villa*, English Heritage, 2003.
Painter, K. S., 'The Lullingstone Wall-Plaster: An Aspect of Christianity in Roman Britain,' *The British Museum Quarterly*, 33: pp. 131–50, 1969.

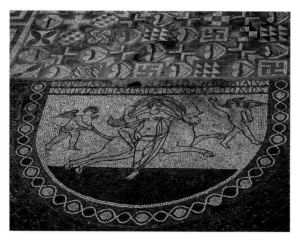

Mosaics at Lullingstone Villa

15

The statue of Boudica, Queen of the Iceni, and her daughters

This wonderful statue encapsulates the dignity of Queen Boudica and her violated daughters. She was the Queen of the British tribe the Iceni, who took on the Roman imperialist invaders and nearly defeated them.

One way in which local British tribes could guarantee peaceful co-existence with Rome was to bequeath to the Romans their lands on the death of the monarch. Prasutagus, prosperous king of the Iceni, did just that, citing Nero as heir, but with a codicil naming his daughters as co-heirs. The Iceni had been on friendly terms with the Romans since the early days of the invasion but on the king's death in AD 60 these same Romans chose to ignore the small print in the king's will, divided up the legacy, took over the erstwhile client kingdom and plundered it. Indeed, Suetonius relates (*Augustus* 48) that Augustus had ordained that many years before client kingdoms (*reges socii*) were always 'integral parts of the empire' (*membra partesque imperii*). Perhaps it was naive of the Iceni to expect an extension of the special relationship after Prasutagus's death, but the aftermath of the Roman decision was shocking, brutal and highly provocative: Prasutagus's daughters were raped, Queen Boudica, his wife, was flogged, the family was treated as slaves and his Roman creditors called in their loans, loans which the Iceni had been led to believe were gifts; grants made by Claudius were also revoked. Boudica was humiliated and outraged.

Elsewhere in Britannia, the time was ripe for revenge and rebellion: the Iceni were joined by the disaffected Trinovantes, the tribe that had been igno-miniously displaced from the native capital Camuodunum and enslaved as labourers to help in the construction of a *colonia* in AD 49–50 with its Temple of Claudius, a citadel unmistakably symbolic of oppressive Roman rule, a beacon of Romanisation which was the focus of an imperial cult dedicated to Claudius with the burden of cost on the native aristocracy. Furthermore, the Romans settled it with a large contingent of army veterans, which would provide a permanent insurance against rebellion, in effect making it a small piece of Rome in Britannia. What they failed to do, however, was fortify the place.

In AD 61 the Iceni under Boudica advanced on the *colonia*. Camulodunum was sacked and the temple fell after two days; the *saevitia*, savagery, of Boudica's forces was uncompromising. The sounds of human sacrifice rang around the sacred groves. The IXth legion under Petillius Cerealis rushed to relieve the defenders but was annihilated. Catus Decianus, the procurator, fled to Gaul. Only the IXth's cavalry escaped to fight another day. Suetonius reached Londinium – then an important but undefended trading port – calculating that it was impossible to defend with the meagre forces at his disposal. The awful decision to abandon Londinium was made and those left behind were slaughtered in the carnage that ensued. Excavations have revealed a thick red layer of burnt detritus covering coins and pottery dating before AD 60.

Euphoric and drunk – metaphorically and actually – on their easy successes, the Britons then devastated Verulamium (St Albans), a stronghold of the pro-Roman Catuvellauni. According to (an exaggerating) Tacitus, up to 80,000 men, women and children were slain in the orgy of destruction visited on the three towns by Boudica's forces. The Britons were not in the habit of taking prisoners: they had no interest in selling slaves: they showed no quarter; the only options were rape, slaughter, hanging, burning alive and crucifixion. Dio's account is even more graphic: he says that the noblest women were impaled the length of their bodies on sharpened spikes and that their breasts were hacked off and sewn onto their mouths, 'to the accompaniment of sacrifices, feasts, and lewd behaviour' sacrilegiously performed in sacred places, like the groves of Andraste, a British goddess of victory.

Suetonius Paulinus hurriedly assembled a force of around 10,000 men and prepared for battle, the battle of Watling Street, to salvage what he could

Opposite: A dignified Boudica and her daughters; she, a queen, was flogged, and they were raped by the Romans. Courtesy of Geoff Cook at Cardiff City Hall.

of the Roman occupation. His army included his own Legio XIV *Gemina* and units from the XX *Valeria Victrix*; Legio II *Augusta* under Poenius Postumus, near Exeter, did not respond to the call for assistance either because Postumus was petrified at the prospect of fighting Boudica or, more likely, he (sensibly) did not want to leave the South West unprotected. Whatever, his insubordination would have fortuitously detained some tribes in the South West, preventing them from joining Boudica.

The 10,000 were massively outnumbered by Boudica's 230,000 – no doubt another huge exaggeration but Boudica certainly enjoyed a substantial superiority; as Dio says, even if the Romans were lined up one deep, they would not have reached the end of Boudica's line. However, British complacency was to be their undoing: so casual, so confident of victory was Boudica's army that women were allowed to attend the battle as grandstand spectators in wagons on the edge of the battlefield. Boudica herself rallied her troops from a chariot, her violated daughters beside her, in a rousing speech, anticipating another easy victory.

Unfortunately for the Britons, there was to be no victory; Boudica was soundly defeated. The Britons were hampered by their poor manoeuvrability and their inexperience of disciplined open-field tactics. Moreover, the narrow battlefield restricted the numbers Boudica could deploy at any one time, thus diminishing her numerical advantage. The Britons were felled in their droves by the Roman javelins which rained down on them.

Women and domestic animals were slaughtered while Boudica's retreating warriors were hampered in their collective flight by the wagons, all full of those hapless spectators. According to Tacitus (exaggerating again), 80,000 Britons died that day to the Romans' loss of 400. No doubt there was more rape and other atrocities carried out by the Romans; the fate of Boudica's daughters is not recorded. Some say Boudica herself committed suicide by poisoning; Dio disputes this, or at least paraphrases the detail out of the same story, and claims that Boudica fell ill and died, and was buried at great expense and with full honours.

Suetonius instigated vicious slash-and-burn reprisals on every tribe involved in the rebellion, but he was eventually replaced by the more conciliatory Publius Petronius Turpilianus, in the interests of averting another revolt. The pretext for Suetonius's (the commander) removal was that he had apparently 'lost' some of the ships of the Roman fleet.

If Suetonius (the biographer), is to be believed, the crisis, as noted, almost made Nero, now emperor, abandon Britannia for good.

Iceni territory was amongst the lands laid waste by Suetonius Paulinus, with many surviving rebels sold into slavery; and 'whatever tribes still wavered or were hostile were ravaged with fire and sword'. The prospect, and reality, of famine became all the more real because the Britons had not bothered to sow seeds for the year's harvest, over-optimistically and naively assuming they could live off plundered Roman supplies. It is likely that Britannia went into recession, even depression: the fields were empty and the agricultural workforce was severely depleted through war casualties, disability and enslavement.

Further information at:

Chrystal. Paul, *Roman Military Disasters*, Barnsley, 2016.
Chrystal, Paul, *Women at War in the Ancient World*, Barnsley, 2020.
Gillespie, C.C., *Boudica: Warrior Woman of Roman Britain*, Oxford, 2018.
Taylor, John W., *Tacitus and the Boudican Revolt*, Dublin, 1998.

16

The Corbridge Lanx

1735 was a good year for Corbridge, for it was then that nine-year-old Isabel Cutter, daughter of a local cobbler, found this magnificent silver lanx on the banks of the River Tyne. Over about 30 years in the early 18th century, a number of silver objects kept turning up in the vicinity, thought likely to be part of a big Roman hoard. Sadly, all other items from the treasure disappeared, with only the Corbridge Lanx remaining. The lanx fell into the hands of the Dukes of Northumberland and remained in their possession until 1993, when it was sold by Henry Percy, 11th Duke of Northumberland, to the British Museum.

The best description of the find is by T.W. Potter in his, *Roman Britain,* second edition:

'A superlative late-Roman "picture plate" designed for display.

This magnificent silver platter was found by nine-year-old Isabel Cutter in the bank of the River Tyne at Corbridge, near Hadrian's Wall, in February 1735. It is probable that gradual erosion of the river bank was washing out part of a fourth-century silver hoard, as other vessels were found there on various occasions between 1731 and 1760.

'The scene shows the god Apollo at the entrance to a shrine, holding a bow, his lyre at his feet. His twin sister Artemis (Diana), the hunter goddess, enters from the left, and the helmeted goddess with her hand raised to indicate conversation is Athena (Minerva) … The entire scene is clearly a shrine of Apollo … In the foreground stands an altar flanked by Artemis's hound and fallen stag and a griffin, a mythical beast associated with Apollo.

'The decoration of the platter and its style indicate a fourth-century AD date … Though no other piece has survived, some were sketched or described when they were originally found. At least one of the lost objects bore Christian symbols. We can compare the treasure with the Mildenhall treasure where high-quality pagan decoration is combined with a few Christian references. The Latin term lanx (tray) was used for vessels of this shape by eighteenth-century scholars.'

Further information at:
Potter, T.W., *Roman Britain*, second edition, London, 1997.
Strong, D., *Greek and Roman Silver Plate*, London, 1996.

The Corbridge Lion in Corbridge Museum

The Corbridge Lion is a dynamic Roman sandstone sculpture of a male lion crouching menacingly over a prone, injured animal, probably a deer. It was originally on top of a piece of decorative funerary ornamentation from a tomb. It is believed to date from the second or third centuries and is now in the site museum.

This famous lion is the best preserved of five lion statues from Corbridge and vividly symbolises the conquest of death over life, or the superiority of Rome over its enemies. *Horribile dictu*, it was subsequently re-deployed as a fountainhead by extracting the teeth and passing a water pipe through its mouth, explaining why it was found in a water tank, in 1907, in what was possibly a mansion.

Of the four other stone lions found at Corbridge, two of them were excavated within the enclosure wall around a second-century mausoleum at Shorden Brae, in the cemetery just west of the Roman town; one was built into a wall in the village, and the other (now lost) was in the private museum owned by Bartholomew Lumley in the early 19th century.

Our mausoleum lion was found *in situ*, lying where it had fallen from the wall of what was a huge mausoleum. The lion was part of a pair set on the mausoleum's outer wall and pre-dates the Corbridge lion by about 50 years. Built in the form of a tower, the tomb is unique in Roman Britain and is one of the largest tower tombs known from the Roman world. Excavated in 1958, it measured 10m² and the thick precinct wall surrounding it would have covered an area of 40m². Whoever was buried in this monument came from a family of some status and wealth, maybe a legionary commander.

Further information at:

Dickinson, G. , *Corbridge – the Last Two Thousand Years*, London, 2000.
Phillips, E.J., *Corpus Signorum Imperium Romani I*, in Corbridge, Hadrian's Wall East of the North Tyne, Oxford, pp. 31–2, No. 82, 1977.

The Corbridge Lion (photographer: Alun Salt).

CHAPTER 3

THE 'DARK' AGES

17

The Sutton Hoo ship burial

Suffolk

Shoulder clasp (closed) from the Sutton Hoo ship-burial 1, Suffolk, now in the British Museum (photographer: Rob Roy, user: https://www.flickr.com/ people/robroy/ or http://www.roblog.com).

Sutton Hoo, near Woodbridge in Suffolk, has yielded two early medieval cemeteries dating from the sixth to seventh centuries in a site which archaeologists have been excavating since 1938. One cemetery offered up a spectacular undisturbed ship burial with a treasure trove of Anglo-Saxon artefacts, most of which are now held by the British Museum. Who was the dignitary buried in the ship? Scholars believe Rædwald of East Anglia is the most likely candidate. Why is the site important in British history? Because it establishes the history of the Anglo-Saxon kingdom of East Anglia as well as illuminating the early Anglo-Saxon period which, hitherto, lacked historical record. It is widely acknowledged that the artefacts comprise the greatest treasure ever discovered in the United Kingdom. Those found in the burial chamber include a suite of metalwork dress fittings in gold and gems, a ceremonial helmet, a shield and sword, a lyre and silver plate from the Byzantine Empire.

The ship burial has led to comparisons with the world of the Old English poem *Beowulf*, which is partly set in Götaland in southern Sweden, a region which has archaeological parallels to some of the finds from Sutton Hoo.

Once the Romans had left Britain in AD 410 to defend their beleaguered empire, invading Germanic tribes such as the Angles and Saxons began to settle in the south-eastern part of the island: the newcomers were particularly drawn to East Anglia, hence the name. Over time, the native Brittonic population absorbed the culture and habits of the new peoples.

The Sutton Hoo grave field contained about 20 barrows; the grave goods tell us that they were reserved for people with exceptional wealth or prestige.

A brief survey of the finds will illustrate the wide variety of goods, many of which originate from far afield.

Mounds 3 to 7

The cremation burials at Sutton Hoo were 'among the earliest' in the cemetery, two being excavated in 1938. Mound 3 gave up the ashes of a man and a horse placed on a wooden trough or dugout bier, a Frankish iron-headed throwing-axe, and imported objects from the eastern Mediterranean, including the lid of a bronze ewer, part of a miniature carved plaque depicting a winged Victory, and fragments of decorated bone from a casket. Under Mound 4 was the cremated remains of a man and a woman, with a horse and perhaps also a dog, as well as fragments of bone gaming-pieces.

In Mounds 5, 6, and 7, archaeologists found cremations in bronze bowls. In Mound 5 more gaming-pieces were uncovered, small iron shears, a cup, and an ivory box. Mound 7 contained gaming-pieces too, as well as an iron-bound bucket, a sword-belt fitting and a drinking vessel, together with the remains of horse, cattle, red deer, sheep and pig that had been burnt with the deceased on a pyre. Mound 6 contained more cremated animals, gaming-pieces, a sword-belt fitting and a comb. In level areas between the mounds, archaeologist Martin Carver found three furnished inhumations: one held a child's remains, along with his buckle and miniature spear. A man's grave included two belt buckles and a knife, and that of a woman contained a leather bag, a pin and a chatelaine.

Mound 17

Mound 17 yields the most impressive of the burials: that of a young man who was buried with his horse. The horse would have been sacrificed for the funeral in a standard ritual. There were two undisturbed grave-hollows side by side under the mound. The man's oak coffin contained his sword to his right and his sword-belt, wrapped around the blade, which had a bronze buckle with garnet cloisonné cell work, two pyramidal strap mounts and a scabbard-buckle. A firesteel and a leather pouch containing rough garnets and a piece of millefiori glass were next to the man's head. Scattered around the coffin were two spears, a shield, a small cauldron and a bronze bowl, a pot, an iron-bound bucket and some animal ribs. There was a bridle, mounted with circular gilt bronze plaques, with interlace ornamentation.

Mound 14

The grave under Mound 14 has been destroyed almost completely by pillaging, but we do know that it had contained exceptionally high-quality goods belonging to a woman. These included a chatelaine, a kidney-shaped purse-lid, a bowl, several buckles, a dress-fastener, and the hinges of a casket, all silver, and also a fragment of embroidered cloth.

Mound 2

Mound 2, also looted, was the source of the many iron ship-rivets found at Sutton Hoo in 1860. In 1938, when the mound was excavated, iron rivets were found, which enabled the Mound 2 grave to be interpreted as a small boat. Carver's re-investigation revealed that there was a rectangular plank-lined chamber 16ft long by 6ft 7in wide, sunk below the surface, with the body and grave-goods laid out in it. A small ship had been placed over this before a large earth mound was raised.

Chemical analysis of the chamber floor has suggested the presence of a body in the south-western corner. The goods found included fragments of a decorated blue glass cup with a trailed decoration. There were two gilt-bronze discs with animal interlace ornament, a bronze brooch, a silver buckle and a gold-coated stud from a buckle. The tip of a sword blade showed elaborate pattern welding; silver-gilt drinking horn-mounts (struck from the same dies as those in Mound 1); and the similarity of two fragments of dragon-like mounts or plaques. Although the rituals were not identical, the association of the contents of the grave shows a connection between the two burials.

The execution burials

But it wasn't all pomp and ceremony; there was a decidedly dark side to the Sutton Hoo grave field. It was also populated by people who died violently – by hanging and decapitation. Often the bones have not survived, but the flesh has stained the sandy soil: the soil was laminated as digging progressed, so that the emaciated figures of the dead were revealed. Casts were taken.

It is believed that a gallows once stood on Mound 5, in a prominent position near to a significant river-crossing point, and that the graves contained the bodies of criminals, possibly executed from the eighth and ninth centuries onwards.

The new grave field

In 2000 the site earmarked for the National Trust's new visitor centre was excavated. When the topsoil was removed, early Anglo-Saxon burials were discovered in one corner, with some containing high-status objects. Interest was kindled with the discovery of part of a sixth-century bronze vessel, of eastern Mediterranean origin, that had probably formed part of a furnished burial. The outer surface of the so-called 'Bromeswell bucket' was decorated with a Syrian or Nubian-style frieze, depicting naked warriors in combat with leaping lions, and had an inscription in Greek that translated as 'Use this in good health, Master Count, for many happy years'.

A group of moderate-sized burial mounds was also identified. One lay in an irregular oval pit that contained two vessels, a sixth-century stamped, black earthenware urn, and a well-preserved large bronze hanging bowl, with openwork hook escutcheons and a related circular mount at the centre. In another burial, a man had been laid next to his spear and covered with a shield of normal size. The shield bore an ornamented boss-stud and two fine metal mounts, ornamented with a predatory bird and a dragon-like creature.

Mound 1

It is commonly agreed that the ship-burial discovered under Mound 1 in 1939 contained one of the most magnificent archaeological finds in Britain for its size and completeness, far-reaching connections, the quality and beauty of its contents, and for the profound interest it generated.

Although very little of the original timber survived, the form of the ship was perfectly preserved through stains in the sand which preserved many construction details.

'Nearly all of the iron planking rivets were in their original places. The ship was 89ft long, pointed at either end with tall rising stem and stern posts and widening to 14ft in the beam amidships with an inboard depth of 4ft 11in over the keel line. From the keel board, the hull was constructed clinker-fashion with nine planks on either side, fastened with rivets. Twenty-six wooden ribs strengthened the form. Repairs were visible: this had been a seagoing vessel of excellent craftsmanship, but there was no descending keel. The decking, benches and mast were removed. In the fore and aft sections along the gunwales, there were oar-rests ... indicating that there may have been positions for forty oarsmen. The central chamber had timber walls at either end and a roof, which was probably pitched'.

A so-called 'ghostly' image of the buried burial ship was revealed during exca-
vations in 1939. The 'ghost' effect was the result of sand discoloured by the
organic matter which had rotted away
(still from a film made by H. J. Phillips, brother of Charles Phillips).

Soil analyses in 1967 found phosphate traces, supporting the view that
a body had dissolved in the acidic soil. The presence of what may have
been a large coffin about 9ft long was indicated and an iron-bound wooden
bucket, an iron lamp containing beeswax, and a bottle of north continental manufacture were found close by. Artefacts near the body have been
identified as regalia, suggesting it was that of a king. Since 1940, when
H.M. Chadwick first posited that the ship-burial was probably the grave
of Rædwald, scholarly opinion has been divided between Rædwald and his
son (or step-son) Sigeberht.

We can tell from the sword hilt that the occupant was left-handed, as
the hilt's malleable gold pieces are worn down on the opposite side from
what you would expect with a right-handed owner.

David M. Wilson asserts that the metal artworks found in the Sutton
Hoo graves were 'work of the highest quality, not only in English but in
European terms'. Sutton Hoo remains fundamental to the study of art in
Britain in the sixth to ninth centuries. George Henderson has described the

ship treasures as 'the first proven hothouse for the incubation of the Insular style'. The gold and garnet fittings show the creative fusion of earlier techniques and motifs by a master goldsmith. Insular art drew upon Irish, Pictish, Anglo-Saxon, native British and Mediterranean artistic sources. 'The Sutton Hoo treasures form a continuum from pre-Christian royal accumulation of precious objects from diverse cultural sources, through to the art of gospel books, shrines and liturgical or dynastic objects.'

Beowulf

As already mentioned, *Beowulf*, the Old English epic poem set in Denmark and Sweden (mostly Götaland) during the first half of the sixth century, opens with the funeral of the great Danish king Skjöldr (Scyld Scefing or Shield Sheafson) in a ship laden with treasure, and has other descriptions of hoards, including Beowulf's own mound-burial. It gives us a unique and astounding picture of warrior life in the hall of the Danish Scylding clan: the formal mead-drinking, minstrel recitation to the lyre and the rewarding of valour with gifts, and the description of a helmet, could all be illustrated from the Sutton Hoo finds. The east Sweden connections seen in several of the Sutton Hoo artefacts reinforce the link to the world of Beowulf.

The spectacular ship-burial treasure was presented to the nation by the owner, Edith Pretty, and was at the time the largest gift made to the British Museum by a living donor. The main items are now permanently on display at the British Museum. A display of the original finds excavated in 1938 from Mounds 2, 3 and 4, and replicas of the most important items from Mound 1, are in the Ipswich Museum.

Further information at:

Bruce-Mitford, Rupert, *The Sutton Hoo Ship-Burial, Volume 1: Excavations, Background, the Ship, Dating and Inventory*, London, 1975.

Bruce-Mitford, Rupert, *The Sutton Hoo Ship-Burial, Volume 2: Arms, Armour and Regalia*, London, 1978.

Bruce-Mitford, Rupert, *The Sutton Hoo Ship-Burial, Volume 3: Late Roman and Byzantine silver, hanging-bowls, drinking vessels, cauldrons and other containers, textiles, the lyre, pottery bottle and other items*, London, 1983.

Bruce-Mitford, Rupert, *The Sutton Hoo Ship-Burial, Volume 3: Late Roman and Byzantine silver, hanging-bowls, drinking vessels, cauldrons and other containers, textiles, the lyre, pottery bottle and other items*, London, 1983.

Campbell, James, 'The Impact of the Sutton Hoo Discovery on the Study of Anglo-Saxon History,' in Kendall, Calvin B. (ed.), 'Voyage to the Other World: The Legacy of the Sutton Hoo,' *Medieval Cultures*, 5, Minneapolis, pp. 79–101, 1992.

Carver, Martin, *The Sutton Hoo Story. Encounters with Early England*, London, 2017.

18

The Sutton Hoo helmet

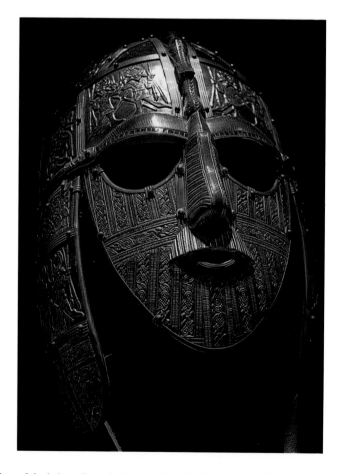

Replica of the helmet from the Sutton Hoo ship-burial 1; produced for the British Museum by the Royal Armouries, Leeds (photographer: Gernot Keller).

The helmet was found wrapped in cloths and placed to the left of the head of the body. It can be described as an ornately decorated Anglo-Saxon helmet which was both a functional piece of armour that would have offered good protection if ever used in warfare and a decorative, prestigious piece of extravagant metalwork. Julian Richards described it as 'the most iconic object' from 'one of the most spectacular archaeological discoveries ever made', and perhaps the most important known Anglo-Saxon artefact. The helmet was made of iron and covered with decorated sheets of tinned bronze. Fluted strips of moulding divided the exterior into panels, each of which was stamped with one of five designs. The visage features eyebrows, a nose and moustache, creating the image of a man joined by a dragon's head to become a soaring dragon with outstretched wings. It has become a symbol of the Early Middle Ages and 'of archaeology in general'. It was excavated as 500 rusted fragments because it was shattered when the ship's canopy came crashing down; it was first displayed following an initial reconstruction in 1945–46, and then in its present form after a second reconstruction in 1970–71.

The Sutton Hoo helmet was discovered over three days in July and August 1939, with only three weeks remaining in the excavation of the ship-burial. The landmark discovery was recorded in the diary of C. W. Phillips as follows:

'*Friday, 28 July 1939*: "The crushed remains of an iron helmet were found four feet east of the shield boss on the north side of the central deposit. The remains consisted of many fragments of iron covered with embossed ornament of an interlace with which were also associated gold leaf, textiles, an anthropomorphic face-piece consisting of a nose, mouth, and moustache cast as *a* whole (bronze), and bronze zoomorphic mountings and enrichments."

'*Saturday, 29 July*: "A few more fragments of the iron helmet came to light and were boxed with the rest found the day before."

'*Tuesday, 1 August*: "The day was spent in clearing out the excavated stern part of the ship and preparing it for study. Before this a final glean and sift in the burial area had produced a few fragments which are probably to be associated with the helmet and the chain mail respectively."'

The helmet exudes both wealth and power, with a modification to the sinister (left) eyebrow subtly linking the wearer to the one-eyed Norse god Odin. It is descended from the Roman helmets of the fourth and fifth-century Constantinian workshops. Its construction – featuring a distinctive crest, solid cap and neck and cheek guards, face mask, and leather lining – bears clear similarities to these earlier helmets.

Design features:

- Dragon motifs: three dragon heads can be seen on the helmet
- Dancing warriors
- Rider and fallen warrior
- Larger interlace depicting a single animal on the cheek guards, the neck guard and the skull cap
- Smaller interlace which covered the face mask and shows 'two animals, upside down and reversed in relation to each other, whose backward-turning heads lie towards the centre of the panel'

Beowulf

Sutton Hoo, especially the helmet, has been inextricably linked with *Beowulf* since its 1939 discovery. According to Rosemary Cramp (1957) '[h]elmets are described in greater detail than any other item of war-equipment in the poem.' The boar imagery, crest and visor all find parallels in *Beowulf*, as does the helmet's gleaming white and jewelled appearance. Though the Sutton Hoo helmet cannot be said to fully mirror any one helmet in *Beowulf*, the many isolated similarities help ensure that 'despite the limited archaeological evidence, no feature of the poetic descriptions is inexplicable and without archaeological parallel.'

Although the helmet is now, by common consent, considered to be one of the most important artefacts ever found on British soil, initially it went unnoticed due to its shattered state. No photographs were taken of the fragments *in situ*, nor were their relative positions recorded, since the importance of the discovery had not been realised. When reconstruction of the helmet began years later, Rupert Bruce-Mitford summed up the task facing the British Museum when he said that it had become 'a jigsaw puzzle without any sort of picture on the lid of the box' not to mention a jigsaw puzzle missing half its pieces.

Excavations at Sutton Hoo were concluded on 24 August 1939, and all items were shipped out the following day. In reality, the dig had been a rescue dig because nine days later Britain declared war on Germany. During World War Two the Sutton Hoo artefacts, along with other treasures from the British Museum such as the Elgin Marbles, were stored in the tunnel connecting the Aldwych and Holborn tube stations. Only at the end of 1944 were preparations made to unpack, conserve and restore the finds from Sutton Hoo.

The 1971 reconstruction of the Sutton Hoo helmet symbolises for us the Middle Ages, archaeology, and England and continues to leave its indelible mark on authors, artists, film makers and designers. The helmet is the face of the Dark Ages, and it brings to life the times of *Beowulf*, its warriors, weapons and echoing halls. Considered 'the most iconic object' from an archaeological find and hailed as the 'British Tutankhamen', in 2006 it was voted one of the 100 cultural icons of England alongside the Queen's head stamp, the double-decker bus and the cup of tea.

The replica helmet is displayed in the British Museum alongside the original (1971) helmet in Room 41.

Further information at:

Bruce-Mitford, Rupert, 'The Sutton Hoo Helmet: A New Reconstruction,' *The British Museum Quarterly*, British Museum, XXXVI (3–4), pp. 120–30, Autumn 1972.

Bruce-Mitford, Rupert, '*The Sutton Hoo Helmet,*' *The British Museum Society Bulletin*, 15, pp. 6–7, February 1974.

Cramp, Rosemary J., 'Beowulf and Archaeology,' *Medieval Archaeology*, Society for Medieval Archaeology 1, pp. 57–77, 1957.

Phillips, C. W., 'The Excavation of the Sutton Hoo Ship-burial,' *The Antiquaries Journal*, Society of Antiquaries of London, XX (2), pp. 149–202, 1940.

Phillips, C. W., '*The Sutton Hoo Ship Burial,*' *Antiques*, XXXVIII (1), pp. 12–14, July 1940.

19

The Lindisfarne Gospels

St Mark, seated, with his symbol, a winged lion, blowing a trumpet and carrying a book, from between AD 710 and 721 (held and digitised by the British Library, and uploaded to Flickr Commons, courtesy of the British Library).

The beautiful Lindisfarne Gospels is an illuminated manuscript gospel book probably produced around AD 715–720 in the monastery at Lindisfarne (Holy Island), off the coast of Northumberland, now kept in the British Library. It features the four gospels recounting the life and teachings of Jesus Christ. Around AD 635 the Irish missionary Aidan had founded the Lindisfarne monastery on Lindisfarne. King Oswald of Northumbria despatched Aidan from Iona to preach to and baptise the pagan Anglo-Saxons, following the conversion to Christianity of the Northumbrian monarchy in AD 627. Aidan died in AD 651, by which time the Christian faith was gaining a foothold in the area.

The Lindisfarne Gospels are presumed to be the work of a monk named Eadfrith, who became Bishop of Lindisfarne in AD 698 and died in AD 721; they were produced in honour of St Cuthbert, an ascetic member of a monastic community in Lindisfarne, before his death in AD 687. The book was commissioned as part of the preparations to translate Cuthbert's relics to a shrine in AD 698.

The manuscript is one of the finest works in the unique style of Hiberno-Saxon or Insular art, combining Mediterranean, Anglo-Saxon and Celtic elements. The Gospels are opulently illustrated in the insular style and were originally encased in a fine leather treasure binding replete with jewels and metals made by Billfrith the Anchorite in the eighth century. During the destructive Viking raids on Lindisfarne, this jewelled cover was lost; a replacement was made in 1852. The text is written in insular script and is the best-documented and most complete insular manuscript of the period.

The tenth century saw an Old English translation of the Gospels: a word-for-word gloss of the Latin Vulgate text, inserted between the lines by Aldred, Provost of Chester-le-Street. This is the oldest extant translation of the Gospels into the English language. We can speculate that the Gospels were appropriated from Durham Cathedral during Henry VIII's Dissolution of the Monasteries and were acquired in the early 17th century by Sir Robert Cotton from Robert Bowyer, Clerk of the Parliaments. Cotton's library came to the British Museum in the 18th century and thence to the British Library in London when this was separated from the British Museum.

The manuscript was produced in a scriptorium in the monastery at Lindisfarne, taking about ten years to create. Its pages are vellum, made using roughly 150 calf skins. The book runs to 516 pages long and is,

Folio 27r from the Lindis-farne Gospels, incipit to the Gospel of Matthew. The main text contains the first sentence of the Gospel According to Saint Matthew: 'Liber gen-erationis Iesu Christi filii David filii Abraham' – 'The book of the generation of Jesus Christ, the son of David, the son of Abraham'.

according to Janet Backhouse (1981), written 'in a dense, dark brown ink, often almost black, which contains particles of carbon from soot or lamp black.' The pens used would have been cut from either quills or reeds. The composition of the Gospels led to two new tools of the trade: the lightbox and the lead pencil. Lavish jewellery, now lost, was added to the binding of the manuscript later in the eighth century.

Eadfrith mixed 90 of his own colours with 'only six local minerals and vegetable extracts'. The variety of individual pigments is huge: the colours are derived from animal, vegetable and mineral sources, some sourced locally but others were imported from the Mediterranean, and rare pigments such as lapis lazuli would have come from the Himalayas. The pages were arranged into signatures of eight.

Janet Backhouse (1981) describes how one of the most prominent characteristic styles evident in the manuscript is the zoomorphic style adopted from Germanic art and revealed through the extensive use of interlaced animal and bird patterns throughout the book. It is possible that the birds populating the manuscript may also have been from Eadfrith's own observations of wildlife on Lindisfarne. The geometric design motifs are also of Germanic influence and appear throughout the manuscript.

Bede (AD 673–735) explains how each of the four Evangelists were represented by their personal symbol: Matthew was the man, representing the human Christ; Mark was the lion, symbolising the triumphant Christ of the Resurrection; Luke was the calf, symbolising the sacrificial victim of the Crucifixion; and John was the eagle, symbolising Christ's second coming. These symbols feature in their miniature portraits in the manuscript: Matthew, Mark, and Luke are shown writing, while John looks straight ahead at the reader holding his scroll. The Evangelists also represent the dual nature of Christ: Mark and John are shown as young men, symbolising the divine nature of Christ, and Matthew and Luke appear older and bearded, representing Christ's mortal nature.

Apart from its huge significance in the history of Christianity and the history of the (illuminated) book *per se*, The Lindisfarne Gospels wielded considerable power in the missionary work of the early Christians: it symbolised, literally, the Word of God in missionary forays while the clergy would have been well aware of the profound impression a book such as the Lindisfarne Gospels made on congregations.

St Matthew (detail), second initial page, f.29.

There is an ongoing campaign to have the gospels housed in the North East of England – where, of course, they belong. Supporters include the Bishop of Durham, *Viz* creator Simon Donald, and the Northumbrian Association; any move is, unsurprisingly, strenuously opposed by the south-centric British Library. Several possible north-east locations have been mooted, including Durham Cathedral, Lindisfarne itself or one of the museums in Newcastle upon Tyne or Sunderland. In 1971 Professor Suzanne Kaufman of Rockford, Illinois, presented a facsimile copy of the Gospels to the clergy of the Island.

In 2000 old sketches were discovered beneath the manuscript: Michelle Brown, now Professor Emerita of Medieval Manuscript Studies at the School of Advanced Study, University of London, came across the sketches of flowers, animals and Latin script beneath the illuminated Latin manuscript of the Gospels themselves. The 60 previously unknown drawings seem to have been inscribed using a metal-tipped pen on the vellum pages, leaving imprints that were visible only through a powerful microscope. They appear to be a series of practice sketches on the back of every page of the manuscript. No other metal point paintings are known to have existed before the year 1100.

> 'The Lindisfarne Gospels is one of the first and greatest masterpieces of medieval European book painting..'
> – Janet Backhouse, *The Illuminated Manuscript*, 1979

Further information at:

Backhouse, Janet, *Lindisfarne Gospels*, Grove Art Online, Oxford Art Online.

Backhouse, Janet, *The Illuminated Manuscript*, Oxford, 1979.

Backhouse, Janet, *The Lindisfarne Gospels*, Ithaca, NY, 1981.

Brown, Michelle P., *The Lindisfarne Gospels: Society, Spirituality and the Scribe*, London, 2003.

Brown, Michelle P., *The Lindisfarne Gospels and the Early Medieval World*, London, 2010.

Chilvers, Ian. (ed.), 'Lindisfarne Gospels,' *The Oxford Dictionary of Art*, Oxford, 2004.

CHAPTER 4

THE VIKINGS

20

Eymund

Jorvik Viking Centre, York

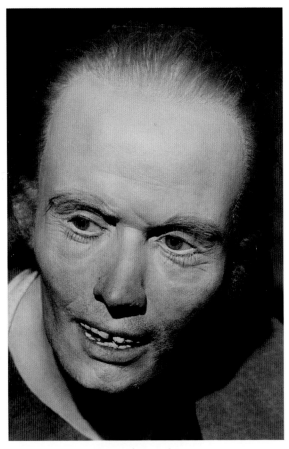

Eymund © York Press.

Meet Eymund. He was a Viking fisherman and very much a part of daily life in Viking York as delineated in the AD 975 Jorvik Cityscape there. Eymund is an unnervingly faithful reconstruction from a Viking skeleton excavated in Fishergate in York. In 1990, when cutting-edge computer technology allowed for the first time the affordable reconstruction of faces from the past, York Archaeological Trust used a skeleton from tenth-century burials at Fishergate to literally bring visitors face to face with the Vikings and their world. The result was a highly realistic presence gazing out at you from the 1,000-year-plus past.

Eymund is joined by Thorfast, the antler bone carver; Lothin, the wood turner; Snarri, the jeweller; and Svein, the leather worker – all working away in their workshops and stalls. Other exhibits feature the toilets, wells, warehouses, workshops and homes faithfully reproduced from the major discoveries by archaeologists from the York Archaeological Trust. The result is a fascinating, almost living, survey of Viking life in tenth-century Jorvik, with noises, smells and sights evoking another world, all conveyed in Time Cars, which silently glide you back through the years.

The importance of Viking York

The Great Heathen Army descended on England in AD 865, probably from a bay in Frisia at the mouth of the River Scheldt in today's Netherlands. In AD 876 the army took York. In AD 878 an Anglo-Scandinavian kingdom of York was established under a Danish Prince, Gudfrid, who importantly had converted to Christianity and had the support of the Church of Saint Cuthbert. Ireland and Pictland were frequently plundered, with a thousand captives taken from Armagh in AD 869, and Dumbarton Rock besieged and destroyed in AD 870 with 200 ships returning to Dublin laden with captives.

During the second half of the ninth century, dynasties of Scandinavian origin controlled territories on either side of the Irish Sea, with urban trading centres in Dublin and York. To the north, the Pictish kingdoms lost territory to Norse-speaking settlers, and the Gaelic Kingdom of Alba, which would become the medieval kingdom of Scotland, was first mentioned around AD900.

To the south, England was partitioned into an area of Danish rule (the so-called Danelaw), while Alfred of Wessex and his descendants worked to unite the remaining realms into what would become England.

A scene from Jorvik in 2010.

The Jorvik Viking Centre

The Jorvik Viking Centre in Coppergate was created by the York Archaeological Trust in 1984 after extensive excavations in the area. Well-preserved remains of some of the timber buildings of the Viking city of Jorvík were discovered, along with workshops, fences, animal pens, privies, pits and wells, together with durable materials and artefacts of the time, such as pottery, metalwork and bones. Unusually, wood, leather, textiles, and plant and animal remains from the period around AD 900 were also discovered

Animatronic tableau of fishermen working and talking at the Jorvik Viking Centre, York (photographer: Chemical Engineer).

to be preserved in oxygen-deprived wet clay. In all, over 40,000 objects were unearthed.

In 2001 the centre was refurbished and enlarged to 'intensify the message' at Jorvik by increasing 'the sensory stimuli to include smells, more sounds, heat, cold and damp'. Visitors (and there have been more than 20 million of them) are taken back to 5:30pm on 25 October AD 975 in a time-capsule, and then embark on a tour of a reconstructed Viking settlement which includes voices speaking in Old Norse as well as aromas and 'life-like animated figures, made by laser technology from skeletons found on the site'.

Beyond this is an extensive museum area, which combines an exhibition of some 800 finds from the site with interactive displays and the opportunity to learn about tenth century life and to discuss it with 'Viking' staff. Among the exhibits is a replica of the famous Coppergate Helmet, which was found near the site of the centre and is now in the Yorkshire Museum.

Further information at:

Hopkins, Joseph S., 'The "Viking Apocalypse," : An Analysis of the Jorvik Viking Centre's Ragnarök and its Media Reception,' *RMN Newsletter*, University of Helsinki, 8, pp. 7–12, 22 February 2014.

Renfrew, Colin, (ed.), 'York and the Public Presentation of Archaeology,' *Archaeology: Theories, Methods and Practice* (4th ed.), London, pp. 536–45, 2004.

Wilson, Peter, 'High-tech wizardry beams Jorvik visitors into Viking past,' *Edmonton Journal*, 16 July 2005.

The Lloyds Bank Coprolite

This is a large paleofaeces, or desiccated human dung specimen, recovered by archaeologists from York Archaeological Trust excavating the Viking settlement of Jorvik. The coprolite was unearthed in 1972 beneath the site of what was to become the York branch of Lloyds Bank and may be the largest example of fossilised human faeces ever found, measuring 8in long and 2in wide. Analysis of the stool reveals that its producer subsisted largely on meat and bread, whilst the presence of several hundred parasitic eggs suggests he or she was riddled with intestinal worms. In 1991 York Archaeological Trust paleoscatologist Andrew Jones made international news with his appraisal of

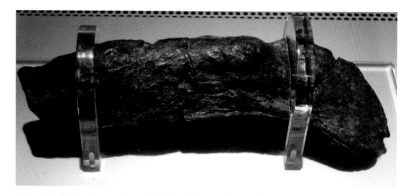

The Lloyds Bank coprolite: fossilised human faeces dug up from a Viking site at Coppergate, York. It contains pollen grains, cereal bran, and many eggs of whipworm and maw-worm. It is on display at the Jorvik Centre in York (photographer: Linda Spashett, Storye book).

the item for insurance purposes: 'This is the most exciting piece of excrement I've ever seen ... In its own way, it's as irreplaceable as the Crown Jewels.'

The specimen was put on display at the city's Archaeological Resource Centre (now known as DIG), the outreach and education institution run by the York Archaeological Trust. In 2003 it broke into three pieces after being dropped whilst on exhibition, and efforts were obviously made to reconstruct it. It has been displayed intact at the Jorvik Viking Centre since 2008.

Further information, if you really want it, at:
Horwitz, Tony . 'Endangered Faeces: Paleo-Scatologist Plumbs Old Privies – It may not be the Lost Ark, but then, Andrew isn't exactly Indiana Jones,', *Wall Street Journal*, p. A1, 9 September 1991.
Simon, Jeffery, 'Museum's broken treasure not just any old shit,' *The Guardian*, 6 June 2003.

21

Ridgeway Hill Viking burial pit near Weymouth

In June 2009 the archaeological world, specifically the Viking archaeological world, was stunned to learn of the discovery of 54 dismembered male skeletons and 51 skulls, decapitated and dumped in an old Roman quarry pit on a road in Weymouth. The skeletons were in a haphazard jumble but the severed heads had been piled up neatly to one side. Forensic examination revealed that the mass grave was filled with executed Vikings: a war grave from the tenth century vividly reminiscent of the atrocities we associate with Nazi Germany, Rwanda and Bosnia. Radiocarbon dating of the remains established that they dated to between AD 970 and AD 1025. An analysis of teeth from ten of the skeletons was carried out by the NERC Isotope Geosciences Laboratory, part of the British Geological Survey. This found that the men had come from Scandinavia, with one thought to have come from north of the Arctic Circle, and had eaten a high-protein diet comparable with human remains found at known sites in Sweden.

The disparity between skulls and skeletons may be accounted for by the fact that three of the heads – perhaps of high-ranking individuals – were kept as souvenirs or put on stakes elsewhere. The men are believed to have been Vikings executed by local Anglo-Saxons. Judging from the absence of any remains of clothing or other possessions, it is thought that the victims were stripped of their clothes and executed at the graveside. They exhibit the typical defensive wounds on their hands, arms and skulls; the hacking injuries and multiple blows to the vertebrae, jawbones and skulls are consistent with a bloodbath in which several strikes were required to effect decapitation. There were a total of 188 wounds visible on the skeletons, an average of four per individual, indicating that they had been the victims of severe violence

The grave was excavated during the creation of the Weymouth Relief Road, in the build-up to the 2012 Olympic Games. © Oxford Archaeology

before being killed. One man had had the top of his skull sliced off, exposing his brain.

But it was not just trauma injuries which the bodies displayed: 'Curiously, many of the individuals had suffered from infections and physical impairment,' says Louise Loe, a member of the Oxford Archaeology team and co-author of a book on the excavation and its findings.

'A spectacular example, on display at the British Museum, is one individual who had osteomyelitis – a chronic bone infection – involving his thigh bone. The bone was twice the size of a normal thigh bone and had openings which would have oozed smelly pus during his life. The leg would have been swollen and painful. It must have caused considerable disability to the individual, and consequently the rest of the group. Other examples of impaired mobility or limb usage were also evident. There was a deformed right leg caused by a fracture to the femur and a collar bone fracture. Bladder or kidney disease was also evidenced by a stone found amongst the disarticulated bones.'

Dental analysis suggests the deceased came from the Arctic and sub-Arctic regions of Norway,

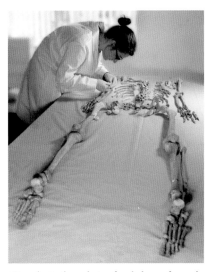

Osteological analysis of a skeleton from the mass grave found in Weymouth, Dorset.
© Oxford Archaeology

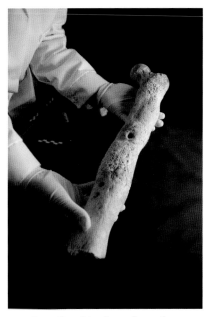

An infected leg bone from the grave.
© Oxford Archaeology

Sweden, Iceland, the Baltic States, Belarus and Russia, with the youngest in his early teens and the oldest over 50.

One surprise was the amount of deliberate cosmetic dental surgery that was revealed; possibly an indication of warrior status that has been observed in other Scandinavian burials. Loe again says:

'There is direct evidence of deliberate modification of the body that rarely survives in archaeological records. All of them were made in more or less the same area of the teeth in all of the individuals and, in several cases, the furrows were identical, even though the skeletons were from different parts of Sweden. Modifying teeth in this way may have been undertaken for the same reasons that we choose to have tattoos today … Given the depth and precision of the filing marks, they are likely to have been created by a skilled person … They may have been created in reference to a person's occupational status, or they may simply have been pure decoration.'

'Several individuals had suspected brucellocis,' says Loe, describing 'a highly contagious infectious [zoonotic] disease that is passed from animals to humans, either by the ingestion of unsterilised milk or meat or by coming into close contact with secretions from infected animals.'

One indisputable conclusion is that these victims suggest a much more fragile mortality than the stereotypical alpha male brutish mightiness usually associated with Vikings.

Gareth Williams, the curator of the 2014 British Museum Norse exhibition, sums up the importance of the find to the history of the Vikings in Britain:

'Not only is it one of the most dramatic Viking finds of recent years, it is particularly important in providing a very different perspective to the usual view of Viking military success in England in that period.'

Further information at:
Loe, Louise, *Given to the Ground: A Viking Age Mass Grave on Ridgeway Hill, Dorset*, British Museum and online, 2014.
Loe, Louise , 'Death on Ridgeway Hill,' *Current Archaeology*, 229, pp. 38–41, February 2015.

22

The Galloway Hoard

A selection of objects from the Viking age Galloway Hoard (courtesy of National Museums Scotland).

When metal detectorist Derek McLennan set out for a spot of detector work one day in September 2014 on Church of Scotland land in Dumfries and Galloway, he could hardly have expected to be later uncovering an early Christian cross and a carefully wrapped vessel along with other spectacular finds in a ninth to tenth-century hoard described by archaeologists as the best to emerge in Scotland in recent years. It contains more than 100 artefacts, including gold, silver, glass, enamel and textiles. The items among the treasure are very diverse and originated across a wide geographic area that includes Anglo-Saxon England, Ireland, and Scandinavia. Many of them are believed to be unique. The bulk of the hoard's contents is silver bullion.

The Christian cross, unearthed from beneath a pile of ingots and rings, is solid sliver. Whoever buried it had carefully wrapped it in cloth with a finely wound silver chain; the Rev. Dr David Bartholomew (who was with Mclennan) said:

'It was tremendously exciting, especially when we noticed the silver cross lying face-downwards. It was poking out from under the pile of silver ingots and decorated arm-rings, with a finely wound silver chain still attached to it. It was a heart-stopping moment when the local archaeologist turned it over to reveal rich decoration on the other side.'

Also of interest are the preserved enamelled decorations, which could be the four evangelists Matthew, Mark, Luke and John. The haul also includes

Pre-conservation image, taken in June 2018, of an ornamented silver pectoral cross with wire chain. The cross is decorated with what appears to be gilding and niello, each arm ornamented with a motif; there appears to be an ornamentation missing from the centre. A chain of coiled silver wire is wrapped around the arms. Loot for later, a personal possession, a votive offering, or a protective amulet?

what was considered the largest silver Carolingian pot ever discovered, with its lid still in place. However, recent research has revealed Zoroastrian symbols across its surface, indicating that it was more likely made in the Sasanian Empire (the Empire of Iranians) pre-seventh century AD. The vessel was one of the older items in the hoard and may have been more than 100 years old by the time it was deposited. It was made of a silver alloy, and was found wrapped in the remains of a cloth. It contains more objects and was examined using X-rays in November 2014 before being opened and emptied. The contents were found to be a collection of silver Anglo-Saxon disc brooches, an Irish silver brooch, Byzantine silk from the area around Constantinople (Istanbul), a gold ingot and gold and crystal objects wrapped in cloth.

National Museums Scotland describes the hoard as:

'The richest collection of rare and unique Viking-age objects ever found in Britain or Ireland … the Galloway Hoard brings together a stunning variety of materials and treasures from Ireland, the Anglo-Saxon kingdoms and as far away as Asia. The Hoard transports us back to a critical moment in history: the formation of the political entities we now know as Scotland, England and Ireland, in a time of Viking raids.'

While Dr Martin Goldberg, Principal Curator of Medieval Archaeology and History adds:

'Nothing like this has ever been found in Scotland . . . research so far is pointing to a new understanding of Scotland in the international context of the earliest Viking Age.

Hoards are usually thought of as buried collections of multiple precious objects hidden for safekeeping, then lost or forgotten due to death or destruction. Viking-age hoards are particularly prone to this stereotype because the Vikings are often clichéd as endlessly raiding, looting, warmongering and terrorising. But there were many reasons for hoarding in the past, and many reasons why hoards might be preserved under the ground for centuries. The Norse sagas give us examples where wealth was buried in the ground deliberately so that it could be accessed in the afterlife; treasures were also

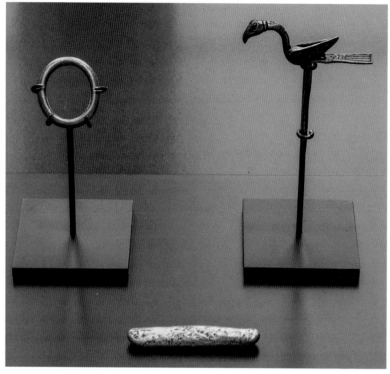

Gold items from the Viking treasure.

buried to seal an oath, or as a claim on land. But Stuart Campbell of the National Museum of Scotland has suggested that this particular hoard was buried for safekeeping, likening it to 'a safety deposit box that was never claimed'. He comments that the discovery may change views of the historical relationship between Scotland and the Vikings: 'We have the idea of Vikings as foreigners who carried out raids on Scotland, but this was a Viking area where they settled and traded, and the people who lived there were culturally and linguistically Norse.'

The Viking Age can be thought of as a Silver Age because of the new sources of silver that became available through connections to Scandinavia, the Baltic Sea and beyond. This abundance of silver is demonstrated through the increase in burial of silver hoards The main sources of Viking-Age silver in Britain were coinage from the Anglo-Saxon and Carolingian kingdoms, and dirhams from the Islamic Caliphates of Central Asia.

The serendipitous discovery of over 100 objects accumulated over several centuries tell the story of hundreds of Viking lives from over 1,000 years ago. Men and women, manufacturers and owners, traders and thieves, the holy and the profane – ongoing analysis will tell us so much more about their social history: we already know a lot more about Viking history than we did before the Galloway Hoard was detected in that field at Balmaghie, Galloway.

More information at:

Owen, Olwyn, 'Galloway's Viking treasure: the story of a discovery,' *British Archaeology*, 140, pp. 16–23, January–February 2015.

Images, videos and 3D objects of the hoard at National Museums Scotland.

CHAPTER 5

THE MIDDLE AGES

23

The Domesday Book

1086

The National Archives at Kew tells how, 'Domesday is by the far the most complete record of pre-industrial society to survive anywhere in the world and provides a unique window on the medieval world.' *Domesday Book* is a manuscript record of the 'Great Survey' of much of England and parts of Wales completed in 1086 by order of William I, William the Conqueror (r. 1066-87). William was no fool: the *Anglo-Saxon Chronicle* states that in 1085 the king sent his agents to survey every shire in England, to list his holdings and calculate the dues owed to him. One of the first rules of conquest: establish what your new territories are worth to you and what they owe you. The survey's main purpose was to determine what taxes had been owed during the reign of King Edward the Confessor (r.1042–66), William's predecessor on the throne of England, thereby allowing William to reassert the rights of the Crown and assess where power lay after a wholesale redistribution of land following the Norman Conquest.

'After this had the king a large meeting, and very deep consultation with his council, about this land; how it was occupied, and by what sort of men. Then sent he his men over all England into each shire; commissioning them to find out "How many hundreds of hides were in the shire, what land the king himself had, and what stock upon the land; or, what dues he ought to have by the year from the shire." Also he commissioned them to record in writing, "How much land his archbishops had, and his diocesan bishops, and his abbots, and his earls"; and though I may be prolix and tedious, "What, or

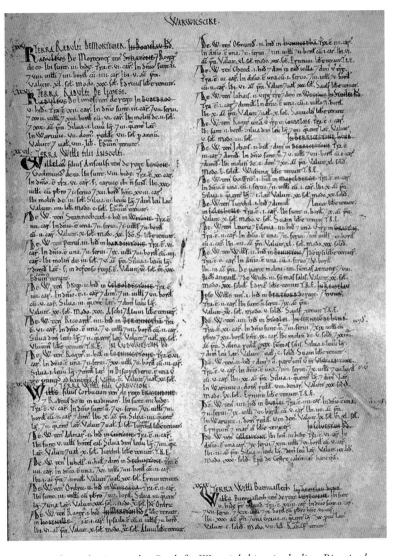

A page from the Domesday Book for Warwickshire, including Birmingham.

how much, each man had, who was an occupier of land in England, either in land or in stock, and how much money it was worth." So very narrowly, indeed, did he commission them to trace it out, that there was not one single hide, nor a yard of land, nay, moreover

105

(it is shameful to tell, though he thought it no shame to do it), not even an ox, nor a cow, nor a swine was there left, that was not set down in his writ. And all the recorded particulars were afterwards brought to him.'

– *Anglo Saxon Chronicle*

It is easy to underestimate the massive political convulsion created by the Norman Conquest and the land grab of landed estates which ensued. William had to be sure that he was not losing out and needed to have official confirmation that the rights of the Crown, which he claimed to have inherited, had not been filched in the process. Scholars believe that the survey was to reassure William in establishing certainty and a definitive reference point as to property holdings across the nation, in case such evidence was needed in disputes over Crown ownership.

The survey, therefore, recorded the names of the new holders of lands and the assessments on which their tax was to be paid. But, importantly for him and every historian of Britain after him, it did more than that; it turned out to be a good attempt to make a national valuation list, estimating the annual value of all the land in the country, the national wealth. After recording the assessment of the manor, the survey sets forth the amount of arable land, and the number of plough teams (each reckoned at eight oxen) available for working it; then the river-meadows, woodland, pasture, fisheries (fishing weirs), water-mills, salt-pans (if by the sea) and other subsidiary sources of revenue; the peasants are enumerated in their several classes; and finally the annual value of the whole, past and present, is roughly estimated.

Where did the apocalyptic name Domesday come from? Richard FitzNeal – a cleric and bureaucrat in the service of Henry II – wrote in the *Dialogus de Scaccario* (c. 1179) – *Dialogue Concerning the Exchequer*, the first administrative treatise of the Middle Ages – that the book was so-called because its decisions were unalterable, like those of the Last Judgement, there was no appeal and its sentence could not be quashed.

The project to publish *Domesday* was begun by Lord North's Government in 1773, and the book appeared in two volumes in 1783 as a partial-facsimile of the manuscript. In 1811, a volume of indexes was added. In 1816, a supplementary volume, separately indexed, was published containing:

- The Exon Domesday – for the south-western counties
- The Inquisitio Eliensis
- The Liber Winton – surveys of Winchester late in the 12th century
- The Boldon Buke (Book) – a survey of the bishopric of Durham a century later than Domesday

The manuscript is held at The National Archives at Kew, London; in 2011 the Open Domesday site made the manuscript available online.

The book is a priceless primary source for modern historians. No survey approaching the scope and extent of *Domesday Book* was attempted again in Britain until the 1873 *Return of Owners of Land* which presented the first complete, post-Domesday picture of the distribution of landed property in the then United Kingdom.

Domesday Book originally encompassed two independent tomes in two separate volumes: 'Little Domesday' (covering Norfolk, Suffolk, and Essex), and 'Great Domesday' (covering much of the rest of England – except for lands in the north that later became Westmorland, Cumberland, Northumberland, and the County Palarine of Durham – and parts of Wales bordering, and included within, English counties). Tax-exempt status meant that no surveys were made of the City of London, Winchester and some other towns. Other areas of modern London were then in Middlesex, Kent, Essex, etc., and are included in *Domesday Book*. Most of Cumberland and Westmorland is missing because in 1086 they were not fully conquered. The County of Durham is missing because the Prince Bishop of Durham (William de St-Calais) had the exclusive right to tax it; in addition, parts of the North East were covered by the 1183 *Boldon Book*, listing areas liable to tax by the Bishop of Durham.

'Little Domesday' is physically smaller than its companion and is the more detailed survey, right down to the last horse, cow and pig. This first attempt resulted in a decision to avoid such micro detail in 'Great Domesday'. Each county's list opens with the king's demesne lands; under the feudal system the king was the only true 'owner' of land in England and was thus the ultimate overlord. This was followed by holdings of bishops, then of the abbeys and religious houses, then of lay tenants-in-chief and lastly the king's serjeants (*servientes*), and Saxon thegns who had survived the Conquest, all in hierarchical order.

Domesday names a total of 13,418 places including entries of interest concerning most of the towns with fragments of older customary agreements, records of the military service due, of markets, mints, and the like. From the towns, from the counties as wholes, and from many of its ancient lordships, the crown was entitled to archaic dues in kind, such as honey. *Domesday Book* lists 5,624 mills – a low estimate since the book is incomplete. For comparison, less than 100 mills were recorded in the country a century earlier. This means a mill for every 46 peasant households and implies a great increase in the consumption of baked bread in place of boiled and un-ground porridge. The book also lists 28,000 slaves, far fewer than the count in 1066.

How did this most ambitious surveys (in 1085) come together? Most shires were visited by a group of royal officers (*legati*), who held a public inquiry, probably in the great assembly known as the shire court. These were attended by representatives of every township as well as of the local lords. The unit of inquiry was the Hundred (a subdivision of the county). The return for each Hundred was sworn to by 12 local jurors, half English and half Norman.

H. C. Darby explains the importance of the *Domesday Book* and, incidentally, why it is in this book:

'[Anyone who uses it] can have nothing but admiration for what is the oldest "public record" in England and probably the most remarkable statistical document in the history of Europe. The continent has no document to compare with this detailed description covering so great a stretch of territory. And the geographer, as he turns over the folios, with their details of population and of arable, woodland, meadow and other resources, cannot but be excited at the vast amount of information that passes before his eyes.'
– H.C. Darby, *Domesday England*, p. 12

Further information at:

Bates, David, *A Bibliography of Domesday Book*, Woodbridge, 1985.
Chrystal, Paul, *The Place Names of County Durham*, Stenlake, 2021.
Chrystal, Paul, *The Place Names of Yorkshire*, Stenlake, 2017.
Darby, H.C., *Domesday England*, Cambridge, 1977.
Finn, R. Welldon, *Domesday Book: a guide*, London, 1973.
Harvey, Sally, *Domesday: Book of Judgement*, Oxford, 2014.
Sawyer, Peter (ed.), *Domesday Book: a reassessment*, London, 1985.

24

Spectacles and Roger Bacon

*The first printed representation of a pair of spectacles,
in Germany, in the 15ᵗʰ century.*

Roger Bacon (c. 1219–c. 1292), also known as Doctor Mirabilis, was a medieval English philosopher and Franciscan friar who emphasised the study of nature through empiricism – the modern scientific method. He was obviously a man of vision because it was he who led the way in the invention of spectacles, or glasses. He was regarded as a wizard and is particularly famous for the story of his mechanical or necromantic brazen head – a legendary automaton which was reputed to be able to correctly answer any question put to it, although it was sometimes restricted to 'yes' or 'no' answers. Bacon, assisted by Friar Bungy, was said to have spent seven years building the device in order to discover whether it would be possible to render Britain impregnable by ringing it with a wall of brass. They only got anywhere once they took on the assistance of a demon. The head either collapsed or exploded or was scrapped for being useless.

Later, he was partially responsible for a revision of the medieval university curriculum, which saw the addition of optics to the traditional *quadrivium* – the four subjects or arts (arithmetic, geometry, music and astronomy). Bacon's major work, the *Opus Majus*, was sent, on request, to Pope Clement IV in 1267, which showcased his views on how to incorporate Aristotelian logic and science into a new theology. One of the seven parts in this was 'On the Science of Perspective' (*De Scientia Perspectivae*). Although gunpowder was first invented and described in China, Bacon was the first in Europe to record its formula.

With the *Opus Majus* he sent his *Opus Minus*, *De Multiplicatione Specierum*, *De Speculis Comburentibus* and an optical lens. He seems to have studied most of the known Greek and Arabic works on optics.

In Part V of the *Opus Majus*, Bacon deals with physiology of eyesight and the anatomy of the eye and the brain, considering light, distance, position, and size, direct and reflected vision, refraction, mirrors and lenses.

Thérèse Schwartze (1851 –1918) – Portrait of Johanna Eugenia Theadora Van Hoorn-Schouwenburg – with glasses. Amsterdam Museum (1887).

Judy in Disguise (with glasses) – rare 7in Brazilian pressing of this hit in 1967, recorded by John Fred & his Playboy Band – said to be a parody of the Beatles' Lucy in the Sky with Diamonds.

His treatment was influenced by the Latin translation of Alhazen's *Book of Optics*. He also draws heavily on Eugene of Palermo's Latin translation of the Arabic translation of Ptolemy's *Optics*; on Robert Grosseteste's work based on Al-Kindi's *Optics*; and, through Alhazen (Ibn al-Haytham), on Ibn Sahl's work on dioptrics – the branch of optics dealing with refraction.

Anyone who wears glasses or other corrective eyeware today owes a debt to Roger Bacon, for it is through his pioneering work in optics that they are able to see clearly now.

Further information at:

Bass, Trystan, L., *A Brief History of Women's Eyeglasses*, 2018 (http://www.trystancraft.com/costume/2018/04/17/a-brief-history-of-eyeglasses/).

Crombie, Alistair Cameron, 'Science, Optics, and Music in Medieval and Early Modern Thought', *Medical History*, 36 (1), p. 119, 1990.

James, R.R., 'The Father of British Optics: Roger Bacon, c. 1214–1294,' *British Journal of Ophthalmology* 12, No. 1, pp. 1–14, 1928.

Wade, Nicholas J., *A Natural History of Vision*, Cambridge, Massachusetts, 1998.

25

Magna Carta

M agna Carta Libertatum ('Great Charter of Freedoms'), commonly called *Magna Carta,* is a royal charter of rights agreed to by King John at Runnymede on 15 June 1215. If the *Domesday Book* was a prudent and largely successful attempt to assess the wealth of the nation by William I and establish what was rightfully owed to him, then *Magna Carta,* some 130 years later, as drafted by Archbishop of Canterbury Stephen Langton, was a failed attempt to make peace between the unpopular king and a faction of troublesome barons. John and his predecessors had ruled using the principle of *vis et voluntas,* or 'force and will', taking executive and sometimes arbitrary decisions, often justified on the basis that a king was above the law. *Magna Carta* guaranteed the protection of church rights, protection for the barons from illegal imprisonment, access to swift justice and limitations on feudal payments to the Crown, to be implemented through a council of 25 barons. Neither side honoured their commitments, and the charter was annulled by Pope Innocent III within a couple of months because it had been extracted by duress; only a few sentences from it remain on the statute book. More to the point, its beneficiaries were not downtrodden serfs who largely remained in slavery, but wealthy Anglo-Norman

Opposite: Engraved 1733 facsimile of the original text of the Magna Carta, surrounded by a series of 25 coats of hand-coloured arms of the Barons, panel at foot containing notes and a representation (hand-coloured) of the remains of King John's Great Seal, all panels surrounded by oak leaf and acorn borders.
Source: Bonhams; John Pine (1690-1756), publisher

barons who themselves were responsible for much of the oppression of the serfs but were desperate to curb the monarch's excesses. And *Magna Carta* promulgated neither jury trial nor *habeas corpus* – both came much later. This impasse resulted in the First Barons' War (1215–17), the civil war led by Baron Robert Fitzwalter who claimed publicly that John had attempted to rape his daughter; he was implicated in a plot to assassinate John in 1212 .

Nevertheless, *Magna Carta* remains one of the most important documents in British, and indeed world, history. Its presence has been evident – cited, referred to and relied on – in many of the more significant episodes in our history: over the last 800 years *Magna Carta* has influenced monarchs and statesmen, lawyers and lawmakers, prisoners, Chartists and suffragettes. But how did this, to use the words of the British Library, 'old piece of parchment become such a powerful symbol of our rights and freedoms?'

In the turbulent 17th century *Magna Carta* was used by the Parliamentarians who were struggling against James I and Charles I and the monarchists who believed that they could wield absolute power. When Charles I came to power with his conviction that he had utter and absolute power, Parliament cited *Magna Carta,* pointing out that there were limits to regal power; this forced the king initially to agree to the Petition of Right, later the Declaration of Right which embodied *Magna Carta* and brought *Magna Carta* out of obscurity.

Sir Edward Coke it was who turned a rather arid, elite constitutional legal document into a viable text that justified resistance against the tyrannous use of prerogative first by James I and then Charles I, justified by the doctrine of the divine right of kings. And the core argument was that *Magna Carta* protected the freedoms, the lives, and the estates of men, free men. 'To no one will we sell, to no one deny or delay right or justice.'

In 1642 *Magna Carta* was the banner under which Parliament fought the Civil War and established the real liberties of the subject, the independence of the judiciary, an end to torture, while at the same time abolishing Star Chamber and the king's power to arrogate to himself the right to punish people.

It became a resource that all sorts of interest groups, whether they were marginal, economic, poor people using *Magna Carta* to justify resisting paying taxes, or radicals. For the 19th-century Chartist movement it provided a template of sorts for their six-point charter; this was their new form of

Magna Carta which was a much more democratic document than the original one, calling for universal suffrage and for annual parliaments. *Magna Carta* allowed some radicals 'to clothe themselves in patriotism'. They were able to assert that their demands were neither disruptive nor iconoclastic. *Magna Carta* demonstrates that the pursuit of liberty is intrinsic to Britain and the British way of life. Elements of the role and function of our Parliament derives from the Council called by *Magna Carta*.

'On the one hand, for many, Magna Carta is alive and well. It remains a bedrock of Britishness; the foundation of all that's good about laws and liberties from Land's End to John O'Groats. The alternative view is that Magna Carta has been reduced to nothing but a symbol; a crumbling relic, redundant at law and in practice. As always, the truth is probably somewhere in the middle.'
– Shami Chakrabarti in 2015

'It is perhaps easiest to think of Magna Carta in two ways: first, as a document of historical and legal significance; and secondly, as a principle underlying how we live, through equality under the rule of law and through accountability. Magna Carta matters both for what it said in 1215 and, perhaps more significantly now, for what it has come to symbolise.'
– Professor Justin Fisher, Professor of Political Science at Brunel University London. He is Director of the University's Magna Carta Institute and chairs the Academic Sub-Committee of the Magna Carta 800 Group.

Human rights

In the late 18th century in the United States of America, *Magna Carta* informed both the Declaration of Independence and the United States Constitution, and it is still held in some esteem. The Constitution's Fifth Amendment guarantees that 'no person shall be deprived of life, liberty, or property, without due process of law,' a phrase that was derived from *Magna Carta*.

When the Universal Declaration of Human Rights was adopted in 1948, it drew on *Magna Carta*, as well as the Bill of Rights (1689) (which stated that it was illegal for the Crown to suspend or dispense with the law, and insisted on due process in criminal trials) and others, for inspiration and asserts that people everywhere should be protected by fundamental human rights, regardless of their citizenship, race, gender or beliefs. The European Convention on Human Rights, drafted in response to the horrors of World War Two, followed close on the heels of the Universal Declaration. Today these vital protections are incorporated into British law by our own Human Rights Act (1998) – a modern day *Magna Carta*? If the main thing we take from the *Magna Carta* is that no power is absolute, the Human Rights Act honours that legacy by exercising constraint.

'Magna Charter was therefore the chief cause of Democracy in England, and thus a Good Thing for everyone (except the Common People).'
– W.C Sellar and R.J. Yeatman, *1066 and All That*

Further information at:

Arlidge, Anthony, *Magna Carta Uncovered*, London, 2014.
Breay, Claire, *Magna Carta: Manuscripts and Myths*, London, 2010.
Danziger, Danny, *1215: The Year of Magna Carta*, London, 2004.
Poole, Austin Lane, *From Domesday Book to Magna Carta 1087–1216* (2nd ed.), Oxford, 1993.

26

Chaucer's *Canterbury Tales*

Geoffrey Chaucer, from the 15ᵗʰ-century Ellesmere manuscript of The Canterbury Tales.

The *Canterbury Tales* is a collection of 24 stories in over 17,000 lines written in Middle English by Geoffrey Chaucer between 1387 and 1400. The tales are mostly written in verse and form part of a story-telling contest by a group of pilgrims as they travel together from London to Canterbury to visit the shrine of Saint Thomas Becket at Canterbury Cathedral. The pilgrims are, in effect, a kind of itinerant book group. The winner's prize for this engaging contest is a free meal at the Tabard Inn at Southwark on their return.

One of the significant contributions *The Canterbury Tales* makes to English literature is in the popularisation of the English vernacular in mainstream literature, as opposed to French, Italian or Latin. English had, however, been used as a literary language centuries before Chaucer's time, and several of Chaucer's contemporaries – John Gower, William Langland, the Pearl Poet, and Julian of Norwich – also wrote major literary works in English.

It seems that *The Canterbury Tales* is incomplete since in the general prologue 30 pilgrims are introduced. Chaucer's intention was to write four stories by each pilgrim, two each on the way to and from Becket's shrine, thus making about 120 stories. Incomplete as it may be, *The Canterbury Tales* is considered one of the most important works in English literature.

These are the salient features of what are, in my opinion, the best of the tales; the tales themselves are only briefly introduced so as not to spoil them for the reader who wants to explore more.

General Prologue – the frame story of the poem, as set out in the 858 lines, is of a religious pilgrimage. The narrator, Chaucer, is in The Tabard Inn in Southwark, where he meets a group of 'sundry folk' who are all on the way to Canterbury, the site of the shrine of Saint Thomas Becket, a martyr reputed to have the power of healing the sinful. The setting is April …

The Knight's Tale – described by Chaucer as the person of highest social standing amongst the pilgrims, though his manners and clothes are unpretentious. We are told that he has taken part in some 15 crusades in many countries and also fought for one pagan leader against another. Chivalry and courtly love are prominent. The epic poem *Teseida* (Teseida delle Nozze d'Emilia, or 'The Theseid, Concerning the Nuptials of Emily') by Boccaccio is the source of the tale. It starts when two cousins and knights, Palamon

Canterbury Tales mural by Ezra Winter (1886–1949). North Reading Room, west wall, Library of Congress, John Adams Building, Washington DC (1939).[1]

and Arcite, are captured and imprisoned by Theseus, Duke of Athens, after being found unconscious following his battle against Creon …

The Miller's Tale – a complete antithesis told by the drunken Miller, Robin, to 'quite' the Knight's Tale; it also involves a conflict between two men over a woman, but with none of the nobility or heritage of classical mythology, but is instead 'a rollicking, bawdy fabliaux', designed to annoy the knight and amuse the other pilgrims with its crude comedy. Robin is 'a stout and evil churl fond of wrestling'. Robin's story is of a carpenter, John, who lives in Oxford with his much younger wife, Alisoun, a local beauty. In order to make extra money, John rents out a room in his house to an Oxford University student named Nicholas, who has taken a liking to Alisoun. The parish clerk, Absolon, also fancies Alisoun …

The Reeve's Tale – Oswald the reeve is the manager of a large estate who reaped huge profits for his master and himself. He is described as skinny, bad-tempered and old; his hair is closely cropped reflecting his social status as a serf. His sword is rusty, while he rides a fine grey horse called Scot. The Reeve is a skilled carpenter, a profession mocked in the 'Miller's Tale'. Oswald responds with a tale that ridicules the Miller's profession. The tale is based on a popular fabliau (also the source of the Sixth Story of the Ninth Day of The Decameron) of the period with many different versions, the 'cradle-trick'. Chaucer improves on his sources with his detailed characterisation and sly humour, linking the act of grinding corn with sex. The north-eastern accent of the two clerks is also the earliest surviving attempt in English to record a dialect from an area other than that of the main writer. Chaucer's works are written with traces of the southern English or London accent of himself and his scribes, but he raises comedy from imitating accents.

The dissolute cook

The Cook's Tale – Chaucer never finished 'The Cook's Tale,' which breaks off after 58 lines. The story starts telling of an apprentice named Perkyn, a lover of drinking and dancing. Perkyn is released by his master and moves in with a friend who also loves to drink, and whose wife is a shopkeeper but really she's a prostitute.

The Wife of Bath's Tale – among the best-known, it is important because It provides rare insight into the role of women in the Late Middle Ages. It was written during the reign of Richard II, when it was increasingly evident that changes needed to be made within the traditional hierarchy at court; a 'feminist' reading of the tale argues that Chaucer chose to address through the prologue the change in *mores* that he had noticed, in order to highlight the imbalance of power within a male-dominated society. Women were typically identified not by their social status and occupations, but solely by their relations with men: a woman was defined as either a maiden, a spouse or a widow – capable only of child-bearing, cooking and other 'women's work'. The tale is an example of the 'loathly lady' motif, that of a woman who appears unattractive (ugly, loathly) but undergoes a transformation upon being approached by a man in spite of her unattractiveness, becoming extremely desirable. It is then revealed that her ugliness was the result of a curse which was broken by the hero's action.

The Franklin's Tale – focuses on issues of providence, truth, generosity and gentillesse in human relationships. The story tells how two lovers, Arveragus and Dorigen, decide that their marriage should be one of equal partnership, although they agree that, in public, Arveragus should appear to have overall authority to preserve his high status. Arveragus then travels to Britain to seek honour and fame, leaving Dorigen alone in France. She misses her husband terribly, and is particularly concerned that his ship will be wrecked on the black rocks of Brittany as he returns home.

While Arveragus is absent, Dorigen is pestered against her will by another suitor, a squire named Aurelius. Finally, to get rid of him, and in a lighthearted

The Wife of Bath. One of a series of illustrations from Chaucer's Canterbury Tales, edited by John Saunders, published by J.M. Dent & Co in 1889, based on those in the Ellesmere Manuscript.

mood, she makes a rash promise and tells Aurelius that he might have her love providing he can dispose of all the rocks on the coast of Brittany …

The Physician's Tale – a domestic drama about the relationship between a daughter and her father, based on the legend of Verginia from Livy and retold in the 13th-century *The Romance of the Rose*. Virginius – the father of the 14-year-old Verginia and a knight – kills his daughter (who was abducted on the way to school) rather than give her up to the corrupt judge Appius. Chastity and consent are everything … Shakespeare's Titus Andronicus references this tale: after Lavinia is raped and mutilated, her father Titus kills her, arguing that she 'should not survive her shame'. He then compares himself to Virginius.

Further information at*:*
Chrystal, Paul, *Women in Ancient Rome*, Stroud, 2014.

The Pardoner's Tale – prompted by the host's wish to hear something positive after the preceding depressing tale of calamity. Briefly narrating his methods of swindling people – he then proceeds to tell a moral tale. Intent on killing Death, three young men encounter an old man who says they will find him under a nearby tree. When they arrive, they discover a hoard of treasure and decide to stay with it until nightfall and carry it away under the cover of night. Out of greed, they murder one another: *Radix malorum est cupiditas* ('Greed is the root of [all] evils').

The Shipman's Tale – the story of a merchant, his wife and her lover, a monk; the story is a retelling of a common type of folktale called 'the lover's gift regained'. The tale describes a merchant whose wife is something of a party girl. A young monk, who is close friends with the merchant, comes to stay with them. After confessing that she does not love her husband, the wife asks the monk for 100 franks to pay her debts. The monk, without her knowledge, borrows the money from the merchant to give to the wife, at which point she agrees with the monk, 'That for these hundred frankes he sholde al nyght Have hire in his armes bolt upright' (315–316). Criticism of the clergy apart, the tale also connects money, business and sex.

The Prioress's Tale – meet Madame Eglantine, with her impeccable table manners, aristocratic way and mispronounced French. She maintains a secular lifestyle, including keeping lap dogs which she favours over people, a fancy rosary and brooch inscribed with 'Amor vincit omnia'. Her story is of a child martyr killed by Jews, a common theme in medieval Christianity; criticism much later focusses on the tale's anti-semitism. The story is typical of a genre popular at the time known as the miracles of the Virgin such as those by Gautier de Coincy.

Further information at:

Louise O. Fradenburg, 'Criticism, Anti-Semitism, and the Prioress' Tale,' in *Chaucer: New Casebooks*, Valerie Allen (ed.) and Ares Axiotis, New York, 2003

The Monk's Tale – a collection of 17 short stories, *exempla*, on the theme of tragedy; a series of brief accounts of toppled despots, criminals and fallen heroes. The tragic endings of these historical figures are recounted: Lucifer, Adam, Samson, Hercules, Nebuchadnezzar, Belshazzar, Zenobia, Pedro of Castile, Peter I of Cyprus, Bernabò Visconti, Ugolino of Pisa, Nero, Holofernes, Antiochus, Alexander the Great, Julius Caesar, and Croesus.

The Nun's Priest's Tale – a beast fable and mock epic based on an incident in the Reynard cycle. The story of Chanticleer and the Fox became even more popular in Britain through this. The fable is set in a world of talking animals who reflect both human perception and fallacy. Its protagonist is

Chauntecleer, a proud rooster who dreams of his imminent doom in the form of a fox. Frightened, he awakens Pertelote, the favourite among his seven wives. She assures him that he only has indigestion and chastises him for worrying over a simple dream. Chauntecleer responds by recounting stories of prophets who foresaw their deaths, dreams that came true, and dreams that were more profound (for instance, Cicero's *Dream of Scipio*). Chauntecleer is reassured and prepares for a new day. Sadly for Chauntecleer, his own dream was also correct. A col-fox, 'ful of sly iniquitee' (l. 3215), who had previously tricked Chauntecleer's father and mother to their downfall, lies in wait for him in a bed of wortes …

The Second Nun's Tale – a hagiography of the life of Saint Cecilia. The prologue contains three sections: 1. four stanzas on the hazards of idleness 2. the Invocation to Mary (nine stanzas) 3. the 'Interpretation of the name Cecilia which Brother Jacob of Genoa put in his legend'. This final section comprises a series of invented etymologies about that name Cecilia. A virgin maiden, Cecilia, with an unwavering faith in God which transformed her into Saint Cecilia, is to marry Valerian. Cecilia asks Valerian to swear not to betray her if she reveals her secret, that she has an angel that watches over her – Christianity was a crime at the time. Every day Cecilia prayed that God would 'protect her virginity'. She then tells Valerian that if he were to 'touch or love [her] ignobly, without delay [the angel] will slay you on the spot; and thus [he] would die in [his] youth.' He respects her wishes. Almachius, a Roman prefect, does not …

St Cecilia by Guido Reni (1575–1642), Norton Simon Museum, Pasadena, California.

Further information at:
Ortiz, Julio Vélez, *The Language of Alchemy in Chaucer's 'The Canon's Yeoman's Tale' and Ben Jonson's The Alchemist*, Universidad de Puerto Rico, 1991.

The Manciple's Tale – the Manciple, a purchasing agent for a law court, tells a fable about Phoebus Apollo and his pet crow, which is both an aetiological myth explaining the crow's black feathers, and a moralistic injunction against gossip. The source for the tale is Ovid's *Metamorphoses*.

The Manciple digresses to assert that you cannot tame a creature to remove its essential nature; no matter how well-fed a tame cat may be, it will still attack mice instinctively. Similarly, mighty Phoebus's wife takes a low-born lover; the crow reveals their secret, and an enraged Phoebus kills his wife. In his grief afterwards, he regrets his act and blames the crow, cursing it with black feathers and an unmelodious voice. The Manciple ends by saying it is best to hold one's tongue and not to say anything malicious even if it is true.

Storytelling was one of the main forms of entertainment in Chaucer's England, and storytelling contests had been popular for hundreds of years. In 14th-century England the English *Pui* was a group with an appointed leader who would judge the songs or stories of the group. The winner received a crown and, as with the winner of *The Canterbury Tales*, a free dinner. Research reveals that the general prologue, in which the innkeeper and host Harry Bailey introduces each pilgrim, is a pastiche of the historical Harry Bailey's surviving 1381 poll-tax account of Southwark's inhabitants.

The Canterbury Tales leans heavily on the *Decameron* by Giovanni Boccaccio (1313-1375) and contains more parallels to it than any other work. In fact, one quarter of Chaucer's work parallels a tale in the *Decameron*. *The Canterbury Tales* is a collection of stories built around a frame tale, the prologue; Chaucer's tales differ from most other story 'collections' in this genre chiefly by virtue of its great variation. Most story collections focus on a theme, usually a religious one. The idea of a pilgrimage to bring such a diverse collection of people together for literary purposes was also novel, though 'the association of pilgrims and storytelling was a familiar one'. Introducing a competition among the tales encourages the reader to compare the tales in all their variety, and allows Chaucer to showcase the breadth of his skill in different genres and literary forms. Chaucer, in the general prologue, describes not the tales to be told, but the people who will tell them, making it clear that structure will depend on the characters rather than a general theme or moral.

In 1386, Chaucer became Controller of Customs and Justice of the Peace and, in 1389, Clerk of the King's Works. This was the period in which Chaucer began working on *The Canterbury Tales*. They were turbulent times: the Catholic Church was embroiled in the Western Schism; and Lollardy, an early English religious movement led by John Wycliffe, was flourishing.

The *Canterbury Tales* is among the first English literary works to mention paper, a relatively new invention that fostered unprecedented dissemination of the written word. Political clashes, such as the 1381 Peasants' Revolt and conflicts ending in the deposing of King Richard II, speak of the turmoil surrounding Chaucer in the time of the *Tales'* writing. Many of his close friends were executed and he himself wisely moved to Kent to distance himself from events in London.

Most of us know that Procol Harum's 1967 hit 'A Whiter Shade of Pale' is often assumed to be referencing *the Canterbury Tales* through the line, 'as the miller told his tale'. However, lyricist Keith Reid has denied this, saying he had never read Chaucer when he wrote the line. I don't believe him.

Further information at:

Bisson, Lillian M., *Chaucer and the late medieval world*, New York, 1998.

Cooper, Helen, *The Canterbury tales. Oxford Guides to Chaucer* (2nd ed.), Oxford, 1996.

Kolve, V.A., *The Canterbury Tales: fifteen tales and the general prologue: authoritative text, sources and backgrounds, criticism* (2nd ed.), New York, 2005.

[1]Photographed in 2007 by Carol Highsmith (1946–), who explicitly placed the photograph in the public domain. According to the inscription, this mural shows (left to right): 'The Miller, in the lead, piping the band out of Southwark; the Host of Tabard Inn; the Knight, followed by his son, the young Squire, on a white palfrey; a Yeoman; the Doctor of Physic; Chaucer, riding with his back to the observer, as he talks to the Lawyer; the Clerk of Oxenford, reading his beloved classics; the Manciple; the Sailor; the Prioress; the Nun; and three priests.' (Source: John Y. Cole, *On These Walls*, Washington DC, Library of Congress, p. 79, 1995.)

27

The Stone of Scone

Replica of the Stone of Scone masquerading at Scone Palace.

It was on Christmas Day 1950 when a group of four Scottish nationalist students from the University of Glasgow broke into Westminster Abbey and removed the Stone of Destiny from King Edward I's Coronation Chair. The students were members of the Scottish Covenant Association, a group that supported home rule for Scotland. By removing the stone, the group hoped to promote their cause for Scottish devolution and to reignite a sense of national identity amongst the Scottish people: at the time, the Scottish National Party had 0.7 per cent of the vote.

But disaster struck when, on removing the stone from under the chair, it crashed to the floor and broke into two pieces. On discovering that the Stone was missing, the authorities closed the border between Scotland and England for the first time in 400 years. In 2008, Ian Hamilton's

The real stone in exile in Westminster Abbey.

book, *The Taking of the Stone of Destiny*, was made into a film entitled *Stone of Destiny*. In April 1951 the police received a message and the stone was found on the site of the High Altar at Arbroath Abbey where, in 1320, the assertion of Scottish nationhood was made in the Declaration of Arbroath. The stone was returned to Westminster Abbey in February 1952, where it remained until 1996, when the then Scottish Secretary, Michael Forsyth, arranged for its transfer to Edinburgh Castle.

The location of the stone has always been imbued with significant symbolism – for centuries the abduction of Scotland's historic coronation stone to London has been a source of grievance for the Scottish nation, and not just for nationalists – it goes deeper than that. The Stone of Scone is of significant historical importance to Scotland.

According to legend, it was Jacob's pillow from Biblical times, which arrived in Scotland by way of Ireland and became the seat on which kings of Scotland were crowned. This, the Stone of Jacob, was taken by Jacob from Bethel while on the way to Haran (Genesis 28:10–22). It was then supposedly taken to ancient Ireland by the prophet Jeremiah.

Historically, it was kept at the now-ruined Scone Abbey in Scone, near Perth, having been brought there from Iona by Kenneth MacAlpin c. AD 841. In 1296, during the First Scottish War of Independence, King Edward I of England plundered the stone as booty and removed it to Westminster Abbey, where it was fitted into a wooden chair – known as King Edward's Chair – on which most subsequent English and then British sovereigns have been crowned. By removing the Stone to London, Edward I was declaring himself 'King of the Scots'; Edward sought to claim the status of the 'Lord Paramount' of Scotland, with the right to oversee its King.

In the 1328 Treaty of Northampton between Scotland and England, the English agreed to return the beleaguered stone to Scotland, but riotous crowds prevented it from being removed from Westminster Abbey. The stone languished in England for another six centuries, even after King James VI of Scotland assumed the English throne as James I of England in 1603. On 11 June 1914, suffragettes protesting for women's rights placed a small explosive device near the Coronation Chair and Stone; the explosion damaged the chair but not the stone.

Further information at:

Breeze, David, *The Stone of Destiny: Symbol of Nationhood*, Historic Scotland, 1997.

Hamilton, Ian R., *No Stone Unturned: The Story of the Stone of Destiny*, London, 1952.

28

A pilgrim badge of Saint Thomas Becket

(1119–70)

A Becket pilgrim badge (museum number: 2001,0702.1)
(source: the British Museum).
© *The Trustees of the British Museum.*

Thomas Becket was Archbishop of Canterbury from 1162 until his murder in 1170. He is venerated as a saint and martyr by both the Catholic Church and the Anglican Communion. He clashed with Henry II over the rights and privileges of the Church and was murdered by followers of the king in Canterbury Cathedral. Soon after his death, he was canonised by Pope Alexander III.

Things erupted in June 1170: Roger de Pont L'Évêque, Archbishop of York, was at York with Gilbert Foliot, Bishop of London, and Josceline de Bohon, Bishop of Salisbury, to crown the heir apparent, Henry the Young King. This breached Canterbury's privilege of coronation and in November 1170 Becket excommunicated all three. Henry the Young King (1155–83) was the eldest surviving son of Henry II of England and Eleanor of Aquitaine and, from 1170, he was titular King of England, Duke of Normandy, Count of Anjou and Maine. Henry the Young King was the only English king since the Norman Conquest to be crowned during his father's reign.

When he heard what Becket had done, Henry was incensed and is said to have uttered words interpreted by his men (Reginald FitzUrse, Hugh de Morville, William de Tracy and Richard le Breton) as wishing Becket killed. The exact wording is in doubt but the most commonly quoted, as invented in 1740 and handed down by oral tradition, is 'Will no one rid me of this turbulent priest?' Rid him they did.

There are several contemporary accounts of what happened; particularly lurid is that of the appropriately named Edward Grim. This is part of his description:

'… the impious knight … suddenly set upon him and [shaved] off the summit of his crown which the sacred chrism consecrated to God … Then, with another blow received on the head, he remained firm. But with the third the stricken martyr bent his knees and elbows, offering himself as a living sacrifice, saying in a low voice, "For the name of Jesus and the protection of the church I am ready to embrace death." But the third knight inflicted a grave wound on the fallen one; with this blow … his crown, which was large, separated from his head so that the blood turned white from the brain yet no less did the brain turn red from the blood; it purpled the appearance of the church … The fifth – not a knight but a cleric who had entered with the knights ... placed his foot on the neck of the holy priest and precious martyr and (it is horrible to say) scattered the brains with the blood across the floor, exclaiming to the rest, 'We can leave this place, knights, he will not get up again.'

It did not take long before the faithful throughout Europe began venerating Becket as a martyr. In 1173 Becket's sister Mary was appointed Abbess of Barking as reparation for the murder of her brother. On 12 July 1174, during the Revolt of 1173–74, Henry humbled himself in public penance at Becket's tomb and at the Church of St Dunstan's, which became a popular pilgrimage site. The assassins meanwhile fled north to skulk in de Morville's Knaresborough Castle for about a year.

Miracles were reported immediately after the martyrdom of Thomas Becket, notably by the monks Benedict of Peterborough and William of Canterbury. The saint was known to cure many illnesses: Benedict notes that Edilda and Wlviva regained the ability to walk; Edmund of Canterbury,

The Cooper Memorial Window, St Peter's Berkhamsted by Nathaniel Westlake, in memory of industrialist William Cooper (1813–85). It shows Becket with a sword in his head (photographer: Cnbrb).

Robert from the Isle of Thanet and Henry of Fordwich all got their eyesight back; Muriel and Agnes were rescued from the jaws of death; Ethelburga's shoulder pain was relieved; and Eilward of Tenham recovered his sense of smell. Pilgrims with health issues could do a lot worse than go on a pilgrimage to Canterbury. Badges of Becket have been discovered in abundance and attest to his flourishing cult. However, this all came to an end in 1538 when Henry VIII ordered the extirpation of his shrine.

Before that, though, by the late Middle Ages it was the done thing for pilgrims to take home souvenirs; badges and *ampullae* were much more practical than relics, so these became the keepsakes of choice. It was only in the mid-20th century that archaeologists, with the aid of metal detectors, unearthed a large number of badges. They came from northern and western parts of Europe, with the majority of them discovered in waterways; for instance, hundreds have been excavated from the River Thames. They were thrown into rivers because it was a ritual for pilgrims to break the badges and throw them into water as wishes or as gestures of thanksgiving.

The image on page 129 depicts a bust of Becket, who wears the pointed mitre and chasuble, liturgical vestments characteristic of a bishop. It corresponds in form with the reliquary bust once displayed in the Corona Chapel at Canterbury Cathedral, which was used to house the martyr's skull.

Further information at:
Blick, Sarah, 'Votives, Images, Interaction and Pilgrimage to the Tomb and Shrine of St. Thomas Becket, Canterbury Cathedral,' *Push Me, Pull Me: Imaginative, Emotional, Physical, and Spatial Interaction in Late Medieval and Renaissance Art*, pp. 21–58, Leiden, 2011.
Chrystal, Paul, *Knaresborough Through Time*, Stroud, 2011.
Guy, John, *Thomas Becket: Warrior, Priest, Rebel*, London, 2012.
Lee, Jennifer, 'Medieval Pilgrims' Badges in Rivers: The Curious History of a Non-Theory,' *Journal of Art Historiography*, 11, no. 1, pp. 1–11, 2014.
Slocum, Kay Brainerd, *The Cult of Thomas Becket: History and Historiography through Eight Centuries*, Oxford, 2019.

29

The 'Pricke of Conscience' window

1410

*The Doom Window showing the death
and destruction which awaits us all.*

All Saints, North Street, in York is a stunning church by any standard; it comprises Early English, Decorated and Perpendicular styles and features an octagonal tower with an unusual 120ft spire. Emma Raughton, a visionary anchorite, lived in an anchorhold here – a two-storey house attached to the aisle.

The church has some of the finest mediaeval stained glass in Europe, including the aisle window which shows the Six Corporal Acts of Mercy (as in *Matthew*) and the famous 1410 Doom Window (or 'Pricke of Conscience' window), which graphically depicts *your* last 15 days before the Day of Judgement. There is also an outstanding 15th-century hammer-beam ceiling decorated with beautiful, colourful angels. Other treasures include a figure in one of the 14th-century windows wearing glasses – one of the earliest depictions of spectacles – and representations of the green man in the aisles and nave.

Further reading:
Chrystal, Paul, *York Churches and Places of Worship*, Stenlake 2016.

30

Caxton's printing press

1476

William Caxton (c. 1422 – c. 1491), merchant, diplomat, and writer, was, in 1476, the first person to introduce the printing press to England, and as a printer was the first English bookseller. In 1476 books in England were still copied out by hand, by scribes: they are called manuscripts which means 'written by hand' in Latin.

In 1438 he was apprenticed to Robert Large, a wealthy London silk mercer, but after his death he moved to Bruges. Here he was elected the 'governor of the English nation' in Bruges – that is he was the leader of all the English people living in the city. In the 1450s Johannes Gutenberg had set up Europe's first printing press in Mainz, Germany – a momentous event that would change the culture of Europe. This new print technology involved setting pages of type from individually cast metal letter forms that were then run off on a hand press. For the first time it was possible to speedily and mechanically reproduce multiple copies of the same work.

His travels enabled Caxton to see the fledgling printing industry while he was in Cologne, which inspired him to set up a printing press in Bruges with Colard Mansion. The first evidence of his interest in this magical new technology was his involvement in the printing there, in 1472, of a massive Latin encyclopaedic work, *Bartholomaeus Anglicus's De Proprietatibus Rerum* ['*On the Properties of Things*']. Wynkyn de Worde, Caxton's associate and successor, who printed an English translation of *Bartholomaeus* in Westminster in 1495, says in the verse epilogue to it that 'William Caxton [was] first printer of this book In Latin tongue at Cologne'.

William Caxton showing specimens of his printing to Edward IV (1442–83) and his queen, Elizabeth Woodville. Published in The Graphic in 1877, referring to The Caxton Celebration, commemorating the 400ᵗʰ anniversary of the first printed book in England, which took place in London in the summer of 1877.

When Margaret of York, sister of Edward IV, married the Duke of Burgundy, they moved to Bruges and befriended Caxton. It was the Duchess who encouraged Caxton to complete his translation of the *Recuyell of the Historyes of Troye*, a collection of stories based on Homer's *Iliad*, which he completed in 1471. In the epilogue, Caxton tells how his 'pen became worn, his hand weary, his eye dimmed' with copying the book by hand, so he 'practised and learnt' how to print it, publishing it in Ghent in 1473. Back in England, this and a healthy demand for his translation prompted Caxton to set up a press at Westminster in 1476.

Although the first book he is known to have produced was the first ever print edition (*editio princeps*) of Chaucer's *The Canterbury Tales*, he went on to publish chivalric romances (the most important of which was Sir Thomas Malory's *Le Morte d'Arthur* in 1485), classical works (for example Cicero's *Of Old Age, Of Friendship and Of Nobility* (1481), and a prose version of Virgil's *Aeneid*, the *Eneydos* (1490), and English and Roman histories (for example, a Latin universal history, the *Polychronicon*), and to edit many others. He printed a second edition of *The Canterbury Tales* in 1483,

William Caxton's printer's mark, 1478.

as well as other poems by Chaucer: his *Parliament of Fowls* and *Anelida and Arcite* (both c. 1477–78), and his *Troilus and Criseyde* and *House of Fame*, both in 1483. He also printed Chaucer's prose translation of Boethius's *Consolation of Philosophy* (1478). Thus, Caxton is responsible for establishing Chaucer in print which has endured over the centuries. He was the first to translate *Aesop's Fables* in 1484. Caxton's translations of the *Golden Legend* (a prose collection of saints' lives, 1483) and *The Book of the Knight in the Tower* (1484) contain the earliest verses of the Bible to be printed in English. The last works from his press included several concerned with spiritual well-being: *The Art and Craft to Know Well to Die* (1490), *The Craft for to Die Well* (1491) and a collection of spiritual writings generally known as *The Book of Divers Ghostly Matters* (1491).

Caxton's involvement in literally changing the world did not end with printing and publishing. He was also an accomplished editor of his projects with an acute awareness of how to make his work accessible and reader friendly. Many of the books he published contain his own prefaces or epilogues, explaining the contents and/or the circumstances that led him to publish them. He made extensive changes to the manuscript of Malory's *Morte Darthur*, dividing it into books and chapters and modifying some parts of the text where he felt the language could be difficult for his readers. Sometimes he added substantial material of his own to a work. He appended an additional *'Liber ultimus'* ['Final Book'] to his edition of the *Polychronicon* to bring its account of history closer to his own modern times.

It is difficult some 700 years later to imagine the revolution in communication and education and the impact that the printed word caused – the nearest we can get to it is the arrival of the Internet.

The John Rylands Library in Manchester holds the second largest collection of printing by William Caxton, after the British Library's collection. In the Rylands collection of more than 60 examples, 36 are complete and four are unique.

Caxton printed 80 per cent of his works in the English language, doing much of the translation and editing work himself. He is credited with printing as many as 108 books, 87 of which were different titles, and translated 26 of the titles himself.

Caxton gets the credit for standardising the English language through printing – that is, homogenising regional dialects and largely adopting the London dialect. This facilitated the expansion of English vocabulary, the regularisation of inflection and syntax, and a widening gap between the spoken and the written word. Richard Pynson started printing in London in 1491 or 1492 and favoured what came to be called Chancery Standard, largely based on the London dialect. Pynson was a more accomplished stylist than Caxton and consequently pushed the English language further toward standardisation.

Caxton was nothing if not prolific: he published over three million words of his own writings during his career, either in direct translation or in passages he added to books. His own prose made important contributions to the English language, including the introduction of a large number of neologisms into the lexicon: his writings provide the first recorded use of such nouns as 'concussion', 'fortification', 'servitude' and 'voyager', for example. In all, he gives us first usage of over 1,300 words.

Innovation in typography, illustration and design did not escape him: he used a variety of different type fonts and he was the first English printer to commission woodcuts to illustrate his books. They appear for the first time in his edition of *Mirror of the World* (1481) and thereafter in a number of other books, perhaps most famously in his second edition of Chaucer's *The Canterbury Tales*, with its portraits of the pilgrims.

Caxton was anxious, too, to develop markets for English publications: English writings became far more widely available than ever before through the proliferation of copies that print technology enabled. After his death, Caxton's press was taken over by his associate Wynkyn de Worde who, initially using Caxton's own type and woodcuts, further extended the range of publications in English, printing over 800 books before his own death in the 1530s. By then the market for English printed books was firmly established.

Further information at:
Blake, Norman Francis, *Caxton: England's First Publisher*, London, 1976.

31

Boar badge from the Battle of Bosworth

22 August 1485

The boar badge

This object is just over an inch high and just under one and a half inches wide, but it is of significant historic importance for all that. The boar badge was commissioned by Richard III, last king of the House of York, and was worn by someone of consequence among his followers, maybe even by someone in the royal household. Richard ordered that 13,000 boar badges be made for his son Edward's investiture at York in 1483, but few have actually been found thereabouts. Similar badges discovered around the country are made of cloth or copper, but for people of status more precious metals were required – such as silver, as in this find.

His son's investiture as Prince of Wales took place at the Archbishop's Palace close to York Minster. Richard himself planned to be buried in York Minster – a radical ambition as English monarchs were traditionally interred at Westminster Abbey. He planned to build a huge chantry chapel at the minster where 100 additional chaplains would pray for his soul. Had he not died in battle at Bosworth leaving his corpse to desecration by Henry Tudor, he would have been the first English king to be buried at York Minster.

Another silver gilt boar badge was discovered on the site of the Battle of Bosworth Field in 2009, leading to speculation that the find gave us the precise spot where Richard III lost his horse before succumbing to death and defeat – two miles away from the Bosworth Heritage Centre on private farmland near Upton, Leicestershire. That boar badge is now on display at the Bosworth Battlefield Heritage Centre.

'The crucial archaeological evidence came from our systematic metal detecting survey,' explained Battlefields Trust archaeologist Dr Glenn Ford, who has no doubts about the provenance of the badge, and is convinced the evidence 'proves exactly' where the battle took place.

'The most important by far is the silver-gilt boar, which was Richard III's own badge, given in large numbers to his supporters. This one is special, because it was almost certainly worn by a knight in King Richard's own retinue who rode with the King to his death in his last desperate cavalry charge. It was found right next to the site of a small medieval marsh, and the King was killed when his horse became stuck in a mire.'

Other treasures unearthed include silver coins belonging to Charles the Bold of Burgundy, a silver-gilt badge found close to where the Duke of Norfolk met his demise, and the largest collection of round shot ever recorded on a medieval battlefield in Europe.

The Stillingfleet badge depicts a more complete boar than the Bosworth version, which is somewhat disabled: Stillingfleet can boast two intact legs and a haunch (Bosworth's has one complete leg and three stumps), and the attachment loop on the back (Bosworth's just has the rectangular solder

Richard III's skull languishing in that Leicester car park with the rest of his remains – he should have been reinterred in York, as he wished.

patch where the loop was once attached). More of the gilding also appears to have survived: on the Stillingfleet badge you can clearly see the glint of gold on the boar's tail, and some very impressive genitalia.

Further information at:

Richard III Museum: the museum and website dedicated to Richard III, Monk Bar, York. https://richardiiiexperience.com/
Chrystal, Paul, *York A-Z*, Stroud, 2014.
Chrystal, Paul, *York: Places of Learning*, Stroud, 2015.

32

Sweating sickness caricature

1485–1551

'Safer on the battlefield than in the city.'
– Thomas More reflecting on the dangers posed by 'the sweats' in a letter to Erasmus, 19 August 1517

'There raged at that time, in London and other parts of the kingdom, a species of malady unknown to any other age or nation, the 'sweating sickness', which occasioned the sudden death of great multitudes though it seemed to be not propagated by any contagious infection, but arose from the general disposition of the air and of the human body. In less than twenty-four hours the patient commonly died, or recovered.'
– *Hume's History of England Vol II*, page 384

Sweating sickness goes by many names including the Sweat, Sweats, English sweating sickness, English sweat, *sudor anglicus,* the Swat, hote iylls, hote sicknes, Stup-Gallant, Stoupe Knave and Know thy Master, Posting Sweat and the New Acquaince. It was a terrifying contagious disease which is still very much shrouded in mystery; it afflicted England and later continental Europe in a series of epidemics beginning in 1485. The last outbreak occurred in 1551, after which the disease seems to have vanished. In between there were outbreaks in 1506, 1517 and in 1528. The 1551 outbreak struck on 7 July and lasted for 23 days, in which time it killed nearly 1,000 people. The onset of symptoms was sudden, with death often occurring within hours. Its cause remains unknown, although there is speculation that an unknown species of hantavirus was responsible. Ague, rheumatic fever and influenza have also been proposed over the years. Ague is fever (such as from malaria) indicated by paroxysms of chills, fever, and sweating recurring at regular intervals.

In 1517 London was thronged with foreign workers, while in 1528 Europe was preoccupied with the military operations of Francis I in Italy – both events obvious facilitators of disease transmission. Whatever the precise nature of the disease, it would be contending with numerous other immune depressing contagions amongst the population of England: spotted fever, brain fever, epidemic flux, scurvy, diphtheria, smallpox, measles, scarlet fever, erysipelas to name but a few. In 1886 the journal *Science* concluded: 'That England was not blotted out of existence by pestilential disease during this epoch is a marvel.'

The Sweat broke in London on 19 September 1485, causing the postponement of the coronation of Henry VII until 30 October. One of the most alarming features of the disease was the speed with which it could claim its victims. There were numerous reports of people suddenly dropping dead in the street. Thomas Forrestier (or Le Forestier), a French physician living in London at the time, wrote of the disease:

A 1799 caricature showing Tom Ruby being tricked by six friends into thinking he has the sweating sickness.

'We saw two prestys standing togeder and speaking togeder, and we saw both of them dye sodenly. Also in die – proximi we se the wyf of a taylour taken and sodenly dyed. Another yonge man walking by the street fell down sodenly.'

Forrestier is our earliest source, writing in 1490; he notes the high mortality at 15,000 lives in London and more in Oxford, and the acute onset of:

'… sudden grete swetyng and stynkyng, with rednesse of the face and of all the body, and a contynual thurst, with a grete hete and hedache because of the fumes and venom …'

He added that some patients presented with black spots. It seems that the most dangerous stage of the disease was the first few hours; those who survived the first 24 hours would go on to make a full recovery.

Both Forrestier and Richard Grafton (in 1569) describe the plague as something 'new'; so it was probably not a recurrence of a previous epidemic. John Caius (or Keys) adds to the symptomatology. Caius, born in 1510, was physician to Edward VI, Mary I and Elizabeth I. He was a practising physician in Shrewsbury in 1551 when an outbreak occurred, and he described the symptoms and signs of the disease in *A Boke or Counseill Against the Disease Commonly Called the Sweate, or Sweatyng Sicknesse* (1552), which is still our main source of knowledge of the disease.

He opens his description with a sonorous 'this disease is not a sweat onely … but a feuer'. The disease had a sudden onset, inducing anxiety, followed by cold shivers which were sometimes very violent, dizziness, headache 'and madness of the same', and severe pains in the back, shoulders and extremities accompanied by exhaustion, 'grief in the liver and nigh stomacke'. The cold stage might last from between half an hour to three hours, after which a feeling of hotness and sweating took over. The characteristic sweat broke out suddenly without any obvious cause. A sense of heat, headache, delirium, rapid pulse and intense thirst accompanied the sweat. Palpitation and chest pain were frequent symptoms as well. No skin eruptions were noted by observers, including Caius. In the final stages, there was either general exhaustion ('marueilous heauinesse') and collapse, or an irresistible urge to sleep, which Caius thought was fatal if the patient submitted. Fluid and electrolyte imbalance may have been the actual cause of death.

Unfortunately, one attack did not confer the consolation of immunity, and some people suffered several episodes before dying. The disease usually occurred in summer and early autumn. The relatively affluent male adult population was most seriously afflicted, particularly the clergy. Unlike many other medieval diseases, it seemed to spare the very young and the very old. It was most prevalent in rural areas but also severely affected the nobility living in London and the student populations of Oxford and Cambridge. Caius, however, noted that the patients most at risk of the disease were 'either men of wealth, ease or welfare or [not one to forego a stereotype] of the poorer sort, such as were idle persons, good ale drinkers and tavern haunters.'

In later outbreaks, Cardinal Wolsey contracted the disease twice, in 1517 and 1528, and recovered on both occasions, although it claimed the lives of many of his household. The sweat may have been what afflicted Arthur, Prince of Wales (the elder brother of Henry VIII), and his wife Catherine of Aragon in March 1502; their illness was described as 'a malign vapour which proceeded from the air': other theories contend that it was tuberculosis, the Black Death or influenza. Catherine recovered, but Arthur died on 2 April 1502 at Ludlow Castle, age 15. Anne Boleyn contracted the disease, but she too survived. Anne's brother-in-law William Carey did not. The disease's predilection for the young and wealthy led to it being dubbed the 'Stop Gallant' by the poorer classes.

The economic effects of the Sweat even invaded Tudor culture when, in 1604, Shakespeare put the sweating sickness up there with the three great population shrinkers – war, executions and poverty – in *Measure by Measure* (Act 1 Scene 2) when Mistress Overdone bemoans the loss of her trade:

'Thus, what with the war, what with the sweat, what with the gallows and what with poverty, I am custom-shrunk.'

A second outbreak occurred in 1507, followed by a third and much more severe epidemic later that year, which also spread to Calais, where it remained mostly confined to the English ex-pat population.

This outbreak was frequently fatal; half the population died in some areas when it reached epidemic proportions in 1528 during its fourth outbreak. It erupted in London at the end of May, causing panic and death, and quickly spread over most of England, and, although it did not infect

A 'danse macabre' (dance of death) from 1493, in deference to the sweats.

Scotland, it did reach Ireland, where Lord Chancellor Hugh Inge was the most prominent victim. It became known as 'The *English* Sweate' for the very reason that it did not spread to Scotland and Wales. It also seemed to affect foreigners living in England less severely. In 1881 Arthur Bordier delivered a paper to the Anthropology Society of Paris entitled, 'On the special susceptibility of the fair-haired races of Europe for contracting sweating Sickness'. In the paper, he presented an interesting, but unproven, theory that sweating sickness did not solely affect Englishmen but instead had a tendency to infect those descended from the Anglo-Saxon and spared those descended from the Celts.

The disease also affected the court of Henry VIII and, as noted, Anne Boleyn is said to have contracted and survived the disease. Chronicler Edward Hall commented on how it affected the king's court and nobility in London:

'Suddenly there came a plague of sickness called the sweating sickness that turned all his [the King's] purpose. This malody was so cruel that it killed some within two houres, some merry at dinner and dedde at supper. Many died in the Kinges courte. The Lorde Clinton, the Lorde Gray of Wilton, and many knightes, gentleman and officiers.'

A good number of Englishmen unsuccessfully tried to escape the disease by fleeing to Ireland, Scotland, and France, only to die there. John Caius wrote that 'it followed Englishmen like a shadow'. Because the mortality rate was so high in London, Henry VIII suspended the court and left there, frequently changing his residence. In 1529 Thomas Cromwell lost his wife and two daughters to the disease.

The last major outbreak of the disease occurred in England in 1551. John Caius wrote his 'eyewitness account' referred to above. Henry Machin made this diary entry:

'… the vii day of July begane a nuw swet in London … the x day of July [1551] the Kynges grace removyd from Westmynster unto Hamtun courte, for ther [died] serten besyd the court, and caused the Kynges grase to be gone so sune, for ther ded in London mony marchants and grett ryche men and women, and yonge men and old, of the new swett … the xvi day of July ded of the swet the ii yonge dukes of Suffoke of the swet, both in one bed in Chambrydge-shyre … and ther ded from the vii day of July unto the xix ded of the swett in London of all dyssesus … [872] and no more in alle.'
– The Diary of Henry Machyn 1550–63

There is a reference in the *Annals* of Halifax parish in 1551 to an outbreak there, resulting in 44 deaths while an outbreak of 'sweating sickness' occurred in Tiverton, Devon, in 1644, recorded in Martin Dunsford's *Historical memoirs of the town and parish of Tiverton*, burying 443 people, 105 of them in the month of October.

What caused the Sweat? The aetiologic agent is still unknown but the most likely guilty suspect is sewage, poor sanitation and contaminated water supplies of the time providing reservoirs for the source of infection. The first confirmed outbreak was in August 1485 as the Wars of the Roses drew to a close; this has prompted the very English speculation that it may have been brought over from France by the French mercenaries whom Henry Tudor enlisted; there are no reports of it affecting the Tudor army. However, an earlier outbreak may have afflicted York in June 1485, before Henry and his army of mercenaries, disaffected Edwardian Yorkists and staunch Lancastrians landed at Milford Haven on 7 August 1485. It is more likely that it entered England somewhere on the Yorkshire–Lincolnshire coast in cargoes or crews trading from Russia and Scandinavia.

The *Croyland Chronicle* reveals that Thomas Stanley, 1st Earl of Derby and a key ally of Richard III, who contributed 30 per cent of the king's army, gave the sweating sickness as an excuse not to join with Richard III and travel from his home in Lancashire to Nottingham, after news of Henry Tudor's landing had broken and before Tudor's victory over Richard at the Battle of Bosworth.

Social and environmental issues may have been a factor. Erasmus, another lucky survivor who contracted the disease whilst in London in the summer of 1511, in a letter to Francis, physician to the Archbishop of York, explained how English houses were not built to make a through-draft possible and that their rush-strewn floors were totally unhygienic because sometimes they were not renewed for around 20 years and so they allowed 'spittle, vomit, dog's urine and men's too, dregs of beer and cast-off bits of fish, and other unspeakable kinds of filth' to fester. The streets were no better, with all manner of refuse casually ejected from windows. Erasmus himself claims that 'if, even twenty years ago, I had entered into a chamber which had been uninhabited for some months, I was immediately seized with a fever'. Others blamed the damp, foggy English climate.

Relapsing Fever could also have been the cause. This disease is spread by ticks and lice, and it occurs most often during the summer months, as did the original sweating sickness. Symptoms may include a sudden fever, chills, headaches, muscle or joint aches and nausea. A rash may also occur. These symptoms usually continue for two to nine days, then disappear. However, Relapsing Fever is marked by a prominent black scab at the site of the tick bite and a subsequent skin rash.

[This is an adapted version of my Sweating Sickness chapter in *A History of the World in 100 Pandemics, Epidemics and Plagues.*]

Further information at:

Chrystal, Paul, *A History of the World in 100 Pandemics, Epidemics and Plagues* Barnsley, 2021.

Evans, E., 'The Sweating Sickness,' *Science*, 8(186), p. 190, 1886.

Heyman, Paul, 'The English Sweating Sickness: Out of Sight, Out of Mind?' *Acta Medica Academica*, 47 (1), pp. 102–11, 2018.

Roberts, L., 'Sweating Sickness and Picardy Sweat,' *British Medical Journal*, 2 (4414), p.196, 1945.

Thwaites, Guy, 'The English Sweating Sickness, 1485 to 1551,' *New England Journal of Medicine*, 336 (8), pp. 580–2, 1997.

CHAPTER 6

THE 16ᵀᴴ AND 17ᵀᴴ CENTURIES

33

The potato

The potato.

Because we eat so many of them in their various forms, we tend to regard the potato and its derivatives (crisps, chips, for example) as something exclusively British. Not so. Potatoes were domesticated about 7,000 to 10,000 years ago around modern-day southern Peru and north-western Bolivia. Potatoes were introduced to Europe in the second half of the 16th century by the Spanish. They arrived in Europe sometime before the end of the 16th century by two different ports of entry: the first in Spain around 1570, and the second via the British Isles between 1588 and 1593. The first written mention of the potato is a receipt for delivery dated 28 November 1567 between Las Palmas de Gran Canaria and Antwerp. Today potatoes are a staple food in many parts of the world and an integral part of much of the world's food supply. Potatoes are the world's fourth largest food crop after corn, wheat, and rice. Following millennia

of selective breeding, there are now over 5,000 different types of potato.

The potato is not quite as innocent as it looks. Like the tomato, the potato is a nightshade in the genus *Solanum*, and the vegetative and fruiting parts of the potato contain the toxin solanine, which is dangerous in human consumption. If green sections of the plant (namely sprouts and skins) are exposed to light, the tuber can accumulate a high enough concentration of glycoalkaloids to adversely affect human health.

In 1845 a plant disease known as late blight, caused by the fungus-like oomycete *Phytophthora infestans*, spread like wildfire through the poorer communities of western Ireland as well as parts of the Scottish Highlands, resulting in the crop failures that led to the devastating Great Irish Famine.

In the UK, potatoes, of course, form one part of that peerless double act: the traditional staple, fish and chips. Roast potatoes, of course, are commonly served as part of a Sunday roast dinner and mashed potatoes form a major component of several other traditional dishes, such as shepherd's or cottage pie, bubble and squeak, and bangers and mash. New potatoes are cooked with mint, often served with butter. The Tattie scone is a popular Scottish speciality; colcannon is a traditional Irish food made with

Potatoes come in all shapes, sizes and colours.

mashed potato, shredded kale or cabbage, and onion; Boxty pancakes are eaten throughout Ireland but especially in the North and in Irish diaspora communities, traditionally made with grated potatoes, soaked to loosen the starch, and mixed with flour, buttermilk and baking powder.

Sir Walter Raleigh (c.1552–1618), adventurer, courtier to Elizabeth I, navigator, author and poet, also gets the credit for bringing back the potato from Guiana (now Venezuela) to England. However, that, it seems, is nothing more than a myth: John Houghton wrote in his weekly bulletin in 1699, that Raleigh returning from Virginia, stopped off in Ireland and planted the potato (Salaman 2000 p.149). This is disputed by Safford in *The Potato of Romance and of Reality* who points out that Raleigh merely financed the five expeditions to Virginia and only one of these stopped in Ireland for provisions on its return. He also states that Raleigh would not have found the potato there. Safford also dismisses the legend that Raleigh brought them from Quito, explaining that he was never within 1,000 miles of the place.

Further information:

Safford, W. E., *The potato of Romance and of Reality*, 1925.
Salaman, R. N., *A Social History of the Potato*, Cambridge, 2000.
Wilson, A., *The Story of the Potato through illustrated varieties*, Balding & Mansell, 1995.

34

Tobacco

1573

*The story of tobacco, the plant and its uses by man
(courtesy of the Wellcome Collection).*

If Raleigh must lose out on claims to the potato, he is on much firmer ground with the introduction of tobacco to Britain. John Lennon cursed him, calling him 'such a stupid get' in his 'I'm So Tired' and, with hindsight, he was just that, given the prodigious death and disease tobacco smoking has caused over the years. But Raleigh was not to know that, and between its arrival here from Virginia on his boats and the early 21st century, many trillions have enjoyed smoking cigarettes and pipes, many, until relatively recently, blissfully oblivious to the damage it was doing.

We know of more than 70 species of tobacco, but the main commercial crop is *N. tabacum*. Dried tobacco leaves are mainly used in cigarettes and cigars, as well as pipes and shishas. They can also be consumed as snuff, chewing tobacco, dipping tobacco and snus.

The writing's on the tin. A 50g tin of John Player Real Red Tubing tobacco.

Tobacco contains the highly addictive stimulant alkaloid nicotine as well as harmala alkaloids. Tobacco use is a cause or risk factor for many deadly diseases, especially those affecting the heart, liver and lungs, as well as many cancers. In 2008, the World Health Organization named tobacco use as the world's single greatest preventable cause of death.

John Hawkins was the first to bring tobacco seeds to England. William Harrison's *English Chronology* mentions tobacco smoking here in 1573; Raleigh brought the first 'Virginia' tobacco to Europe from the Roanoke Colony, referring to it as *tobah* as early as 1578. In 1595 Anthony Chute published *Tabaco*, which reinforced earlier arguments about the benefits of the plant and emphasised the healthy properties of pipe-smoking. A popular song of the early 1600s by Tobias Hume proclaimed that 'Tobacco is Like Love'.

However, not everyone was happy with the fast-growing use of tobacco in Britain. In 1604, James I, with remarkable perspicacity, wrote a polemic entitled *A Counterblaste to Tobacco* in which he denounced tobacco use as:

'[a] custome lothsome to the eye, hatefull to the Nose, harmefull to the braine, dangerous to the Lungs, and in the blacke stinking fume thereof, neerest resembling the horrible Stigian smoke of the pit that is bottomelesse.'

Something had to be done, so that year a law was enacted that placed a heavy protective tariff on tobacco imports. The duty rose from 2p per £ to 6s 10p, a 40-fold increase, but English demand remained strong despite the high price; Barnabee Rych reported that 7,000 shops in London sold tobacco and calculated that at least £319,375 was being spent on tobacco annually. Because the fledgling Virginia and Bermuda colonies' economies were affected by the high duty, James, in 1624, instead created a royal monopoly. No tobacco could be imported except from Virginia, and a royal licence that cost £15 per year was required to sell it. To help the colonies, Charles II banned tobacco cultivation in England, but allowed it in herb gardens for medicinal purposes.

In 1665, London was laid low by yet another bubonic plague epidemic. Then it was believed that the disease was spread by bad smells and invisible

A smoking club'. An illustration included in Frederick William Fairholt's Tobacco, its history and associations (1859).

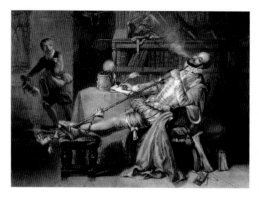

Raleigh's first pipe in England, in Tobacco, its history and associations (1859). The servant can't believe his eyes.

'miasmas', so people used smoke as a screen to protect themselves. Tobacco was especially recommended to ward off the plague, and those tasked with disposing of the dead smoked a clay pipe to keep the disease at bay.

This misguided belief that tobacco smoke could ward off disease persisted for centuries. A pipe or cigarette was an essential accoutrement for the doctor, surgeon or medical student, and for the latter, especially in the dissecting room where the anatomist and his students were advised to smoke freely to camouflage the smell of the corpse and to protect themselves from potential diseases seeping out from the cadaver.

More alarmingly, smoking was recommended by physicians as part of their armamentarium to treat illness. Inhaling smoke was seen to be an effective way of delivering medicine to the lungs. Brands like Potter's asthma cigarettes used the plant *stramonium* rather than tobacco. This can help to relieve the symptoms of asthma, but in reality the benefits would have been more than offset by the toxic irritation of the smoke in the patients' lungs.

The astronomer Thomas Harriot, who accompanied Sir Richard Grenville on his 1585 expedition to Roanoke Island, thought that the plant 'openeth all the pores and passages of the body' so that the bodies of the natives 'are notably preserved in health, and know not many grievous diseases, wherewithal we in England are often times afflicted.'

In 1618, the Royal College of Physicians (RCP) of London published *Pharmacopoeia Londinensis*, the first standard reference book of medicines in England. In it, the hot and dry tobacco leaf is recommended as an efficacious drug for counteracting the symptoms of cold and lethargy.

Attempts to resuscitate a victim of drowning by smoke enema (courtesy of the Wellcome Collection).

One of the more bizarre medical uses for tobacco was the smoke enema used to resuscitate drowning victims in the 18th century. Physicians commonly believed that tobacco smoke combated cold and drowsiness, making it a logical choice in the treatment of drowned people in need of warmth and stimulation. Tobacco-smoke enema kits were provided along the River Thames by the Royal Humane Society.

In the late 19th century US inventor James Bonsack invented a machine to automate cigarette production. This expedited further tremendous growth in the tobacco industry.

Perhaps the most sinister and cynical marketing of cigarettes came in the guise of sweet cigarettes which were routinely packaged in tobacco company branded packs licensed by confectionery companies to imitate cigarette packs.

Health concerns related to smoking started to emerge in the 1920s and 1930s, causing big tobacco companies some anxiety. To reassure their customers, companies such as Camel deployed the image and endorsement of the physician to help sell their products. Advertisements famously claimed that doctors recommended smoking and, what is more, smoked themselves. It would not have been part of the patient consultation at this time for doctors to actively encourage patients to renounce their smoking habits.

One of the few beneficial things to come out of Nazi Germany was the first modern anti-smoking campaign; the Nazi Government condemned tobacco use, funded research against it, levied increasing sin taxes on it, and in 1941 banned tobacco in public places as a health hazard.

A real breakthrough came in 1948 when the British physiologist Richard Doll published the first major studies proving that smoking could cause

Every doctor in private practice was asked...

Yes, your doctor was asked too, along with thousands of others from Maine to California! Family physicians, surgeons, nose and throat specialists ... doctors in every branch of medicine were asked.

Three nationally known independent research groups ... hundreds of trained research specialists ... put the question: "What cigarette do you smoke, Doctor?"

The answers came in by the thousands from all over the country... the actual statements of doctors themselves. Figures were checked and re-checked with scientific precision. The answer? Right! Camels! And by a very convincing margin!

R. J. Reynolds Tobacco Company, Winston-Salem, North Carolina

ACCORDING TO THIS RECENT NATIONWIDE SURVEY:

MORE DOCTORS SMOKE CAMELS

THAN ANY OTHER CIGARETTE!

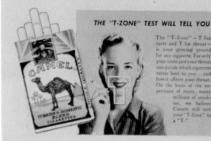

THE "T-ZONE" TEST WILL TELL YOU

The "T-Zone" – T for taste and T for throat – is your proving ground for any cigarette. For only your taste and your throat can decide which cigarette tastes best to you ... and how it affects your throat. On the basis of the experience of many, many millions of smokers, we believe Camels will suit your "T-Zone" to a "T."

Now it's down in black and white. Based on the actual statements of doctors themselves to 3 outstanding independent research organizations.

This was no study of "trends." No mere "feeling the pulse" poll. This was a nationwide survey to discover the *actual fact* ... and from statements of doctors themselves.

And the men in white have put their answers down in black and white: As the brand they smoke, the most named Camel!

Doctors smoke for the same enjoyment as the rest of us. Camel's full, rich flavor is as appealing to the doctor as to you. And Camel's mildness and coolness are as welcome to his throat as to yours ... and to those millions of other smokers the world over!

Advertising using doctors as key opinion leaders to promote the 'benefits' of healthy smoking.

serious health damage. In 1950 he published research in the *British Medical Journal* proving a close link between smoking and lung cancer. In 1954 the British Doctors Study, a study of some 40,000 doctors over 20 years, confirmed this, based on which the Government issued public health advice that smoking and lung cancer rates were related. The hugely popular *Reader's Digest* magazine over many years published frequent anti-smoking articles. In 1962 the RCP published *Smoking and Health*, which used the research of Richard Doll and Austin Bradford Hill to demonstrate that smoking causes cancer. The report sold 33,000 copies in year one and was widely translated, but the public response was hostile. *The Daily Telegraph* moaned that the RCP was 'taking the place of the Church as the main threat to human freedom'.

Controls and regulatory measures followed in much of the developed world, including partial advertising bans, minimum age of sale requirements, and basic health warnings on tobacco packaging. Unfortunately, the habit of smoking and associated ill health continued to rise in the developed world in the first three decades following Richard Doll's ground-breaking discovery, with Governments reluctant to curtail a popular habit; tax revenues may also have had something to do with their inaction. Increasingly, organised disinformation efforts by the tobacco industry did nothing to help. Eventually it was realised that a multi-pronged policy response was needed; this combined positive health messages with help to quit and effective marketing restrictions, as initially indicated in a 1962 overview by the Royal College of Physicians.

Production of tobacco leaf increased by 40 per cent between 1971, when 4.2 million tons of leaf were produced, and 1997, with 5.9 million tons produced; the record-high production was in 1992 when 7.5 million tons of leaf were produced. This growth was almost entirely due to increased productivity by developing nations, where production increased by 128 per cent.

Further information at:

Burns, Eric, *The Smoke of the Gods: A Social History of Tobacco*, Philadelphia, 2007.

Charlton ,A ., 'Medicinal uses of tobacco in history,' *J R Soc Med*, 97 (6), pp. 292–6, 2004.

Chrystal, Paul, *The History of Sweets*, Barnsley, 2021 pp. 48-50, sweet cigarettes.

Gately, Iain, *Tobacco: A Cultural History of How an Exotic Plant Seduced Civilization*, Grove Press, 2003.

Goodman, Jordan, *Tobacco in History: The Cultures of Dependence*, 1993.

35

John Harington's flushing toilet

1590

A priuie in perfection.
Here is the same all put together, that the worke-
man may see if it be well.

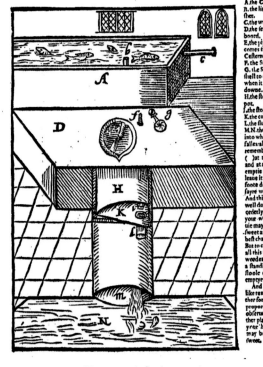

A. the Cesterne,
B. the litle wa-
ther.
C. the waft pipe.
D. the seate
board.
E. the pipe that
comes from the
Cesterne,
F. the Screw,
G. the Scallop
fhell to couer it
when it is fhut
downe.
H. the ftoole
pot.
I. the ftopple,
K. the current,
L. the fluce,
M.N. the vault
into which it
falles: alwayes
remember that
( )at noone
and at night,
emptie it, and
leaue it halfe a
foote deepe in
fayre water.
And this being
well done, and
orderly kept,
your worft pri-
uie may be as
fweete as your
beft chamber.
But to conclude
all this in a few
wordes, it is but
a ftanding clofe
ftoole eaffilie
emptyed.
  And by the
like reafon (o-
ther formes and
proportions
obferued) all o-
ther places of
your houfe
may be kept
fweet.

Harington's flushing toilet.

Sir John Harington (baptised 1560 and died in 1612) was an English courtier, author and translator – but it is by his invention of the flush toilet that history remembers him, and always will.

He came to prominence at Elizabeth I's court, and was known as her 'saucy Godson', but his poetry and other writings caused him to fall in and out of favour – Harington was inclined to overstep the mark in his somewhat Rabelaisian pieces: his attempt at a translation of Ariosto's *Orlando Furioso* caused his banishment from court for some years. Angered by the raciness of his translations, Elizabeth told Harington that he was to leave and not come back until he had translated the entire poem. She chose this punishment rather than actually banishing him, because she considered the task of translation so difficult that it was assumed Harington would not bother to comply. Harington, however, chose to follow through with the challenge and completed the translation in 1591. It received great praise and is still read today.

Oddly, the description of a flush-toilet forerunner installed in his Kelston, Somerset, house turns up in his *A New Discourse of a Stale Subject, called the Metamorphosis of Ajax* (1596), a political allegory and coded attack on the monarchy, written under the pseudonym Misacmos and which remains his best-known work. The book cast aspersions on the Earl of Leicester, which annoyed Elizabeth. It was a coded attack on the stercus or excrement that was poisoning society with torture and state-sponsored 'libels' against his relatives Thomas Markham and Ralph Sheldon. After its publication, he was again banished from the court. Elizabeth's mixed feelings for him may have been the only thing that saved Harington from being tried at Star Chamber.

Ajax was a 'jakes', then a vulgar word for toilet and, much later, a brand of toilet cleaner. Ajax was a forerunner to the modern flush toilet which had a flush valve to let water out of the tank, and a wash-down design to empty the bowl. What it crucially lacked was an S-bend or U-bend to stifle noxious smells; this was later invented by Alexander Cumming.

Further information at:
Kinghorn, Jonathan, 'A Privvie in Perfection: Sir John Harrington's Water Closet,' *Bath History*, 1, pp. 173–88, 1986.

36

Gunpowder and the Gunpowder Plot

1605

Gunpowder, also known as black powder, is the earliest-known chemical explosive. It consists of a mixture of sulphur, carbon (in the form of charcoal) and potassium nitrate (salt peter). The sulphur and carbon act as fuels while the salt peter is an oxidiser. Gunpowder is widely used as a propellant in firearms, artillery, rocketry, and pyrotechnics, including use as a blasting agent for explosives in quarrying, mining, and road building.

But it is the explosive of choice in the 1605 attempt to blow up the House of Lords that it is of interest to us.

The plot was a failed assassination attempt against King James I by a group of provincial English Catholics led by Robert Catesby, whose aim was to restore the Catholic monarchy to England after decades of Protestant intolerance against Catholics. When Henry VIII took control of the English Church away from Rome between 1533 and 1540, it was the start of decades of religious tension in England. Henry's daughter, Queen Elizabeth I, responded to the growing religious divide by introducing the Elizabethan Religious Settlement, which required anyone appointed to a public or church office to swear allegiance to the monarch as head of the Church and state. The penalties for refusal were severe; fines were imposed for recusancy, and repeat offenders risked imprisonment and execution. Catholics became marginalised, but despite the threat of torture or execution, priests continued to practise their faith in secret.

Gunpowder for muzzleloading firearms in granulation size.

The plan was to blow up the House of Lords during the State Opening of Parliament on 5 November 1605, as an opening act to a popular revolt in the Midlands during which James's nine-year-old daughter, Elizabeth, was to be installed as the Catholic head of state. His fellow traitors included John Thomas Wintour, Thomas Percy, Guy Fawkes, Robert Keyes, Thomas Bates, John Grant, Ambrose Rookwood, Sir Everard Digby and Francis Tresham. Fawkes, as Captain Guido Fawkes, had 10 years' military experience fighting in the Spanish Netherlands in the failed suppression of the Dutch Revolt and was in charge of the explosives.

However, the plot was betrayed to the authorities in an anonymous letter sent to William Parker, 4th Baron Monteagle, on 26 October 1605. Monteagle (1575–1622), the brother-in-law of one of the conspirators, was warned not to attend Parliament on 5 November. Monteagle alerted the Government, and hours before the attack was to have taken place Fawkes and the explosives were discovered.

Fawkes had smuggled 36 barrels of gunpowder under the House of Lords – enough to reduce the House of Lords to rubble – ready for its royal opening on 5 November 1605. Just before midnight he was arrested, *'booted and spurred'*,

The lantern which Guy Fawkes used during the plot.

ready to make his get-away, having on his person a watch, lantern, tinder-box and slow fuses. He was interviewed by King James, taken to the Tower to be tortured, and finally *'hanged, drawn and quartered'* as a traitor on 31 January 1606. Though he is still burnt in effigy on 5 November ('Plot Night' as it is called in parts of Yorkshire) no Guy is ever burnt at St Peter's, his old school in York.

Most of the conspirators fled from London as they learned of the plot's discovery, trying to enlist support along the way. Several made a stand against the pursuing Sheriff of Worcester and his men at Holbeche House; in the ensuing battle, Catesby was one of those shot and killed.

There were other plots before the famous Guy Fawkes Plot. Elizabeth's successor, James I, was more tolerant towards Catholics but Catholics wanted a decisive end to the persecution and decided to take matters into their own hands in what became known as the Bye Plot: the priests William Watson and William Clark planned to kidnap James and hold him in the Tower of London until he agreed to be more tolerant. At about the same time, Lord Cobham, Lord Grey de Wilton, Griffin Markham and Walter Raleigh hatched what became known as the Main Plot, which involved removing James and his family and supplanting them with Lady Arbella Stuart (1575–1615). Amongst others, they approached Philip III of Spain for funding, but were unsuccessful.

The Bye Plot had been revealed by Catholics and James was grateful enough to allow pardons as well as postponing payment of their fines for a year.

James was the 1605 conspirators' main objective, but he was by no means the only one, and there were many other important targets at the State Opening, including the monarch's nearest relatives, members of the Privy Council, the senior judiciary, most of the Protestant aristocracy, and

*The Gunpowder Plot Conspirators: An illustration from Old and New
London: A Narrative of its History, its People and its Places, Vol II
by Walter Thornbury, 1872-8.*

the bishops of the Church of England. And then there was that plan to
kidnap the King's daughter, Elizabeth, as a follow up to the assassinations.
On the death of the king the plotters intended to kidnap the nine-year-old
Elizabeth from Coombe Abbey and place her on the throne of England – and
presumably the thrones of Ireland and Scotland – as a Catholic monarch.

But by the evening of the 6th the game was up. Johnson (Fawkes) persisted with pleading innocence and along with the gunpowder he was found
with, was moved to the Tower of London, where the King had decided that
'Johnson' would be tortured. The use of torture was forbidden, except by
royal prerogative or a body such as the Privy Council or Star Chamber. On
6 November James wrote: 'The gentler tortours [tortures] are to be first used
unto him, et sic per gradus ad ima tenditur [and thus by steps extended
to the bottom depths], and so God speed your good work.' 'Johnson' was
probably placed in manacles and hung from the wall, but he was almost
certainly subjected to the horrors of the rack. On 7 November his resolve
was broken; he confessed late that day, and again over the following two
days. The foiling of the plot set off a wave of national relief and inspired in
the ensuing Parliament a mood of loyalty and goodwill.

Catesby and Percy escaped the executioner, but their bodies were
exhumed and decapitated, and their heads exhibited on spikes outside the

House of Lords. On a cold 30 January, Everard Digby, Robert Wintour, John Grant, and Thomas Bates were tied to wooden panels and dragged through the streets of London to St Paul's Churchyard. Digby, the first to mount the scaffold, pleaded for forgiveness; he was stripped of his clothing, and, wearing only a shirt, climbed the ladder to place his head through the noose. He was quickly cut down, and while still fully conscious was castrated, disembowelled, and then quartered, along with the three other prisoners. Next day Wintour, Rookwood, Keyes and Guy Fawkes were hanged, drawn and quartered, opposite the building they had planned to blow up, in the Old Palace Yard at Westminster. Keyes did not wait for the hangman's command and jumped from the gallows, but he survived the drop and was led to the quartering block. Although weakened by his torture, Fawkes managed to jump from the gallows and break his neck, thus avoiding the agony of the quartering.

What was the effect of the plot? Later, in 1606, laws against recusancy were tightened up by way of the Popish Recusants Act which returned England to the Elizabethan system of fines and restrictions, introduced a sacramental test and an Oath of Allegiance. The cellars beneath the Houses of Parliament continued to be leased out to private individuals until the Popish Plot in 1678; it was then considered prudent to search the cellars on the day before each State Opening of Parliament, a ritual that continues to this day.

Further information at:

Chrystal, Paul, *York Places of Education*, Stroud, 2013.

Fraser, Antonia, *The Gunpowder Plot*, London, 2005.

Haynes, Alan, *The Gunpowder Plot: Faith in Rebellion*, London, 2005.

Hogge, Alice, *God's Secret Agents: Queen Elizabeth's Forbidden Priests and the Hatching of the Gunpowder Plot*, London, 2005.

37

The King James Bible

1611

The 1612 First Quarto edition of the King James Bible.

The *King James Version (KJV)* is a landmark English translation of the Christian Bible for the Church of England, which was commissioned in 1604 and published in 1611, sponsored by King James I. It includes the 39 books of the Old Testament, an inter-testamental section containing 14 books of the Apocrypha, and the 27 books of the New Testament. It is famous for its 'majesty of style', and has been described as one of the most important books in English culture and a powerful force in the development of the English-speaking world. Not since the Septuagint – the Greek-language version of the Hebrew Scriptures, Old Testament, produced between the third and the second centuries BC – had a translation of the Bible been undertaken under royal sponsorship on so grandiose a scale.

The *KJV* was, in fact, the third translation into English language approved by the English Church: the first had been the *Great Bible*, commissioned in the reign of Henry VIII in 1535, and the second was the *Bishops' Bible*, commissioned during the reign of Elizabeth I in 1568. Before these, however, the acolytes of John Wycliffe gave us the first complete English translations of the Christian scriptures in the 14th century. These translations were banned in 1409 due to their association with the Lollards. The Wycliffe Bible pre-dated the printing press, but it was circulated extensively in manuscript form, often inscribed with a date which was earlier than 1409 in order to avoid the legal ban.

Then in 1525 William Tyndale, contemporary with Martin Luther, translated the New Testament – the first printed Bible in English. Over the next ten years, Tyndale revised his New Testament and embarked on a translation of the

Opposite: Frontispiece to the King James Bible, 1611, shows the Twelve Apostles at the top. Moses and Aaron flank the central text. In the four corners sit Matthew, Mark, Luke and John, authors of the four gospels, with their symbolic animals. At the top, over the Holy Spirit in a form of a dove, is the Tetragrammaton "יהוה" ('YHWH').
The title page text reads:
'THE HOLY BIBLE, Conteyning the Old Teſtament, AND THE NEW: Newly Tranſlated out of the Originall tongues: & with the former Tranſlations diligently compared and reuiſed, by his Maiesties speciall Comandement.
Appointed to be read in Churches.
Imprinted at London by Robert Barker, Printer to the Kings moſt Excellent Maiestie.'
ANNO DOM. 1611 . At bottom is "C. Boel ſecit in Richmont."

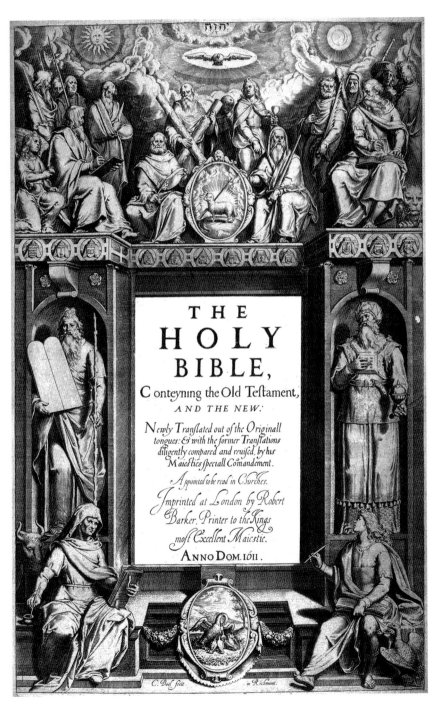

THE
HOLY
BIBLE,
Conteyning the Old Testament,
AND THE NEW:

Newly Translated out of the Originall
tongues: & with the former Translations
diligently compared and reuised, by his
Maiesties speciall Comandement.

Appointed to be read in Churches.

Imprinted at London by Robert
Barker, Printer to the Kings
most Excellent Maiestie.

ANNO DOM. 1611.

Old Testament. Despite Tyndale's execution on charges of heresy for having translated the Bible, the merits of Tyndale's work and prose style made his translation the ultimate basis for all subsequent renditions into Early Modern English. With these translations lightly edited and adapted by Myles Coverdale, in 1539, Tyndale's New Testament and his incomplete work on the Old Testament became the basis for the *Great Bible*. When Mary I succeeded to the throne in 1553, she returned the Church of England to the communion of the Roman Catholic faith and many English religious reformers fled the country, some establishing an English-speaking colony in Geneva. Under the leadership of John Calvin, Geneva became the chief international centre of Reformed Protestantism and Latin biblical scholarship. These English expatriates undertook a translation that became known as the *Geneva Bible*. This translation, dated 1560, was a revision of Tyndale's Bible and the *Great Bible*.

The *KJV* translation was carried out by six panels of translators: two based in each of the University of Oxford, the University of Cambridge, and Westminster, making 47 men in all, most of whom were leading English biblical scholars – the Old Testament was entrusted to three panels, the New Testament to two, and the Apocrypha to one. The New Testament was translated from Greek, the Old Testament from Hebrew and Aramaic, and the Apocrypha from Greek and Latin.

Two editions were printed in 1611, later distinguished as the 'He' and 'She' Bibles because of the variant readings 'he' and 'she' in the final clause of Ruth 3:15 ('and he went into the city'). Perhaps the most notorious error is the so-called 'Wicked Bible' (1631), which gets its name from the omission of 'not' in the injunction against adultery in the Ten Commandments ('Thou shalt commit adultery'). The printers were fined £300 for the error.

During the 18th century, the *KJV* supplanted the Latin Vulgate as the standard for English-speaking scholars. With the development of stereotype printing at the beginning of the 19th century, this version of the Bible became the most widely printed book in history, almost all such printings presenting the standard text of 1769 extensively re-edited by Benjamin Blayney at Oxford, and nearly always omitting the books of the Apocrypha.

A complete New King James Version (NKJV) with modernised spellings was published in 1982.

Further information at:

Bobrick, Benson, *Wide as the waters: the story of the English Bible and the revolution it inspired*, New York, 2001.

Bruce, Frederick Fyvie, *History of the Bible in English*, Cambridge, 2002.

Crystal, David, *Begat: The King James Bible and the English Language*, Oxford, 2011.

Daniell, David, *The Bible in English: its history and influence*, New Haven, 2003.

Nicolson, Adam, *Power and Glory: Jacobean England and the Making of the King James Bible*, London, 2003.

38

Shakespeare's First Folio

1623

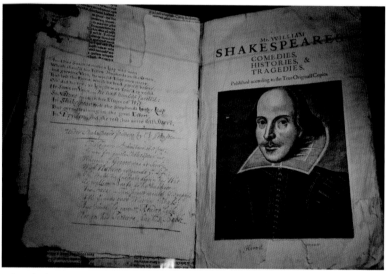

The Shakespeare First Folio.

Only 11 years after publication of the *KJV* another momentous publishing event took place with the release of *The Shakespeare First Folio* – the first collected edition of William Shakespeare's plays, put together and published in 1623, seven years after his death. Folio editions were large and expensive books; they were highly visible prestige items.

Shakespeare wrote around 37 plays, 36 of which are contained in the *First Folio*. Most of these plays were performed in the Globe, an open-air playhouse built on the south bank of the Thames in 1599. As none of

Shakespeare's original manuscripts survive (except, possibly, *Sir Thomas More*, which Shakespeare is believed to have revised a part of) our only source for his work comes from printed editions such as this. It is considered one of the most influential books ever published. The *First Folio* is arguably the only reliable text for about 20 of the plays, and an invaluable primary source for many of those previously published.

What is the historical and literary significance of the First Folio? Of the 36 plays within it, 17 were published in Shakespeare's lifetime in various smaller quarto editions, one was printed after his death, but the remaining 18 had not been printed at all. This is what makes it so important; without it, 18 of Shakespeare's plays, including *Twelfth Night, Measure for Measure, Macbeth, Julius Caesar* and *The Tempest*, might never have seen the light of day. The Folio includes all of the plays generally accepted to be Shakespeare's, with the exception of *Pericles, Prince of Tyre, The Two Noble Kinsmen, Edward III*, and the two lost plays, *Cardenio* and *Love's Labour's Won*.

The text was collated by two of Shakespeare's fellow actors and friends, John Heminge and Henry Condell, who edited it and supervised the printing. They feature in a list of the 'Principall Actors' who performed in Shakespeare's plays, alongside Richard Burbage, Will Kemp and Shakespeare himself. The members of the Stationers' Company who published the book were the booksellers Edward Blount and the father–son team of William and Isaac Jaggard.

Significantly, Heminge and Condell took the decision to divide the plays into comedies, tragedies and histories, an editorial decision that has shaped our perception of the Shakespearean canon ever since. Anxious to produce as authoritative a text as possible, they compiled it from the good quartos and from manuscripts (now lost) such as prompt books, authorial fair copy and foul papers (working drafts). The *First Folio* corrected the bad quartos – spurious and corrupt pirate editions, probably based on memory: 'stol'n and surreptitious copies, maimed and deformed by frauds and stealths of injurious impostors'. When completed, a transcript or fair copy of the foul papers would be prepared by the author or by a scribe. Such a manuscript would have to be heavily annotated with accurate and detailed stage directions and all the other data needed for performance, and then could serve as a prompt book, to be used by the prompter to guide a performance of the play. Any of these manuscripts, in any combination, could be used as a source for a printed text.

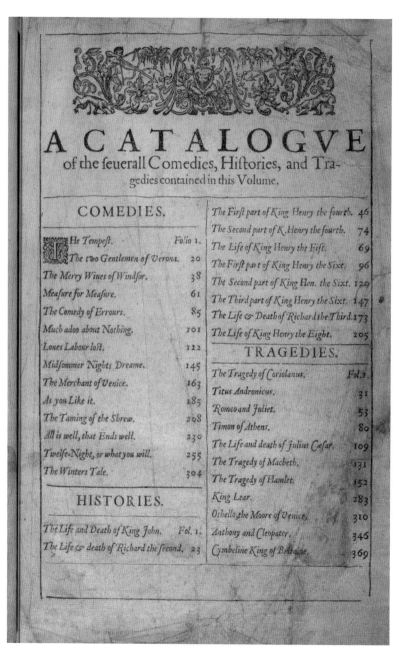

A CATALOGVE
of the seuerall Comedies, Histories, and Tragedies contained in this Volume.

COMEDIES.

He Tempest.	Folio 1.
The two Gentlemen of Verona.	20
The Merry Wiues of Windsor.	38
Measure for Measure.	61
The Comedy of Errours.	85
Much adoo about Nothing.	101
Loues Labour lost.	122
Midsommer Nights Dreame.	145
The Merchant of Venice.	163
As you Like it.	185
The Taming of the Shrew.	208
All is well, that Ends well.	230
Twelfe-Night, or what you will.	255
The Winters Tale.	304

HISTORIES.

The Life and Death of King John.	Fol. 1.
The Life & death of Richard the second.	23

The First part of King Henry the fourth.	46
The Second part of K. Henry the fourth.	74
The Life of King Henry the Fift.	69
The First part of King Henry the Sixt.	96
The Second part of King Hen. the Sixt.	120
The Third part of King Henry the Sixt.	147
The Life & Death of Richard the Third.	173
The Life of King Henry the Eight.	205

TRAGEDIES.

The Tragedy of Coriolanus.	Fol.1.
Titus Andronicus.	31
Romeo and Juliet.	53
Timon of Athens.	80
The Life and death of Julius Cæsar.	109
The Tragedy of Macbeth.	131
The Tragedy of Hamlet.	152
King Lear.	283
Othello, the Moore of Venice.	310
Anthony and Cleopater.	346
Cymbeline King of Britaine.	369

Mr. William Shakespeare's Comedies, Histories, & Tragedies or The First Folio contents page, 1623. It was printed by Edward Blount and Isaac Jaggard.

We believe that around 750 *First Folios* were printed, of which 233 are currently known to survive worldwide. The British Library owns five. The Folger Shakespeare Library in Washington DC owns 82 copies – more than one third of all known surviving copies.

It was probably printed between February 1622 and early November 1623. Presumably the printer expected to have the book ready early, since it was listed in the Frankfurt Book Fair catalogue as a book to appear between April and October 1622. Delayed publishing and books missing Frankfurt continues to dog publishers to this day. The first impression had a publication date of 1623, and the earliest record of a retail purchase is an account book entry for 5 December 1623 of Edward Dering (who purchased two copies); the Bodleian Library, in Oxford, received its copyright copy in early 1624 (which it subsequently sold for £24 as a superseded edition when the *Third Folio* became available in 1663/64).

Before the *First Folio*, Shakespeare's work enjoyed a flourishing publishing history. From the first publications of *Venus and Adonis* (1593) and *The Rape of Lucrece* (1594), 78 individual printed editions of his works are known. About 23 of these editions are his poetry, and the remaining 55 his plays. Counting by number of editions published before 1623, the best-selling works were *Venus and Adonis* (12 editions), *The Rape of Lucrece* (six editions), and *Henry IV, Part 1* (six editions).

The Globe Theatre.

39

The dreaded plague doctor's costume – 17th century PPE

The dreaded Plague doctor. During the 17th-century European plague physicians wore beaked masks, leather gloves, and long coats in an attempt to fend off the disease, as depicted in this 1656 engraving of a doctor in Rome.

In times of bubonic pestilence in the 17th century, plague doctors prowled the streets 'diagnosing' victims in their terrifying and hideous garb and mask. They were usually hired by city and town authorities to treat infected patients, regardless of income, especially the poor who could not afford to pay. No doubt freelancers were in the market as well; we know of a plague doctor who was a fruit salesman before his employment as a physician. Their contractual responsibility was to treat plague patients, and plague patients only, to prevent spreading the disease to the uninfected.

Many of these oddities had no form of medical training whatsoever; they were a double-edged sword in the fight against plague, their presence giving some people a reason to move away (and potentially spread the disease). Others charged patients and their families exorbitant fees for special treatments or bogus cures. Some practiced bloodletting and other remedies such as putting frogs or leeches on the buboes to 'rebalance the humours'. In cities like Florence and Perugia, plague doctors were asked to conduct post-mortems to help establish cause of death and the role of plague in the death. They were often witnesses to wills, dispensing advice to the dying which no doubt involved more extortion. Generally plague doctors had a poor cure rate and ended up merely recording death tolls and the number of infected people in a given area. Often, these plague doctors were the last thing a patient would see before death, so the doctors were seen as a presage of death.

A plague doctor had to serve a lengthy quarantine after attending a plague patient. He was regarded as a 'contact' who by agreement had then to live in isolation.

According to Michel Tibayrenc's *Encyclopedia of Infectious Diseases*, we first meet the sinister looking plague doctor during the 1619 plague outbreak in Paris, in the written work of royal physician Charles De Lorme, in the service of Louis XIII at the time. After De Lorme, German engraver Gerhart Altzenbach published a famous illustration in 1656, which publisher Paulus Fürst's iconic Doctor Schnabel von Rom is based upon. In this satirical work, Fürst describes how the doctor does nothing but terrify people and extort money from the dead and dying.

In the 14th century the Italian city of Orvieto hired Matteo fu Angelo in 1348 for four times the normal rate of a doctor of 50-florin per year. Pope Clement VI engaged several extra plague doctors during the Black Death to tend to the sick people of Avignon. Of 18 doctors in Venice, only one was

A physician wearing a 17th-century plague preventive costume. Courtesy of the Wellcome Collection.

left by 1348: five had died from the plague, and 12 were missing and had presumably fled.

The aim of the frightening costume was intended to protect them from airborne infection, often regarded as a symbol of death and disease. In reality, the costume was worn by a comparatively small number of medieval and later physicians studying and treating plague patients.

Typically, it consisted of an ankle-length waxed overcoat and a macabre bird-like beak mask, often filled with sweet or strong-smelling substances such as lavender to deflect the miasma, along with gloves, boots, a wide-brimmed hat and an outer over-clothing garment. The mask had glass openings for the eyes while the curved beak had straps that held it in front of the doctor's nose. The mask had two small nose holes and was a type of respirator for the aromatic items packed in there: these might be dried flowers such as roses and carnations, herbs like peppermint, camphor, or a vinegar sponge as well as juniper berry, ambergris, cloves, labdanum, myrrh and storax.

'I never had much sympathy for the plague doctor. To me, the image represented the triumph of fear and superstition over the more noble impulses I hoped would drive me in a time of crisis. How could a physician don such a terrifying costume to approach a suffering or dying patient? And the cane? Formalizing a distance between doctor and patient seemed egregious; prodding the patient with a cane as a means of examination was unthinkable…[Later] I imagined what it would have been like to care for patients during the Black Death. I realised I'd been far too hard on my predecessors from the Middle Ages. A 14th-century plague doctor faced risks far higher than mine.'
– Mark Earnest, MD, PhD, *On Becoming a Plague Doctor*, 2020

The wide-brimmed leather hat was a badge of the profession, while the wooden cane was for indicating areas needing attention and to examine patients without touching them, but not without prodding them – no bedside manner there. The canes were also used to keep people socially distanced and to remove clothing from plague victims, again without having to come into contact with them.

John Paulitious was Edinburgh's first plague doctor, but he died in June 1645 of bubonic plague only weeks after beginning employment. He was succeeded by George Rae, who was appointed on 13 June on the promise

The plague doctor in York's Barley Hall.

of £100 a month – an enormous sum of money – as it was expected that he, too, would die before he could collect. However, Rae survived and spent ten years attempting to collect his promised payment, but it is believed that he died without ever receiving it.

Further information at:

Byrne, Joseph Patrick, *Daily Life During the Black Death*, Greenwood Publishing, 2006.

Chrystal, Paul, *Secret York*, Stroud, 2017.

Chrystal, Paul, *History of the World in 100 Pandemics, Epidemics & Plagues*, Barnsley, 2021.

Cipolla, Carlo M., 'The Medieval City,' in *Miskimin*, Harry A. (ed.), *A Plague Doctor*, Yale, pp. 65–72, 1977.

Earnest, Mark, 'On Becoming a Plague Doctor,' *New England Journal of Medicine*, 383 (10): 64, 2020.

Fitzharris, Lindsey, 'Behind the Mask: The Plague Doctor,' *The Chirurgeons Apprentice*, 6 May 2014.

Tibayrenc, Michael (ed.), *Encyclopedia of Infectious Diseases: Modern Methodologies*, Hoboken, 2007.

40

Charles I's execution vest

1649

The bloody vest (photograph courtesy of the Museum of London).

Seven years of internecine civil war claimed the lives of thousands, including the King of England himself. Tuesday, 30 January 1649 was Charles I's last day on earth. After years of fractious political and military conflicts between the royalists and the Parliamentarians during the English Civil War, England's king was arrested and tried on Saturday, 27 January: the Parliamentarian High Court of Justice declared

Charles to be guilty of attempting to 'uphold in himself an unlimited and tyrannical power to rule according to his will, and to overthrow the rights and liberties of the people'. Treason. Accordingly, he was sentenced to death.

The King's final two days were spent in St James's Palace, surrounded by his most loyal subjects and his family. Charles spent much of the 29th praying with the Bishop of London, William Juxon. That same day he burnt his personal papers and correspondence. Because he had not seen his children for 15 months, the Parliamentarians allowed him to talk to his two youngest children, Henry Duke of Gloucester, aged 9, and Princess Elizabeth, who was 11. He instructed Elizabeth to be faithful to 'true Protestant religion' and to tell her mother that 'his thoughts had never strayed from her'. He instructed the ten-year-old Henry to 'not be made a king' by the Parliamentarians, since many suspected they would install the boy as a puppet king. Charles divided his jewels among the children, leaving him with only his George – an enamelled figure of St. George, worn as a part of the ceremonial dress of the Order of the Garter.

On 30 January, Charles rose early and began dressing at 5am in fine clothes, all black, and a blue sash. He instructed the Gentleman of his Bedchamber, Thomas Herbert, on how to dispose of the few possessions he had left. He requested one extra shirt from Herbert, so that the crowd would not see him shiver from the cold and attribute it to cowardice. Before leaving, Juxon gave Charles the Blessed Sacrament, so that he would not faint out of hunger on the scaffold. At 10am, the Colonel Francis Hacker instructed Charles to leave for Whitehall. At noon, Charles drank a glass of claret wine and ate a piece of bread.

A large crowd had gathered to gawp. Just before 2pm, Colonel Hacker called Charles to the large scaffold that was draped in black; staples had been driven into the wood for ropes to be run through if Charles needed to be restrained. The execution block was so low that the king would have had to prostrate himself to place his head on the block, a submissive pose when compared to kneeling before the block. A Colonel John Hewson was tasked with finding an executioner, offering 40 soldiers the position of executioner or assistant in exchange for £100 and accelerated promotion, though none came forward immediately. The eventual executioners concealed their identities behind sinister face masks and under wigs.

Charles came through the window of the Banqueting Hall to the scaffold in what Herbert described as 'the saddest sight England ever saw'. Charles saw the crowd and must have realised that the barrier of guards and the scaffold prevented the crowd from hearing any speech he would make, so he delivered his speech direct to Juxon and the regicide Matthew Thomlinson; Juxon took the speech down in shorthand. Charles maintained his innocence, claiming to be a 'martyr of the people' and that he would be killed for their rights; he declared his faithfulness to Christianity and that Parliament had been the cause of all the wars before him. Charles asked Juxon for his silk nightcap to put on, so that the executioner would not be troubled by his hair. He turned to Juxon and declared he 'would go from a corruptible crown to an incorruptible crown' – claiming his perceived righteous place in Heaven. Charles gave Juxon his George, sash, and cloak – uttering one cryptic word: 'Remember'.

Charles then put his head on the block. He paused for a few moments and, on a prearranged signal, the executioner decapitated the king in one clean blow. He held Charles's head up to the crowd before dropping it into the crowd of soldiers who, in a frenzy, dipped their handkerchiefs in his blood and cut off locks of his hair. The body was then placed in a coffin and covered with black velvet. It was temporarily placed in the 'former 'lodging chamber' within Whitehall.

The silk nightcap. The nightcap was donated by Queen Victoria to Carisbrooke Castle Museum where it can be seen today. Charles I was confined at Carisbrooke Castle from November 1647 to November 1648, before being brought to trial in London.

And the gloves: a beautifully worked pair of gauntlet gloves left behind after a Royal visit to an aristocratic family in Derbyshire in the 1630s. 'They are made of light brown doeskin leather, dressed on the flesh side to give a sueded finish. The gloves are embroidered in fine silver gilt wire thread in an abstract design round the gauntlet, on the back of the hand, at the base of the thumb and along the finger and thumb seams. The top edges are trimmed with silver gilt bobbin lace with silver gilt spangles, and the side ribbons are also trimmed with narrow strips of silver gilt lace. Each glove is inscribed on the inside in ink: "Gloves of King Charles I. W.B. Redfern's Collection." (Source: https://www.fashionmuseum.co.uk/news/glove-story-week-king-charles-i%E2%80%99s-gloves)

As to be expected, news of the regicide received a mixed response. It has been described as one of the most significant and controversial events in English history. Some consider it to be the martyrdom of an innocent man, with Restoration historian Edward Hyde describing 'a year of reproach and infamy above all years which had passed before it; a year of the highest dissimulation and hypocrisy, of the deepest villainy and most bloody treasons that any nation was ever cursed with,' and the Tory Isaac D'Israeli in his *Commentaries on the Life and Reign of Charles the First* (1828) writing of Charles as 'having received the axe with the same collectedness of thought and died with the majesty with which he had lived,' dying a 'civil and political' martyr to Britain. Others saw it as a key step towards democracy in Britain, with the King's prosecutor, John Cook, declaring that it 'pronounced sentence not only against one tyrant but against tyranny itself,' while Whig historian Samuel Rawson Gardiner, wrote that 'with Charles's death the main obstacle to the establishment of a constitutional system had been removed ... The monarchy, as Charles understood it, had disappeared forever.'

The image of Charles's execution was of course central to the flourishing cult of St Charles the Martyr in English royalism. Soon after his death, relics of his execution circulated and were supposed to perform miracles – with handkerchiefs of his blood curing the King's Evil among peasants. (The King's Evil was scrofula, a tuberculous swelling of the lymph glands.) Many elegies and works of devotion were produced to glorify the dead Charles and his cause. After the Restoration of the English monarchy in 1660, this was transformed into official worship; in 1661, the Church of England declared 30 January a solemn fast for the martyrdom of Charles and he assumed a saint-like status in contemporary prayer books. During Charles II's reign (1660–85) around 3,000 sermons were given annually to commemorate the martyrdom of Charles. Few saw anything fallible in Charles I.

Further information at:
Carlton, Charles, *Charles I: The Personal Monarch*, London, 1983.
Edwards, Graham, *The Last Days of Charles I*, Stroud, 2001.
Skerpan-Wheeler, Elizabeth, 'The First "Royal": Charles I as Celebrity,' *PMLA*, 126 (4): pp. 912–34, 2011.

41

The cricket bat

1624

E ven those of us who do not particularly relish a good game of cricket
have to admit that the image, and sound, of 22 men or women
playing on a neatly trimmed pitch on a sunny mid-summer's day
captures the very essence of Britishness.

The cricket bat can be described, somewhat fussily, as follows:

'As a specialised piece of equipment used by batsmen in the sport of
cricket to hit the ball, typically consisting of a cane handle attached
to a flat-fronted willow-wood blade. It may also be used by a batter
who is making their ground to avoid a run out, if they hold the bat
and touch the ground with it. The length of the bat may be no more
than 38 inches and the width no more than 4.25 inches.'

Its use is first mentioned in 1624. Since 1979, the law demands that
cricket bats can only be made from wood.

The blade of a cricket bat is a wooden block that is generally flat on the
striking face and with a ridge on the reverse that concentrates wood in the
middle where the ball is generally hit. The bat is traditionally made from willow
wood, specifically from a variety of white willow called cricket bat willow
(*Salix alba var. caerulea*), treated with raw linseed oil to give protection. This
variety of willow is used as it is very tough and shock-resistant, and does not
dent or splinter on impact with a high speed cricket ball, while also being light.

The blade is connected to a long cylindrical cane handle by means of a
splice. The current design of a cane handle spliced into a willow blade through

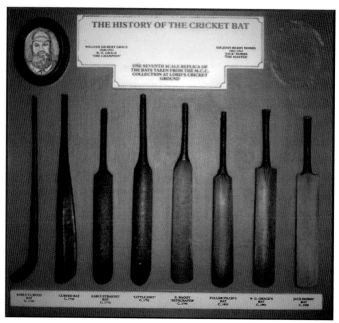

The history of the cricket bat.

The head of the main title plate reads: THE HISTORY OF THE CRICKET BAT

The text centred and below reads: ONE SEVENTH SCALE REPLICA OF THE BATS TAKEN FROM THE M.C.C COLLECTION AT LORDS CRICKET GROUND.

The text on the left of the main plate reads: WILLIAM GILBERT GRACE ~ 1848-1915 ~ W.G.GRACE ~ 'THE CHAMPION'

The text on the right of the main plate reads: SIR JOHN BARRY HOBBS ~ 1882-1963 ~ 'JACK' HOBBS ~ 'THE MASTER'

The text below the replica bats is as follows (from left to right):

EARLY CURVED BAT C.1720

CURVED BAT C.1750

EARLY STRAIGHT BAT C.1774

'LITTLE JOEY' C.1792

E.BAGOT 'SKYSCRAPER' C.1793

FULLER PILCH'S BAT C.1835

W.G. GRACE'S BAT C.1901

JACK HOBBS' BAT C.1930

a tapered splice was the invention, in the 1880s, of Charles Richardson, a pupil of Brunel and the first chief engineer of the Severn Railway Tunnel.

Before the 18th century, bats were shaped like modern hockey sticks, perhaps a throwback to the game's origins. It may be that cricket was first played using shepherd's crooks.

The oldest surviving bat is dated 1729 and is on display in the Sandham Room at The Oval.

Cricket goes back to the late 16th century. Originating in south-east England, it became the country's national sport in the 18th century and has developed globally in the 19th and 20th centuries. International matches have been played since 1844 and Test cricket began in 1877. Cricket is the world's second most popular spectator sport after association football. The name was an early spelling of 'craic', 'fun and games in general'.

It may be that cricket was derived from bowls by the intervention of a batsman trying to stop the ball from reaching its target by hitting it away. Playing on sheep-grazed land or in clearings, the original kit may have been a matted lump of sheep's wool (or even a stone or a small lump of wood) as the ball; a stick or a crook or another farm tool as the bat; and a stool or a tree stump or a gate (e.g. a wicket gate) as the wicket.

First grand match of cricket played by members of the Royal Amateur Society on Hampton Court Green, 3 August 1836 (courtesy of the Yale Centre for British Art).

Further information at:

Altham, H.S., *A History of Cricket, Volume 1* (to 1914), London, 1962.

Bateman, Anthony, *Cricket, literature and culture: symbolising the nation, destabilising empire*, London, 2016.

Birley, Derek, *A Social History of English Cricket*, Aurum, 1999.

Warner, P.F., *Imperial Cricket*, The London and Counties Press Association Ltd, 1912

Women's cricket

We can trace the history of women's cricket back to a mildly sarcastic report in *The Reading Mercury* on 26 July 1745 and a match that took place between the villages of Bramley and Hambledon near Guildford.

The Mercury reported:

'The greatest cricket match that was played in this part of England was on Friday, the 26th of last month, on Gosden Common, near Guildford, between eleven maids of Bramley and eleven maids of Hambledon, all dressed in white. The Bramley maids had blue ribbons and the Hambledon maids red ribbons on their heads. The Bramley girls got 119 notches and the Hambledon girls 127. There was of bothe sexes the greatest number that ever was seen on such an occasion. The girls bowled, batted, ran and catches as well as most men could do in that game.'

Maybe this report is responsible for the term 'maiden over'? A match, on 13 July 1747, held at the Artillery Ground between a team from Charlton and another from Westdean and Chilgrove in Sussex continued into the following day after it was interrupted by crowd trouble. The first women's county match was held in 1811 between Surrey and Hampshire at Ball's Pond in Middlesex. Two 'gentlemen' underwrote the game with 1,000 guineas, and its participants ranged in age from 14 to 60.

The first women's cricket club was formed in 1887 at Nun Appleton near York and called the White Heather Club. In 1890, a team known as the Original English Lady Cricketers toured England, playing in exhibition matches to large crowds. The team was highly successful until its manager absconded with the profits, forcing the women to disband.

The Women's Cricket Association was founded in 1926. The England team first played against The Rest at Leicester in 1933 and undertook the first international tour to Australia in 1934–5, playing the first Women's Test match between England and Australia in December 1934. After winning two tests and drawing one, England travelled on to New Zealand, where Betty Snowball scored 189 in the first Test in Christchurch.

Further information at:

Case, Roy, *The Pebble in My Shoe: An Anthology of Women's Cricket*, Milton Keynes, 2018.

Duncan, Isabelle, *Skirting the Boundary: A History of Women's Cricket*, London, 2013.

Heyhoe Flint, Rachael, *Fair Play: The Story of Women's Cricket*, London, 1976.

Nicholson, Rafaelle, *Ladies and Lords: A History of Women's Cricket in Britain*, Oxford, 2019.

Threlfall-Sykes, Judy, *A History of English Women's Cricket, 1880-1939*, thesis for PhD Degree awarded by De Montfort University, Leicester, 2015.

Women's Test Cricket. Anne Palmer (out lbw and stumped), with Spear, Snowball and Partridge (England), second women's Test match in Sydney, 1935.

42

The coffee house

1652

'Mad dog runs riot in coffee house',
Thomas Rowlandson (1757–1827), 1809.
Note the reference to Cerberus – guard dog of Hades – on the sign.
The scene is the chaos caused by a dog running riot through a coffee
house. The dog stands on top of a table, knocking over the contents
of a jug that spills over a man who has fallen from his seat and is
lying on the floor. On the right, a bearded Jewish man looks up
from his papers to where the commotion is, whilst various gentlemen around
the room attempt to eject the dog from the room using
brooms, umbrellas and clubs. Others flee in terror.

According to Samuel Pepys, England's first coffee house was estab-lished in Oxford in 1650 at the Angel in the parish of St Peter in the East by a Jewish gentleman called Jacob in the building now known as 'The Grand Café'; the café still trades today. Given Oxford's reputation for scholarly enquiring and enlightenment, it seems natural that coffee society be born here in the light of how the coffee houses were to develop into informal, refined if unruly havens of education – cauldrons of polemic, debate and discussion.

What compelled men to congregate in coffee houses? It was surely some-thing more than celebrating the Restoration and its restored liberation and freedoms, something more than escaping the home and family, or the drudgery of the workplace. Dispensing and receiving information – news, tittle-tattle, ships' movements, commodity prices, rumour and scandal were the draw to the coffee house. Never before had there been such a focal point for what was an information revolution. Word of mouth, newspapers and pamphlets all conspired in these places to provide a font of knowledge about all manner of things: the coffee house was the Google, the Wikipedia, the world wide web of its day.

7 November 1665 saw a revolution in newspaper publishing when the official Government newsheet was remodelled and published, twice weekly, first as the *Oxford Gazette* and then as the *London Gazette*; again the success of this major publishing event was assisted by its ubiquity in the coffee houses where the avid readers – the Westminster wannabees – could pride themselves on being privy to the same news as Government officials and diplomats, British and foreign. The *London Gazette* was our first newspaper and provided the template for all subsequent newspapers – and it was there for all to read in the coffee houses. Foreign newspapers were available too, especially the enemy Dutch, so that anyone who could translate them would get a Dutch eye view of affairs in England, just as the English did of affairs in the Netherlands from scanning the London papers.

Pamphlets covered a whole range of issues. A random selection of the many pamphlets and broadsheets published from Tom's Coffee House at 17 Russell Street, Covent Garden, includes expatiations on such diverse topics as dentistry (*A Dissertation on Artificial Teeth in General*, in French and English), medicine (*A Problem Concerning the Gout*), the Treaty of Utrecht, France, Hull, slavery (*A Proposal for the Better Supplying of Churches in or*

Plantations. And for Converting the Savage Americans to Christianity) and astrology. Politics, science, medicine and religion were, not surprisingly, the most popular subjects. *An Anatomical Account of the Elephant Accidentally Burnt in Dublin* printed in 1681 must have been fascinating, as indeed *The Cudgel, or a Crab-tree Lecture by Hercules Vinegar Esq* (1742). Boswell was a customer.

Satirical prints (forerunners of the political cartoon) and broadside ballads also found a home in the coffee houses, contributing much to the torrid debates and discussions. Early day *Financial Times* and *Lloyd's List* were also must-have staples in the coffee house reference library. Publications gave daily news of bills of entry (*London, Imported*, from 1660), commodity price lists (*Prices of Merchandise in London*, from 1667); stock prices and exchange rates (the twice-a-week *Course of the Exchange* from 1698); and shipping lists and movements (*Lloyd's News* from 1697). Indeed, Lloyd's of London grew from Edward Lloyd's coffee house in Tower Street in the 1680s, moving in 1692 to Abchurch Lane off Lombard Street. Lloyd made special arrangements to receive news of shipping activity there; *Lloyd's List*, Lloyd's insurance institution as well as the Register of Shipping, originated in his coffee house. It is easy to see why the coffee house became a commercial centre and a trading floor. People would go to the Virginian and Maryland (later the Baltic) to subscribe to new investment schemes in Russia. The daily *Votes of the House of Commons* appeared in 1688, anticipating *Hansard*, and recording speeches and resolutions. Cutting edge science could be read about in 1665's *Philosophical Transactions* – the equivalent of today's *Nature* and *New Scientist*. Literary tastes were satisfied by the *Universal Historical Bibliotheque* from 1687. New books were listed in the *Term Catalogues* – the forerunner of *Whitaker's Books in Print* and *The Bookseller* – for those too busy declaiming in the coffee house to browse in the bookshop.

For a while, coffee houses were the best place to go for books. In 1819 the British Museum acquired the book and pamphlet stock of three London coffee houses: Tom's in Devereux Court, George's in Temple Bar (both close to the Inns of Court) and the Bank coffee house in Threadneedle Street. This collection gives us a unique picture of the sort of books that were bought for the delectation of coffee-house readers. From this, and from books from Tom's found in other libraries, we can be sure that Tom's had at least 135 books and pamphlets for the edification and education of its clientele. Most

Lloyd's coffee house from a coloured aquatint by William Holland, 1798.

were political, military and religious, with some poetry, and translations from Tasso and Aristotle, and a Milton translated into Latin. Lists of names in some of the books would suggest that they could be borrowed. In the 1840s there may have been as many as 500 coffee-house libraries providing this valuable public service well before the advent of public libraries.

Coffee shops, then, became the go-to places for conversation, debate and gossip amongst tradesman, politicians, journalists and lawyers; shares and commodities were bought and sold here. As the numbers of coffee houses proliferated, they became more specialised, with different professions or with different interests congregating at a particular house. For example, booksellers and publishers met at the Chapter Coffee House in Paternoster Row – Charlotte and Anne Brontë were (rare) female visitors there when they arrived in London to resolve a problem with their publishers, Smith and Elder; Will's was the place for actors, or Wright's or the Bedford, all in Covent Garden; opera singers and dancing masters chorused in the Orange; lawyers adjudicated at Alice's and Hell Coffee House, and artists canvassed at the Old Slaughter in St. Martin's Lane. Up the road at the Rainbow and at Garraway's, there were artists' clubs and exhibitions of prints. Child's coffee house in St Paul's Churchyard was where the clergy preached, as they did at St. Paul's coffee house, also under the cathedral, visited once by Benjamin Franklin. Jonathan's in Exchange Alley had been the centre of 'jobbing', as the *Annual Register* of 1762 puts it, it 'had been a market, time out of mind, for buying and selling Government securities'. This came about because in 1697 the merchants had the stock-jobbers removed from the Royal Exchange so they took their business dealings to the neighbouring coffee houses. It became The Stock Exchange in July 1773 and the brokers there 'christened the house with punch, according to the *Old and New London*, Walter Thornbury 1883–85. Other financial industries such as life assurance, general insurance and reinsurance, and investment banking were all born in the coffee houses at this time. Officials of the East India Company, Hudson's Bay Company, and the African, Russian and Levant Companies met in coffee houses in the early days. Coffee houses occasionally witnessed slave trading. Like Edward Lloyd, many used their coffee house as a *poste restante*: the penny post had been established in 1680; the ideal place to direct the mail was to the four or five hundred shops or coffee houses now often called 'penny post houses'.

For one penny, customers bought a cup of coffee and admission, with access to newspapers and the opinions, advice and attitude of fellow patrons. The early coffee houses also served tea and chocolate but not alcohol: it is this that did much to foster an atmosphere in which it was possible to engage in more serious and nuanced conversation than was usually possible in the rowdy alehouse. The low admission price made them comparatively inclusive, in Oxford (and presumably Cambridge) they became an exciting alternative to the exclusive and much more formal university lecture and tutorial.

The famous Grecian Coffee House was first established in about 1665 at Wapping Old Stairs by a Greek sailor called George Constantine. The enterprise was a resounding success and by 1677 Constantine could afford to move to more salubrious premises in Devereux Court, off Fleet Street. In the 1690s the Grecian was the favoured meeting place of the Whigs, the opposition party at the time. Soon it was to become a haunt of members of the Royal Society, including Sir Isaac Newton, Sir Hans Sloane, Edmund Halley and the poet and politician Joseph Addison. Isaac Newton once dissected a dolphin on the table there. Classics scholars were frequent patrons and on one occasion amused themselves by trying to arrange the events of the Iliad into chronological order. Another time, two of them, friends, fought a duel in the street outside because they could not agree on where to put the accent on a Greek word. The loser was run through with a sword and died there and then. By 1803, however, the Grecian was overtaken by lawyers and it finally closed in 1843 to become the Devereux Public House, host to many a Freemasonry Meeting, and Oliver Goldsmith's local. The Grecian was the favourite coffee house of famous Shakespearean scholar Edmond Malone.

But coffee was not just about cosmopolitan London or academic Oxford. What we see proliferating in the commercial capital and amongst the dreaming spires was replicated, naturally on a smaller scale, throughout the kingdom. In York, for example, coffee houses were legion. The rise of the coffee house coincided with a flood of books, pamphlets and newspapers which facilitated the transmission of political argument and made it more accessible than ever before. Charles II, seeing that the printed word could be as much an ally as an enemy, passed *An Act for Preventing the frequent Abuses in Printing Seditious, Treasonable, and Unlicensed Books and Pamphlets; and for the Regulating of Printing and Printing.* The Act – better known as the *Printing or Licensing Act* – passed into law on 10 June 1662 restricting printing to a limited number of presses, mostly in London. Apart from Oxford, Cambridge and York, printing was outlawed in provincial England until the Act was allowed to lapse in 1695, freeing printers to set up presses in provincial towns. Nowhere exemplifies better the link between the coffee house and printing and publishing than the city of York: one fed the other.

Disorder of one sort or another – be it prostitution at Moll King's, brawling or highwaymen conspiring to waylay well-healed guests – led coffee houses and chocolate houses such as St. James and the Cocoa-Tree to follow White's into a private membership business model; this paved the way for the demise of the coffee shop and its culture.

Many coffee houses were eccentric and individualistic; for example, the walls of Don Saltero's Chelsea coffee house were exotically adorned with stuffed birds and animals; at Lunt's in Clerkenwell Green, patrons could sip coffee and have a haircut by owner John Gale Jones; at John Hogarth's Latin Coffeehouse, also in Clerkenwell, patrons were encouraged to speak in Latin at all times; there was even a floating coffeehouse, the *Folly of the Thames*, moored outside Somerset House, where dancing went on until the early hours. There was nothing remotely Spanish about Don Saltero – he was really just plain James Salter; coffee apart, Salter offered impromptu dental extractions, hair cuts, fiddle-playing and set up a museum in his house.

In Covent Garden, the Bedford Coffee house had a 'theatrical thermo-metre' with 'temperatures' on a scale from 'excellent' to 'execrable': a veritable trial by coffee for playwrights who must at times have dreaded walking into the place after the opening performance of their latest play; politicians suffered the same ordeal in the Westminster coffee houses after delivering speeches to Parliament. The Hoxton Square coffee house was notorious for its mock insanity trials, where a suspected lunatic would be tied up and wheeled into the coffee room. A jury would examine, prod and interrogate the alleged madman and then vote on whether to imprison the accused in one of the local asylums.

There were coffee houses, and there were coffee houses. In the mid-18th century, Tom King's coffee house was a notorious establishment in Covent Garden, operating until dawn each night as nothing less than a thinly-disguised brothel. The key to its survival was the absence of beds: without beds King could swerve round any charges of keeping a bawdy house, an offence which could attract a whipping and a prison sentence.

Tom came from good stock: he was born in 1694 to Thomas King, a squire from Thurlow, Essex, and Elizabeth Cordell, the daughter of Baronet Sir John Cordell. He was educated at Eton and King's College, Cambridge. Around 1720, after a short-lived marriage, he and second-wife Moll reunited after a break-up, and opened a coffee house in one of the shacks in Covent

The inscrutable Moll King.

Garden which they rented from the Duke of Bedford for £12 a year. She was a lowly market girl. Also known as Elizabeth Adkins, Mary or Maria Godson, Moll was a prostitute, pickpocket and a thief. She may even have been the protagonist in Daniel Defoe's *Moll Flanders.*

The King's coffee house was a spectacular success, with the owners' connections at both ends of the social spectrum – all united by that universal common denominator – sex. A second and third shack followed, to which was added the attraction of the pretty black barmaid Black Betty (also known as Tawny Betty). One of the slogans for Tom King's coffee house was the place where anybody could find a willing partner, open to 'all gentlemen to whom beds were unknown'. Over time Hogarth, Alexander Pope, John Gay and Henry Fielding were all clients. Fielding mentions it in both *The Covent Garden Tragedy* and *Pasquin,* and Tobias Smollett in *The Adventures of Roderick Random.*

It was not just men in search of sex (and maybe some coffee?) who were attracted to Tom King's. That fervent moral campaigner Sir John Gonson of the Society for the Reformation of Manners, and inveterate brothel raider, regularly sent incognito informers in to try and uncover illegalities. To counter this, Tom and Moll developed their own secret language, this was *Talking Flash* (similar to thieves' can't or rogues' can't, or peddler's French – a far cry from the polite and urbane conversation of Steele or Addison), to render their conversations quite incomprehensible to outsiders.

On Tom's death, the coffee house became known as Moll King's coffee house – business continued much as before. Moll, however, took to drinking the stock and the establishment's reputation for violence, corruption and disorder grew apace. That did not, however, deter the patronage of fashionable society: one night George II paid a visit and was challenged to a fight for ogling the companion of another client, thus occasioning a hasty regal exit. After a spell in prison for riotous behaviour and refusing to pay a £200 fine, Moll ran the coffee house until around 1745, when she retired to live in her villa at decidedly up-market Haverstock Hill. She died on 17 September 1747, leaving a fortune.

Carpenter's coffee house (later known as 'The Finish', 'The Queen's Head' and 'Jack's') was a coffee house of similar ilk and reputation, also in Covent Garden; it was established by George Carpenter around 1762. As with King's, coffee was low down on the price list. The quality of what coffee there was was decidedly poor. In 1766 William Hickey, lawyer and author, described it as: *'a spartan mixture difficult to ascertain the ingredients but which was served as coffee'.*

Beer and punch were also served. By 1768 Carpenter's was known by the nickname 'The Finish', describing its terminal (in both senses of the word at times) role for those out for a night on the town; when all else was shut, there was always Carpenter's.

Carpenter died around 1785; from 1788 it was run by Elizabeth Butler, a former brothel-keeper, who had run a successful business in King Street nearby. The reputation deteriorated yet further: thieves and murderers would lie in wait there for victims. At the beginning of the 19th century it had become a favourite haunt of boxers. A far cry indeed from the glittering *literati* in other coffee houses.

(Adapted from the author's *Coffee: A Drink for the Devil* (2016))

Further information at:

Berry, Helen, 'Rethinking Politeness in Eighteenth-Century England: Moll King's Coffee House and the significance of "Flash Talk",' *Transactions of the Royal Historical Society*, 11, pp,. 65–81, 2001.

Cessford, C., '"To Clapham's I go": a mid to late 18th-century Cambridge coffeehouse assemblage,' *Post-Medieval Archaeology*, No.51(2), pp. 372–426, 2017.

Chrystal, Paul, *Coffee: A Drink for the Devil*, Stroud, 2016.

Cowan, Brian William, *The Social Life of Coffee: The Emergence of the British Coffeehouse*, New Haven, 2005.

Ellis, Aytoun, *The Penny Universities: A History of the Coffee-houses*, London, 1956.

Whitewall, Bryant, *London Coffeehouses. A Reference Book of Coffee Houses of the Seventeenth, Eighteenth and Nineteenth Centuries*, London, 1963.

43

The nice cup of tea

1725 Posh English Family at Tea, Richard Collins d. 1732?

How British is the cup of tea?

'Tea is more important than bullets,' said Winston Churchill. To the historian A.A. Thompson tea was England's secret weapon, 'what keeps 'em together is tea,' 'em being the armed services and the Women's Institute. Within two days of the declaration of war against Germany, the Government requisitioned all tea stocks and dispersed the supplies around the country to spare them from destruction by German bombing. Rationing was introduced in 1940 in response to the German naval blockades: two ounces of tea per person per week for those over the age of five, enough for two or three cups a day of weak tea.

Milk first?

George Orwell (1903–50) in *A Nice Cup of Tea: Evening Standard*, 12 January 1946, was an incurable tea lover with strong views:

'*Tea is one of the mainstays of civilisation in this country* and causes *violent disputes over how it should be made.*' Orwell was a strictly 'no sugar, tea in first' man. He goes on to expatiate on his 11 cardinal points regarding the only correct way to make a cup of tea.

Then there was *Monty Python (ca. 1972):* 'Make tea, *not* war.'

The ubiquitous cup of tea is as much a part of British life as indifferent weather, the BBC or the queue at the Post Office. Tea, since its arrival here in the 17th century, has shaped our lives, our history, our work, our culture and even our bodies. Not surprisingly, for a drink that many of us take throughout the day, every day, there is a fascinating story to tell about its origins and how it took Britain by storm to become our second most popular beverage after tap water.

Britain has an intimate love affair with tea; tea has an intimate love affair with Britain: look at the facts. On average we each drink three-and-a-half cups of tea every day, or 130,000 tonnes in a year, 96 per cent of which are from tea bags. We Britons drink 165 million cups per day or sixty-two billion cups per year; 70 per cent of the population (over age 10) drank tea yesterday; over 25 per cent of all the milk consumed in the UK goes into your cup of tea. In the two minutes or so it has taken me to type these two paragraphs, the tea-ometer on the Tea Council UK website has clocked up a staggering 191,000 cups of tea consumed in the UK; 70 million cups had been made by 11am that day.

Tea drinking became something quintessentially British when it slowly but surely insinuated itself into our culture, language and society: afternoon tea, tea gardens, tea dances, Lyons tea houses, tea-time, tea breaks, tea for two; storms in tea cups and builders' tea are all ingrained in the British way of life. Our loss of the American colonies, the Opium Wars, votes for women,

A little piece of Britain in Rome. Inside Babington's Tea Shop next to the Spanish Steps. It was founded in 1893 by Isabel Cargill and Anne Marie Babington to cater for the many British ex-pats in Rome.

victory in the two world wars and tea in the 'Troubles' all owe something to a nice cup of tea. English literature mentions tea and tea-time all the time; the Beatles, Kinks and the Rolling Stones all took tea.

The story of our intimate relationship with tea is in effect the social history of Britain, reflecting aspects of the nation's trade, manners, fashion, culture, drinking habits, industrial legislation, foreign policy and its health. Tea has defined us and informed our way of life over the last 500 years. Like Samuel Johnson, we just can't get enough of it: '*You cannot make tea so fast as I can gulp it down*'. So, put the kettle on, and read on ...

According to the barber Thomas Rugg, writing in his *Diurnal*, 'Coffee, chocolate and a kind of drink called *tee*' were 'sold in almost every street in 1659.' The Navy's Clerk of the Acts, Samuel Pepys, ever keen to try anything new, had his first cup of tea on 25 September 1660 while discussing foreign affairs relating to Spain, Holland and France with friends. His diary entry reads: 'I did send for a Cupp of Tee (a China drink), of which I had never drunk before.' Nearly seven years later on 28 June 1667 we find Pepys confirming for us the alleged medicinal benefits of tea: 'I went away and by coach home, and there find my wife making of tea, a drink which Mr. Pelling, the Potticary, tells her is good for her cold and defluxions'. If Susanna Centlivre's 1718 play *A Bold Strike for a Wife* is anything to go by, Bohea tea was just as popular in Jonathan's coffee house (where the play was set) as coffee.

Given Portugal's involvement in the early importation of tea to the Netherlands, it comes as no surprise that it was a popular drink in affluent Portuguese circles. The British East India Company presented the newly restored Charles II with 2lbs 2oz in 1660, shipped in from Portugal; two years later his queen, Catherine of Braganza, ensured its popularity amongst the nobility by being seen to be imbibing. Charles himself would take little persuading to join her: he had spent many years in exile in Amsterdam where tea was readily available. Catherine's tea arrived in chests as part of the dowry sent by her father King John IV: ship-loads of luxury goods, some as gifts and some to be sold to pay off Charles's debts. The tea qualified as a gift and was enjoyed at and by the English court. Legend has it that when Catherine landed at Portsmouth on 13 May 1662 she asked for a calming cup of tea after her somewhat stormy crossing; there was no tea to be had anywhere so she was offered a glass of ale instead.

The social and cultural importance of the arrival of tea in Britain was perfectly captured by the American essayist Agnes Repplier in her 1931 essay, *To Think of Tea!*

'Tea had come as a deliverer to a land that called for deliverance; a land of beef and ale, of heavy eating and abundant drunkenness; of grey skies and harsh winds; of strong-nerved, stout-purposed, slow-thinking men and women. Above all, a land of sheltered homes and warm firesides – firesides that were waiting – waiting for the bubbling kettle and the fragrant breath of tea.'

Repplier is absolutely spot on. Catherine of Braganza not only made tea drinking fashionable in Britain, to some extent she changed the drinking habits of the nation by providing an alternative to stultifying ale or wine. Who knows what long-term effect that had on national productivity, political decision-making, and behaviour generally at the time? After dinner, women of means started to withdraw from the table, distancing themselves from their rumbustious, wine fuelled, cigar-smoking men-folk, to the relative calm of the ante-room and its sewing, conversation and a nice cup of tea. Although increasing numbers of men imbibed, Henry Savile must have spoken for many when in 1674 he vilified his tea-drinking friends 'who call for tea, instead of pipes and bottles after dinner, a base, unworthy Indian practice'. If Charles's queen was a force for tea then so was the British East India Company; their monopoly on Chinese tea ensured an increasingly ready supply and a market in London where eager traders enjoyed high margins. This, and the virtual exclusion of Britain from the Mediterranean and the coffee-exporting Levant during wars with Spain and France, ensured Britain as a nation of tea drinkers while the rest of the continent remained hooked on coffee.

One of the first airings of the health debate relating to tea came with the translation and publication of a volatile French tract, '*Wholesome Advice against the Abuse of Hot Liquors*', in 1706. The author, a Dr Duncan from the noted health resort Faculty of Montpelier, argued that while moderate consumption was fine, an excess of hot drinks raised the temperature of blood and internal organs, concluding that 'Excess of Heat is the most Common Cause of Sickness and Death'.

There are countless tenuous references to Bible stories and analogies with Greek and Roman mythology to support this; one, for example, claimed that Methuselah never drank hot liquors and lived for nearly 1,000 years. Duncan warned that hot liquors heated up the womb, destroying a woman's fertility; as evidence, it took Rachel, the Biblical figure notorious for her hot temper, years to conceive. Before that Sir Kenelm Digby, in his 1669 *Book of Receipts,* recommended a wholesome snack after a hard day at the office which comprised two egg yolks mixed into a pint of tea. This was guaranteed to 'satisfy all rawness of the stomach' when it 'flew all over the body and into the veins'.

In 1674 women registered their disapproval in a satirical petition against coffee and the family-wrecking coffee houses. Tea, because it was served in these 'Stygian Tap-houses', 'a Pimp to the Tavern', was culpable by association. The petition begins: 'The … Address of Several Thousands of Buxome Good-Women, Languishing in Extremity of Want' and goes on to expatiate on the numerous malicious effects coffee and the coffee houses have on family and married (sex) life:

'For the continual flipping of this pitiful drink is enough to *bewitch* Men of two and twenty, and tie up the *Codpiece-points* without a Charm. It renders them that use it as *Lean* as Famine, as *Rivvel'd* as *Envy*, or an old meager Hagg over-ridden by an Incubus. They come from it with nothing *moist* but their snotty Noses, nothing *stiffe* but their Joints, nor *standing* but their Ears ... Men by frequenting these *Stygian Tap-houses* will usurp on our Prerogative of *tattling*, and soon learn to exceed us in *Talkativeness* ... that our Husbands may give us some other *Testimonial* of their being Men, besides their *Beards* and wearing of empty *Pantaloons*: That they no more run the hazard of being *Cuckol'd* by *Dildo's*: But returning to the good old strengthening Liquors of our Forefathers; that Natures *Exchequer* may once again be replenisht, and a Race of Lusty Hero's begot.'

'The evil effects of tannin in tea are readily seen by its ravages on the throats and stomachs of tea tasters. Dyspepsia ... is often caused and increased by tea drinking. In flatulent dyspepsia few substances are more to be avoided than tea ... women are the chief sufferers from this most distressing and unpleasant variety of indigestion, being great tea drinkers ... The mental depression is often distressing, varying in degree from slight dejection ... to the extremes of melancholia or suicidal monomania.'

The distinguished Quaker John Coakley Lettsom wrote his MD thesis at Leiden University in 1769: *The Natural History of the Tea Tree*. In 1773 he founded the prestigious Medical Association of London, which survives today as the oldest medical society in the United Kingdom. When he inherited his father's sugar plantations in the British Virgin Islands, the first thing he did was free the slaves. His opposition to tea was a selfless act performed in full knowledge that any reduction in consumption would have impacted on his sugar business – tea being routinely sweetened with sugar. Lettsom experimented with tea, injecting the stomachs of frogs and dogs with green and black tea of differing strengths: paralysis occurred in the frogs injected with the black tea, but not the green. To Samuel Johnson he was one of the doctors who 'extend the art of torture'. Experiments with beef showed that when immersed in weak tea it turned putrid, thus leading to the correct conclusion that tea is an antiseptic. Lettsom believed that tea had good and bad points; in the healthy person it was fine, in the infirm it caused them to be 'fluttered' with trembling in the hands in the anxious and nervous. A tea broker called Marsh ingested a good deal of tea dust and suffered from 'giddiness, headache, universal spasms, and loss of speech and memory' – cause of death was 'effluvia of tea'. In a similar case, the patient was bled and electric-shocked but to no avail; Lettsom conceded that it may have been the shocks which killed him.

The truth of it all clearly lay somewhere between the pernicious and the panacea. The curmudgeonly, beer-swigging William Cobbett did not approve; he wrote in his *Cottage Economy*, published in 1822:

'It is notorious that tea has no useful strength in it; and that it contains nothing nutritious; that it, besides being good for nothing, has badness in it, because it is well-known to produce want of sleep in many cases, and in all cases, to shake and weaken the nerves.'

He calculated precisely how much the working classes could save if they drank beer instead. In conclusion, tea was a harbinger of social disaster and doom; he ranted:

'I view tea drinking as a destroyer of health, an enfeebler of the frame, an engenderer of effeminacy and laziness, a debaucher of youth and a maker of misery for old age.'

Patriotic tea advertising around 1900.

What could be worse? Surely not beer. Beer is much cheaper than tea, suitable for all except the youngest child; five quarts (just over a pint) a day should be enough for everyone except drunkards. Tea, on the other hand, is a weak form of laudanum, a complete waste of time and money. Tea kills pigs:

'Give him the fifteen bushels of malt and he will repay you in ten score of bacon or thereabouts. But give him the 730 tea messes, or rather begin to give them to him, and give him nothing else, and he is dead from hunger, and bequeaths you his skeleton, at the end of about seven days ... tea drinking has done a great deal in bringing this nation into the state of misery in which it now is.'

Tea leads men and boys to idleness; it encourages 'a softness, an effeminacy, a seeking for the fireside, a lurking in the bed, and, in short, all the characteristics of idleness.' Tea leads girls to prostitution: it 'does little less for the girls, to whom the gossip of the tea-table is no bad preparatory school for the brothel.'

The argument raged on up to the late 19th century. Amongst other polemics is a nothing-if-not-blunt article by Dr J.E. Cooney in the *Windsor Magazine* entitled *The Dangers of Tea Drinking* and syndicated to the *San Francisco Call*, 27 October 1895, and the New York *London Queen*, 10 November 1895.

But by then it was all over; tea was here to stay, like it or not – and most people liked it. The Duke of Wellington liked to drink tea from a Wedgwood tea pot during his battles, because it kept his head clear – what could be more British? What part could be more crucial for tea to play in British history? C.H. Denyer, in an article entitled *The Consumption of Tea and Other Staple Drinks* published in *The Economic Journal* in 1983, concurred with, 'We are now almost justified in calling tea the English national drink; the more so as we take of it as much as all the rest of Europe put together.'

'Tea' and 'British' were now synonymous, they were officially one. George Gissing summed it up when he said, 'Nowhere is the English genius of domesticity more notably evident than in the festival of afternoon tea. The mere chink of cups and saucers turns the mind to happy repose.'

By the 1880s tea rooms had become popular and fashionable, especially with women of the comfortable classes who now had a respectable place in which they could meet, chat and relax in safety, with dignity and in comfort.

In her online article *Tea and Women – How the Tearoom Supported Women's Suffrage,* Jane Pettigrew points out how many local branches of the Suffragette movement evolved from local temperance societies; tea was served at these meetings where attendees were urged to reject alcohol and drink 'the cup that cheers but does not inebriate'. But, apart from this rather *ad hoc*, transient place of refuge, there was still nowhere suitable for the middle-class, politically motivated, independent-minded woman to meet.

(Extracted from the author's *Tea: A Very British Beverage*, 2014.)

Further information at:
Chrystal, Paul, *Tea: A Very British Beverage*, Stroud, 2014.
Heiss, Mary Lou, *The Story of Tea: A Cultural History and Drinking Guide*, Ten Speed Press, 2007.
Mair, Victor H., *The True History of Tea*, London, 2009.
Martin, Laura C, *Tea: The Drink that Changed the World*, Tuttle Publishing, 2007.

44

Laudanum

1676

Various laudanum preparations.

pothecary John Quincy, in his *A Compleat English Dispensatory* (1718), noted: 'A very mischievous way some Nurses have got, of giving their Children this Medicine to make them sleep, more for their own Ease than anything else.'

By the mid-19th century the practice seemed to have reached epidemic proportions, especially among mercenary 'nurses' accused of caring for numerous babies by drugging them with laudanum-based products. One Manchester druggist admitted selling a half-gallon of the market leader, Godfrey's Cordial, and up to six gallons of a generic equivalent, euphemistically called 'quietness', each week.

Hodgson's Genuine Patent Medicines: infants preservative. The text reads: 'Mrs Easy your house says it's going to tumble down, upon the spot, and your child is in the cockloft. Never you mind Miss Fume, I gave it a bottle of Infant's Preservative before I come out so there is no danger.'

If neither a jug of coffee nor a cup of tea satisfied your needs then a spoonful or two of laudanum might do the trick – as it commonly did for some from the mid-17th century. Also known as opium tincture, laudanum is a powerful, bitter-tasting oral formulation of morphine. Basically, it is prepared by dissolving extracts from the opium poppy (*Papaver somniferum Linnaeus*) in alcohol (ethanol). Its principal use was as a pain medication and cough suppressant. Until the early 20th century, laudanum was sold without prescription and was a constituent of many patent medicines.

Today, laudanum is recognised as addictive and is strictly regulated and controlled. Accidental or deliberate overdose was common; overdose and death may occur with a single oral dose of between 100 and 150 mg of morphine in a healthy adult – the equivalent of between two to three teaspoons of laudanum. Overdose can result in severe respiratory depression, collapse and death. Victorian women were prescribed the drug, marketed as 'women's friends', for problems with menstruation and childbirth, and even for fashionable female maladies of the day such as 'the vapours', which included hysteria, depression and fainting fits. Nurses spoon-fed laudanum to infants as a soporific. Twenty or twenty-five drops of laudanum could be bought for a penny (1d).

Here is a 19th century recipe for a cough mixture:
Two tablespoons of vinegar, two tablespoons of treacle; 60 drops of laudanum. One teaspoonful to be taken night and morning.

Theophrastus von Hohenheim, better known as Paracelsus, an itinerant Swiss alchemist and physician, found fame from his exotic travelling and criticism of classical authority relating to pharmacology. From 1517 until his death in 1541, he criss-crossed Europe and the Near East demonstrating that Greek and Roman medicine was no longer good enough for his modern age. His alternative lay in concentrated and refined substances – vitriols, elixirs, powdered metals in distilled alcohol – which he described as 'nature fortified beyond its grade'. Something he called Laudanum was in his medicine bag; 'Laudanum, as listed in the *London Pharmacopoeia* (1618), was a pill made from opium, saffron, castor, ambergris, musk and nutmeg.' (Hodgson 2001).

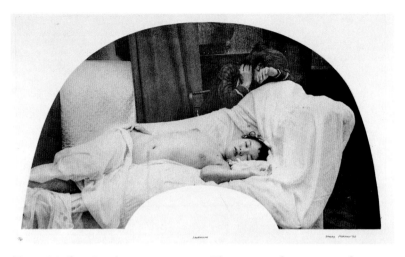

Tracey Moffatt, Laudanum #10, 1999. This image is from a series of 19 photogravures by Tracey Moffatt called Laudanum.

Thomas Sydenham (1624 –89), however, popularised and perfected laudanum; his recipe would become the standard preparation – a proprietary opium tincture that he also named laudanum, although it differed substantially from the laudanum of Paracelsus. In 1676 Sydenham published a seminal work, *Medical Observations Concerning the History and Cure of Acute Diseases*, in which he promoted his brand of opium tincture, and advocated its use for a range of medical conditions. By the 18th century, the medicinal properties of opium and laudanum were well known, and the term 'laudanum' came to refer to any combination of opium and alcohol.

Sydenham was a physician known as 'the English Hippocrates' for his belief that medicine was all about close observation of patients rather than fixed theories. He won for himself the epithet 'Opiophilos' for the regard in which he held opium: the queen of medicines, revered since antiquity, unequalled in the relief of pain, the suppression of coughs and respiratory ailments, the treatment of diarrhoea and dysentery and the provision of deep and refreshing sleep: as he himself said, 'Of all the remedies it has pleased almighty God to give man to relieve his suffering, none is so universal and so efficacious as opium.' Many doctors and apothecaries concocted their own laudanums, but Sydenham's preparation was considered the best: two ounces of opium in a pint of strong red wine or port, spiced with saffron, cloves and cinnamon. For two centuries, pharmacy jars filled with this tincture would be decorated in gold leaf with *Laudanum Sydenhamii.*

In the 18th century one work that gained much traction was by George Young, who published a *Treatise on Opium*, emphasising its dangers. To challenge Young, an essay on opium by his contemporary Charles Alston, professor of botany and materia medica at Edinburgh, had recommended the use of opium for a wide variety of conditions. Young countered this by emphasising the risks '... that I may prevent such mischief as I can, I here give it as my sincere opinion ... that opium is a poison by which great numbers are daily destroyed.' Young gives a comprehensive account of the indications for the drug including its complications. As it gained popularity, opium, and after 1820, morphine, was mixed with a wide variety of dubious agents, drugs and chemicals including mercury, hashish, cayenne pepper, ether, chloroform, belladonna, whisky, wine and brandy.'

The Edinburgh surgeon-apothecary and physician George Young was an empiric who emphasised observation, practical experience and a healthy sceptical approach to evidence in medicine. He was an early member of the Rankenian Club, a group of young intellectuals whose ideas were to be at the heart of Scottish Enlightenment thinking.

According to Goodman and Gilman, *Pharmacological basis of therapeutics*, 'Paregoric is a four per cent opium tincture in which there is also benzoic acid, camphor and anise oil ... Paregoric by tradition is used especially for children.' The name paregoric has also been used for a kind of boiled sweet, originally (and by some reports still currently) containing paregoric – in particular, the army and navy brand sweet produced by British confectioner Paynes.

Laudanum: The poor child's nurse.
Courtesy of the Wellcome Collection.

By the 19th century, laudanum found its way into many patent medicines to 'relieve pain ... to produce sleep ... to allay irritation ... to check excessive secretions ... to support the system ... [and] as a soporific.' The limited pharmacopoeia of the day meant that opium derivatives were among the most effective of available treatments, so laudanum was widely prescribed for ailments from colds to meningitis to cardiac diseases, in both adults and children. Laudanum was also used to combat yellow fever.

Many a Victorian woman was prescribed the drug for relief from period pain and vague aches (general ill feeling or lethargy). As noted, nurses also spoon-fed laudanum to infants. The Romantic and Victorian eras saw the widespread use of laudanum in Europe and the United States. Mary Todd Lincoln, the wife of the US president Abraham Lincoln, was a laudanum addict, as was Coleridge, who was famously interrupted during an opium-induced writing session of (the unfinished) *Kubla Khan* by a 'person from Porlock'. Initially a drug of the working classes, laudanum was cheaper than a bottle of gin or wine, because it was treated as a medication and not taxed as an alcoholic beverage.

'To understand the popularity of a medicine that eased—even if only temporarily—coughing, diarrhoea and pain, one only has to consider the living conditions at the time.' In the 1850s, 'cholera and dysentery regularly ripped through communities, its victims often dying from debilitating diarrhoea,' and dropsy, consumption, ague and rheumatism were all too common. (Hodgson, 2001).

Laudanum is implicated in this murder story from 1822:

'A changed will in 1815 was the cause of the murder by poisoning of an old lady in Ravensworth near Richmond, Yorkshire. Robert Peat was put out, to say the least, when his half cousin, also Robert Peat, altered his will, removing his namesake from the list of beneficiaries to the advantage of his wife. Peat was a regular visitor to his half cousin's – despite the fact that he was less than welcome – and one June day in 1822 told a neighbour he was going there because of the woman "who wanted to wrong him out of the brass he had" and that he had a bottle of laudanum which "would do her a trick". When he got to the house in Ravensworth he surreptitiously added the laudanum to a leg of lamb that was simmering on the stove, concealing the consequences of his actions by suggesting there was bad water about which was making people ill. Peat had bought the laudanum from John Smith's chemist in Darlington, allegedly for "some ladies in Middleton".'

'Neighbours, too, were given some of the stew and remarked on its strange taste and colour; in due course they and Peat's half cousin and wife were violently ill, particularly the wife. One neighbour, Mary Bolam, told Peat to call a doctor for her but he demurred. She died later that night. Suspicions were raised and Peat was arrested and hanged at Durham.'

English literature has a number of references to laudanum, illustrating its ubiquity in the general population:

In Mary Shelley's *Frankenstein* (1818), Victor Frankenstein takes laudanum as his only way of getting some sleep, and thus preserving his life:

'Ever since my recovery from the fever I had been in the custom of taking every night a small quantity of laudanum; for it was by means of this drug only that I was enabled to gain the rest necessary for the preservation of life. Oppressed by the recollection of my various misfortunes, I now swallowed double my usual quantity and soon slept profoundly. But sleep did not afford me respite from thought and misery; my dreams presented a thousand objects that scared me.'
– Shelley M., *Frankenstein*, pp. 197–198

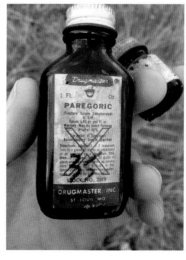

A bottle of Paregoric, circa 1940s. The large red X on the label indicates that it was classified as an 'exempt narcotic', sold without prescription even though it contained morphine (photographer: User:Jwilli74; this file is licenced under the Creative Commons Attribution-Share Alike 3.0 Unported licence).

Confessions of an English Opium-Eater (1821) is an autobiographical account by Thomas De Quincey about his laudanum addiction and its effect on his life.

In *Silas Marner* by George Eliot (1861), Silas finds and adopts a two-year-old girl who had wandered into his house. The girl had been abandoned while walking with her opium-addicted mother, Molly Farren, who had fallen asleep in the snow and died. Earlier in the novel we learn that she uses laudanum … 'if Molly should take a drop too much laudanum some day, and make a widower of you.'

In Wilkie Collins's *The Moonstone* (1868), laudanum is 'as an essential ingredient of the plot'. Collins based his description of the drug's effects on his own experiences with it. A laudanum-addicted character also appears in his novel *Armadale* (1864–66).

Further information at:

Berridge, Virginia, *Opium and the People: Opiate Use in Nineteenth-Century England*, New Haven, 1987.

Chrystal, Paul, *Yorkshire Murders, Manslaughter, Madness, and Executions*, Stenlake Publishing, 2018.

Davenport-Hines R., 'Early History', *The Pursuit of Oblivion*, 2004.

Hodgson, Barbara, *In the Arms of Morpheus: The Tragic History of Laudanum, Morphine, and Patent Medicines*, Buffalo, NY, 2001.

Sigerist H.E., 'Laudanum in the Works of Paracelsus,' *Bulletin of the History of Medicine*, 9, pp. 530–44, 1941.

45

Celia Fiennes's peregrinations

1885

'The only permanent memorial in the whole country in memory of Celia Fiennes', this 'Waymark' stands in No Man's Heath, near Malpas, Cheshire

Daniel Defoe (1660–1731) was not the only traveller and writer to leave for us a fascinating and detailed description of England, although, for some reason, his is the more famous account. Celia Fiennes's *Through England on a Side Saddle in the Time of William and Mary* (1698) is an equally remarkable description of much of England.

The journeys took place between 1684 and about 1703, 'to regain my health by variety and change of aire and exercise' (*Journeys*). In these times the notion of travel for its own sake was still unusual, particularly for woman travellers.

The intrepid lady traveller journeyed the length and breadth of the country from Cornwall to Newcastle upon Tyne, often accompanied by only one or two maids. As with any competent travel journalist, Fiennes worked up her notes into a travel memoir in 1702, which she never published, intending it only for family consumption. It gives us a vivid portrait

Detail from Woman on Horseback in a Landscape by Gesina ter Borch; Image Source: Rijksmuseum, Amsterdam. This image adorns the cover of a number of editions of Through England on a Side Saddle in the Time of William and Mary.

of a still largely unenclosed countryside with few and primitive roads, although signposts ('posts and hands pointing to each road with the names of the great towns or market towns that it leads to') were starting to appear. Robert Southey published extracts in 1812, and the first complete edition appeared in 1888 under the title *Through England on a Side Saddle*. A scholarly edition called *The Journeys of Celia Fiennes* was

Celia's blue plaque in Hackney: 'Celia Fiennes, 1662–1741, traveller and diarist, lived in a house near this site from 1738, and died here'.

produced by Christopher Morris in 1947. Since then the book has remained in print in various editions.

The newly fashionable spa towns such as Bath and Harrogate were favourites of hers; she was what we would now call a devotee of the staycation and domestic tourism; her avid interest in the 'production and manufactures of each place' anticipated the genre of 'economic tourism', which was made famous with Defoe's *A Tour through the Whole Island of Great Britain* (1724–26). She saw and described many of the finest baroque English country houses while they were still being built and helped establish a tourist industry for them; her comments remain the most interesting sources of information about many of them. At Stonehenge she counted the exact number of stones and at Harrogate visited 'the sulphur or stinking spaw'. She also clambered over the rocks at Land's End.

This is how she described the Old Sulphur Well at Harrogate in her *Great Journey to Newcastle and to Cornwall* in 1698:

'There is the Sulpher or Stincking spaw, not Improperly term'd for the Smell being so very strong and offensive that I could not force my horse Near the Well ... the taste and smell is much of Sulpher' tho' it has an additionall offenciveness Like Carrion.'

Fiennes visited York in 1697. This is her description of the the River 'Ouise' and the mean streets of the city:

'Thence we go much on a Causey [causeway] to Yorke 8 miles more, it stands high but for one of the Metropolis and the see of ye Archbishopp it Makes but a meane appearance. The Streetes are Narrow and not of any Length, save one wch you Enter of from the bridge that is over the Ouise which Lookes like a fine River when full after much raine. It is but Low in Comparison of Some Rivers, it bears Great Barges, it Looks muddy, its full of good ffish. We Eate very good Cod fish and Salmon and that at a pretty Cheape rate, tho' we were not in the best jnn for the Angel is the best in Cunny Streete. The houses are very Low and as indifferent as in any Country town and the Narrowness of ye Streetes makes it appear very mean.'

A few years later Daniel Defoe, in his *A Tour Through the Whole Island of Great Britain* (1724–1727), concurs after his visit to York:

'There is abundance of good company here, and abundance of good families live here, for the sake of the good company and cheap living; a man converses here with all the world as effectually as at London.'

When she called in at Leeds she gives us a marvellous insight on the price and strength of beer there and opens a debate as to whether her bar meals should be free or not:

'Leeds is a Large town, severall Large streetes, Cleane and well pitch'd and good houses all built of stone. Some have good Gardens and Steps up to their houses and walls before them. This is Esteemed the Wealthyest town of its bigness in the Country its manufacture is ye woollen Cloth-the Yorkshire Cloth in wch they are all Employ'd and are Esteemed very Rich and very proud. They have provision soe plentiful y^t they may Live wth very Little Expense and get much variety; here if one Calls for a tankard of Ale wch is allwayes a groate its the only dear thing all over Yorkshire, their ale is very strong, but for paying this Groat for yo^{ur} ale you may have a slice of meate Either hott or Cold according to the tyme of day you Call, or Else butter and Cheese Gratis into the bargaine; this was a Generall Custom in most parts of Yorkshire but now they have almost Changed it, and tho' they still retaine the great price for the ale, yet Make strangers pay for their meate, and at some places at great rates, notwithstanding how Cheape they have all their provision. There is still this Custome on a Market day at Leeds, the sign of ye bush just by the Bridge, any body y^t will goe and Call for one tanchard of ale and a pinte of wine and pay for these only shall be set to a table to Eate wth 2 or 3 dishes of good meate and a dish of sweetmeates after. Had I known this and ye Day wch was their Market I would have Come then but I happened to Come a day after ye market, however I did only pay for 3 tankards of ale and w^t I Eate, and my servants was gratis.'

Further information at:

'June 7th 1662: Birth of Celia Fiennes,' *History Today* LXII/6, June 2012.
Chrystal, Paul, *Harrogate Through Time*, Stroud, 2011.
Chrystal, Paul, *Central Leeds Through Time*, Stroud, 2020.
Chrystal, Paul, *Harrogate Pubs*, Stroud, 2017.
Chrystal, Paul, *Pubs in and Around York*, Darlington, 2018.

CHAPTER 7

THE 18ᵀᴴ AND 19ᵀᴴ CENTURIES

46

The mantua

1700

1750s court mantua showing the stylised back drapery at the Metropolitan Museum of Art, New York.

Originally a loose gown, the later mantua was an overgown or robe typically worn over stays, stomacher and a co-ordinating petticoat. Putting it on, dancing and moving in it took skill, patience and practice. The mantua (from the French *manteau*) style was introduced to Britain in the 1670s and remained fashionable until the beginning of the

A British court Mantua at the Victoria and Albert Museum, London. Arnold van Westerhout (Italian, 1651–1725). Gentildonna Venetiana, 1688. Engraving; hand-colouring; printing ink; watercolour. London: Victoria and Albert Museum, E.21581-1957. Given by the House of Worth.

18th century. It started off as an informal style, and was banned for its informality from the French court by Louis XIV. The mantua gradually became acceptable as formal dress and remained a popular choice for court dress in England. For the very well to do it replaced the stiff constricting boned bodice-and-skirt style. This loosely draped style of gown was thought to display silk designs to their best advantage, as they were draped rather than cut.

The skirts of the mantua were used to show off luxurious fabrics that reflected a wearer's wealth, taste and status. The use of gold, silver and silk, as well as the technical skill required to weave such complex patterns, made these fabrics very expensive. It is probable that the fabric of this dress would cost around the equivalent of £5,000 today.

According to the National Museum Scotland:

'There were many layers underneath, including stockings, held with a garter, a linen or cotton shift and stays, which fastened at the back. The hooped petticoat would have been arranged on the floor with the outer skirts over it for the lady to step into; both were then pulled up and tied at the waist. Small hip pads, or panniers, may also have been added at the waist to support the width of the skirt. The bodice and the stomacher – the triangular insert of fabric that sits in the open front of the garment – was arranged and pinned or sewn to the stays at the front. Finally, it was accessorised with the finest European lace and jewels. The process required the assistance of a lady's maid, who would have been expected to attend their mistress for any change of clothes.'

– *https://www.nms.ac.uk/explore-our-collections/stories/art-and-design/ court-mantua/*

Further information at:

Mantua [British] (33.54a,b). *In Heilbrunn Timeline of Art History*, New York: The Metropolitan Museum of Art, 2000.

Ribeiro, Aileen, on the 'Origins of the Mantua in the late 17th Century', in *Dress in Eighteenth Century Europe 1715–1789*, Ashelford, Jane, *The Art of Dress.*

Blue silk and gold-embroidered court mantua dress at Tullie House Museum, Carlisle. It belonged to the 18th-century Carlisle miser Margery Jackson (1722–1812) and dates from around 1750. It is unusual in that it still retains the stomacher (front bodice panel) (photographer: Storye book).

47

Jethro Tull's seed drill and the Agricultural Revolution

1701

The seed drill.

Jethro Tull (baptized 30 March 1674–d.1741) helped to bring about the British Agricultural Revolution of the 18th century. He perfected a horse-drawn seed drill in 1701 that economically sowed the seeds in neat rows, and later developed a horse-drawn hoe. Tull's methods were adopted by many landowners and helped to provide the basis for modern agriculture.

Agriculture was by no means Tull's first career choice. He grew up in Bradfield, Berkshire, moving on to St John's College, Oxford. He trained as a lawyer, became a member of Staple Inn, and was called to the bar in 1693 at Gray's Inn. On marrying Susanna Smith, they settled on Tull's father's farm at Howberry, near Crowmarsh Gifford, Oxfordshire, where they had one son and two daughters.

Tull then fell ill with a pulmonary disorder and travelled to Europe in search of a cure, staying for a long period at Montpellier. Here he had the time to compare the agricultural practices of France and Italy with that of Britain. More than once did he allude in his work to the similarity of his own horse-hoe husbandry to the practice followed by the vine-dressers of the south of Europe in constantly hoeing or otherwise stirring their ground. On his return to England in 1709, he took on the farm called Prosperous, at Shalbourne (now in Wiltshire) near Hungerford. This is where he wrote his *Horse-hoeing Husbandry* (1731).

Jethro Tull was one of the early pioneers of a scientific approach to agriculture. He helped transform agricultural practices by inventing or improving a number of implements. The seed drill was his greatest invention – a mechanical seeder that sowed efficiently at the correct depth and spacing and then covered the seed so that it could grow. Before this the usual practice was to plant seeds by broadcasting – evenly throwing – them across the ground by hand on the prepared soil and then lightly harrowing the soil to bury the seeds to the correct depth. Some would germinate and some would fail. It was a very inefficient, hit-and-miss way of seeding that did not always produce good crops.

Tull had observed that traditional heavy sowing densities were not very efficient, so he instructed his staff to drill at very precise, low densities. By 1701, his frustration with their lack of cooperation prompted him to invent a machine to do the work for him. He designed his drill with a rotating cylinder. Grooves were cut into the cylinder to allow seed to pass from the hopper above to a funnel below. They were then directed into a channel dug by a plough at

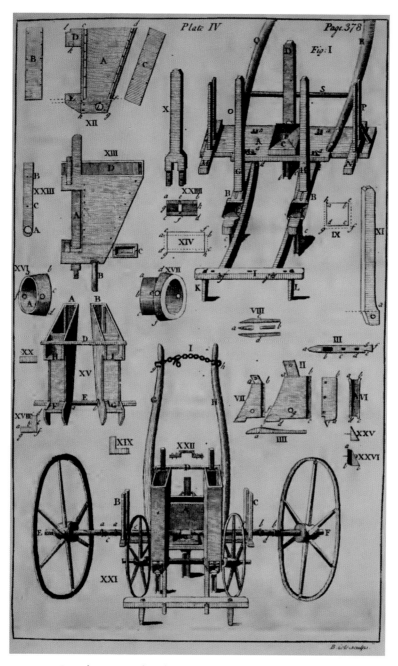

Horse-hoeing Husbandry by Jethro Tull, 4th edition (1762), plate IV.

the front of the machine, then immediately covered by a harrow attached to the rear. This limited the wastage of seeding and made the crop easier to weed.

This was the first agricultural machine with moving parts. It started as a one-man, one-row device, but later designs sowed seeds in three uniform rows, had wheels and were drawn by horses. Using wider spacing than previous practices allowed horses to draw the equipment and not step on the plants.

Tull was the first to demonstrate the advantages of hoeing cultivated soils. His work in the fields started a new movement in 18th-century agriculture called 'horse-hoeing husbandry' or 'new husbandry'. His system was supported by Henri-Louis Duhamel du Monceau in France, Michel Lullin de Chateauvieux in Switzerland, John Mills in England, and many others. It offered two major innovations:

Scarifiers and horse hoes: these were implements unknown until the 18th century.

> 'Hoeing by manual labour had, in very early ages, been partially prac-tised; for the earliest writers [...] recommended particular attention to the cutting down and destroying of weeds. But to Jethro Tull, is indisputably due the honour of having first demonstrated the importance of frequent hoeing, not merely to extirpate weeds, but for the purpose of pulverising the soil, by which process the gases and moisture of the atmosphere are enabled more freely to penetrate to the roots of the crop.'
> – Cuthbert W. Johnson, *The Farmer's Encyclopaedia, and Dictionary of Rural Affairs*, 'Agriculture', p. 41, 1844.

Throughout the 18th century, the *Georgics*, a didactic poem by the Roman poet Virgil from around 37–30 BC, was still held in great esteem in Britain, not just as an exemplar of fine poetry, but as an authoritative manual of husbandry. The number of English translations and editions of the *Georgics* between 1690 and 1820 is testament to its cultural significance in British society. In the preface to his translation, William Benson declares his certainty that 'the Husbandry of England in General is Virgilian'. Tull disagreed: in a chapter entitled 'Remarks on the Bad Husbandry, that is so finely Express'd in Virgil's First Georgic,' Tull criticises it for several apparent deficiencies in farming techniques.

In 1759 one in four families in Britain were engaged in agriculture, and one in seven by 1801. Agriculture had a critical role to play as a stimulus to, and in the development of, the Industrial Revolution. The Agricultural Revolution took place in Britain in the 1700s and with it came farm machinery inventions and innovations (Tull's seed machine being a good example) that led to an increase in food production; this in turn spawned an increase in the population of Britain which had two major consequences for the Industrial Revolution. First, the increased population provided, in time, a reservoir of workers for the factories and mines; second, this larger population eventually generated a market for the goods being produced in the factories and for the raw materials coming off production lines such as iron and steel for civil engineering infrastructure projects.

One of the most significant innovations on the farms was the introduction of crop rotation, prompted by the Royal Society. Hitherto, farmers planted the same crop in the same field every year, which compromised the quality of the soil and meant having fields lie fallow every couple of years. Charles Townshend (Turnip Townshend) saw a way out of this which would increase productivity and soil quality: in the 1730s, he discovered that simply by growing different types of crops in the fields year after year British farmers could avoid leaving a field fallow. More food meant increased population and bigger markets. During the century animal husbandry went from strength to strength, with the average weight of a sheep at Smithfield ballooning from 28lb to 80 lb. The invention of labour-saving machinery was crucial, too; for example, Jethro Tull's invention of the mechanical seed drill had a profound effect on productivity, seed costs and on labour costs when it replaced the laborious and labour intensive less efficient process of manual seed drilling.

Further information at:

Brachfeld, Aaron , *Jethro Tull's Horse Hoeing Husbandry*, 5th edition, 2010.
Bruyn, Frans De, 'Reading Virgil's Georgics as a Scientific Text: The Eighteenth-Century Debate between Jethro Tull and Stephen Switzer,' *ELH*, 71 (3), pp. 661–89, 2004.
Fussell, G.E., *Jethro Tull: His Influence on Mechanized Agriculture*, Osprey, 1973.

48

The Acts of Union

1707

An 1809 engraving showing James Douglas, the '2nd Duke of Queensberry and 1st Duke of Dover' presenting the Act of Union to Queen Anne in 1707.

The Acts of Union (Scottish Gaelic: Achd an Aonaidh) were two Acts of Parliament: the Union with Scotland Act 1706, passed by the Parliament of England, and the Union with England Act, passed in 1707 by the Parliament of Scotland. They effected the terms of the Treaty of Union that had been agreed on 22 July 1706.

6 March 1707 was a momentous day for England and Scotland – for it was on that day that The Acts of Union, passed by the English and Scottish

Parliaments in 1707, led to the creation of the United Kingdom of Great Britain. By the two Acts, the Kingdom of England and the Kingdom of Scotland – which at the time were separate states with separate legislatures, but sharing the same monarch – were, in the words of the Treaty, 'United into One Kingdom by the Name of

The flag of Great Britain (1707–1800).

Great Britain'. The UK Parliament convened for the first time in October 1707. The two countries had shared a monarch since the Union of the Crowns in 1603, when King James VI of Scotland inherited the English throne from his double first cousin twice removed, Queen Elizabeth I.

The idea of a union between England and Scotland first gained serious traction in spring 1689 during the deliberations of the Convention Parliament in Edinburgh. William III (r. 1689-1702) wrote to the Convention saying how pleased he was that so many members of the Scots nobility and gentry favoured the proposal, especially since both nations shared the same 'landmass, language and attachment to the Protestant religion'. Union would also, of course, help against ex-King James and the Jacobites. So, the Convention appointed commissioners to negotiate with the English: the English showed no interest. A proposal for union was made in the House of Lords in 1695, but that, too, was dismissed.

The parlous state of the Scottish economy, however, kept hope alive among the Scottish political elite during the 1690s; the Scots had hopes for a union of trade with access to English colonial markets. The Scottish economy was badly damaged by the English Navigation Acts of 1660 and 1663 and England's wars with the Dutch Republic, Scotland's major export market. Nevertheless, in 1699 things progressed with discussions between 62 commissioners in London and Edinburgh when the English acknowledged that a union might be in both nations' interest.

The Act ratifying the Treaty of Union was finally carried in the Parliament of Scotland by 110 votes to 69 on 16 January 1707, with a number of key amendments. News of the ratification and of the amendments was received in Westminster, where the Act was passed quickly through both Houses and received the royal assent on 6 March.

The Downsitting of the Scottish Parliament' from Châtelain and Gueudeville's Atlas Historique, 1720.

According to G.N. Clark, Scotland benefitted by gaining 'freedom of trade with England and the colonies' as well as 'a great expansion of markets'. The agreement guaranteed the permanent status of the Presbyterian Church in Scotland, and the separate legislature system in Scotland. Clark argues that in exchange for the financial benefits and bribes that England bestowed, what it gained was priceless. Scotland accepted the Hanoverian succession and gave up her power of threatening England's military security and complicating her commercial relations ... 'The sweeping successes of the eighteenth-century wars owed much to the new unity of the two nations.' (Clark, 1956, *pp 290–93*)

When Samuel Johnson and James Boswell made their tour in 1773, as recorded in *A Journey to the Western Islands of Scotland*, Johnson noted that Scotland was 'a nation of which the commerce is hourly extending, and the wealth increasing' and in particular that Glasgow had become one of the greatest cities of Britain.

Further information at:

Campbell, R. H., 'The Anglo-Scottish Union of 1707. II. The Economic Consequences,' *Economic History Review*, vol. 16, no. 3, 1964.

Clark, G.N., *The Later Stuarts, 1660–1714* (2nd edition), 1956.

Whatley, C., *Bought and sold for English Gold? Explaining the Union of 1707*, East Linton, 2001.

Whatley, C., *The Scots and the Union*, Edinburgh, 2006.

49

Powdered wigs and syphilis

'Her Ladyship, with a head so smooth, throws up her hands in horror at the coloured rag which is about to be placed on her head. In the background the glamorous daughter looks forlornly at her image in the glass, her fashionable white locks replaced with brown curls. There is an interesting contrast between the picture on the wall of Charles II, resplendent in his full wig, and the young blade looking at his reflection in the mirror. Only father seems unconcerned by all the fuss: he is happy with the brown rug sitting atop his pate.'

For nearly 200 years, powdered wigs – perukes – were all the rage. The in- vogue hairpiece owes some of its popularity amongst the well to do to three factors: a syphilis pandemic, two vainglorious monarchs and bad hair hygiene.

Between the 16th and 19th centuries, syphilis was one of the biggest public-health burdens in terms of prevalence, symptoms, and disability, although records of its true prevalence are scanty because of the frightening and stigmatic nature of sexually-transmitted infections at the time. According to a 2020 study, more than 20 per cent of individuals aged between 15 and 34 years in late 18th-century London were treated for syphilis. At the time no one really knew exactly what caused it, but it was well-known that it was spread sexually and also often from mother to child. Its association with sex, especially sexual promiscuity and prostitution, amplified the fear and revulsion. Much of the damage it wreaked was caused not so much by great sickness or death early in the course of the disease, but rather by its gruesome and horrendous effects decades after primary infection as it progressed to neurosyphilis with *tabes dorsalis* – a late

Leaving off POWDER, —or— A Frugal Family saving the Guinea.

James Gillray 'Leaving off powder – a frugal family saving the guinea.'

consequence of neurosyphilis, characterised by the slow degeneration, specifically, demyelination, mainly of the neural tracts. Mercury compounds and isolation were commonly used, with treatments often worse than the disease itself.

So, by 1580 syphilis had become one of the worst epidemics to strike Europe since the Black Death. According to William Clowes, an 'infinite multitude' of syphilis patients clogged London's hospitals, and more shuffled in each day. Without antibiotics, victims endured the full horror of the disease: open sores, nasty rashes, blindness, dementia – and alopecia. Baldness swept the land.

This was in a time when visible hair loss was 'a one-way ticket to public embarrassment'. Long hair was the fashion with men and women and a bald head would irreparably destroy any reputation. When Samuel Pepys's brother contracted syphilis, the diarist wrote, 'If [my brother] lives, he will not be able to show his head – which will be a very great shame to me.' Hair, or the lack of it, told the world what you had been up to.

Enter the wigmaker and his wigs. They were a perfect solution, enabling the follically challenged to conceal their baldness and, at the same time, any indiscretion, or suggestion thereof. Wigs were made of horse, goat or human hair and coated with powder – scented with lavender or orange – to mask any embarrassing smells.

Richard Newton: Sketches in a Shaving Shop (1794).

Powdering was obligatory – a fashion copied from the French. Gentlemen generally wore white powder, ladies a slightly bluish white. Wig powder was made from finely ground starch that was scented with orange flower, lavender or orris root. It was occasionally coloured violet, blue, pink or yellow, but was most often off-white; the powders were highly toxic since they were made from white lead. The prudent covered their face with a conical mask while the dresser applied the poisonous powder, otherwise the ingestion of lead might well lead to nausea, dizziness, headaches, paralysis and in some cases even death.

Samuel Pepys recorded the day in 1665 when a barber shaved his head and he tried on his new periwig for the first time, but in a year of plague he was uneasy about wearing it:

'3rd September 1665: Up, and put on my coloured silk suit, very fine, and my new periwig, bought a good while since, but darst not wear it because the plague was in Westminster when I bought it. And it is a wonder what will be the fashion after the plague is done as to periwigs, for nobody will dare to buy any haire for fear of the infection? That it had been cut off the heads of people dead of the plague.'

Plague fear was not the only problem, as Pepys noted on 27 March 1663:

'I did go to the Swan; and there sent for Jervas my old periwig-maker and he did bring me a periwig; but it was full of nits, so as I was troubled to see it (it being his old fault) and did send him to make it clean.'

Different professions cultivated their own style of wig – different ones for the clergy, the services, the judiciary and so on. Shortly after the coronation of George III, William Hogarth published a satirical print implying that the choice of wig was actually a branch of science.

In 1655, 17-year-old Louis XIV of France started losing his hair so he hired 48 wigmakers to save his image. Five years later, Louis's cousin, England's Charles II, did likewise when his hair started to grey. These wigs were shoulder-length or longer, imitating the long hair that had become fashionable among men since the 1620s. That was all it took for courtiers and other aristocrats to ape the two kings and the fashion percolated down to the upper-middle class.

The price of wigs increased so perukes became a badge for conspicuous wealth. An everyday wig cost about 25 shillings—a week's pay for a common Londoner. The bill for ostentatious, elaborate perukes ballooned to as high as £40. The word 'bigwig' was coined to describe those who could afford big perukes.

Perukes remained popular. Head lice were crawling everywhere, and nit-picking was painful and time-consuming. Wigs, however, solved the problem. Lice gave up infesting people's hair – which had to be shaved for the peruke to fit – and decamped to the

William Hogarth parodying contemporary pseudo-scientific treatises and manuals. The 'Five Orders of Periwigs' shows 'Episcopal or Parsonic' as well as 'Old Peer-ian or Aldermanic', 'Lexonic", and 'Composite or Half Natural' and 'Queerinthian'.

wigs instead. Delousing a wig was a lot easier than delousing a head of hair: your infested headpiece was simply sent to a wigmaker, who would boil the wig and exterminate the lice.

'The Five Orders of Periwigs as they were Worn at the Late Coronation Measured Architectonically,' is a 1761 engraving by William Hogarth which contains several levels of satire. First, and most clearly, it lampoons the fashion for outlandish wigs in the mid- to late-18th century. Second, in classifying the wigs into 'orders', it satirises the formulation of canons of beauty from the analysis of surviving pieces of classical architecture and sculpture from ancient Greece and ancient Rome, particularly the classical remains at Athens, Rome, Baalbek and Palmyra, and the precise architectural drawings of James 'Athenian' Stuart (published in the *Antiquities of Athens,* the first volume of which appeared in 1762).

Women in the 18th century did not wear wigs, but wore a coiffure supplemented by artificial hair or hair from other sources – forerunners of today's extensions.

Later, all manner of wildlife shared head space with the wearer. Women used a special rod to scratch their insect-infested wigs.

In France, the French Revolution of 1789 did once and for all for the peruke, symbol, as it was, of the old order. The British renounced wigs after William Pitt levied a tax on hair powder in 1795 – The Duty on Hair Powder Act. Thenceforth, wig-wearers who wished to powder their tresses were obliged to go to the stamp office, fill in a form and apply for an annual certificate at a cost of one guinea. Various exemptions applied – for instance for poorer clergymen and certain classes of the armed forces. The law was repealed in 1869, by which time fewer than 1,000 annual licences were being granted – and most of them were for servants.

Short, natural hair was the new fashion for men and largely remained so until the 1960s.

Further information at:
Chaudhary, Amit, 'History of Hair Wigs – Why It is in Trend Today – Artificial Heads of Hair,' *Planetofhaircloning.com,* 10 July 2018.
McDowall, Carolyn, 'Adventures in Hair for 18th Century Gentlemen,' *The Culture Concept Circle.*

50

The smallpox vaccine

1796

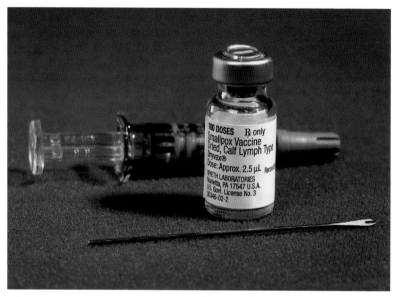

Components of a smallpox vaccination kit, including the diluent, a vial of Dryvax® smallpox vaccine and a bifurcated needle.

Smallpox is spread by an inhaled virus that causes fever, vomiting and a rash which soon covers the body with pus-filled blisters. These turn into scabs that leave scars. Fatal in approximately one-third of cases, another third of those afflicted with the disease typically go blind. Smallpox existed in ancient times, invading, among other places, Egypt, India and China. Although the origin of smallpox remains unknown, it is thought to date back to Egypt around the third century BC based on a smallpox-like rash found on three mummies. The earliest written description of a disease clearly resembling smallpox emerged in China in the fourth century AD. We also have early written accounts from India in the seventh century and in Asia Minor in the tenth century.

As with other pandemics, the global spread of smallpox goes hand in hand with the growth and spread of crowded civilizations, war, exploration and expanding trade routes and colonisation over the centuries: smallpox came to Europe during the Crusades of the 11th century. When Europeans began to explore and colonise other parts of the world, smallpox went with them. Smallpox has had a major impact on world history, particularly on indigenous populations where smallpox was non-native, such as the Americas and Australia; these peoples were rapidly weakened by smallpox, sometimes deliberately by the colonists, along with other imported diseases, during periods of early foreign contact.

At the end of the 15th century Christopher Columbus led the way when he shipped into the Americas a raft of deadly diseases for which the indigenous populations had no natural immunity: measles, smallpox, whooping cough, chickenpox, bubonic plague, typhus and malaria all had a role to play as efficient native population killers in the New World. Worldwide, smallpox was a leading cause of death in the 18th century, killing an estimated 400,000 Europeans each year, including five reigning European monarchs. Then, every seventh child born in Russia died from smallpox. Most people were infected at some point during their lifetime, and about 30 per cent of people died from the disease. Smallpox was responsible for a third of all cases of blindness. Between 20 and 60 per cent of all those infected – and over 80 per cent of infected children – died from the disease.

In the 20th century, smallpox was probably responsible for a staggering 300-500 million deaths worldwide. In the early 1950s an estimated 50 million cases of smallpox occurred in the world each year. In 1967 the World Health Organization estimated that 15 million people contracted the disease and that two million died in that year. After successful vaccination campaigns during the 19th and 20th centuries, the WHO certified the global eradication of smallpox in December 1979. Given these terrifying statistics, who today would reject a smallpox vaccination? They did not, however, deter the Anti-Vaccine Society members (See image on page 244).

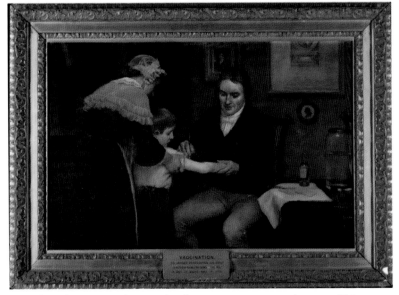

Dr Edward Jenner performing his first vaccination on eight-year-old James Phipps, 14 May 1796. Painting by Ernest Board circa 1910 (images.wellcome.ac.uk).

Variolation

One of the earliest methods for controlling the spread of smallpox was the use of variolation. Variolation involved infecting a person via a cut in the skin with exudate from a patient with a relatively mild case of smallpox (variola) to bring about a manageable and recoverable infection that would provide later immunity. With variolation, people usually went on to develop the symptoms associated with smallpox, such as fever and a rash. However, fewer people died than if they had acquired smallpox naturally.

This practice of smallpox inoculation (as opposed to the later practice of vaccination) was developed possibly in eighth-century India or tenth-century China, spreading into 17th-century Turkey. By the beginning of the 18th century, the Royal Society in England was discussing the practice of inoculation, and the smallpox epidemic in 1713 spurred further interest. It was not until 1721, however, that England recorded its first case of inoculation.

Further information at:

Chrystal, Paul, *A History of the World in 100 Pandemics, Plagues and Epidemics*, Barnsley, 2021.

Hopkins D.R. , *The Greatest Killer: Smallpox in history*, University of Chicago Press, 2002 (originally published as *Princes and Peasants: Smallpox in History,* 1983).

Whipps, Heather, 'How Smallpox Changed the World,' *LiveScience*, 23 June, 2008.

Inoculation and vaccination

Edward Jenner, FRS FRCPE [1749–1823), pioneered the concept of vaccines, including creating the smallpox vaccine, the world's first. The terms vaccine and vaccination are derived from *Variolae vaccinae* (smallpox of the cow), as devised by Jenner to denote cowpox. He used it in 1798 in his *Inquiry into the Variolae vaccinae known as the Cow Pox*, in which he described the protective effect of cowpox against smallpox. Jenner is often called 'the father of immunology,' and his work is said to have 'saved more lives than the work of any other human'.

In 1768 English physician John Fewster had realised that prior infection with cowpox rendered a person immune to smallpox. In the years following 1770, at least five investigators in England and Germany successfully tested a cowpox vaccine against smallpox in humans. One, Dorset farmer Benjamin Jesty, successfully vaccinated and induced immunity with cowpox in his wife and two children during a smallpox epidemic in 1774; a similar observation was made in France by Jacques Antoine Rabaut-Pommier in 1780.

Observing that milkmaids were generally immune to smallpox, Jenner postulated that the pus in the blisters that milkmaids received from cowpox (a disease similar to smallpox, but much less virulent) protected them from smallpox.

Jenner's hypothesis was that the initial source of infection was a disease of horses, called 'the grease', which was transferred to cattle by farm workers, mutated, and then presented as cowpox. On 14 May 1796, Jenner tested his hypothesis by inoculating James Phipps, an eight-year-old boy who was the son of Jenner's gardener. He scraped pus from cowpox blisters on the hands of Sarah Nelmes, a milkmaid who had caught cowpox from a cow called Blossom whose hide now decorates the wall of the St. George's Medical School Library, Tooting. Phipps was the 17th case described in Jenner's first paper on vaccination.

Jenner inoculated Phipps in both arms that day, subsequently producing in the boy a fever and some anxiety, but no full-blown infection. Later, he injected Phipps with variolous material, the routine method of immunisation at that time. No disease ensued. The boy was later inoculated with variolous material and again showed no sign of infection.

The medical establishment deliberated at length over Jenner's findings before accepting them. Eventually, vaccination was given approval, and in 1840 the British Government banned variolation – the use of smallpox to induce immunity – and provided vaccination using cowpox free of charge through the Vaccination Acts of 1840, 1853, 1867 and 1898.

British satirist James Gillray caricatured a scene at the Smallpox and Inoculation Hospital at St. Pancras, showing cowpox vaccine being administered to frightened young women, and cows emerging from different parts of people's bodies. The cartoon was inspired by the controversy over inoculating against the dreaded disease, smallpox. Opponents of vaccination had depicted

An 1802 caricature by James Gillray depicting the early controversy surrounding Jenner's vaccination theory: The Cow-Pock – or – the Wonderful Effects of the New Inoculation! – vide. the Publications of ye Anti-Vaccine Society. Published 12 June 1802 by H. Humphrey, St. James's Street (Library of Congress, Prints & Photographs Division).

cases of vaccinees developing bovine features and this is picked up and exaggerated by Gillray. The boy holds a container labelled 'VACCINE POCK hot from ye COW' and papers in the boy's pocket are labelled 'Benefits of the Vaccine'. The tub on the desk is labeled 'OPENING MIXTURE'. A bottle next to the tub is labeled 'VOMIT'. The painting on the wall depicts worshippers of the Golden Calf, a painting by Nicolas Poussin.

Although the World Health Organisation declared the disease eradicated in 1979, some pus samples still remain in laboratories in the Centers for Disease Control and Prevention in Atlanta, USA, and in the State Research Center of Virology and Biotechnology, VECTOR, in Koltsovo, Novosibirsk Oblast, Russia. Both are under WHO supervision. The US smallpox stockpile, which includes samples from Britain, Japan and the Netherlands, is stored in liquid nitrogen.

However, *The Guardian* reported in 2014 that:

'A government scientist cleaning out an old storage room at a research center near Washington made a startling discovery last week – decades-old vials of smallpox packed away and forgotten in a cardboard box.'

The virus samples were found in a cold room connecting two laboratories at the National Institutes of Health in Bethesda, Maryland, that has been used by the Food and Drug Administration since 1972. The implications for possible bioterrorism if similar vials exist unrecorded are horrendous.

Further information at:
Chrystal, Paul, *A History of the World in 100 Pandemics, Plagues and Epidemics*, Barnsley, 2021.
Chrystal, Paul, *Bioterrorism: Weaponising Nature*, Barnsley, 2022.
Durbach, Nadja, *Bodily Matters: The Anti-Vaccination Movement in England, 1853–1907*, Raleigh, NC, 2004.
Jenner, Edward, 'An Inquiry Into the Causes and Effects of the Variolæ Vaccinæ, Or Cow-Pox. 1798,' *The Harvard Classics*, 1909–1914.
Riedel, Stefan, 'Edward Jenner and the history of smallpox and vaccination,' *Proceedings of the Baylor University Medical Center*, 18 (1), pp. 21–5, 2005.
van Oss C.J., 'Inoculation against smallpox as the precursor to vaccination,' *Immunological Investigations*, 29 (4), pp. 443–6, 2000.

51

The Davy Safety Lamp

1815

A Davy safety lamp, circa 1880.

Coal mining was undisputedly the most dangerous of all dangerous work activities in the 18th and 19th centuries. Between 1705 and 1838 there were over 140 mining incidents where more than five workers were killed – and that is just the incidents that were actually reported. Add to this the numerous life-changing injuries which resulted in life-long disability and ill health and we have a prodigious number of casualties of one sort or another. In the West Riding of Yorkshire alone, it is estimated that from 1810 to 1835 346 mine workers lost their lives and a high proportion of those were women and children. Naked flames from guttering candles and oil lamps meeting with firedamp were the chief culprits. One eye-witness to one such firedamp explosion describes how, 'it lasted a quarter of a minute, like a flash. It blew trap doors in bits, blew the punches out and the corves to pieces, threw one upon the other and the men against the face of the coal.'

The Felling Colliery Disaster, 1812

The Felling Colliery (Brandling Main) endured four disasters in the 19th century: in 1812, 1813, 1821 and 1847. Much the worst of the four was the 1812 disaster, which claimed 92 lives on 25 May 1812; this terrible tragedy was one of the triggers for the development of the miners' safety lamp. Before its invention the only way to shed light was by the naked flame of a candle. Where explosive gas was suspected, a Spedding mill was used, that is a steel cylinder which revolved at high speed against a flint with the resulting shower of sparks shedding some light. Although safer than candles, the Wallsend Colliery explosion of 1785 had shown that these mills could cause explosions too. It is worth pointing out that smoking and smoking materials were allowed in many pits including Felling at this date. It was not commonly realised at the time that firedamp was essentially methane rather than hydrogen.

So, 25 May 1812 was indeed a black day for Felling – that was the day when, despite the colliery having state-of-the-art, cutting-edge safety measures in place, methane gas ignited, and at around 11.30am 'one of the most tremendous explosions in the history of coal mining took place'. For half a mile around, the earth shook and the explosion could be heard up to four miles away when clouds of dust and coal debris were thrown up from both William Pit and John Pit. The dust fell like a shower for up to a mile and a half downwind. The pit-heads carrying the pulleys at both pits were blown off, set on fire and the pulleys broken. The pulleys for the horse-whim at John Pit were mounted in a crane kept away from the shaft. As a result, they were undamaged and could still be swung over the shaft. Men on the surface worked the whim in place of the horses and brought 33 survivors and two bodies out of the colliery. Three of the survivors subsequently died. 87 men and boys were left entombed below ground:

> 'Immense quantities of dust and coal rose high into the air in an inverted cone … In the village of Heworth, this cloud caused a darkness like that of early twilight and covered the roads so thickly that the footsteps of passengers were deeply imprinted in it. As soon as the explosion was heard, wives and children of the workmen ran to the pit. Wildness and terror were pictured in every countenance. The crowd soon collected to several hundreds, some crying out for a husband, others for a parent or a son, and all affected by a mixture of horror, anxiety and grief.
> – Baldwin, *The annual register or a view of the history, politics and literature for the year 1813,* Baldwin, Cradock, & Joy, 1823

At 12.15am a rescue team went down the shaft with Spedding mills to light their way. They were forced back with difficulties breathing and retreated to the pit bottom. The party ascended, but while two were still below at 2pm the second blast occurred. All in all some 29 men were saved, but the remaining 92 men and boys were killed.

The rescue team all agreed that there was no possibility of the men left below ground being alive. Two explosions, blackdamp, fire and the lethal afterdamp put paid to any rescue attempt. Two days later the decision was made to seal the colliery to starve the fire of oxygen. However, local recollections of three men who had survived for 40 days in a pit near Byker led to shouts of 'murder' and physical obstruction.

The parish priest for Jarrow and Heworth was the Reverend John Hodgson (1779–1845). As well as giving comfort to the bereaved, he persuaded them to accept a common, speedy burial. The bodies had lain for seven weeks in the pit while the fires were extinguished and were badly decomposed. Dr. Ramsay gave his opinion that if the bodies were returned to their homes for a normal wake and burial, 'putrid fever' might spread throughout the neighbourhood.

Identification was obviously problematic. Mothers and widows could not identify most of the bodies as 'they were too much mangled and scorched to retain any of their features'. Most were identified by clothes, tobacco-boxes, shoes and other personal items. On Sunday, 20 September, 117 days after the explosion, the pit was inspected by candle light. The furnace below William Pit was relighted and the whole mine brought back into production.

Just one year later, on Christmas Eve 1813, a further catastrophe occurred:

'About half-past one o'clock on the morning, an explosion took place in Felling Colliery, by which nine men and thirteen boys were hurried into eternity, several others severely burnt, and all the underground horses but one destroyed. The accident occurred at the time of calling course, or when one set of men were relieving another. Several of the morning shift men were standing round the mouth of the pit, waiting to go down, when the blast occurred, and the part who had just descended met it soon after they had reached the bottom of the shaft; these were most miserably burnt and mangled.'
– Richardson, Moses Aaron, *Local Historian's Table Book of Remarkable Occurrences Connected with the Counties of Newcastle-Upon-Tyne, Northumberland and Durham,* J.R Smith, London, 1844

On Tuesday, 22 June 1847, just after 9pm, yet another explosion led to the death of six miners: four outright by a fall of rock from the roof, the other two by afterdamp, and two died from their injuries over the following two days. Eighteen horses were also killed either by the explosion or by the afterdamp. Many of the victims of the explosion here were children.

So what was to be done to stop this atrocious and negligent absence of worker protection in the workplace?

After a number of serious explosions in north-east coal mines due to pockets of firedamp, Humphry Davy was asked by the Rector of Bishopwearmouth to find a way of lighting coal mines safely. Davy got to work and came up with various prototype lamps. The final design was disarmingly simple: a basic lamp with a wire-gauze chimney encapsulating the flame. The holes allowed light to pass through, but the metal of the gauze absorbed the heat. The lamp was, by and large, safe to use because the flame was unable to heat enough flammable gas to cause an explosion, although the flame itself changed colour.

The lamp was successfully trialled in Hebburn Colliery in January 1816 and quickly went into production. The introduction of the lamp had an immediate effect, decreasing enormously the number of fatalities per million tons of coal produced and also increasing the amount of coal produced as it allowed miners to mine deeper seams. In this way, it made a fundamental contribution to the ongoing industrialisation of Britain and to many other mining countries during the 19th century.

Before Davy's invention a safety lamp came from William Reid Clanny, an Irish doctor at Bishopwearmouth, who delivered a paper to the Royal Society in May 1813. The more cumbersome Clanny safety lamp was successfully tested at Herrington Mill; the Royal Society of Arts awarded him medals. Then there was George Stephenson, 'Father of the Railways', who devised a lamp, the Geordie Lamp, in which the air entered via tiny holes, through which the flames of the lamp could not pass. A month before Davy presented his design to the Royal Society, Stephenson demonstrated his own

Illustration of George Stephenson experimenting with his safety lamp in a mine.

lamp to two witnesses by taking it down Killingworth Colliery and holding it in front of a fissure from which firedamp was issuing.

As noted, the inaugural trial of a Davy lamp with a wire sieve was at Hebburn Colliery on 9 January 1816. A letter from Davy (intended to be kept private) described his findings and various suggestions for a safety lamp was made public at a meeting in Newcastle on 3 November 1815. A paper describing the lamp was formally presented at a Royal Society meeting in London on 9 November for which Davy was awarded the society's Rumford Medal and £2,000 worth of silver raised by public subscription. Stephenson was accused of stealing the idea from Davy, because the fully developed 'Geordie lamp' had not been demonstrated by Stephenson until after Davy had presented his paper at the Royal Society, and, it was alleged, previous versions had not actually been safe.

In 1833 a House of Commons committee found that Stephenson had equal claim to having invented the safety lamp. Davy went to his grave claiming that Stephenson had stolen his idea. The Stephenson lamp was used almost exclusively in north-east England through most of the 19th century, until the introduction of electric lighting while the Davy lamp was used in most other mines. The experience gave Stephenson a lifelong distrust of London-based, theoretical, scientific experts.

In 1816, the *Cumberland Pacquet* reported a demonstration of the Davy lamp at William Pit, Whitehaven. Placed in a blower:

'… the effect was grand beyond description. At first a blue flame was seen to cap the flame of the lamp, then succeeded a lambent flame, playing in the cylinder; and shortly after, the flame of the firedamp expanded, so as to completely fill the wire gauze. For some time, the flame of the lamp was seen through that of the firedamp, which became ultimately extinguished without explosion. Results more satisfactory were not to be wished …'

Another correspondent to the paper commented:

'The Lamp offers absolute security to the miner … With the excellent ventilation of the Whitehaven Collieries and the application of Sir HUMPHRY's valuable instrument, the accidents from the explosion of (carburetted) hydrogene which have occurred (although comparatively few for such extensive works) will by this happy invention be avoided.'

However, this was not to be: over the next 30 years, firedamp explosions in Whitehaven pits killed 137 people. More worryingly, the Select Committee on Accidents in Mines reported in 1835 that the introduction of the Davy lamp had actually caused an increase in coalmining accidents, the main reason being that the false security the lamp engenderedencouraged the working of mines and seams that had previously been off limits for safety reasons, as we have noted. For example, in 1835 102 men and boys were killed by a firedamp explosion in a Wallsend colliery working the Bensham seam, described at the subsequent inquest by John Buddle as 'a dangerous seam, which required the utmost care in keeping in a working state,' which could only be worked with the Davy lamp.

Interestingly, the miners had to buy their own lamps. Miners still preferred the better illumination afforded by a naked light, and while mine regulations mandated that only safety lamps be used, in practice they were neither observed nor enforced. After two accidents in two years (1838–39) in Cumberland pits, both, ironically, caused by safety checks being carried out by the light of a naked flame, the Royal Commission on Children's Employment commented both on the failure to learn from the first accident, and on the 'further absurdity' of:

'carrying a Davy lamp in one hand for the sake of safety, and a naked lighted candle in the other, as if for the sake of danger. Beyond this there can be no conceivable thoughtlessness and folly; and when such management is allowed in the mine of two of the most opulent coal-proprietors in the kingdom, we cease to wonder at anything that may take place in mines worked by men equally without capital and science'.'

The unreliability of the lamps themselves were another cause of continuing accidents. The bare gauze was easily damaged, and as soon as just a single wire broke or rusted away, the lamp became unsafe. The 'South Shields Committee', a body set up by a public meeting there (in response to an explosion at the St Hilda pit in 1839) to consider the prevention of accidents in mines had shown that mine ventilation in the North-East was generally deficient, with an insufficient supply of fresh air giving every opportunity for explosive mixtures of gas to accumulate. A subsequent select committee in 1852 agreed; firedamp explosions could best be prevented by improving mine ventilation (by the use of steam ejectors: the committee specifically advised against fan ventilation), which had been neglected because of over dependence on the safety of the Davy lamp.

Even then, new and clean illumination from the safety lamps was limited, and remained problematic until electric lamps became widely available in the late 19th century. However, the net benefit of the Davy Safety Lamp and others like it was that it saved countless lives and injuries throughout the UK over the years. Lamps are still made in Eccles, Greater Manchester; in Aberdare, South Wales; and in Kolkata, India.

Further information at:

Chrystal, Paul, *Factory Girls: Women & Children at work from the Industrial Revolution to 1914,* 2022.

Davy, Humphry, 'On the Fire-Damp of Coal Mines, and on Methods of Lighting the Mines So as to Prevent Its Explosion,' *Philosophical Transactions of the Royal Society of London*, 106: 1, 1816.

James, Frank A.J.L., 'How Big is a Hole?: The Problems of the Practical Application of Science in the Invention of the Miners' Safety Lamp by Humphry Davy and George Stephenson in Late Regency England,' *Transactions of the Newcomen Society*, 75 (2), pp. 175–227, 2005.

52

The Football Association Laws of the Game

1863

The Football Association, English football's governing body, kicked off on 26 October 1863 when what we might call 'organised football' or 'football as we know it' was formalised.

We have Ebenezer Morley, a London solicitor who formed Barnes FC in 1862, to thank. He is remembered as the 'father' of the Association. He himself did not attend a public school but old boys from several independents joined his club and there ensued 'feverish' disputes about the way the game should be played.

Morley wrote to *Bell's Life*, a popular newspaper, suggesting that football should have a set of rules in the same way that the MCC had them for cricket. His letter led to the first historic meeting at the Freemasons' Tavern in Great Queen Street, near to where Holborn tube station now stands.

The captains, club secretaries and other representatives of a dozen London and suburban clubs each playing their own versions of football met 'for the purpose of forming an Association with the object of establishing a definite code of rules for the regulation of the game.'

The clubs present were: Barnes, War Office or Civil Service FC (Crusaders, Forest (Leytonstone), No Names (Kilburn), Crystal Palace (nothing to do with the present league club), Blackheath, Kensington School, Perceval House (Blackheath), Surbiton, Blackheath Proprietory School and Charterhouse.

Civil Service FC, who now (2021/22) play in the Southern Amateur League Senior Division Two, are the only surviving club of the 11 who

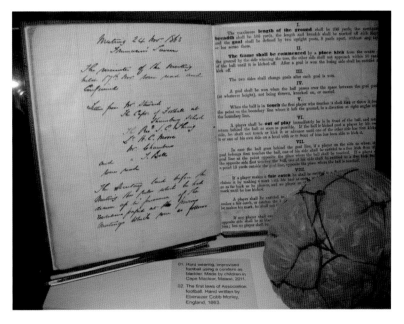

*The original hand-written 'Laws of the game' for Association Football drafted
for and behalf of The Football Association by Ebenezer Cobb Morley in 1863
on display at the National Football Museum, Manchester. The handwriting
on the left is that of Cobb Morley and reads:
'Meeting 24th November 1863 Freemasons Tavern
The minutes of the meeting held 17th Nov were read and confirmed.
Letters from Mr Steward. The Captain of Football at Shrewsbury School;
Lt H C Moore; Mr Chambers; and Mr J Bell.
The Secretary laid before the meeting the [illegible] which had been drawn up in
[illegible] of the [illegible] at previous meetings which were as follows …'*

signed up to be FA members at that first meeting, when they were listed as
the War Office. They helped create and played in the first-ever FA Challenge Cup competition in the 1871/72 season and provided both umpires
for the first final. The club originally played both Association Football and
Rugby Football and the Civil Service, along with Blackheath FC, is one of
the two clubs that can claim to be a founder member of both the Football
Association and the Rugby Football Union. Some say Clapham Rovers also
played both. The club took part in the first-ever official football match at

Buckingham Palace in October 2013 to mark the Football Association's 150th anniversary.

Six meetings took place over 44 days before the fledgling Association could start to function. The FA was formed at the first; the rules of the Association were formulated at the second. There was an annual subscription of a guinea and alterations to rules or laws were to be advertised in sporting papers. A discussion on drafting the laws took place at the third.

The intention was that 'football', despite the name, would be a blend of handling and dribbling. Players would be able to handle the ball: a fair catch accompanied by 'a mark with the heel' would win a free kick. A bone of contention was 'hacking', best described as the gentlemanly art of kicking an opponent in the shins, tripping and holding, which Blackheath FC wanted to keep. Other English rugby clubs followed and did not join the FA but instead in 1871 formed the Rugby Football Union. The term 'soccer' dates back to this schism to refer to football played under the 'association' rules.

The laws originally drafted by Morley were finally approved at the sixth meeting, on 8 December, and hacking was out. They were published by John Lillywhite of Seymour Street in a booklet that cost 1s/6d. The FA were anxious to see their laws in action so an inaugural game using the new rules was initially scheduled for Battersea Park on 2 January 1864, but enthusiastic members of the FA could not wait for the new year: the first game under FA rules was played at Mortlake on 19 December 1863 between Morley's Barnes FC and their neighbours Richmond (who were not members of the FA), ending in a goalless draw. The Richmond side were obviously unimpressed by the new rules in practice because they subsequently helped form the Rugby Football Union in 1871 at Limes Field in Barnes, also on 19 December. Unfortunately from a media point of view, it was another 0-0 draw.

Some clubs in the north were all for profit and success, and for paying a man for doing his job. According to Ricaard Jolly, 'The turning point, north replacing south, working class defeating upper and professionals impinging upon the amateurs' territory, came in 1883.' Hitherto, public school sides had played a dribbling game punctuated by violent tackles, but a new passing style developed in Scotland was successfully adopted by some Lancashire teams, along with a more organised approach to training. Blackburn Olympic reached the FA Cup Final in March 1883 and defeated Old Etonians. Blackburn Rovers started to pay players, and the following season won the first of three consecutive FA Cups. The FA initially tried to outlaw professionalism but, in the face of a threatened breakaway body, the British Football Association, by 1885 were forced to permit payments to players. Three years later, in 1888, the first Football League was established, formed by six professional clubs from north-west England and six from the midlands. William McGregor, an Aston Villa committee man, had seen that football needed an organised system of regular fixtures involving the top clubs. The FA was still the ultimate authority but the League would live as a self-contained body within it.

The FA Cup

At a meeting at the office of *The Sportsman* newspaper on 20 July 1871, the announcement of the birth of 'the Football Association Challenge Cup' ran to a mere 29 words: 'That it is desirable that a Challenge Cup should be established in connection with the Association for which all clubs belonging to the Association should be invited to compete.'

The FA Cup held aloft by Bobby Moore after West Ham's splendid 3-2 victory in the 1964 FA Cup Final over Preston North End. Ken Brown is at the front. Martin Peters and Geoff Hurst are on either side of the jubilant Moore – the famous trio who, of course, helped West Ham defeat West Germany in the 1966 World Cup Final 4-2.

Questionable crowd control and ticketing at the 1923 (first) FA Cup Final at Wembley between West Ham and Bolton Wanderers: mounted police fail to keep more than 300,000 fans from spilling onto the Wembley pitch, including constable George Scorey and his white horse Billy.

'The Cup' was the idea of one man, namely Charles Alcock, then 29; he had remembered playing in an inter-house 'sudden death' competition during his schooldays at Harrow and his proposal was eagerly agreed. The rules of the new competition were drafted and 15 clubs were accepted: Barnes, Civil Service, Crystal Palace, Clapham Rovers, Hitchin, Maidenhead, Marlow, Queen's Park (Glasgow), Donington Grammar School (Spalding), Hampstead Heathens, Harrow Chequers, Reigate Priory, Royal Engineers, Upton Park and Wanderers.

Good as it seems, this was a rather disappointing entry, because the FA had 50 member clubs by that time. Apparently, many of them felt that competition would lead to unhealthy rivalry and even bitterness. The first cup season was plagued with withdrawals and byes. Only 12 clubs actually played and there were just 13 matches in total, but Wanderers beat Royal Engineers 1-0 in front of 2,000 spectators at Kennington Oval in a final described by *The Sporting Life* as 'a most pleasant contest'.

A home international between England and Scotland was another of Alcock's excellent ideas. He wrote to *The Glasgow Herald* on 3 November 1870 to announce that such a fixture would be played at the Oval in 16 days' time. 'In Scotland, once essentially the land of football, there still should be a spark left of the old fire,' he said. 'England' won this unofficial international 1-0; all the players, English and Scottish, lived in London.

The Scottish FA was yet to be formed, but the Queen's Park club agreed to organise the first official international between England and Scotland; it was to take place at Hamilton Crescent, the Partick home of the West of Scotland Cricket Club, on 30 November 1872. The admission fee, as it had been for the first Cup Final, was a shilling. A 4,000-crowd – men and women – was present for (another) 0-0 draw that *Bell's Life* saw as 'one of the jolliest, one of the most spirited and most pleasant matches that have ever been played according to Association rules.' Things would change.

Women's football

An article on the history of Shrove Tuesday refers to a game between married and unmarried women at Inveresk, Midlothian, which was apparently already of some age when it was reported in *A Statistical Analysis of Scotland* in 1795 (*Bolton Chronicle*, 28 February 1846, p.6). There are other references to women playing a form of football, for example in Bath, as long ago as 1726 (*Ipswich Journal*, 8 October 1726).

In 1921 the FA scored what must be the most spectacular own goal in the organisation's history, indeed in the history of football. It was an embarrassing and disgraceful act of sexism in tune with the male 'clubbism' which was prevalent at the time. By 1921 women's football had become increasingly popular through the charitable games played by women's teams during and after World War One, with one match attracting over 53,000 spectators in 1920 in a packed Goodison Park to watch a Dick, Kerr's Ladies England Munitionettes team. In 1917, 'The team not only regularly drew large crowds but raised more than £70,000 for ex-servicemen, hospitals and needy children,' – about £14 million in today's money.

Bolckow, Vaughan & Co. Munitionettes
Munitionette Cup Finalists 1918
back: Emily Milner, Amelia Farrell, Greta Kirk, Violet Sharples
front: Elizabeth Powell, Mary Mohan, Mercy Page, Winnie McKenna, Gladys Reece, Olive Percival, Annie Wharton
(photograph courtesy of Peter McNaughton)

The 1918 Bolckow Vaughan of Middlesbrough steel works team.

In 1918, Bolckow Vaughan of Middlesbrough, like other north-eastern manufacturing firms, had its own women's football team. Many factories had been converted to munitions work during the war. Bolckow, Vaughan's Munitionettes team, were runners-up in a replayed final tie for the Tyne, Wear & Tees Alfred Wood Munition Girls Cup. Sadly, they were beaten 5-0 by Blyth Spartans. See the website for more details in the most complete account of the history of early women's football: http://www.donmouth.co.uk/womens_football/munitionettes.html

Other clubs included Dorman, Long & Co; Teesside Ladies; Ridley's, Skinningrove; Skinningrove Ironworks; Smith's Docks; Richardson, West-garth (Hartlepool) and Christopher Brown (West Hartlepool). These were not just casual kick-arounds, but highly organised matches played at venues such as Ayresome Park and St James's Park. By 1918 munitionettes numbered more than 900,000, producing 80 per cent of the weapons and shells used by the British Army.

The palpable success of the Munitionette teams, particularly in the north of England, added to the enthusiasm the general public had for the women's

The Football Association has confirmed that it moved to give the Lionesses equal pay to their male counterparts at the start of the year (2020), ensuring that international players are rewarded with the same salary regardless of gender. 'The FA pays its women's players exactly the same as their male counterparts for representing England, both in terms of match fees and match bonuses. This parity has been in place since January 2020.'

game. The 'suits' at the FA obviously felt threatened by this and, in a move that was widely seen as motivated by insecurity and jealousy of the crowds' interest in women's games, which frequently exceeded that of the top men's teams, in 1921 the Football Association banned all women's teams from playing on grounds affiliated to the FA – because, they said, they thought football damaged women's bodies.

For nearly five decades this extraordinary decision meant that women's football virtually disappeared from England. It was only reversed after 1969 when, after the explosion of interest in football caused by England's 1966 World Cup triumph, the Women's Football Association was founded, although it took a further two years – and an order from UEFA – to force the (men's) Football Association to remove its restrictions on the playing rights of women's teams. It was not until 1983 that the WFA was able to affiliate to the FA as a 'County Association' and only in 1993 did the FA found the 'Women's Football Committee' to run women's football in England. Just look at the progress the women's game at club and international level has enjoyed since then.

Further information at:

Brennan, Patrick, *The Munitionettes: A History of Women's Football in North-East England During the Great War.*
Grainey, Timothy F., *Beyond Bend It Like Beckham: The Global Phenomenon of Women's Soccer*, University of Nebraska Press, 2012.
Harvey, Adrian, *Football, the First Hundred Years: The Untold Story of the People's Game*, Routledge, 2005.
Jolly, Richard, 'Football's working-class roots,' The National, 23 October 2010.
Lewis, R.W., '"Touched Pitch and Been Shockingly Defiled": Football, Class, Social Darwinism and Decadence in England, 1880-1914', in Mangan, J.A., *Sport in Europe: Politics, Class, Gender*, Frank Cass, London, pp.117–43, 1999.
Tate, Tim, *Women's Football: The Secret History*, London, 2013.

53

The rugby ball

1870

Early shape, four-panel rugby ball

A rugby ball is an elongated ellipsoidal ball used in rugby football. Its measurements and weight are specified by World Rugby and the Rugby League International Federation, the governing bodies for both codes, Rugby Union and Rugby League respectively. Formerly known as the 'quanco', the ellipsoid shape makes it easier to pass.

Two enterprising cobblers, Richard Lindon (1816–87) and William Gilbert (1799–1877) gave us the distinctive rugby ball. The Rugby School wanted an oval ball to further distinguish their game from soccer. So Lindon and Gilbert started making a more egg-shaped buttonless ball for the school out of hand-stitched, four-panel leather casings and pigs' bladders. This was the first specifically designed four-panel rugby ball and the start of sizes being standardised. In 1892 the RFU made it compulsory for all rugby balls to be oval in shape.

By 1877 the family business was hand-stitching over 2,800 balls a year. 'Gilberts' then began exporting their balls to Australia. Both men owned boot- and shoe-making businesses located in the High Street, which led to Rugby School's quad entrance where the boys played football (quad ball) before Rugby School got its playing fields.

A Rugby Football Match between England and Scotland. Illustration circa 1893 (Source: Rugby Pioneers).

The shape of the pig's bladder determined the ball's distinctive oval shape so balls of those days were more plum-shaped than oval. The balls also varied in size depending on how large the bladder was. In those days you had to get volunteers to inflate the ball because the bladder needed to be blown up while still in its very smelly 'green state' by lung power down the snapped stem of a clay pipe, which was inserted into the opening. Unfortunately, Richard Lindon's wife (one of the volunteers) contracted a lung disease thought to have been caused from years of blowing up pig's bladders, some of which were most probably diseased, and died as a result.

Around 1862 Richard Lindon introduced Indian rubber bladder inner-tubes so, because of the pliability of rubber, the shape of the balls gradually morphed to the shape we know today. Lindon also invented the Brass Hand Pump, after observing how the ordinary ear syringe worked, as rubber bladders were impossible to inflate by mouth. Unfortunately for Lindon, he omitted to patent either the ball, the bladder or the pump, with the result that by the 1880s there were several manufacturers of 'footballs' in England all using the same process.

Women's Rugby

Information relating to the early days of women's rugby is scant to say the least, most probably because sports journalists were all men. But we do know that in 1884 Portora Royal School in Enniskillen, Co Fermanagh, Ireland, formed the school's first rugby team which included a young woman called Emily Valentine, making her the first official woman to play rugby.

How did that happen? In 1884 student numbers at Portora were so low Mr Steele – the elderly headmaster – delegated the day-to-day running of the school to classics master and assistant headteacher William Valentine, who had joined the school the year before. Valentine had at least three children at the school: William (aged about 16), John (aged about 10/11), and 'Miss E. F Valentine'. The three children were keen to play rugby, and with the help of several friends they started playing. To begin with this was not supported by the school, who denied them access to the main school field, but they still practised and played intra-school matches every Saturday. The first official matches against external opposition took place in 1887,

Mini-Rugby is all the rage in England — but how many clubs have a girl in their side? Morpeth (Northumberland) have. She is nine-year-old Dawn Laidlaw, daughter of the club secretary. In a tournament last season Morpeth were one short, and Dawn filled in. She has played ever since. Here is Dawn in possession, followed by a bunch of likely lads. Bit harum-scarum, eh?

Early female participation (source http://www.rugbyrelics.com/Museum/topics/ womens-rugby-history.htm).

but several records suggest that there were games as early as 1885 against local opposition, possibly in combination with Enniskillen Rugby Club.

School records, and letters from Miss Valentine (later Mrs Galway) in the 1950s show that she definitely took part in the practices and intra-school games, and some records suggest the external games as well. Several sources say that the entire three-quarter line was made up of Valentines, with Miss Valentine playing on the wing.

According to Andy Carter (2017), what is probably the earliest reference to women playing rugby proper dates from 1881 with an England versus Scotland game at Liverpool. The game was one of a series on both sides of the border, which appear to have mainly been played according to Football Association rules, but reports of the game on 25 June made definite references to touchdowns, indicating that something akin to rugby was played on that occasion.

Carter adds, whichever code of football was being played, the events that surrounded the 1881 series led to the suspension of women's involvement as players and gave an early indication of the controversy and resistance which their participation provoked.

'Reactions to the games in the press ranged from amusement to expressions of concern that women's football was unladylike and dangerous for their delicate constitutions. The matches in 1881 drew large attendances, but on more than one occasion sections of the crowd rioted, although the exact reasons for the disorder are not entirely clear.'

1881 became a template for the fall out accompanying women's rugby for many years: a few women would start a game attracting public interest, then objections and obstacles would be raised. For the women there was also a degree of social risk attached to their participation and many played under pseudonyms such as the suffragist Helen Matthews. In choosing to play rugby, seen as that most masculine of sports, Matthews was 'challenging male hegemony at its core and setting out to prove that women were neither weak nor feeble' (Carter, 2017).

Another problem was the kit. Playing a contact sport in the restrictive clothing prescribed for Victorian women was not realistic, so new clothing had to be designed – another fundamental challenge to male dominance, linked to the emergence of the Radical Dress Society. It certainly made the game easier for the women, but the hypocritical moral standards which

An early women's rugby team.

characterised late-Victorian Britain, what the *Luton Times and Advertiser*, 22 November 1895, reported as the 'daring novelty and unconventionality' of women's football, became a doubled-edged sword. The new kit was anything but revealing, but representations such as that on an Ogden's cigarette card of 1895 sexualised and exaggerated the close fit of the attire. This may explain the crowd disorder at women's matches: maybe male outrage at the very fact that women were playing or else disappointment that the players were not as erotic as they would have liked. Then, as now, women who challenged norms of dress and behaviour were open to being misunderstood and wilfully misrepresented. This in turn led to hostility from other women who were known to hurl stones at women footballers (*Hull Daily Mail*, 28 October 1895, p.3).

In 1891, records speak of an attempt at a women's touring team in New Zealand; however, this was banned due to it being socially unacceptable, and the team were forced to disband. Women had to play the sport in secret to avoid public outrage, and it is only in 1917 that a first official charity match at Cardiff Arms Park featuring female teams, Cardiff Ladies and Newport Ladies took place. Cardiff won 6-0.

The inter-war years saw women's rugby relegated to the shadows, with undue emphasis on rugby as a man's game and the alleged sexual gratification sought by male spectators. Despite this sexist stereotyping, Colonel Phillip Trevor included a chapter on rugby for girls in his 1923 *Rugby Union Football*, and in 1937 the Lord Mayor of Plymouth was pleased to see that there was an increase in the numbers of women interested in playing rugby (*Western Morning News, 24 June 1937, p.5*). After World War Two, women's rugby began to gain some traction. In 1950 a women's rugby match took place at Nottingham University (*Nottingham Journal*, 30 March 1950, p.5), which marked the birth of women's rugby in British universities (*Nottingham Journal*, 21 April 1950, p.6). In the middle of the following decade the game began to slowly emerge at other universities and, following the pattern of the men's game 100 years earlier, soon began to emerge from colleges with the rapid establishment of club sides in later years. In 1962 a Rugby Union team was formed, for example, at Edinburgh University and the first fully documented women's club match took place at Toulouse Femina Sports in France. This led to the first national association for women's rugby union, the AFRF, and the formation of women's rugby unions in universities across

Canada, the USA, the Netherlands and Spain. In 1978 Canada and the Netherlands were the first to form non-university rugby clubs, and other countries across the world were soon to follow.

This section in parts owes much to Andy Carter's *Playing like a girl: a brief background to women's rugby*.

Further information at:

http://www.rugbyfootballhistory.com/ball.htm

Carle, Alison, 'Crossing the Line: Women Playing Rugby Union,' in Timothy J. L. Chandler (ed.), *Making the Rugby World: Race, Gender, Commerce* (Sport in the Global Society), London, 1999.

Carter, Andy, *https://hindzeit.wordpress.com/2017/07/25/playing-like-a-girl-a-brief-background-to-womens-rugby/*

Collins, Tony, *The Oval World: A Global History of Rugby*, London, 2015.

54

The tennis racket

1874

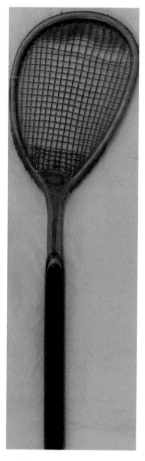

Antique, lopsided tilt-top lawn tennis racket – 1874 Wimbledon Special.

CHAPTER 7: THE 18TH AND 19TH CENTURIES

Tennis rackets were invented in the middle of the 18th century, but long before that French monks were playing a game very similar to tennis, only without rackets. Instead, they simply used their bare hands to hit the ball back and forth over something resembling a net; the monks later progressed to wearing leather gloves.

This was still causing hand injuries so they moved on to using solid wooden paddles, graduating to what we would call rackets in the 14th century. This early medieval racket had strings made of gut and it was bound in a large wooden frame. They were teardrop-shaped, with a long wooden handle, and used to hit a dead ball over a net-type structure.

The modern wooden tennis racket was invented several centuries later, and the game started to resemble more what we recognise as tennis today. These early tennis rackets borrowed their design from the older sport of real tennis, an early racket sport dating back to around the 16th century and played by the rich and elite. Made of wood, they had long handles and small, lopsided heads, which made it easier for the player to bring the hitting surface close to the ground to hit the low bouncing balls typical of real tennis. They soon disappeared as tennis developed as a sport in its own right.

In 1874, Major Walter C. Wingfield registered his patent in London for the equipment and rules of outdoor lawn tennis that is generally considered the first version of what we play today: his racket was large, heavy and made of solid wood, and could deliver some serious damage. This coincided with the time when lawn tennis was gaining popularity. Laminated rather than solid wooden rackets started to gain popularity in 1947.

Metal rackets repeatedly tried to gain popularity; they had been around since 1889 but never caught on.

The dawn of the open era in 1968, when players started to compete for cash prizes, was the engine behind the rapid development of tennis rackets around this period. During the 1960s wooden rackets were still the most common, but fibre-reinforced composite materials such as fibreglass started to appear as a reinforcement on wooden frames; examples are the Challenge Power by Slazenger and the Kramer Cup by Wilson.

By the 1970s, racket engineers were experimenting with a range of materials, such as wood, fibre-reinforced composites, aluminium and steel. Around this time Jimmy Connors used his famous steel racket, which showed just how powerful metal rackets could be against wooden ones. A key racket

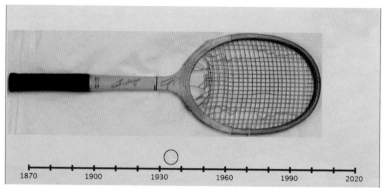

A 1930s racket, in need of restringing.

A vintage wooden racket.

from this period was the Classic by Prince, based on a 1976 patent owned by Howard Head. The Classic was made of aluminium, which allowed for a much larger head than its wooden predecessors and made it easier to hit the ball.

Further information at:

Gillmeister, Heiner, *Tennis : A Cultural History*, New York, 1998.

55

The public toilet

George Jennings (1810–82) was an English sanitary engineer and plumber who invented the first *public* flush toilets; we all owe him an eternal debt of gratitude. Jennings specialised in designing toilets that were 'as perfect a sanitary closet as can be made'. However, he also excelled in public sanitation projects such as the design of the once ubiquitous subterranean 'public convenience'. The familiar entrances to these were surrounded by elaborate metal railings and arches lit by lamps, with interiors built of slate and, later, of ceramic tiles. They took up minimal space on busy streets and station concourses (such as at King's Cross and Charing Cross) and hid the 'objectionable contrivances' from the view of prudish Victorians.

A beautiful example of a public convenience from a period a little after Jennings's death is the Gentlemen's Convenience at Wesley's Chapel, City Road, London, built in 1891 by Thomas Crapper (who was *not* the inventor of the flush toilet).

At the Great Exhibition at Hyde Park in 1851, George Jennings installed his Monkey Closets in the Retiring Rooms of the Crystal Palace. These were the first public toilets, and they caused huge excitement. During the exhibition, 827,280 visitors paid one penny to use them; for that they got a clean seat, a towel, a comb and a shoe shine. 'To spend a penny' remains a euphemism for going to the toilet.

When the exhibition finished and moved to Sydenham, the plan was to close down the toilets. However, Jennings persuaded the organisers to keep them open, and the toilet went on to earn over £1,000 a year. Jennings astutely said that 'the civilisation of a people can be measured by their domestic and sanitary appliances'.

In 1855, during the Crimean War, Jennings headed up the sanitary commission sent out by the British Government to improve conditions at Selimiye Barracks hospital at Scutari, Sebastopol, at the request of Florence Nightingale.

In the 1860s Jennings supplied Khedive of Egypt, Tewfik Pasha, with an elaborate mahogany shower cabinet. He also supplied the Empress Eugenie of France with a magnificent copper bath. In 1870 he supplied the water closet

On Monday, 15 March 1926, Hull City Council posted a notice in the local press inviting builders to tender for a new public convenience adjacent to Victoria Pier in Nelson Street. The new toilets served both sexes, replacing an earlier 'men only' cast-iron urinal. Result: these wonderful public toilets: inside … These award-winning public lavatories are, according to The Hull Daily Mail, 'hailed as a shrine to sanitation, with generous displays of potted plants, gleaming cream tiles and polished brass, this is a fine place to "spend a penny".' In 2017 Historic England bestowed a Grade II listing on the toilets. This accolade was in recognition of their architectural merit and their role in illustrating and acknowledging the changing social status of women during the 1920s. The photo shows Douglas Glasby, attendant of the pier toilets, who won the Hull 1992 festival award, old town floral award on 23 July 1992 (Source: Hull Daily Mail).

with his patented flushing mechanism in Lord Bute's Victorian bathroom in the Bute Tower at Cardiff Castle.

In 1872 Jennings supervised the public facilities at the thanksgiving service for the Prince of Wales at St Paul's Cathedral to celebrate his recovery from typhoid. *The Sanitary Record* records:

'The Prince Consort greatly encouraged this indefatigable Engineer. In sanitary science he was *avant coureur* in his day and generation, and was among the first Engineers to practically carry out the theories of the wise men of the time. *"Sanitas sanitatum"* was Mr Jennings's motto before Disraeli adopted it as his political maxim (*Sanitas sanitatum, omnia sanitas*) ... and he implored a shocked city of London to accept his public lavatories free, on the condition that the ... attendants whom he furnished were allowed to make a small charge for the use of the closets and towels.'

1884 saw the opening of the first underground convenience at the Royal Exchange, designed by Jennings.

The subterranean toilets in Parliament Street, York – sometime in the 1940s (courtesy York Press).

The only thing wrong with all this sanitary splendour was that most of the early public toilets catered for the needs of men. Women were often left out in the cold, even with a penny to hand. So what was the woman about town, the women who lunch, to do in this slowly liberating society?

Further information at:

Borzello, F., 'Pre-WWI Women's Clubs in London: Tea, Toilets & Typewriters,' *History Today,* 58, 12, 2008.

Chrystal, Paul, *Tea: A Very British Beverage*, Stroud, 2014.

Penner, Barbara, 'A World of Unmentionable Suffering: Women's Public Conveniences in Victorian London,' *Journal of Design History*, 14, no. 1, 35–51, 2001.

Routh, Jonathan, *The Good Loo Guide: Where to Go in London*, Wolfe Publishing, London, 1968.

Yuko, Elizabeth 'The Glamorous, Sexist History of the Women's Restroom Lounge,' Citylab, 3 December 2018.

The grand interior of the Ladies' lavatory at Charing Cross Station. The photograph was taken by Bedford Lemere & Company in 1912.

CHAPTER 9

THE INDUSTRIAL REVOLUTION, 1760–1840

56

Coal

'The story of coal is the story of Britain,' Jeremy Paxman, 2021

Coal, of course, has been around for tens of thousands of years – long, long before the Industrial Revolution. But it was with the Industrial Revolution that this combustible black or brownish-black sedimentary rock came to prominence when, along with the steam engine, it provided the force which drove the machines in the factories. In 2020 coal supplied about a quarter of the world's primary energy and over a third of its electricity. Some iron and steel making and other industrial processes still burn coal. While it has provided much needed warmth and power down the years, it is also inextricably associated with chronic industrial disease, fatal and debilitating accidents, urban pollution, and is the biggest source of carbon dioxide significantly contributing to manmade climate change. Fourteen billion tonnes of carbon dioxide were emitted by burning coal in 2020 – 40 per cent of the total fossil fuel emissions and over 25 per cent of total global greenhouse gas emissions.

Apart from the essential part coal played in factories, power plants and steel works in Britain, coal fires were the primary source of domestic heating until the 1960s and 1970s; for people of a certain age, the smell of a coal-burning fire was everywhere, as was the sight of smoking chimneys, domestic and industrial; the coal man, the coal hole, the pit pony, the coal pit and slag heap were an unmissable part of many an industrial landscape. But with the now-romanticised, nostalgic images conjured up by the cosy coal fire – just look at the opening footage of early episodes of *Coronation Street* – comes a legacy of terrible social and physical exploitation of men, women and children 'down t' pit', of fatal or chronic industrial disease, of

Coal

deadly and life-changing accidents and occasionally fatal industrial relations disasters. That warm, homely coal fire came at a terrible cost.

Just as an example, a 2017 study in the *Economic Journal* found that for Britain from 1851–60, 'a one standard deviation increase in coal use raised infant mortality by 6–8 per cent and that industrial coal use explains roughly one-third of the urban mortality penalty observed during this period.'

Ever since there have been factories, women have worked in those factories. What is perhaps less well-known is that women also worked underground in coal mines, and what is certainly more shocking to us is that young children were also put to work in hazardous, unhealthy factories and coalmines.

With industrial demand, coal, of course, soon became king and ruled as such with cotton; as a source of power and energy it replaced wood in seemingly limitless quantities; coal thus made wood less vital so the land could now be used to grow more food crops. Output of coal in the 18th century increased from three million tons to ten million and then to 50 million tons between 1800 and 1850. Subterranean though it was, its consumption in the towns and cities had an indelible choking, blackening impact on the urban landscapes of Britain as row after row of chimneys, industrial and domestic, belched out the smoke, soot and chemicals into a suffocating and suffocated atmosphere.

One of the most influential inventions of the time was the Watt steam engine, the first steam engine to be powered by coal as developed by James Watt and Matthew Boulton. This world-changing innovation demonstrated the possibilities afforded by steam power produced by coal in a myriad of industrial contexts: it made it possible to power machines, leading to the emergence of those factories in which these ranks of machines could be housed and operated. Coal it was that drove our trains, transporting the emerging hoards of tourists and the mountains of manufactured goods from factory to port or high street.

Coal meant iron. It was in Shropshire's Coalbrookdale that Abraham Darby, an unassuming, typically modest Quaker, changed the world in 1708 when he took out a lease on a dilapidated blast furnace and some forges. Soon, quality pig iron smelted with coke was rolling off the production lines and with it the bridges, pipes, girders, railway engines, railway lines and

carriages, cannons and cannon balls, shot and other materiel, machines and their parts, ships – all the things that shaped the Industrial Revolution – created its landscape and still to this day leaves its indelible mark on the post-industrial world of the 21st century. The humble Darbys never took out a patent on this transformative process; on the contrary, they shared a world view of their achievement, believing that their process was a universal good which everyone should be able to share in and that 'it would be wrong to deprive the public of such an acquisition'.

Underground women pit workers in Wigan.

Further information at:

Chrystal, Paul, *Factory Girls: The Working Lives of Women & Children from the Industrial Revolution to the 20th Century*, Barnsley, 2022.

Chrystal, Paul, *Female Factory Workers in World War I and World War II*, Barnsley, 2022.

Elliott, Brian, *Coal Mine Disasters in the Modern Era c. 1900–1980*, Barnsley, 2018.

Freese, Barbara, *Coal: A Human History*, London, 2003.

Haskell, Rachel, *Notes and documents, a literate woman in the mines: The diary of Rachel Haskell*, Torch Press, 1944.

Paxman, Jeremy, *Black Gold: The History of How Coal Made Britain*, London, 2021.

Thurber, Mark, Coal. London, 2019

Pit brow women workers in Wigan.

In the Industrial Revolution the most dramatic growth in productivity came in the textile industries. The invention of James Hargreaves' spinning jenny, Richard Arkwright's 'throstle' or 'water frame' (1769), and Samuel Crompton's spinning mule (1779) transformed textile manufacturing. Britain began to manufacture cotton cloth, and falling prices for cloth fuelled both domestic consumption and exports. Machines also emerged for other sectors of the cloth-making process, the most important of which was Edmund Cartwright's power loom, which was widely used by the 1830s. While cotton was the most important textile of the Industrial Revolution, there were also significant developments in machinery for silk, flax and wool production. Mechanised cotton-spinning powered by steam or water increased the output of a worker by a factor of around 500. The power loom grew the output of a worker by a factor of over 40. The cotton gin escalated productivity of removing seed from cotton by a factor of 50.

57

The spinning jenny

1764

An early spinning wheel.

James Hargreaves's (b. circa. 1720) 'Spinning Jenny' revolutionised the process of cotton spinning; it was the first machine to improve upon the spinning wheel. At the time, cotton producers could barely meet the demand for textiles, as each spinner produced only one spool of thread at a time. Hargreaves found a way to ramp up the supply of thread – a major factor in the industrialisation of the textile industry. The hand-driven machine used eight spindles onto which the thread was spun, so by turning a single wheel, the operator could now spin eight threads at once; this later increased to 80.

Before the spinning jenny, weaving was done at home, in 'cottage industries'. But when the machines grew, to 16, 24, and eventually to 80 and 120 spindles, the work moved into factories. Significantly, the new production process lowered the manufacturing price of fabric, making textiles more available to more people.

The spinning jenny was used in the cotton industry until about 1810 when the spinning mule replaced it. The British Library tells how 'Richard Arkwright's cotton factories in Nottingham and Cromford, for example, employed nearly 600 people by the 1770s, including many small children, whose nimble hands made light-work of spinning.'

Further information at:

Aspin, Chris, *James Hargreaves and the Spinning Jenny*, Helmshore Local History Society, 1964.

Baines, Edward, *History of the cotton manufacture in Great Britain*, London, 1835.

Timmins, Geoffrey, *The Last Shift: The decline of handloom weaving in nineteenth-century Lancashire*, Manchester, 1993.

The water frame, 1769

Richard Arkwright (1732 –92), 'father of the modern industrial factory system', inventor and a prominent entrepreneur during the early Industrial Revolution, is credited with the development of the spinning frame, known as the water frame, after it was adapted to use water power; moreover, he patented a rotary carding engine to convert raw cotton to 'cotton lap' before spinning. He was the first to build factories housing both mechanised carding and spinning operations.

A spinner using a spinning jenny, circa 1880.

A working example of Arkwright's water frame, Helmshore Mills Textile Museum, Rossendale (Source: ClemRutter/Wikimedia Commons).

Before all that, he began his working life as a barber and wig-maker, setting up a shop at Churchgate in Bolton in the early 1760s, where he invented a waterproof dye for use on the fashionable periwigs of the time; the income from this later funded his cotton machinery. In 1769 Arkwright patented the spinning frame, which could spin four strands of cotton yarn at a time. This machine, initially powered by horses, greatly reduced the cost of cotton-spinning and led to yet more major changes in the textile industry. The spinning frame was a significant advance over Hargreaves's spinning jenny.

Further information at:

Chapman, S. D., *The early factory masters: the transition to the factory system in the midlands textile industry*, 1967.

Fitton, R. S. *The Arkwrights: spinners of fortune*, Manchester, 1989.

Tann, Jennifer, 'Richard Arkwright and technology,' *History*, 58 (192), pp. 29–44, 1973.

Tann, Jennifer, *The development of the factory*, 1970.

Tann, Jennifer, 'Arkwright's Employment of Steam Power,' *Business History*, 21 (2), pp. 247–50, 1979.

The spinning mule, 1775

Samuel Crompton (1753 –1827) was born in Bolton; he, like Hargreaves, and Arkwright before him took spinning technology to another level. Crompton's spinning mule combined the best features of the moving carriage of the spinning jenny with the Arkwright frame's rollers. The Crompton machine could not only turn out hundreds of spindles of yarn at once, but also yarns of different types and qualities.

There was, of course, a serious social downside to all of these efficient labour-saving innovations – a price to pay for the vastly increased scales of production in the factories: that price was labour force lay-offs and redundancies. This in turn ignited social unrest and rioting – not least amongst what came to be known as the Luddites: unemployed workers who smashed machinery and set fire to mills and factories. The new machinery wrecked the livelihoods of the skilled workers, leaving people destitute and famished.

Crompton, like Hargreaves before him, omitted to patent his design. Others naturally jumped on his bandwagon on a massive industrial scale. By 1812 between four and five million mule spindles were in use. The principles of his design continued to be used until the early 1980s.

This machine was called a spinning 'mule' because it combined features of two machines. A mule is a cross between a horse and a donkey, and all three were commonly used working animals of the time. A female donkey is called a 'Jenny'.

Spinning machinery at work in Quarry Mill, Styal.

A Chartist poster at Quarry Mill, Styal.

58

Stephenson's 'Rocket'

1829

Stephenson's 'Rocket' at the Science Museum, London
(photographer: William M. Connolley).

Robert Stephenson's 0-2-2 steam locomotive 'Rocket', designed by Robert Stephenson (1803–59), and made by Robert Stephenson & Co., Newcastle upon Tyne, was the outright winner in the locomotive trials held at Rainhill in October 1829 to decide on the motive power to be used on the Liverpool & Manchester Railway and to prove that the new locomotives would be more efficient than stationary steam engines.

Five locomotives competed at the Rainhill trials – 'Cycloped', built by Thomas Shaw Brandreth; 'Novelty', built by John Ericsson and John Braithwaite; 'Perseverance', built by Timothy Burstall; 'Sans Pareil', built by Timothy Hackworth; and the 'Rocket'.

The 'Rocket' was the only one to successfully complete the trials, averaging 12 miles per hour and achieving a top speed of 30 miles per hour. So it passed the trial requirement of achieving an average speed of ten miles per hour over 70 miles (110 km) by over 40 per cent. Demonstrations also saw 'Rocket' consistently and easily haul a carriage of over 20 persons up the Whiston incline at over 15 miles per hour and light engine running of around 30 miles per hour. Stephenson won the £500 prize and was duly awarded the contract to produce locomotives for the Liverpool & Manchester Railway.

The locomotive sported a tall smokestack chimney at the front, a cylindrical boiler in the middle, and a separate firebox at the rear. The large front pair of wooden wheels was driven by two external cylinders set at an angle. The smaller rear wheels were not coupled to the driving wheels, giving a 0-2-2 wheel arrangement.

When the Liverpool & Manchester Railway opened in 1830, 'Rocket', driven by John Locke, George Stephenson's assistant and future eminent engineer in his own right, was approaching Parkside Station where dignitaries were gathered on the track after getting off their own special train, despite orders to the contrary. William Huskisson MP was unable to get off the track and 'Rocket' mangled his leg as he tried to get out of the way. His injury proved fatal. Ironically, Huskisson had recently been diagnosed with strangury, an inflammation of the kidneys. He had undergone surgery and had been advised by Royal doctor William George Maton to cancel all forthcoming engagements, which included the opening of the Liverpool and Manchester Railway. Huskisson chose to ignore this advice. He rode down the line in the special train built for the prime minister, Duke of Wellington, and his guests and dignitaries, pulled by the locomotive 'Northumbrian', which was driven by George Stephenson himself. This train was the only train on the south track; the other seven were in procession on the northern track. At Parkside railway station, near the midpoint of the line, the locomotives made a scheduled stop to take on fuel and water. A shout went up, 'An engine is approaching. Take care, gentlemen!'

Stephenson's 'Rocket' represented a substantial technical advance over previous designs, bringing together in one machine such developments as the multi-tube boiler and the blast-pipe. Because railway engineering was moving so quickly, however, the 'Rocket' was substantially rebuilt within only 18 months and laid aside within ten years. It was preserved in 1862 incomplete and left semi-derelict. But it had nevertheless created a template for most steam engines in the following 150 years and remains the most significant of all early railway locomotives.

In 1862, 'Rocket' was donated to the Patent Office Museum in London, which became the Science Museum. It is now in the National Railway Museum in York.

Further reading:

Bailey, Michael R., *The Stephenson's Rocket*, York, 2002.
Chrystal, Paul, *York and Its Railways*, Stenlake Publishing, 2015.
Garfield, Simon, *The Last Journey of William Huskisson*, London, 2002.
Thomas, R. G. H., *The Liverpool & Manchester Railway*, London, 1980.

Soldiers in 1992 winching a replica of the 'Rocket' ahead of a 200-mile journey from the National Railway Museum at York (courtesy of York Press).

59

'Am I not a man and a brother?'

The official medallion of the British Anti-Slavery Society, 1787

The Official Medallion of the British Anti-Slavery Society (Source: British Abolition Movement). The image is from a book published in 1788. 'Josiah Wedgewood ... produced the emblem as a jasper-ware cameo at his pottery factory. Although the artist who designed and engraved the seal is unknown, the design for the cameo is attributed to William Hackwood or to Henry Webber, who were both modellers at the Wedgewood factory.'

Probably the most significant and poignant object in the book, this is the first and most identifiable image of the 18th century abolitionist movement: a kneeling African man.

Members of the Society of Friends, Quakers, were among the first leaders of the abolitionist movement in Britain and the Americas. By 1765, Quakers had graduated from viewing slavery as a matter of individual conscience, to seeing the abolition of slavery as a Christian duty.

When Quakers, despite their reservations about frippery and the frivolous in the arts, met in London in 1787 at the Society for Effecting the Abolition of the Slave Trade founded in 1787 by Granville Sharp and Thomas Clarkson, three of its members were tasked with preparing a design for 'a Seal [to] be engraved for the use of this Society'. Later that year, the society approved a design 'expressive of an African in Chains in a Supplicating Posture'. Surrounding the naked man was engraved a motto whose wording echoed an idea widely accepted during the Enlightenment among Christians and secularists: 'Am I Not A Man and A Brother?' The design was approved by the Society, and an engraving was commissioned.

As well as evoking classical art, the figure's nudity signified a state of nobility and freedom, yet it was, paradoxically, bound by chains. Black figures, usually depicted as servants or supplicants, are typically depicted as kneeling in the art of the period, at a time when members of the upper classes did not even kneel when praying; this particular image combined the European theme of conversion from heathenism and the idea of emancipation into a posture of gratitude.

Josiah Wedgwood, who was by then a member of the Society, produced the emblem as a jasper-ware cameo at his pottery factory; the design for the cameo is attributed to William Hackwood or to Henry Webber, who were both modellers at the Wedgwood factory.

In 1788 a consignment of the cameos was shipped to Benjamin Franklin in Philadelphia, where the medallions became a fashion statement for abolitionists and anti-slavery sympathisers. Thomas Clarkson wrote:

'… ladies wore them in bracelets, and others had them fitted up in an ornamental manner as pins for their hair. At length the taste for wearing them became general, and thus fashion, which usually confines itself to worthless things, was seen for once in the honourable office of promoting the cause of justice, humanity and freedom.'

Krasnodar (Russia) and Chelsea players taking the knee in solidarity with the anti-racism movement at a Champions League match on 28 October 2020 (source https://www.soccer.ru/galery/1212130/photo/875158, (photographer: Damitry Pukalik).

Although the intent and the effect of the emblem was to focus public opinion on the evils of the African slave trade, in reality its ultimate effect was to underscore the perception of black inferiority. The supplicant posture of people of colour endured as a standard feature of Western art long after slavery was abolished.

More confusingly, although the image became the emblem of the anti-slavery movement, the society was insistent that its only goal was the abolition of the slave trade, not of slavery *per se*.

Nevertheless, the Wedgwood medallion was the most famous image of a black person in all of 18th-century art.

The symbol and gesture has endured into the 21st century with one of its most visible and powerful manifestations, being athletes of all cultures 'taking the knee' before sporting competitions. At the time of going to press Russia has been banned from sporting competitions the world over on account of its illegal invasion of Ukraine.

Further information at:

https://sites.duke.edu/blackatlantic/2014/02/10/am-i-not-a-man-and-a-brother-the-political-power-of-the-image/

Hochschild, Adam, *Bury the Chains: The British Struggle to Abolish Slavery*, London, 2012.

Olusoga, David, *Black and British: A Forgotten History*, London, 2021.

CHAPTER 10

VICTORIANA AND AFTER

60

Big Ben

1859

Elizabeth Tower and Big Ben in 1897.

Big Ben is the popular name for the Great Bell of the famous striking clock at the north end of the Palace of Westminster, although the name is usually extended to include the clock and the clock tower. The official name of the tower was originally the Clock Tower, but it was renamed Elizabeth Tower in 2012 to mark the Diamond Jubilee of Elizabeth II.

The neo-Gothic tower was designed by Augustus Pugin. On completion in 1859, its clock was the largest and most accurate four-faced striking and chiming clock in the world. The tower stands at 316ft high, and will require you to scale 334 steps with 290 stone steps up to the clock room, followed by 44 to reach the belfry, and an additional 59 to the Ayrton Light at the very top of the tower. All four nations of the UK are represented on the tower on shields featuring a rose for England, thistle for Scotland, shamrock for Northern Ireland and leek for Wales.

Some statistics:

- It is 316ft high, making it the third-tallest clock tower in the UK.
- Each dial is 22.5ft in diameter.
- The minute hands are 14ft long and weigh about 220lbs, including counterweights. Big Ben has gun-metal hour hands and copper minute hands.
- The numbers are approximately 23in high.
- There are 312 pieces of glass in each clock dial.
- Originally the frame and hands were Prussian blue, but were painted black in the 1930s to disguise the effects of air pollution.
- There is a small stack of pre-decimal penny coins on top of the pendulum to adjust the time of the clock. Adding a coin has the effect of minutely lifting the position of the pendulum's centre of mass, reducing the effective length of the pendulum rod and hence increasing the

Big Ben's other face.

rate at which the pendulum swings. Adding or removing a penny will change the clock's speed by 0.4 seconds per day. It keeps time to within a few seconds per week. It is hand wound, taking about 1.5 hours, three times a week. Big Ben has rarely stopped. Even after a bomb on 10 May 1941 damaged two of the clock's dials and sections of the tower's stepped roof and destroyed the House of Commons chamber below, the clock tower survived and Big Ben continued to strike the hours.

- Accumulations of snow on the clock hands have caused the clock to stop a number of times, but on 12 August 1949, the clock slowed by four and a half minutes after a flock of starlings perched on the minute hand.

- The chimes of Big Ben were first broadcast by the BBC on 31 December 1923, a tradition that continues to this day.

- The Latin under the clock face reads DOMINE SALVAM FAC REGINAM NOSTRAM VICTORIAM PRIMAM, which means 'O Lord, keep safe our Queen Victoria the First'.

How did Big Ben come about? The original Palace of Westminster was destroyed by fire in 1834. In 1844, it was decided the new buildings for the Houses of Parliament should include a tower and a clock. A huge bell was required, but the first attempt made by John Warner & Sons at Stockton-on-Tees kept cracking irreparably. The metal was melted down and the bell recast on 10 April 1858 at the Whitechapel Bell Foundry.

Big Ben first rang out across London on 31 May 1859. But in the September, Big Ben cracked; a lighter bell hammer was fitted and the bell rotated to present an undamaged section to the hammer. This is the bell we hear today.

There is an oak-panelled prison room inside the tower, which can only be accessed from the House of Commons. It was last used in 1880 when atheist Charles Bradlaugh, newly elected Member of Parliament for Northampton, was imprisoned by the Serjeant at Arms after he refused to swear a religious oath of allegiance to Queen Victoria. Officially, the Serjeant at Arms can still make arrests, as they have had the authority to do since 1415.

In 1873 Acton Smee Ayrton, then First Commissioner of Works and Public Buildings, added the Ayrton Light. This is a lantern sited above the belfry and it is lit when-ever the House of Commons sits after dark, which can be seen from across London. Originally, it shone towards Buckingham Palace so that Queen Victoria could look out of a window and see when the Commons were in session.

Big Ben face wash.

In 2008 a survey of 2,000 people found that the tower was the most popular land-mark in the United Kingdom. It has also been named as the most iconic film location in London. ITN's *News at Ten* opening sequence features an image of the tower with the sound of Big Ben's chimes punctuating the announce-ment of the news headlines of the day. The Big Ben chimes (known within ITN as 'The Bongs') continue to be used during the headlines and all ITV News bulletins use a

Still British after the 2017–21 face lift. Black faced for years, the restoration work has transformed Big Ben back to the original Victorian Prussian blue-and-gold colour scheme.

graphic based on the Westminster clock dial. Big Ben can also be heard striking the hour before some news bulletins on BBC Radio 4 (6pm and midnight, plus 10pm on Sundays) and the BBC World Service, a practice that began on 31 December 1923. The sound of the chimes is sent live from a microphone permanently installed in the tower and connected by line to Broadcasting House.

Big Ben Aden is a clock tower built by British engineers and locals, beside Aden Harbour in Yemen when Aden Province (later called Aden Colony) was in the British Empire.

Big Ben Aden, 20 March 2010.

Further information at:

McKay, Chris, *Big Ben: the Great Clock and the Bells at the Palace of Westminster,* Oxford, 2010.

Weinreb, Ben, 'Big Ben,' *The London Encyclopaedia* (3rd ed.) London, 2011.

61

The incandescent light bulb

fiat lux, 1879

Early Mazda (General Electric) electric light bulbs.

Thomas Edison (1847–1931) often gets the credit for inventing the light bulb, but lights were coming on all over the place long before he patented his in 1879 and 1880 and brought it to market. In 1761, Ebenezer Kinnersley demonstrated heating a wire to incandescence. Humphry Davy (1778–1829), he of the safety lamp, in 1802 used what he described as 'a battery of immense size', consisting of 2,000 cells housed in the basement of the Royal Institution of Great Britain, to create an incandescent light by passing the current through a thin strip of platinum, chosen because the metal had an extremely high melting point. It caused a glow and did not last long enough, but it did mark the beginning of incandescent light development. He had already discovered the first electric lamp type – the carbon arc lamp; the incandescent lamp was the second form of electric light to be developed for commercial use after the carbon arc lamp. In 1835 the first constant electric light was demonstrated: for the next 40 years, scientists all over the world worked on the incandescent lamp, perfecting the filament (the part of the bulb that produces light when heated by an electrical current) and the bulb's atmosphere (whether air is vacuumed out of the bulb or it is filled with an inert gas to prevent the filament from oxidising and burning out). These early bulbs were not commercially viable: they had very short life spans, were too expensive to produce or used too much energy.

Three key factors allowed Edison to forge ahead: an effective incandescent material, a higher vacuum than others were able to achieve by his use of the Sprengel pump, and a high resistance that made power distribution from a centralised source economically viable. Edison and his team at Menlo Park, California, had concentrated on improving the filament – first testing carbon, then platinum, before finally returning to a carbon filament. By October 1879 Edison's team had produced a light bulb with a carbonised filament of uncoated cotton thread that could last for 14.5 hours. They continued to experiment with the filament until settling on one made from bamboo that gave Edison's lamps a lifetime of up to 1,200 hours – this filament became the standard for the Edison bulb for the next ten years. The story goes that in 1883 Edison was using a fan on a hot day, he unwound fine bamboo on a fold-out oriental fan, carbonised it and tested it as a filament. He then sent researchers to Japan to find the type of bamboo that was used in that fan. They found it and imported the filaments.

Werner von Bolton (a Georgian living in Germany) discovered that using tantalum for a filament allowed for lower energy consumption and greater brightness. Siemens and Halske Company produced these bulbs so successfully they posed a serious threat to General Electric's sales.

Edison also made other improvements to the light bulb, including creating a better vacuum pump to fully remove the air from the bulb and developing the Edison screw which became the standard socket fittings for light bulbs.

Edison, though, was not alone. William Sawyer and Albon Man received a US patent for the incandescent lamp, and Joseph Swan patented his light bulb in England. His house, Underhill, Low Fell, Gateshead, was the first in the world to be lit by a light bulb. Eventually Edison's US lighting company merged with the Thomson-Houston Electric Company who were making bulbs under the Sawyer-Man patent – to form General Electric, and Edison's English lighting company merged with Swan's company to form Ediswan in England.

In 1881 the Savoy Theatre in London was lit by Swan's incandescent light bulbs, which was the first theatre, and the first public building in the world, to be lit entirely by electricity. The first street in the world to be lit by an incandescent light bulb was Mosley Street, Newcastle upon Tyne, lit by Joseph Swan's incandescent lamp on 3 February 1879.

The quality that made Edison stand out in this crowded market was his wider vision: bulbs apart, he also developed a range of inventions that made light bulbs

Light bulbs enjoy their finest hours at Christmas time. This is a small part of the display which takes place every year in 'Twinkepike' Way, a cul-de-sac in Wigginton, near York. Donations go to support Yorkshire Air Ambulance, St Leonard's Hospice and Breast Cancer Now.

practical. Edison modelled his lighting technology on the existing gas lighting system and in 1882, with the Holborn Viaduct in London, he demonstrated that electricity could be distributed from a centrally located generator through a series of wires and tubes (conduits). At the same time he improved the generation of electricity, developing the first commercial power utility called the Pearl Street Station in lower Manhattan. And to track how much electricity each customer was using, Edison developed the first electric meter.

Other enlightened scientists were working hard to improve the efficiency of the bulb and the filament. Filaments have to be made from materials that have a high melting point. Tungsten can reach up to 3,422 °C before it melts. This is a higher temperature than any lamp will reach (except the carbon arc lamp which gets to 3,500 °C). Other materials have made good filaments or parts of filaments including tantalum, molybdenum and carbon. 1904 saw the invention of the tungsten filament by European inventors; they lasted longer and gave off a brighter light compared to the carbon filament bulbs.

In 1913 Irving Langmuir discovered that placing an inert gas like nitrogen inside the bulb doubled its efficiency. By the 1950s, researchers could still only convert about 10 per cent of the energy the incandescent bulb used into light; the rest is lost as heat.

Two Germans – glassblower Heinrich Geissler and physician Julius Plücker – discovered that they could produce light by removing almost all of the air from a long glass tube and passing an electrical current through it; this became known as the Geissler tube – a type of discharge lamp that only gained popularity in the early 20th century; discharge lamps became the basis of many lighting technologies, including neon lights, low-pressure sodium lamps for outdoor lighting such as streetlamps, and fluorescent lights.

Today, one of the fastest developing lighting technologies today is the light-emitting diode (or LED). A type of solid-state lighting, LEDs use a semiconductor to convert electricity into light, are often small in area (less than one square millimeter) and emit light in a specific direction, obviating the need for reflectors and diffusers that can trap light.

More information at:

Challoner, Jack; et al., *1001 Inventions That Changed The World*, Hauppauge NY, 2009.

Levy, Joel, *Really useful: the origins of everyday things*, New York, 2002.

62

The Oxford English Dictionary

1884

Seven volumes of the Second Edition of the Oxford English Dictionary, 1989
(Source https://www.flickr.com/photos/mrpolyonymous/6953043608,
photographer: Dan (mrpolyonymous on Flickr)).

The *Oxford English Dictionary (OED)* is *the* historical dictionary of the English language, published by Oxford University Press (OUP). By tracking the historical development of the English language it provides a unique, comprehensive resource as well as describing usage in its many variations throughout the world. The *Dictionary* features entries in which the earliest ascertainable recorded sense of a word, be it current or obsolete, comes first, and each additional sense is presented in historical order. Following each definition are several brief illustrative quotations.

Work began on the dictionary in 1857, and it started to see the light of day in 1884 when it was published in unbound fascicles as a work in progress with the name of *A New English Dictionary on Historical Principles; Founded Mainly on the Materials Collected by The Philological Society.* In 1895 the title *The Oxford English Dictionary* was first used unofficially on the covers of the series, and in 1928 the full dictionary was republished in ten bound volumes. In 1933 the title *The Oxford English Dictionary* replaced the former name in its reprinting as 12 volumes with a one-volume supplement. More supplements came over the years until 1989, when the second edition was published, comprising 21,728 pages in 20 volumes. Since 2000 work has been proceeding on a third edition, approximately half of which was complete by 2018; the third edition of the dictionary will probably appear only in electronic form.

The first electronic version came out in 1988. The online version has been available since 2000 and by April 2014 was receiving over two million visits per month.

The publishers tell us ('Dictionary Facts') that:

'… it would take a single person 120 years to "key in" the 59 million words of the OED second edition, 60 years to proofread them, and 540 megabytes to store them electronically. As of 30 November 2005, the Oxford English Dictionary contained approximately 301,100 main entries. Supplementing the entry headwords, there are 157,000 bold-type combinations and derivatives; 169,000 italicised-bold phrases and combinations; 616,500 word-forms in total, including 137,000 pronunciations; 249,300 etymologies; 577,000 cross-references; and 2,412,400 usage quotations. The dictionary's second edition (1989) was printed in 20 volumes, comprising 291,500 entries in 21,730 pages. The longest entry in the OED2 was for the verb *set*, which required 60,000 words to describe some 430 senses. As entries began to be revised for the OED3 in sequence starting from M, the longest entry became *make* in 2000, then *put* in 2007, then *run* in 2011.'

*The Compact Oxford English Dictionary, 1991, including the content of all
20 volumes of the second edition of the Oxford English Dictionary, 1989
(Photographer: Aalfons).*

The *OED* is by no means alone in the lexicography world: it is neither
the world's largest nor the earliest exhaustive dictionary of a language. Take,
for example, an earlier large dictionary that is the Grimm brothers' dictionary of the German language, begun in 1838 and completed in 1961.
The first edition of the *Vocabolario degli Accademici della Crusca* is the first
great dictionary devoted to a modern European language (Italian) and was
published in 1612; the first edition of *Dictionnaire de l'Académie française*
dates from 1694. The official dictionary of Spanish is the *Diccionario de
la lengua española* (produced, edited, and published by the Real Academia
Española); its first edition was published in 1780. *The Kangxi Dictionary of
Chinese* was published in 1716. The largest dictionary by number of pages
is believed to be the Dutch *Woordenboek der Nederlandsche Taal.*

How did the *OED* happen? As is often the case, dissatisfaction with the
current state of affairs provided the motivation to improve things. Our dictionary began life as a Philological Society project in 1844 of a small group
of intellectuals in London (unconnected to Oxford University): Richard
Chenevix Trench, Herbert Coleridge, and Frederick Furnivall, but it was
not until June 1857 that they began by forming an 'Unregistered Words
Committee' to track down words that were absent from or poorly defined
in current dictionaries. In November, Trench's report was nothing like a

list of unregistered words; rather, it was the study *On Some Deficiencies in our English Dictionaries*, which identified seven distinct shortcomings in contemporary dictionaries:

- Incomplete coverage of obsolete words
- Inconsistent coverage of families of related words
- Incorrect dates for earliest use of words
- History of obsolete senses of words often omitted
- Inadequate distinction among synonyms
- Insufficient use of good illustrative quotations
- Space wasted on inappropriate or redundant content

How damning can that be? The society soon realised that the number of unlisted words would be far more than the number of words in the English dictionaries of the 19th century. Trench suggested that a new, truly comprehensive dictionary was needed, and on 7 January 1858, the society approved the idea of a comprehensive new dictionary titled *A New English Dictionary on Historical Principles (NED)*. Volunteer readers would be assigned particular books, copying passages illustrating word usage onto quotation slips.

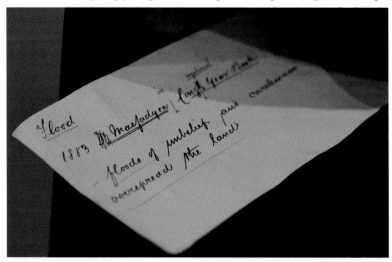

The quotation slip for the word 'flood', museum of the Oxford University Press, Great Clarendon Street, Oxford (Photographer: Daphne Preston-Kendal).

Richard Chenevix Trench (1807–86) was initially the main force in the project's first months, but his appointment as Dean of Westminster meant that he could not give the dictionary the time that it required. He withdrew and Herbert Coleridge became the first editor, working from his house as the editorial office. He set out 100,000 quotation slips in a 54 pigeon-hole grid – a primitive spread sheet. In April 1861 the group published the first sample pages; later that month, Coleridge died of tuberculosis, aged 30.

Furnivall took over but, though enthusiastic and knowledgeable, was ill-suited for the work and many volunteer readers eventually lost interest in the project, as Furnivall failed to keep them motivated. Furthermore, many of the slips were getting lost.

But Furnivall proved invaluable in a different respect. The other problem with the project was that since many printed texts from earlier centuries were not readily available, it would be impossible for volunteers to efficiently locate the quotations that the dictionary needed. As a result, Furnivall founded the Early English Text Society in 1864 and the Chaucer Society in 1868 to publish old manuscripts. Furnivall's efforts lasted 21 years and provided numerous texts for the use and enjoyment of the general public, as well as crucial sources for lexicographers, but they did not actually involve compiling a dictionary … Furnivall recruited more than 800 volunteers to read these texts and record quotations. While enthusiastic, the volunteers were not well trained and often made inconsistent and arbitrary selections. In the end, Furnivall handed over nearly two tons of quotation slips and other materials to his successor.

James Murray had accepted the post of editor.

But who was going to publish such a prodigious, and very expensive, work? In the late 1870s, Furnivall and Murray met with several publishers; in 1879, Oxford University Press agreed with Murray to proceed with the massive project after two years of negotiating; 20 years after its conception, the dictionary finally had a publisher. It would, though, take another 50 years to complete. Murray started the project, working in a corrugated iron shed called the 'Scriptorium' which was lined with wooden planks, bookshelves and 1,029 pigeon-holes to house the innumerable quotation slips.

Unfortunately, on inspection by Murray, Furnivall's slips were found to focus on arcane and abstruse words rather than common usages. For instance, there were ten times as many quotations for 'abusion' as for 'abuse'. What to do? He appealed, through newspapers, bookshops and libraries, for readers who would report 'as many quotations as you can for ordinary words' and for words that were 'rare, obsolete, old-fashioned, new, peculiar or used in a peculiar way'. Murray enlisted American philologist Francis March to manage the collection in North America; 1,000 quotation slips arrived daily to the Scriptorium, and by 1880 there were 2,500,000.

The first dictionary fascicle was published on 1 February 1884 – 23 years after Coleridge's sample pages. The pithy title was *A New English Dictionary on Historical Principles; Founded Mainly on the Materials Collected by The Philological Society*; the 352-page volume, words from A to Ant, cost 12s 6d (equivalent to £60 in 2020). Total sales were a meagre 4,000 copies.

Murray later learned that one particularly prolific reader named W. C. Minor was confined to a mental hospital suffering from what we would now call schizophrenia. Minor was a Yale University-trained surgeon and a military officer in the American Civil War who had been confined to Broadmoor Asylum for the Criminally Insane after killing a man in London. Minor invented his own quotation-tracking system, allowing him to submit slips on specific words in response to editors' requests. The story of how Murray and Minor worked together has been retold in *The Surgeon of Crowthorne*, later the basis for an illuminating 2019 film *The Professor and the Madman*.

Troubling times followed with the near collapse of the project and the firing of Philip Gell, the harassing OUP editor. But sense prevailed and new editors were hired on the death of Murray. In 1919–20, J. R. R. Tolkien was employed to research etymologies from Waggle to Warlock; later he parodied the principal editors as 'The Four Wise Clerks of Oxenford' in the story *Farmer Giles of Ham*.

The 125th and last fascicle covered words from Wise to the end of W, published on 19 April 1928, and the full dictionary in bound volumes followed immediately. William Shakespeare is the most-quoted writer in the completed dictionary, with *Hamlet* his most-quoted work. George Eliot is the most-quoted female writer. Collectively, the Bible is the most-quoted work; the most-quoted single work is *Cursor Mundi* (or '*Over-runner of the World*').

This is an early 14th century religious 30,000-line poem (published 1874–92) in Middle English that presents a detailed retelling of the history of Christianity from the Creation to Doomsday and is more-or-less completely unknown outside medievalist and lexicographical circles. Yet it provides the *Oxford English Dictionary* with over 1,000 new words – words that were unknown before they appeared for the first time in the *Cursor*

Mundi. Examples include: anyway, anywhere, backward, blister, brimstone, chastise and chess to virginity, weakness, wickedness, willing, written, yonder, and zealot. The poem has also furnished over 11,000 quotations, making it the second most heavily quoted work in OED1/2 after the Bible and the fifth most quoted source altogether.

A one-volume supplement of omitted material was published in 1933, with entries including many words and senses newly coined –famously appendicitis, which was coined in 1886 and gained popularity when Edward VII's 1902 affliction with appendicitis postponed his coronation, – and some previously excluded for being too obscure – most famously 'radium,' omitted in 1903, a few short months before its discoverers Pierre and Marie Curie won the Nobel Prize in Physics.

At the launch of the first OED online site in 2000, the editors began a major revision project to create a completely revised third edition of the dictionary (OED3), expected to be completed in 2037 at a projected cost of about £34 million. Improvements include computerised searching, more etymological information, and a general change of focus away from individual words towards more general coverage of the language as a whole. Other important computer uses include internet searches for evidence of current usage and email submissions of quotations by readers and the general public.

Further information at:
Brewer, Charlotte, *Treasure-House of the Language: the Living OED*, Yale University Press, 2007.
Gilliver, Peter, 'Make, put, run: Writing and rewriting three big verbs in the OED,' *Dictionaries: Journal of the Dictionary Society of North America*, 34 (34), pp. 10–23, 2013.
Gilliver, Peter, *The Making of the Oxford English Dictionary*, Oxford, 2016.
Ogilvie, Sarah, *Words of the World: a global history of the Oxford English Dictionary*, Cambridge, 2013.
Willinsky, John, *Empire of Words: The Reign of the Oxford English Dictionary*, Princeton University Press, 1995.
Winchester, Simon, *The Surgeon of Crowthorne: A Tale of Murder, Madness and the Oxford English Dictionary*, London, 1999.
Winchester, Simon, *The Meaning of Everything: The Story of the Oxford English Dictionary*, Oxford, 2003.

63

Radium

1898

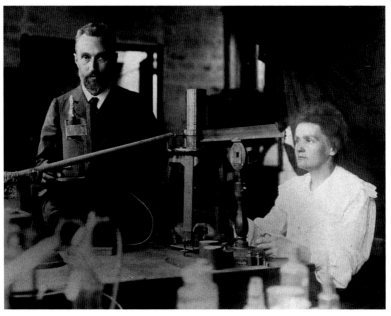

Pierre and Marie Curie – discoverers of radium.

Radium is the most radioactive natural element, a million times more so than uranium. It is so radioactive that it gives off a pale blue glow. Pure radium is silvery-white, but it readily reacts with nitrogen (rather than oxygen) on exposure to air, forming a black surface layer of radium nitride (Ra_3N_2). All isotopes of radium are highly radioactive, with the most stable isotope being radium-226, which has a half-life of 1,600 years and decays into radon gas (specifically the isotope radon-222). Radium, in the form of radium chloride, was discovered by Marie and Pierre Curie in 1898 from ore mined at Jáchymov in the Czech Republic. They succeeded in painstakingly extracting 1mg of radium from ten tonnes of the uranium ore pitchblende (uranium oxide, U_3O_8); their samples glowed with a faint blue light in the dark, caused by the intense radioactivity exciting the surrounding air. They published the discovery at the French Academy of Sciences five days later. Radium was isolated in its metallic state by Marie Curie and André-Louis Debierne through the electrolysis of radium chloride in 1911. Among the many papers that the Curies published in the years after its discovery, one particularly significant article showed that radium could treat cancer by killing cancer cells more readily than healthy cells. Radium became used as one of the first radiation treatments for cancer and skin diseases.

The Radium Girls

Radium was once used in self-luminous paints for watches, nuclear panels, aircraft switches, clocks, and instrument dials. A typical self-luminous watch that uses radium paint contains around one microgram of radium. In the mid-1920s, a lawsuit was filed against the United States Radium Corporation in New Jersey by five dying 'Radium Girls' – dial painters who had painted radium-based luminous paint on the dials of watches and clocks. The dial painters were told to lick their brushes to give them a fine point, thereby ingesting radium. Their exposure to radium caused serious health issues which included sores, anaemia and bone cancer, injuring, disfiguring and killing many of the 2,000 workers estimated to have been employed at peak. The company's scientists and management had taken considerable precautions to protect themselves from the effects of radiation, but they did not protect their employees. Additionally, for several years the companies had attempted to cover up the effects and avoid liability by insisting that the Radium Girls were instead suffering from syphilis. This complete disregard for employee welfare had a significant impact on the formulation of occupational disease industrial law. From the 1960s the use of radium paint was discontinued.

The UK is still dealing with the legacy of radium-painted dials used in World War Two, with Dalgety Bay in Fife just one area affected by radium displaced from old waste dumps. Since the 1990s more than 2,500

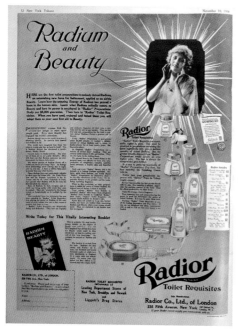

Advertisement for Radior cosmetics which the manufacturer boasted contained radium. The radium was supposed to be good for your skin. Powders, skin creams and soap were part of this line, which was made in London.-(New York Tribune Magazine, 10 November 1918).

radioactive hotspots have been found on the Dalgety Bay foreshore. They come from an eroded landfill that contains debris from World War Two aircraft that had radium dials. Another radiation hotspot is an area of walled and wooded land in an urban area close to the former naval dockyard at Chatham in Kent. Up to 1,000 sites could be polluted, though the best guess is that between 150 and 250 are; the MOD figure is 15 or so sites contaminated with radium from old planes and other materiel. They include the old SAS headquarters at Stirling Lines in Hereford, HMS *Daedalus*, near Portsmouth, a former naval air base; Defence Aviation Repair Agency, Gosport, Hampshire, a former aircraft repair depot; and RAF Little Rissington, Gloucestershire, an air base and former home to Red Arrows; RM Condor, Arbroath, Royal Marines base; Forthside, Stirling, a former army luminising depot, and RAF Carlisle, a former military equipment depot.

Nowadays, other than its vital use in nuclear medicine, radium has few commercial applications, although it is used increasingly in atomic, molecular, and optical physics and as a radiation source in some industrial radiography devices to check for flawed metallic parts. Nuclear medicine is a medical specialty involving the application of radioactive substances in the

'Tho-radia powder' box, based on radium and thorium, according to the formula by Dr Alfred Curie, on display at the Musée Curie, Paris. An example of radioactive quackery. This Curie was unrelated to Marie and Pierre (photographer: Rama).

diagnosis and treatment of disease. Nuclear medicine imaging, in a sense, is 'radiology done inside out'. Single photon emission computed tomography (SPECT) and positron emission tomography (PET) scans are the two most common imaging modalities in nuclear medicine.

Radioactive quackery

Radioactive quackery deceptively promotes radioactivity as a therapy for illnesses; quackery pseudo-scientifically promotes involving radioactive substances as a method of healing for cells and tissues. It was most popular during the early 20th century. The practice is condemned and has largely declined, but is still actively practised by some.

Astonishingly, radium became an ingredient in sweets and throat lozenges, and a constituent of make-up. The complexions of children eating Radium Schokolade may have appeared rubescent for a rather worrying reason. Before the terrible effects of radiation exposure were fully understood, radium found itself in all manner of products, with consumers keen to benefit from its purported magical healing properties and its glow-in-the-dark fascination. Radium and thorium were contained in toothpaste (Doramad Radioactive Toothpaste: 'Your teeth will shine with radioactive brilliance', courtesy of Alfred Curie – no relation to Marie), skin cream, Vita Radium Suppositories ('for restoring sex power'), baby blankets and Hippman-Blach bakery's Radium Bread, for example. Its wide use in cosmetics in the popular Tho-Radia brand of make-up included radioactive powders and creams that promised

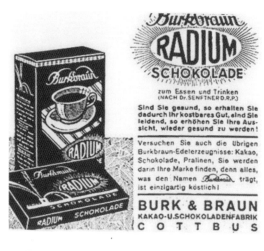

*Radium Chocolate containing real radium.
You could also get uranium ice cream for your
own personal nuclear winter.*

*You could even soothe your sore throat with these pas-
tilles full of radium salts – not just a shelf life but a
half-life too.*

to rejuvenate and brighten the skin. The wonderful German 'wunder bar', Radium Schokolade, sold by Burk & Braun from 1931 to 1936, could claim among its contents not just cocoa and milk, but also an unhealthy dose of radium salts, endowing it with a half-life as well as the more usual shelf life. To really make you better there was always Heidelberger Radium-Pastillen and, if you fancied a change to your radioactive fix, then you could try Snowflake uranium ice cream. Then there was Radithor, a solution of radium salts, which was claimed by its developer William J. A. Bailey to have curative properties. And lethal properties – industrialist Eben Byers died in 1932 from ingesting it in large quantities between 1927 and 1930.

Jewellery, pendants, wristbands and athletic tape were touted as incorporating 'negative ion technology' – also advertised under other names such as 'quantum scalar energy', 'volcanic lava energy', and 'quantum science'. These products were marketed as conferring health benefits or as a means of improving emotional well-being.

Further information at:

Chrystal, Paul, *A History of Sweets*, Barnsley, 2021.

Clark, Claudia, *Radium Girls: Women and Industrial Health Reform, 1910–1935*, University of North Carolina Press, 1987.

Fröman, Nanny, 'Marie and Pierre Curie and the Discovery of Polonium and Radium,' *Nobel Foundation*, 1 December 1996.

Goldsmith, Barbara, *Obsessive Genius: The Inner World of Marie Curie*, New York, 2005.

Moore, Kate, *The Radium Girls, The Dark Story of America's Shining Women*, *sourcebooks.com*, p. 366, 2017.

Rumble, John, *CRC Handbook of Chemistry and Physics* (101st edition), Boca Raton (FL), 2020.

Santos, Lucy Jane, *Half Lives: The Unlikely History of Radium*, London, 2020.

64

Aspirin

1899

A 1923 French advertisement for aspirin.

Many of us will have taken aspirin at one time or another; what it was actually prescribed for depends largely on how old you are: the indications for aspirin have changed markedly since its early use primarily as an analgesic.

Aspirin – acetylsalicylic acid (ASA) – is a non-steroidal anti-inflammatory drug (NSAID). It was originally manufactured and patented by Bayer of Leverkusen in 1853. Specific inflammatory conditions in which aspirin is used include Kawasaki disease, pericarditis and rheumatic fever. Aspirin is a first-line treatment for the fever and joint-pain symptoms of acute rheumatic fever.

Aspirin administered shortly after a heart attack decreases the risk of death; it is also used long-term to help prevent further heart attacks, ischaemic strokes and blood clots in people at high risk. There is evidence that aspirin has chemoprotective properties and may reduce overall cancer incidence and mortality in colorectal, oesophageal and gastric cancers, with smaller effects on prostate, breast and lung cancer. A review of randomised control trials showed that doses between 75 and 300mg daily reduced overall cancer incidence by 12 per cent after three years and also demonstrated a 33 per cent reduction in mortality and 25 per cent reduction in the incidence of colorectal cancer with a median follow up of 18.3 years.

The large studies on the use of low-dose aspirin to prevent heart attacks that were published in the 1970s and 1980s helped spur reform in clinical research ethics and guidelines for human subject research, and are often cited as examples of clinical trials that included only men, but from which people drew general conclusions that did not hold true for women.

Aspirin, however, life-saver that it is, has its dark side. In 2018 Cynthia Connolly published her *Children and Drug Safety,* a disturbing, but vitally important, book which, according to the blurb:

'[T]races the development, use, and marketing of drugs for children in the twentieth century, a history that sits at the interface of the state, business, health care providers, parents, and children. This book illuminates the historical dimension of a clinical and policy issue with great contemporary significance – many of the drugs administered to children today have never been tested for safety and efficacy in the pediatric population. Each chapter of Children and Drug Safety engages with major turning points in pediatric drug development; themes of children's risk, rights, protection and the evolving context of childhood; child-rearing; and family life in ways freighted with nuances of race, class, and gender. Cynthia A. Connolly charts the numerous attempts by Congress, the Food and Drug Administration, the American Academy of Pediatrics, and leading pediatric pharmacologists, scientists, clinicians, and parents to address a situation that all found untenable. '

Indeed, the intentional blurring of safety considerations with the pursuit of profit in over the counter (OTC) children's medicine where drugs are developed and made to masquerade as more palatable sweets is probably the most sinister manifestation of the (deliberate) confusing of pharmaceuticals with sweets.

In 1947 the Plough Company, founded by entrepreneur Abe Plough, successfully reformulated an old, off-patent medication – aspirin – into a flavoured, small-dose chewable tablet designed to appeal to the finicky palates of medicine-averse children. Plough had made his money buying ailing proprietary drug companies and remarketing their products aggressively. Plough purchased one of these companies, St. Joseph, in 1921, but by the 1940s things were not going so well.

But the boom in births after World War Two gave him an opportunity. Plough set St. Joseph chemists to work developing a paediatric aspirin formulation that would be attractive to children through colour and taste. In September 1947 the company released the bright orange St. Joseph Aspirin for children amid a frenzy of aggressive creative marketing in all media. Particularly insidious though was his use of newspaper and magazine adverts, particularly those in *Parents* magazine, in which he depicted homely and idealised scenarios and a stereotyped, class and racially exclusive vision of the comfortable American family in well-appointed living rooms.

Mothers appeared relaxed, but no. The copy implied that parenting was stressful and difficult. According to Cyntha Connolly, 'the ads were designed to tap into mothers' anxieties by persuading them that post-war parenting was much more complex. As a result, the ads implied, children could face danger if a mother purchased a product that had not been scientifically formulated to accommodate her children's physiological and psychological needs.'

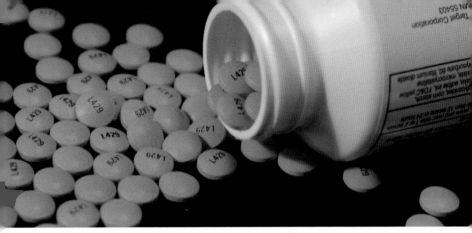

Regular strength enteric-coated 325mg aspirin tablets, distributed by Target Corporation (photographer: Ragesoss).

Plough's new product achieved blockbuster status almost immediately. By the early 1950s, low-dose, flavoured aspirin was the number-one drug ingested by children, far outstripping its chief competitor, penicillin. Plough's profits increased by double digits, in some years by as much as 50 per cent. All of this spurred Bayer and other generic manufacturers to bring competing versions to market.

Connolly goes on to tell us that 'within a few years the American Academy of Pediatrics (AAP) recorded an alarming dramatic increase in aspirin poisoning in young children. The statistics seemed irrefutable: by 1951, three years after St. Joseph Aspirin for Children became available, pre-school-age children represented 80 per cent of aspirin deaths. Children loved the taste of St. Joseph Aspirin for Children.'

There was nothing anywhere in Plough's advertisements that mentioned the importance, the necessity indeed, of keeping these pills away from toddlers and pre-school children; many parents remained blithely unaware of the threat from an overdose. They were, no doubt, 'horrified to learn that a toxic dose of aspirin could cause ringing in the ears, sleepiness, rapid and deep breathing, vomiting, and vision problems. An especially high dose could result in seizures, coma, even death.' Stomach bleeds too must have been an issue.

In the event, some parents did inadvertently overdose their children. There was no requirement or regulation for a standardised children's aspirin preparation. Each generic company decided themselves how much acetylsalicylic acid to put in a tablet. The AAP reported that 50 per cent of accidents in children were now poison-related: paediatricians, nurses and public-health officials began tracking all accidental swallowings in children. In most cases, aspirin topped the list.

Plough were certainly not the only ones.

Indeed, sweets and medicine are inextricably associated with each other; so much so that in the early days of sweets in Europe, it was the apothecary who was the key player in the production of sugar-based preparations. Medieval European physicians were well-versed in the medicinal uses of sugar, having learnt them from the Arabs and Byzantine Greeks. For example, one Middle Eastern remedy for rheums (a thin mucus naturally discharged from the eyes, nose or mouth during sleep) and fevers was little twisted sticks of pulled sugar which the Arabs called *al fānäd* or *al pänäd*. These became known in Britain as alphenics, or, more commonly, as penidia, penids, pennet or pan sugar. They were the precursors of barley sugar and modern cough drops. In 1390 we know that the Earl of Derby paid 'two shillings for two pounds of penydes'.

Further information at:

Chrystal, Paul, *The History of Sweets*, Barnsley, 2021.

Jeffreys, D., *Aspirin the remarkable story of a wonder drug*, New York, 2008.

Ravina, E., *The Evolution of Drug Discovery: From Traditional Medicines to Modern Drugs*, Chichester, 2011.

Schiebinger, L., 'Women's health and clinical trials,' *The Journal of Clinical Investigation*, 112 (7), pp. 973–7, 2003.

65

UK WSPU Hunger Strike Medal

30 July 1909

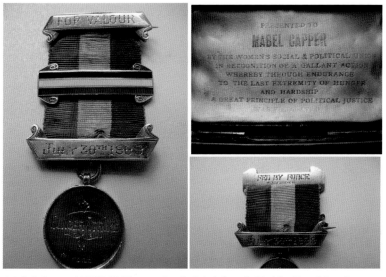

Mabel Capper's WSPU Hunger Strike Medal with 'Fed by Force' Bar September 1909 (photographer: Johnny Cyprus).

The Hunger Strike Medal was a silver medal awarded by the Women's Social and Political Union (WSPU) to suffragette prisoners who went on hunger strike. The Hunger Strike Medals were first presented at a ceremony in early August 1909 to women who had gone on hunger strike while serving a prison sentence at Holloway Prison for some act of militancy. It was intended to win them recognition as political prisoners. Many women were force-fed: a terrifying and painful form of torture.

*Mabel Capper Outside
Bow Street Court,
1 January 1912
(photographer:
Johnny Cyprus).*

The medal was one of a number of military-style campaign medals the WSPU awarded to raise morale and encourage continued loyalty and commitment to the cause. Later the medals would be presented at a breakfast reception on a woman's release from prison. The round and hallmarked silver medals hang on a length of ribbon in the purple, white and green colours of the WSPU from a silver pin bar engraved 'FOR VALOUR', in imitation of the Victoria Cross. The obverse of the medal is inscribed 'HUNGER STRIKE'. About 100 medals were awarded and could be issued with more than one bar representing multiple hunger strikes or force-feedings.

Mabel Capper (1888–1966) was imprisoned six times, went on hunger strike and was one of the first suffragettes to be force-fed. Amongst her many militant actions, she, in October 1908, took part in the Rush on the House of Commons, together with Christabel Pankhurst, Emmeline Pankhurst and other suffragettes, like Clara Codd, with whom she conspired to cause a distraction to get Codd past the police line. Capper ended up in the dock charged with 'wilful obstruction', sporting a costume composed entirely of the colours of the WSPU, together with a sash, waist belt and hatband bearing the words 'Votes for Women'. She spent one month in Holloway for refusing to pay the fine that was imposed.

Emily Wilding Davison

Emily Davison was an English suffragette who fought, and died for, votes for women in Britain. A member of the WSPU and a militant fighter for her cause, she was arrested on nine occasions, went on hunger strike seven times and was force-fed on 49 occasions.

On 4 June 1913 Davison caught a train from Victoria to Epsom, where she took up her place at the rail on Tattenham Corner, and after a first group of horses raced past, ducked under the rail and leapt towards the King's horse, Anmer, as it galloped towards her. She was hurled 30ft on impact; a suffragette flag was found tacked on the inside of her coat. She died four days after she sustained internal injuries and a basilar skull fracture. Emily was 40 years old. Her clever use of cutting-edge newsreel technology, entering the race track at a spot near the finish line where she knew all the cameras were pointed, ensured her place in history.

King George V and Queen Mary were present at the racecourse and witnessed the incident. The Queen damned Emily as 'the horrid woman'. Both Herbert Jones and his mount were unharmed.

Emily Davison is hit by the King's mount at Epsom.

Emily Davison
(1872 – 8 June 1913)
wearing her Hunger Strike Medal
and Holloway brooch c. 1910–12,
(source: The Day Book,
Chicago, 9 June 1913).

Further information at:

Atkinson, Diane, *Rise up, women!: the remarkable lives of the suffragettes*, London, 2018.

Calling all Women, Newsletter of the Suffragette Fellowship, Review of 'Up Hill to Holloway' by Mabel Capper, February 1963.

Collette, Carolyn, 'Faire Emelye: Medievalism and the Moral Courage of Emily Wilding Davison', *The Chaucer Review*, 42 (3), pp. 223–43, 2008.

Crawford, Elizabeth, *The Women's Suffrage Movement*, London, 1999.

Fisher, Lucy, *Emily Wilding Davison The Martyr Suffragette*, Biteback, 2018.

Liddington, Jill, '"Women Do Not Count, Neither Shall They Be Counted": Suffrage, Citizenship and the Battle for the 1911 Census,' *History Workshop Journal*, (17), pp. 98–127, 2011.

Sleight, John, *One-way Ticket to Epsom: Journalist's Enquiry into the Heroic Story of Emily Wilding Davison*, Morpeth, 1988.

CHAPTER 11

WORLD WAR ONE

66

Unexploded shells and the bombardment of Hartlepool

16 December 1914

Germans – be scared! But that's probably not the best way to handle an unexploded high explosive shell …

In the space of 40 minutes on the morning of 16 December 1914, about 1,000 shells were unleashed on Hartlepool from three German heavy cruisers, *Blucher*, *Seydlitz* and *Moltke*. Most of the resulting dead were taken to the Public Mortuary in Market Yard, Lynn Street: 35 bodies were processed in one day in a building designed to hold four; others were sent to Gray, Peverell, in Victoria Street.

The German fleet shelled the towns killing 63 civilians and nine soldiers in Hartlepool and 56 civilians in West Hartlepool; 400 or so civilians were injured and much housing stock was damaged or destroyed.

The raid killed the first British soldier to die on British soil in World War One: Private Theophilus Jones of the 18th Battalion of the Durham Light Infantry aged 27. Hartlepool's gun batteries were the only ones in Britain to open fire in anger on the enemy during the war.

The reference is presumably to the cemented steel armour protecting the German battleships, manufactured by Krupps, and to the corrupt nature of the Kaiser. To the Germans, Hartlepool was strategically more significant a target than Whitby or Scarborough, the other targets that day. It had thriving

A pastiche of German Kaiser Wilhelm II made from shell fragments harvested from the two towns.

dockyards and factories, one of which was a converted munitions works and was defended by 3 BL 6-inch Mk VII naval guns on the seafront. The guns were manned by the 11 officers and 155 men of the Durham Royal Garrison Artillery. *The Yorkshire Post* reported the raid as follows:

'It is even more difficult to give an estimate of the wounded. During the day the CAMERON HOSPITAL DEALT WITH 160 CASES, of which 60 were serious enough to be detained; in fact, the hospital is full, and all day the honorary staff has been busy conducting splinters of metal. Seventeen casualties are being accommodated in the Masonic Hall, Tunstall Hall has been turned into a hospital, and all the available beds at the Workhouse are being utilised. Sorrow, in fact, has entered so many homes, and the street scenes of the deadly half-hour in the morning were so ghastly that the twin towns are for the moment stunned and damaged. People who have passed through it tell you that they never wish to see the like again, and that the only consolation which one philosopher could extract from the experience was perhaps now England would wake up.'

There were 5,611 casualties from German air and naval raids on the British mainland during World War One, a large number but largely unreported, due, presumably, to it being a relatively small number compared to the massive casualties reported from the front lines.

The Yorkshire Post continues its disturbing Hartlepools report:

'The bulk of the men in the town were out that time working, and in their absence the women and children at home were terribly frightened. The little ones, in fact, were mostly getting up for the day, and women, some of them scantily clad, rushed into the streets. CARRYING TROUBLED INFANTS IN THEIR ARMS and others crying at their skirts. This was a general spectacle in the town during the attack, and it was pathetic in the extreme, of course the folks ought to have kept indoors, but their instinct was to get away at all costs, though in doing so some of them were blown to pieces in the street. In a short time the westward road in Elwick was crowded with women and children, who had rushed away with just what they were wearing at the time, with many of them being only half dressed.'

Many years later, *The Northern Echo*, first published the following on Tuesday 10 March 2009 in 'Bombardments'

This horrific account was related by H. Bell:
'We lived on Belk Street at the time of the bombardment. I was working at Gray's Central Shipyard … everybody in the blacksmith's shop where I worked went out to see what was happening. In a few seconds a shell hit the offices and blew nearly all of it in the air. At the same time railway wagons were being blown sky high … I noticed a young boy stretched across the tram-lines face downwards and when I ran over to him I found out he was dead, with nearly half his chest blown away. His name was John McGuire. He lived on Cameron Road and had only recently started work at Gray's dockyard. A few yards further on I saw Barney Hodgson of Water Street, pinned up against the Swedish Church wall bleeding very badly. I went to run towards him but he shouted, "Keep on running son, I'm done for." When I reached Belk Street and home, mother was propped up against

the wall outside the house with blood running from her like water from a tap. In the road opposite her lay the body of a boy, Joseph Jacobs. At the mortuary I had to identify my youngest brother, little Henry, who had been killed. Another brother was in hospital with leg injuries. Our family's casualties were mother who lost a leg and suffered multiple injuries, a brother killed, a brother with leg injuries and a nephew killed.'

The raid on the Hartlepools was followed by similar assaults on Scarborough and Whitby in which 18 and three people were killed respectively. At Hartlepool the two coastal defence batteries (Heugh Battery and Lighthouse Battery with three six-inch guns) responded, firing 143 shells and damaging the three German ships – eight German sailors were killed and 12 wounded.

For the next few nights, the people of Hartlepool camped out in barns away from the shore. King George V, though, sent 'a large number of pheasants' to the homeless, and each wounded person was given a pheasant feather. A true royal pheasant plucker.

The following report also featured in *The Northern Echo* on 10 March 2009 relating to the mortuary in Lynn Street and was given by Robert Wood, a well-known West Hartlepool historian:

'My father was the Superintendent of the public market ... At 9.00am there was a hammering at our back door and the driver of the Corporation coop cart demanded the key of the "Dead House". My father asked why he needed it and he said he had a body in the cart. "What is it?" asked my father. "A young lad," replied the driver. "What happened to him?" "He's been shot." "Good heavens!" exclaimed my father. "Who did it?" "Why man! Don't you know?" cried the astonished cart-man. "The Germans have been shelling us for the past hour. Do you mean to say I'm the first with a load? Get the place open quick because there'll soon be plenty more!" Sure enough there were. Thirty-five bodies were brought into a place built to accommodate four ... but I can remember the wails of distraught relatives ... I too had my own small tragedy, for my mother took all my shirts to make decent the bodies of the children.'

The Royal Navy had received advance warning of the raid from the naval intelligence unit (the 'Room 40' group) and Admiral Warrender was despatched with six battleships, four battlecruisers, four heavy cruisers, six light cruisers and eight submarines to intercept the German raiding force. Just before the attack on Hartlepool, Warrender spotted the Germans but, astonishingly, mistook them for an insignificant raiding party.

Mrs Farnham's Clock.

According to Taylor Downing in his *Secret Warriors: Key Scientists, Code-breakers and Propagandists of the Great War* (2014), the First Lord of the Admiralty was having a bath when news was given to him about the bombardment of the Hartlepools. Churchill leapt out, realising that Admiral Sir John Jellicoe, commander of the Grand Fleet, was in a perfect position to ambush the raiders. Unfortunately, fog intervened and allowed the German battle cruisers to sail right past Jellicoe's squadron unscathed. Despite howls of protest from the British press ('where was our Navy?'), the Admiralty could not respond for fear of divulging the top secret that we had decrypted the Germans' codes and were able to read all of their signals – intelligence that had allowed Jellicoe to be where he was in the first place.

Mrs Farnham of 14 Collingwood Road, West Hartlepool, had the unhappy privilege of receiving one of the first shells of the bombardment: the damage to her house was considerable as this picture shows. The clock poignantly records the precise time the shell hit Mrs Farnham's house. It now resides in Hartlepool's Gray Art Gallery.

This dramatic painting by James Clark has come to symbolise the horror that was visited on local residents that morning. Apparently, a number of the characters are identifiable in this tragic Moor Terrace scene. Sarah

'The Bombardment of the Hartlepools (16 December 1914)' (copy after James Clark), C. Fenwick (photo credit: Hartlepool Museums and Heritage Service).

Ann Stringer is the lady in the background carrying her son Jonathon in a desperate bid for safety; unfortunately, she was hit in the back by a piece of shrapnel which exited through her stomach and then took off Jonathon's foot. The boy survived but Sarah died 13 years later from, it seems, sepsis caused by her injury. Ethel Stringer is the little girl in the foreground being ushered away by the fisherman; sadly, she too was hit, losing both her legs and dying 11 days later.

Further information at:

Chrystal, Paul, *Hartlepool Through the Ages*, Stroud, 2014.

Chrystal, Paul, *Old Hartlepool & West Hartlepool*, Stenlake Publishing, 2019.

Massie, Robert K., *Castles of Steel: Britain, Germany, and the Winning of the Great War at Sea*, London, 2004.

Staff, Gary, 'German Bombardment of Hartlepool, Whitby and Scarborough on 15th and 16th December 1914,' from the Kriegsmarine's Official History (Krieg zur See).

Witt, Jann M., *Scarborough Bombardment: Der Angriff der deutschen Hochseeflotte auf Scarborough, Whitby und Hartlepool am 16. Dezember 1914* (Scarborough Bombardment: The Attack by the German High Seas Fleet on Scarborough, Whitby and Hartlepool on 16 December 1914), Berlin, 2016.

67

The Barnbow Lasses
Roll of Honour

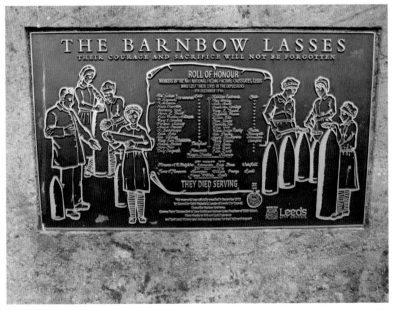

The Barnbow Lasses Roll of Honour in Leeds.

By 1918 there were more than 900,000 munitionettes producing 80 per cent of the weapons and shells used by the British Army.

In 1914 approximately 24 per cent of working-age women were already employed, mainly in domestic service jobs, as shop assistants, or doing menial work in small factories. By the end of the war the number of women who had taken up employment was approximately 1,600,000 – with around a million of those working in munitions factories. These girls and women were called munitionettes. The employment which women found open to them throughout the war not only increased, but became diversified, doing less of the traditionally female roles they had before the war and taking their place in typically male-dominated areas.

To get as many women into the workforce as quickly as possible, many skilled jobs were (patronisingly) segmented into smaller, more simple tasks – the 'dilution of labour'. The unions opposed this, fearful that this diluting, in addition to the lower levels of pay women earned, would lead to fewer jobs for their male members when they came home from the front. *The Factory Times* magazine in 1916 wrote:

> 'We must get women back into the home as soon as possible. That they ever left is one of the evil results of the war!'

Munitionettes were paid less than half the rate of male workers; however, striking was made illegal and so there was no recourse to address this. The War Cabinet Committee on Women in Industry claimed to agree with equal pay in principle, but believed that due to their 'lesser strength and special health problems' (whatever they were!) the output of women was inferior to that of the male workers.

Right: Munionettes and their munitions.

Left: A munitions worker recruitment poster invoking patriotism with an attempt to introduce a touch of glamour into work that was anything but glamorous.

With many of their men – brothers, husbands and fathers – away at the front, the women of the land rose to the challenge of stepping into the breach and doing their very best to keep the country going: women volunteered in their droves – the University of Leeds championed the formation of a Voluntary Aid Detachment (VAD) and signed volunteers for concerted sewing, knitting and bandage making. Just as importantly, women found themselves driving and working as conductors on buses and trams, cleaning trains, filling volatile and toxic shells, clerking in banks and insurance offices, toiling in warehouses and factories – each of these former male bastions fell to girls and women – and these girls and women could hardly be blamed for expecting fairer treatment than they actually got post-1918. For example, during the war there were 1,473 women conductors working in Leeds; by October 1919 this had fallen to 64.

Wherever and whenever there is war, there are victims.

Fire practice drill at Barnbow.

Shells being assembled at Newlay.

Barnbow girls and women making box lids for cartridge packing cases out of empty propellant boxes They are using circular saws (without protective guards) to cut the wood to size to make the box lids. 'Matériel from waste material' (courtesy of Leodis; © Leeds Library & Information Services).

Mary Dorrian, fleet-footed winger for Christopher Brown, saw mills in Stranton, West Hartlepool and England.

Many are male combatants but many more usually are civilians – non-combatants who include women among their number. Women are often left to pick up the pieces during and after war, sometimes literally. Women wait anxiously at home always expecting the worst news; for women, more often than not, their war is not over when the actual war is over. Where there is loss of a husband, father or brother they are left to grieve and mourn and to struggle on with their lives, often bringing up young, fatherless children. Where the husband is wounded, they may have to spend their new lives as unpaid carers working without state support, tending limbless or otherwise traumatised ex-servicemen, coping with all the grinding physical and psychological issues disabling injury brings. To some extent it has always been thus, and to some extent it still is today.

Flora Lion (1878 –1958)

Flora Lion, a celebrated English portrait painter, was commissioned by the Ministry of Information (MoI) to paint factory scenes on the home front. The Ministry issued her permits to set up her easel in factories in Leeds and Bradford. In Leeds she sketched scenes in a factory building wooden flying-boats. In Bradford, Lion painted women working in a munitions factory. Both paintings were finished in 1918, by which time the Ministry of Information had unfortunately been wound up and the Imperial War Museum (IWM) had taken over the MoI artist's scheme. Sadly, the IWM had no funds available to purchase new artworks, and so could not accept Lion's paintings despite her offering them at only 150 guineas each. Lion was also one of three women artists, alongside Anna Airy and Dorothy Coke, considered for commissions by the British War Memorials Committee, but this came to nothing.

68

British Brodie pattern steel helmet

1916

The memorial to George Easton and comrades in St Mary's, Kilburn, North Yorkshire, churchyard wearing his Brodie-pattern helmet.

George Easton's citation reads:

'EASTON George Herbert. Meritorious Service Medal. (Memorial has M.M.) Private 27241. 8th Battalion Yorkshire Regiment. Killed in action on the 17th October 1917. Aged 21. Born Oldstead, Malton, Yorkshire. Lived Scawton, Thirsk. Enlisted Richmond, Yorkshire. Son of Thomas and Clara Easton, of Bagby, Thirsk. Brother of Robert who also fell.'
– *Edinburgh Gazette* dated 5 November 1917

'His Majesty the King has been graciously pleased to award the Meritorious Service Medal to the undermentioned Non-Commissioned Officers and Men for gallantry in the performance of Military duty: … 27241 Pte. G. H. Easton, York. R. (Malton), and many others. Commemorated on the Tyne Cot Memorial, West-Vlaanderen, Belgium.'

George's grave in Kilburn was originally marked with a wooden cross, later to be replaced by a stone one.

Kilburn is the location of the famous White Horse above the village and the home and workshops of Robert Thompson (1876 –1955), the famous mouseman.

Here is the life story of George's brother, Robert, who succumbed to Spanish flu:

'EASTON Robert. Sapper 145281, 26th Field Coy, Royal Engineers died 30th November 1918 aged 25. Born at Oldstead. Son of Thomas and Clara Easton, of Bagby, Thirsk, brother of George who also fell. He joined up on the 17th February 1916 aged 22 and 4 months at the Royal Engineers Depot at Chatham. Occupation prior to enlistment was joiner, wheelwright. Lived at his parents at Oldstead. He embarked for the B.E.F. on the 27th July 1916. Granted leave to his home in November 1918 and died of influenza at his home, Oldstead, Coxwold, Molton, Yorkshire on the 30th November 1918. At rest in St Mary's churchyard, Kilburn, Yorkshire.'
Source: https://www.militaryimages.net/media/kilburn-war-memorial-yorkshire.102139/

The Brodie helmet is a steel combat helmet designed and patented in London in 1915 by John Leopold Brodie. It goes by many names: the shrapnel helmet, battle bowler, Tommy helmet, tin hat, and in the United States the doughboy helmet. It was also known as the dishpan hat, tin pan hat, washbasin, battle bowler (when worn by officers) and Kelly helmet. The Germans called it the *Salatschüssel* (salad bowl).

Astonishingly, at the outbreak of World War One, none of the fighting armies provided steel helmets for their troops. Soldiers of most nations went into battle wearing cloth, felt or leather headgear that offered no protection whatsoever from modern armaments and shrapnel of the day.

Lethal head wounds inflicted by modern artillery soon proliferated and led the French Army to introduce the first modern steel helmets in the summer of 1915. The first French helmets were bowl-shaped steel 'skullcaps' worn under the cloth caps. These basic helmets were soon replaced by the Model 1915 Adrian helmet, designed by August-Louis Adrian.

The British War Office similarly recognised a need for steel helmets; the War Office Invention Department was tasked to evaluate the French design

Troops of the Loyal North Lancashire Regiment showing off their new steel helmets (1916) (original image obtained from http://www.gwpda.org/photos/ greatwar.htm).

Robert 'Mouseman' Thompson's trademark carving on the altar rail in Kilburn Parish Church (picture taken by Dave Sumpner).

and concluded that it was not strong enough and too complex to be speedily manufactured. British industry generally was not prepared for an all-out war production effort, a shortcoming which also led to the shell shortage of 1915.

John Leopold Brodie (1873–1945), born in Riga, was an entrepreneur and inventor who had made a fortune in the gold and diamond mines of South Africa. His design, patented by him in August 1915, was better than the French helmet, constructed as it was in one piece that could be pressed from a single thick sheet of steel, giving it added strength and making it easy to mass manufacture.

British Army troops first took delivery of the Brodie helmets in September 1915, with 50 issued per battalion. Obviously, this was nowhere near enough, so they were designated as 'trench stores', to be kept in the front line and used by each unit that occupied the sector. By early 1916, about 250,000 had been manufactured: the first action in which the Brodie was worn by all ranks was the Battle of St Eloi Craters in the Ypres salient, in April. By the end of the war some 7.5 million Brodie helmets had been produced, including 1.5 million M1917 helmets, for use by American forces.

The helmet of choice for the German army was the *Stahlhelm* ('steel helmet') which began to replace the traditional boiled leather *Pickelhaube* ('spiked helmet') in 1916.

Further information at:

'Brodie's Steel Helmet, War Office Pattern,' *The Brodie Helmet and its derivatives,* 2015.

Chrystal, Paul, *In and Around Easingwold, the Passage of Time, Easingwold* (for Kilburn), 2012.

Tenner, Edward, *Our own devices: The past and future of body technology,* New York.

69

The gas mask

A gas alert practice in Hartlepool during World War One.

Much work in and around the World War One years was focussed on chemical warfare and mainly involved toxic, asphyxiating and blistering gases. The associated images, artworks, memoirs, novels, films and poetry are all etched in our minds. Who, once they have read it once, can forget?

'Drunk with fatigue; deaf even to the hoots
Of gas-shells dropping softly behind.
Gas! GAS! Quick, boys! – An ecstasy of fumbling
Fitting the clumsy helmets just in time,
But someone still was yelling out and stumbling

And flound'ring like a man in fire or lime. –
Dim through the misty panes and thick green light,
As under a green sea, I saw him drowning.
In all my dreams before my helpless sight,
He plunges at me, guttering, choking, drowning.'
– Wilfred Owen, from *Dulce et decorum est,* 1920

The threat of and actual use of gas and other airborne toxins during World War One led to a desperate need to provide some protection. Gases used included chlorine, mustard gas and phosgene. Early masks, including the Hypo Mask, were dipped in anti-gas chemicals such as sodium hyposulphite, washing soda, glycerine and water. Most gas masks were also respirators; the gas mask only protects the user from digesting, inhaling, and also contact through the eyes (many agents attack through eye contact). Most combined gas-mask filters will last around eight hours in a biological or chemical episode.

Early versions of the modern mask were developed by the Scottish chemist John Stenhouse in 1854 and the physicist John Tyndall in the 1870s. The 'Safety Hood and Smoke Protector' invented by Garrett Morgan in 1912 was patented in 1914: it was a rudimentary device consisting of a cotton hood with two hoses which hung down to the floor, allowing the wearer to breathe the safer air circulating there. In addition, moist sponges were inserted at the end of the hoses in order to better filter the air. This was later modified to include its own air supply, leading to gas masks as used in World War One.

World War One required mass production by all armies due to the explosion in chemical weapon use. The German army successfully used poison gas for the first time against Allied troops at the Second Battle of Ypres, Belgium, on 22 April 1915. Allied armies responded by issuing cotton wool wrapped in muslin followed by the Black Veil Respirator, invented by John Scott Haldane, which was a cotton pad soaked in an absorbent solution, secured over the mouth using black cotton veiling.

An improvement on the Black Veil Respirator was Cluny MacPherson's mask made of chemical-absorbing fabric which fitted over the entire head; it comprised a canvas hood and was fitted with a transparent mica eyepiece. Macpherson presented his idea to the British War Office Anti-Gas Department

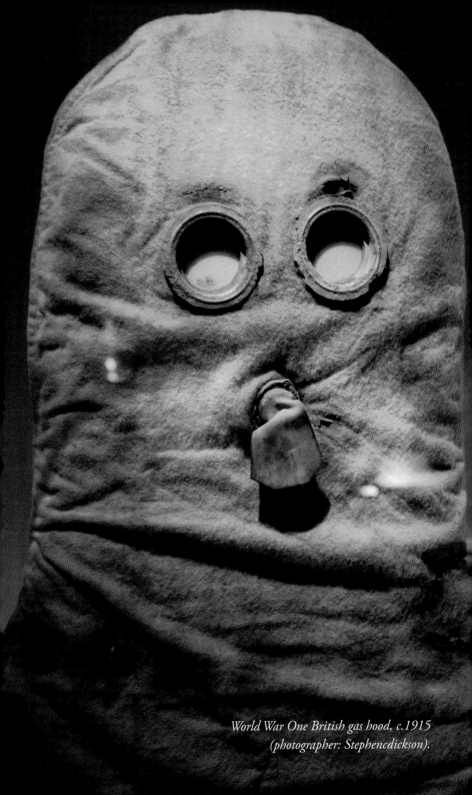

World War One British gas hood, c.1915
(photographer: Stephencdickson).

Two German soldiers and their mule wearing gas masks in World War One, 1916 (source: https://rarehistoricalphotos.com/).

on 10 May 1915; prototypes were developed soon after and the design was adopted by the British Army and introduced as the British Smoke Hood in June 1915. More sophisticated absorbent compounds were added later to counter other respiratory poison gases used, such as phosgene, diphosgene and chloropicrin. In 1915 the Large Box Respirator was developed: this canister gas mask was essentially a tin can containing the absorbent materials by a hose and began to be issued in February 1916. A compact version, the Small Box Respirator, was universal issue from August 1916.

For the first gas masks of World War One, wood charcoal was a good absorbent of poison gases, but in 1918 it was found that charcoals made from the shells and seeds of various fruits and nuts, such as coconuts, chestnuts, horse-chestnuts and peach stones, performed much better than wood charcoal. These waste materials were collected from the public in recycling programs to assist the war effort.

Dogs, horses, donkeys and mules all benefitted from specially adapted gas masks throughout the war.

Further information at:

Chrystal, Paul, *Biological Warfare and Bioterrorism: Weaponising Nature*, Barnsley, 2022.

Mayer-Maguire, Thomas, *British Military Respirators and Anti-Gas Equipment of the Two World Wars*, Crowood, 2015.

Wetherell, Anthony, 'Respiratory Protection,' in Marrs, Timothy (ed.), *Chemical Warfare Agents: Toxicology and Treatment*, , pp. 157–74, Wiley, New York, 2007.

70

The ambulance train

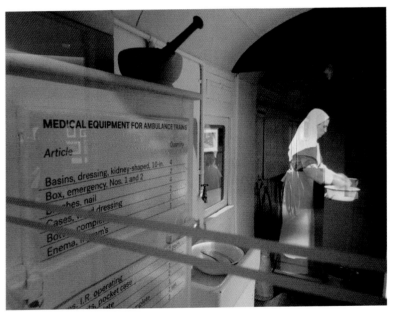

A reconstruction of an ambulance train carriage in the National Railway Museum, York.

I n the early days of the war the first British ambulance trains were rudimentary to say the least, consisting of French goods wagons with straw strewn on the floor. By August 1914 things started to improve when the Royal Army Medical Corps (RAMC) was given three loco-motives, some goods wagons and carriages. These were converted and divided into three 'trains' comprising wards, surgical dressing rooms and dispensaries and were designated British Ambulance Trains 1, 2 and 3 respectively. During 1915 they carried 461,844 patients.

One of the marvellous productions, which rolled out of York Carriage Works in the early 20ᵗʰ century, was the World War One ambulance train, made from existing carriage rolling stock; it comprised 16 carriages and was known as '*Continental Ambulance Train Number 37*'. It was 890ft 8in long and weighed 465 tons when loaded, without a locomotive. Painted khaki, it bore the Geneva Red Cross painted on the window panels and frames on each of the carriages on both sides. This mobile field station featured:

- A brake and infectious lying-down car carrying a guard and 18 patients in two self-contained sections, each with bathroom and own water supply to prevent cross-infection.
- A staff car occupied by four RAMC officers and four St John's Ambulance nurses – it featured two mess rooms, one for the officers, the other for the nurses; three bedrooms for the officers and two for the nurses, one of which contained a bunk bed – all bedrooms had a wardrobe, book shelf, table, chair, net racks and a steam heated radiator; the nurses' bathroom contained a shower and hot and cold running water; that of the officers was in the Kitchen Car, which accommodated 20 cases and three cooks who lived in a single room with a three-bed bunk.
- The Kitchen Car was fitted out with an Army Dixie Range Oven, copper boiler and two sinks; as well as the officers' lavatory, this coach also had a pantry for the officers and room for 20 sick officers.
- Eight Ward Cars constituted as one sick officer's lying down car, three ordinary lying down cars and four ordinary ward cars – each car contained 36 beds (or 'cots' as they were termed), arranged on each side of the carriage – for safety, each bed was fitted with two leather straps; the mattresses were filled with wood fibre, the two pillows with white flock; for extra comfort there was an ash tray and a bracket for a spitting cup; there was a lavatory at one end and a sink at the other end of the carriage.
- A Pharmacy Car comprising a dispensary and a treatment room with operating table, portable electric lamp and facilities for sterilisation, an office, a pantry for 'medical comforts', and a linen room.

- An Infectious Sitting Car with room for 56 sitting up cases and 14 lying down divided into seven compartments accessed by a side corridor. Three of these were 'specially fitted for Mental Cases' fitted with iron bars over the windows and swing doors separating it from the rest of the train, a lavatory at one end and a pantry at the other.
- A Kitchen and Mess room for three more cooks; the two mess rooms were for the use of NCOs and for 'other men'.
- A Personnel Car for 33 medical orderlies.
- A Brake and Stores Car with another guard and his living room, and three store rooms, a meat safe with electric fan and chopping board.

Overall, the Ambulance Car could carry between 445 and 659 patients and staff, depending on how it was configured. Obviously, good ventilation, light and infection control were paramount; there were electric fans everywhere with extra ones for gassed patients. To promote hygiene, round corners were used and the toilets, wash rooms and treatment room all had concrete floors. The kitchen was floored with lead, while other areas were covered in linoleum. A smooth ride was essential for the injured: to that end the train had bolster, side bearing and auxiliary springs on the four-wheeled bogies which ran on 'patent cushioned wheels'.

Two beds arranged for sitting up cases; this one was built in Swindon in 1915 at the GWR works.

RAMC conversions continued up to train number 11. It was decided that a number of 'standard' trains should be built by various British railway companies to War Office specifications. In November 1914, the first specially built medical train was sent out from the UK, designated number 12. No train was given number 13; the last to arrive in France was number 43. The UK Flour Millers' Association presented the Red Cross with two ambulance trains, specially built and equipped, constructed by Great Western and Eastern Railways. The movement of the injured from the trains soon became highly efficient: Boulogne was the main port for embarkation for the wounded and it is recorded that on one occasion it took only 19 minutes to detrain 123 casualties. The main disembarkation points in the UK were Dover and Southampton. Over the course of the war, Dover dealt with 1,260,506 casualties, unloaded 4,076 boats and loaded 7,781 ambulance trains. The patients were then sent by one of the 20 'home standard' ambulance trains, or by an emergency ambulance train, to a receiving station, where they were transferred to road vehicles, usually by volunteer first aiders, which took them to their destination hospital. There were 196 receiving stations in the UK, including one at York.

York's *Number 37* was one of 42 British Ambulance Trains pressed into service overseas, mainly on the Western Front, but three were also

'Guerre 1914' – this postcard was published in Paris; it shows RAMC soldiers having just unloaded casualties at a French port for on shipment to the UK.

deployed in Italy and one in Egypt. A further 22 saw action in the UK, while the American Expeditionary Force used 19 more conversions, including one being built in York, identical to *Number 37*, which was unfinished when the armistice was signed. Before it left for the front in 1917, *Number 37* was used as an exhibition which was attended by 36,404 people touring the train and raising £1,802, 5s for the Red Cross.

The tragedy and pathos of the circumstances surrounding the work of the ambulance trains is admirably captured by Phillip Gibbs of the *Daily Chronicle* after seeing an ambulance train near the village of Choques filling up with men suffering all manner of trauma. The first to board were thousands of '*lightly wounded*,' he said, who:

> 'crowded the carriages, leaned out of the windows with their bandaged heads and arms, shouting at friends they saw in the other crowds. The spirit of victory, and of lucky escape, uplifted these lads ... And now they were going home to bonny Scotland, with a wound that would take some time to heal.'

Next were stretcher cases 'from which no laughter came'. One young Londoner 'was so smashed about the face,' reported Gibbs, 'that only his eyes were uncovered between the bandages, and they were glazed with the first film of death.' Another young soldier 'had his jaw blown clean away. A splendid boy of the Black Watch, was but a living trunk,' he said, 'both his arms and legs were shattered and would be one of those who go about in boxes on wheels.' A group of blinded men 'were led to the train by wounded comrades, "groping", very quiet, thinking of a life of darkness ahead of them ...'

We get an equally harrowing picture of the practical difficulties of working on an ambulance train from the *Anonymous Diary of a Nursing Sister on the Western Front*:

> 'October 25 couldn't write last night: the only thing was to try and forget it all. It has been an absolute hell of a journey – there is no other word for it ... They were bleeding faster than we could cope with it; and the agony of getting them off the stretchers on to the

top bunks is a thing to forget. A train of cattle trucks came in from Rouen with all the wounded as they were picked up without a spot of dressing on any of their wounds, which were septic and full of straw and dirt. The matron, a medical officer, and some of them got hold of some dressings and went round doing what they could in the time, and others fed them. Then the [censored] – got their Amiens wounded into cattle trucks on mattresses, with Convent pillows, and has a twenty hours' journey with them in frightful smells and dirt … they'd been travelling already for two days.'

World War Two also saw the deployment of ambulance trains to transfer the wounded to the many temporary and permanent UK Military Hospitals. The train companies supplied and converted ambulance trains sanctioned by the Railway Executive Committee. There were about 30 or so ambulance trains in operation at the beginning of that war.

Further information at:
Chrystal, Paul, *York and its Railways 1839–1950*, Stenlake, 2015.
Parsons, Mark, *The Ambulance Trains and Hospital Barges of France – World War I*, Parsons Publishing Company, 2017.
Peart, Mike, *Trains of Hope*, Friends of the National Railway Museum, York, 2017.
Robinson, D.C., *Ambulance Trains, British Railways in the Great War*, 2019.

CHAPTER 12

BETWEEN THE WARS

71

The council house

1919

This evocative photo could have been taken in any number of council estates, certainly in the North East where this is: Stockton-on-Tees to be exact.

Note the younger children sidelined on the right (they certainly won't be going in to bat or bowl) and the mothers in the background (just in case). Did the girl at the back get a game? Langham Walk is still there; in December 2018 a three bedroomed terrace sold for £110,000.

Council or social housing is public housing built by local authorities; a council estate is a building complex usually containing a number of council houses and other amenities like schools and shops. Construction of council housing started in earnest from 1919 after the Housing Act 1919; by the 1980s there was much less council housing. By the late 1970s almost a third of UK households lived in what we now call social housing.

From the 1950s, for many 'working-class' people, this housing model provided their first experience of private indoor toilets, private bathrooms and hot running water, as well as gardens and electric lighting. For tenants in England and Wales it also usually offered the first experience of private garden space, usually front and rear. The Housing Acts of 1985 and 1988 facilitated the transfer of council housing to not-for-profit housing associations with access to private finance; they became the providers of most new public-sector housing. By 2003, 36.5 per cent of the social rented housing stock was held by housing associations.

In World War One Woolwich Borough Council led the way with the Well Hall Estate designed for workers at the munition factories at Woolwich Arsenal. The estate and the house were built to the garden-suburb philosophy: houses were all to be different. The estate received the royal seal of approval when, in March 1916, Queen Mary made an unannounced visit. After the war, as a result of Liberal prime minister David Lloyd George's Housing Act of 1919, the 'Addison Act' introduced subsidies for council-house building and aimed to provide 500,000 'homes fit for heroes' within a three-year period, although less than half of this target was ever met. The houses built comprised three-bedroom dwellings with parlour and scullery: larger properties also included a living room.

1950s semi-detached council houses on the Parkway, Seacroft, Leeds, in 2009 (photographer: Chemical Engineer).

The 31-storey Red Road estate in Glasgow were the tallest public-housing towers in Europe at the time of their construction. Like many 1960s British high-rises, they were condemned and have now been demolished (photographer: Nico Hogg).

The Housing Act 1930 energised slum clearance – the destruction of often insanitary houses in the inner cities that had been built before the Public Health Act 1875. This released land for housing and helped satisfy the need for smaller two-bedroomed houses and smaller three-bedroom properties to replace the two-up two-down houses that had been demolished. World War Two brought a halt to this, while enemy bombing significantly depleted housing stock.

By 1951 the Emergency Factory Made housing programme and its derivatives had created one million new council houses, resulting in 15 per cent of all the dwellings in Britain being state-owned, more than the proportion in the Soviet Union at that time.

The first residential tower block, 'The Lawn', was built in Harlow, Essex, in 1951; it survives as a Grade-II listed building. Tower blocks were seen as a quick-fix to cure the housing problems referred to above. They were cheaper to build too. Despite their earlier popularity, as the buildings themselves deteriorated, they were soon regarded as undesirable low-cost housing, which attracted rising crime levels. Tower blocks became even more offensive to many after the partial collapse of Ronan Point in East London in 1968. The shameful circumstances leading up to and following the Grenfell Tower tragedy in 2017 encapsulates the thinly disguised corruption, Government ineptitude and the unspeakably bad treatment of the surviving tenants. Poor maintenance of electrical equipment, fire doors, lethal cladding, and other safety features has resulted in widespread fire hazards here and in many other properties, with residents currently forced to pay part of the substantial cost of putting this right, though the problems are clearly due to inept and disinterested councils and housing associations, greedy landlords, poor maintenance and design errors.

Further information at:

Dunleavy, Patrick, *The politics of mass housing in Britain, 1945–1975*, Oxford, 1981.

Hanley, Lynsey, *Estates: an intimate history*, London, 2007.

Power, A., *Estates on the edge*, Basingstoke, 1997.

University of the West of England, *The History of Council Housing*.

72

Marie Stopes and her *Married Love or Love in Marriage*

1918

*Marie Stopes patented this Racial Cap, a form of diaphragm, in 1921.
It illustrates her racist and ableist conviction that selective breeding
would perfect the human race.*

Marie Charlotte Carmichael Stopes (1880–1958), author, eminent palaeobotanist and activist for eugenics and women's rights. She made significant contributions to plant palaeontology and coal classification, and was the first female academic on the faculty of the Victoria

University of Manchester from 1904 to 1910. With her second husband, Humphrey Verdon Roe, Stopes founded the first birth-control clinic in Britain. She edited *Birth Control News*, which offered explicit practical advice. Her sex manual *Married Love* (1918) was both controversial and influential, and brought the subject of birth control into the public narrative. Stopes publicly opposed abortion, arguing that the prevention of conception was all that was needed, though her actions in private were often at odds with what she said in public.

Her espousal of eugenics led her 'to furnish security from conception to those who are racially diseased'. In a bid to distance itself from this, in 2020 Marie Stopes International changed its name to MSI Reproductive Choices.

Despite rejections from a number of publishers because they considered it too controversial, her *Married Love* was published in March 1918 by Fifield & Co with financial help from Humphrey Verdon Roe – Stopes's future second husband. The book was an overnight success, going into five editions in the first year, and elevating Stopes to national celebrity status. The book opens by stating that 'More than ever to-day are happy homes needed. It is my hope that this book may serve the State by adding to their number. Its object is to increase the joys of marriage, and to show how much sorrow may be avoided.' The preface states that it is a book geared to teaching married couples how to have a happy marriage, including 'great sex' – and it was thus offering a service to 'the State' by reducing the number of people affected by failed marriages.

It was the first book to say that a women's sexual desire coincides with ovulation and the period just before menstruation. The book argued that marriage should be an equal relationship between partners. Although officially derided in the UK, the book went through 19 editions and sales of almost 750,000 copies by 1931.

The US Customs Service banned the book as obscene until 6 April 1931, when Judge John M. Woolsey overturned that decision. Woolsey was the same judge who in 1933 would lift the ban on James Joyce's *Ulysses*.

In 1935 a survey of American academics reported that *Married Love* was one of the 25 most influential books of the previous 50 years, beating *Relativity* by Albert Einstein, *Interpretation of Dreams* by Sigmund Freud, *Mein Kampf* by Adolf Hitler and *The Economic Consequences of the Peace* by John Maynard Keynes.

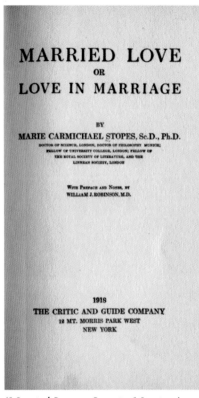

MARRIED LOVE
OR
LOVE IN MARRIAGE

BY
MARIE CARMICHAEL STOPES, Sc.D., Ph.D.
DOCTOR OF SCIENCE, LONDON; DOCTOR OF PHILOSOPHY MUNICH;
FELLOW OF UNIVERSITY COLLEGE, LONDON; FELLOW OF
THE ROYAL SOCIETY OF LITERATURE, AND THE
LINNEAN SOCIETY, LONDON

WITH PREFACE AND NOTES, BY
WILLIAM J. ROBINSON, M.D.

1918
THE CRITIC AND GUIDE COMPANY
12 MT. MORRIS PARK WEST
NEW YORK

'Married Love or Love in Marriage'.

The success of *Married Love* led to a follow-up; the already written *Wise Parenthood: a Book for Married People*, a manual on birth control published later in 1919. *Wise Parenthood* was aimed at married women, middle-class married women, that is, as Stopes believed birth control to be necessary for married couples to help protect mothers against the exhaustion of serial childbearing. Although many were scandalised by Stopes's advocacy of birth control, *Wise Parenthood* went to ten editions.

The following year, Stopes published *A Letter to Working Mothers* on how to have healthy children and avoid weakening pregnancies, a condensed version *of Wise Parenthood* aimed at the poor – a 16-page pamphlet to be distributed free of charge. Until now Stopes had shown little interest in, or respect for, the working-class woman. The aim of *the Letter* was to redress her bias. Stopes naively sent a Mrs E. B. Mayne to distribute the *Letter to Working Mothers* in the slums of East London, approaching 20 families a day, but after several months it soon became clear that the working class was 'mistrustful of well-intentioned meddlers'.

Aged 38, on 16 July 1919, Stopes – pregnant and a month overdue – went into a nursing home where she and her doctors clashed over the method of birth – she was refused permission to give birth on her knees. The child was stillborn, with the doctors suggesting it was due to Stopes having syphilis, a fabrication later disproved on examination. Stopes was furious and claimed her baby had been murdered.

Marie Stopes's ill-judged *Letter* was followed by more tactlessness when she sent a letter to the Anglican bishops which began 'My Lords, I speak to you in the name of God. You are his priests. I am his prophet. I speak to you of the mysteries of man and woman.' This was followed in 1922 with *A New Gospel to All Peoples* which the bishops snubbed and rejected her 'deliberate cultivation of sexual union' and 'indecent literature, suggestive plays and films [and] the open or secret sale of contraceptives'. The Catholic Church's reaction was even more outraged, marking the start of a conflict that lasted the rest of Stopes's life.

Stopes resigned her lectureship at University College London at the end of 1920 to concentrate on the clinic she planned to open for poor mothers in London. She founded the Society for Constructive Birth Control and Racial Progress, a support organisation for the clinic, whose letterheads paraded a list of prominent supporters which included the militant suffragette Lady Constance Lytton, Vera Brittain, Emily Pethick-Lawrence (former Treasurer of the Women's Social and Political Union), and the Rev Maude Royden (Women's Suffrage Societies); later supporters included John Maynard Keynes. Three months later, she and Roe opened the Mothers' Clinic at 61 Marlborough Road, Holloway, North London, on 17 March 1921. The clinic was run by midwives and supported by visiting doctors. It offered mothers birth-control advice, taught them birth-control methods and dispensed Stopes's own 'Pro-Race' (and later the 'Racial') cervical caps.

The free clinic was open to all married women who sought education about reproductive health. Stopes, as noted, opposed abortion; she was trying to discover alternatives for families and increase knowledge about birth control and the reproductive system. Options included the cervical cap – which was the most popular – *coitus interruptus*, and spermicides based on soap and oil. Stopes rediscovered the use of olive oil-soaked sponges as an alternative birth control – using olive oil as a spermicide dates back to Greek and Roman times. Her techniques proved very effective: she tested many of her contraceptives on patients at her clinics.

In 1925 the Mothers' Clinic moved to central London. Stopes gradually built up a small network of clinics across Britain: she opened clinics in Leeds and Aberdeen in 1934; Belfast in 1936; Cardiff in 1937 and Swansea in 1943.

The clinics continued to operate after Stopes's death, but by the early 1970s they were in financial difficulty and in 1975 they went into voluntary receivership. Marie Stopes International was established a year later as an international non-governmental organisation working on sexual and reproductive health. The global partnership took over responsibility for the main clinic, and in 1978 it began its work overseas in New Delhi. Since then the organisation has grown steadily; in 2019, it was operating in 37 countries, had 452 clinics and offices in London, Brussels, Melbourne and the USA.

Stopes and abortion

Publicly, Stopes was ardently opposed to abortion and, during her lifetime, abortion was not offered in her clinics. She hunted down abortion providers and worked with the police and the courts to prosecute them. It was Stopes's conviction that contraceptives were the method of choice by which families should voluntarily limit their number of offspring. Nurses at Stopes's were required to sign a declaration not to 'impart any information or lend any assistance whatsoever to any person calculated to lead to the destruction in utero of the products of conception'.

'Attempted revolution in Dublin' cartoon in the Evening Standard, 6 December 1930. A cartoon by David Low showing, in the Irish Free State, a man arrested, found in possession of Marie Stopes's literature on birth control – followed by his wife and many children (Wellcome Images).

However, in private there was a disconnect: in a 1919 letter she outlined a method of abortion to an unidentified correspondent and she 'was even prepared in some cases to advocate abortion, or, as she preferred to put it, the evacuation of the uterus'. In *Wise Parenthood* she had promoted the 'Gold Pin' or 'Spring', which was a 'method [that] could be described as an abortifacient'.

Stopes and eugenics

In her 1992 biography of Stopes, June Rose claimed 'Marie was an elitist, an idealist, interested in creating a society in which only the best and beautiful should survive,' a view echoed by Richard A. Soloway in the 1996 Galton Lecture:

> 'If Stopes's general interest in birth control was a logical consequence of her romantic preoccupation with compatible sexuality within blissful marriage, her particular efforts to provide birth control for the poor had far more to do with her eugenic concerns about the impending "racial darkness" that the adoption of contraception promised to illuminate.'

Stopes was by no means alone in these odious beliefs: her enthusiasm for eugenics was consistent with a number of intellectuals and public figures of the time, on the right and the left: Havelock Ellis, Cyril Burt and George Bernard Shaw, for example. She joined the Eugenics Education Society in 1912 and became a life fellow in 1921, although she was shunned by the society's inner circle.

The objects of her Society For Constructive Birth Control and Racial Progress exhibited eugenic aims, summarised as follows:

> 'In short, we are profoundly and fundamentally a pro-baby organisation, in favour of producing the largest possible number of healthy, happy children without detriment to the mother, and with the minimum wastage of infants by premature deaths. In this connection our motto has been "Babies in the right place", and it is just as much the aim of Constructive Birth Control to secure conception to those married people who are healthy, childless and desire children, as it is to furnish security from conception to those who are racially diseased, already overburdened with children, or in any specific way unfitted for parenthood.'

Stopes advocated the compulsory sterilisation of those considered unfit for parenthood in 1918 and in 1920.

In her 1920 book *Radiant Motherhood: A Book for Those Who are Creating the Future* Stopes discussed race and said that the 'one central reform' was 'The power of the mother, consciously exerted in the voluntary procreation and joyous bearing of her children, is the greatest power in the world.' But she added that two 'main dangers' stood in the way. The first of these was ignorance and the second was the:

'inborn incapacity which lies in the vast and ever-increasing stock of degenerate, feeble-minded and unbalanced who are now in our midst and who devastate social customs. These populate most rapidly and tend proportionately to increase and these are like the parasite upon the healthy tree sapping its vitality.'

Stopes then stated that 'a few quite simple acts of Parliament' could deal with 'this prolific depravity' through sterilisation by x-rays and assured the reader that:

'When Bills are passed to ensure the sterility of the hopelessly rotten and racially diseased, and to provide for the education of the child-bearing woman so that she spaces her children healthily, our race will rapidly quell the stream of the depraved, hopeless and wretched lives which are at present increasing in proportion in our midst.'

In November 1922, on the eve of the general election, she sent a questionnaire to parliamentary candidates asking that they sign a declaration that:

'I agree that the present position of breeding chiefly from the C3 population and burdening and discouraging the A1 is nationally deplorable, and if I am elected to Parliament I will press the Ministry of Health to give such scientific information through the Ante-natal Clinics, Welfare Centres and other institutions in its control as will curtail the C3 and increase the A1.'

She received 150 replies.

In July 1931 the Women's Co-operative Guild at their conference passed a resolution advocating compulsory sterilisation for the mentally or physically unfit. In 1934, in an interview published in the *Australian Women's Weekly*, Stopes revealed her views on mixed-race marriages: she advised readers against them and believed that all half-castes should be sterilised at birth … 'thus painlessly and in no way interfering with the individual's life, the unhappy fate of he who is neither black nor white is prevented from being passed on to yet unborn babes.' On her death in 1958, Stopes bequeathed her clinics to the Eugenics Society.

Further information at:

Brand, Pauline, *Birth Control Nursing in the Marie Stopes Mothers' Clinics 1921–1931*, Leicester.

Cohen, Deborah A., 'Private Lives in Public Spaces: Marie Stopes, the Mothers' Clinics and the Practice of Contraception,' *History Workshop*, 35, pp. 95–116, 1993.

Davey, C., 'Birth control in Britain during the interwar years: evidence from the Stopes correspondence,' *Journal of Family History*, 13 (3), pp. 329–45, 1988.

Debenham, Clare, *Marie Stopes' Sexual Revolution and the Birth Control Movement*, London, 2018.

Fisher, Kate, 'Contrasting cultures of contraception: birth control clinics and the working-classes in Britain between the wars,' *Clio Medica*, 66, pp. 141–57, 2002.

Geppert, A. C. T. , 'Divine sex, happy marriage, regenerated nation: Marie Stopes's marital manual Married Love and the making of a best-seller, 1918–1955,' *Journal of the History of Sexuality*, 8 (3), pp. 389–433, 1998.

Hall, Ruth, *Passionate Crusader*, Harcourt, Brace, Jovanovich, 1977.

Maude, Aylmer, *Marie Stopes: Her Work and Play*, John Bale & Sons and Danielsson, 1933.

Neushul, Peter, 'Marie C. Stopes and the Popularization of Birth Control Technology,' *Technology and Culture*, 39 (2), pp. 245–72, 1998.

Rose, June, *Marie Stopes and the Sexual Revolution*, London, 1992.

Searle, G.R., *Eugenics and Politics in Britain 1900–1914*, Leiden, 1976.

Soloway, Richard, *Marie Stopes Eugenics and the English Birth Control Movement*, London, The Galton Institute, 1997.

Sutherland, Mark H., *Exterminating Poverty: The true story of the eugenic plan to get rid of the poor, and the Scottish doctor who fought against it*, 2020.

73

The K6 telephone box

1936

The K6, made of cast iron, was designed by Sir Giles Gilbert Scott (1880–1960), who was also responsible for designing Battersea Power Station, Bankside Power Station, now the Tate Modern, and Liverpool's Anglican Cathedral. In 2006, the K2 telephone box was voted one of Britain's top-10 design icons, which included Concorde, the Mini, Supermarine Spitfire, the London tube map, World Wide Web and the AEC Routemaster bus.

The first standard public telephone kiosk was introduced in 1921 by the United Kingdom Post Office. It was made from concrete and was designated K1 (Kiosk No.1). By then the Post Office had taken over most of the country's telephone network. Some local authorities held out and refused to give permission for the K1: Eastbourne Corporation insisted that the kiosks could only be installed if they had thatched roofs. As at 2021, there are only 14 K1 boxes surviving in the UK, including seven that are in museums and museum collections. A further two remain in the Republic of Ireland. Seven of the UK's 14 have been listed Grade II by Historic England, including one in Trinity Market in Kingston-upon-Hull, and another in Bembridge High Street, Isle of Wight.

Opposite: Classic red K2 telephone box and London double-decker bus in front of the Queen Elizabeth Tower and Big Ben. The bus is London United VLE45 (reg. PO54 OOG), (photographer: wiki+spam@eindruckschinderdomain.de Permission cc-by-sa-2.5).

In 1936 the K6 (kiosk number 6) was designed and produced to commemorate the Silver Jubilee of George V and is sometimes known as the 'Jubilee' kiosk. It was the first red telephone kiosk to be extensively used outside London, with many thousands sited in virtually every village, town and city, replacing most of the existing kiosks and establishing thousands of new sites. In 1935 there were 19,000 public telephones in the UK: by 1940, thanks to the popularity of K6, there were 35,000. The design was again by Scott, and was essentially a smaller and more streamlined version of the K2, intended to be produced at a considerably cheaper cost, and to take up less pavement space. Two K6 kiosks were installed in France during 1995 for the 50th anniversary of the 1944 D-Day landings.

Under-used red telephone boxes can be adopted by parish councils in England for other uses. A kiosk may be used for any legal purpose other than telephony; variants include defibrillator stations and libraries or book exchanges. In 2009 Settle in North Yorkshire established the Gallery on the Green in a K6. The Gallery ('possibly the smallest public art gallery in the world) has featured a range of exhibitions; its most famous exhibitor was Brian May, with his stereoscopic photography show 'A Village Lost and Found'.

Why is it cream and not red like all the others? Until 2007 Hull was the only place in the UK to have maintained an independent, municipal telephone network provider operating under the name of Hull Telephone Department – now it is privatised as KCOM, once known as Kingston

Communications, founded in 1902. KCOM have retained 125 or so K6s which are still in use today; the company allocated approximately 1,000 for sale to the public. So, in Hull you will see distinctive cream phone boxes and its residents used to get the White Pages telephone directory, and 'Colour Pages' for business numbers, as opposed to the 'Yellow Pages'.

Unlike the red version, Hull's boxes do not feature the imperial crown. In 2012, a K6 in Market Place was painted gold to honour Hull Olympic medallist

K1 with dog.

A phone box as a library in Whitwell, Isle of Wight, in June 2017 (photographer: Mypix).   *A cream telephone K6 box in Hull.*

Luke Campbell. Several K6 kiosks in Hull are now officially listed as historic buildings of architectural importance. The distinctive cream telephone boxes are highly symbolic locally, communicating to visitors the proud independence that characterises the city and its citizens.

Further information at:

Chrystal, Paul, *Hull in 50 Buildings*, Stroud, 2017.

Johannessen, Neil (ed.), *Ring up Britain: the early years of the telephone in the United Kingdom*, London, 1991.

Johannessen, Neil, *Telephone Boxes* (2nd ed.), Princes Risborough: Shire, 1999.

Stamp, Gavin, *Telephone Boxes*, London, 1989.

www.galleryonthegreen.org.uk

K6 Gallery on the green in mosaic.

74

Percy Shaw's cat's eyes

1934

A cat's eye, or a Lightdome road stud (photographer: ELIOT2000)

A cat's eye, or road stud, is a retroreflective safety device used in road marking and was the first of a range of raised pavement markers. It immediately made an inestimable contribution to road safety. The design originated in the UK in 1934 and today enjoys global usage. The very first examples comprised two pairs of retroreflectors set into a white rubber dome, mounted in a cast-iron housing. This marks the centre of the road, with one pair of cat's eyes showing in each direction. A single-ended form has become widely used in other colours at road margins and as lane dividers. Cat's eyes are particularly valuable in fog and are largely resistant to damage from snow ploughs.

A key feature of the cat's eye is the flexible rubber dome which is occasionally deformed by the passage of traffic. A fixed rubber wiper cleans the surface of the reflectors as they sink below the surface of the road – the base tends to hold water after a shower of rain, making this process even more efficient. The rubber dome is protected from impact damage by metal 'kerbs' – which also give tactile (physical bumping) and audible feedback (bumping sounds) for 'wandering drivers'.

Percy Shaw of Boothtown, Halifax, is the man we need to thank for inventing cat's eyes. How did it happen? Percy realised that when the tramlines were removed in nearby Ambler Thorn, he had been habitually using the polished steel rails to navigate at night. The name 'cat's eye' obviously comes from Shaw's inspiration for the device: the eyeshine reflecting from the eyes of a cat. In 1934 he patented his invention and in March 1935 founded Reflecting Roadstuds Ltd in Halifax to manufacture the items; the name 'Catseye' is their trademark. As it happened, the retroreflecting lens had been invented six years earlier for use in advertising signs by Richard Hollins Murray, an accountant from Herefordshire, and, as Shaw acknowledged, it had contributed to his idea.

World War Two blackouts and the shuttered car headlights then in use demonstrated the value of Shaw's invention and helped promote their mass use in the UK. In 2006, Catseye was voted one of Britain's top-10 design icons in the Great British Design Quest organised by the BBC and the Design Museum, a list which, as we have seen, included Concorde, Mini, Supermarine Spitfire, K2 telephone box, World Wide Web and the AEC Routemaster bus.

In the United Kingdom, different colours of cat's eyes are used to denote different situations:

- White is used to indicate the centre line of a single carriageway road or the lane markings of a dual carriageway.
- Red and amber cat's eyes denote lines that should not be crossed. Red is used for the left side of a dual carriageway, while amber is used for the right side of a dual carriageway.
- Green indicates a line that may be crossed, such as a slip road or lay-by.

The inspiration behind Percy's invention.

Solar-powered cat's eyes are called solar road studs and display a red or amber LED to traffic; they have been introduced on roads regarded as particularly dangerous at various locations. However, the devices, which flash at an almost imperceptibly fast rate of 100 times a second, were found to potentially cause epileptic fits so the Highways Agency suspended the programme until 2015, when LED cat's eyes began to be installed along newly re-paved sections of the A1 and A1(M) in County Durham and Tyne and Wear.

Flashing blue LED cat's eyes alert the driver to potential ice on the road when a low enough temperature, provisionally set at 3 °C (37 °F), is reached. Proposed enhancements in 2013 were to change the standard white light to amber for four seconds after the passing of a vehicle, or red if the following vehicle is too close or traffic ahead is stationary.

Further information at:
'Chapter 5 - Road Markings,' *Traffic Signs Manual*, London: The Stationery Office, 2018.

75

Leslie Hore-Belisha
and his beacons

1934

Belisha beacons everywhere.

A Belisha beacon can be defined as an orange ball containing a flashing light, mounted on a striped post on the pavement at each end of a zebra crossing. The beacons got their name from Leslie Hore-Belisha (1893–1957), the Minister of Transport who, in 1934, to make them safer, added beacons to pedestrian crossings, marked by large metal studs in the road surface. These crossings were later painted with black and white stripes and became known as zebra crossings. Legally, pedestrians have priority over wheeled traffic on zebra crossings.

Since 1997 the number of zebra crossings and Belisha beacons has declined in the northern counties of England, being replaced by pelican crossings or puffin crossings, with pedestrian-controlled traffic signals. A waiting pedestrian can stop vehicular traffic by pressing a button and waiting for the pedestrian signal of a red man to change to green. The green man may be accompanied by a green bicycle to indicate that the crossing is designated for pedestrians and cyclists; continuing the bird-name theme, this type of crossing is called a toucan crossing, as in 'two can' cross. Another variation is the pegasus crossing where the pedestrian is accompanied by a green horse to indicate that the crossing is designated for pedestrians and horses; for example, at Hyde Park Corner, London.

The most photographed Belisha beacon ever – although later cropped from the famous Abbey Road album cover, here is one of them in a photo of the Beatles getting ready for that historic walk across the most famous zebra crossing in the world on 8 August 1969.

The beacons and crossing as a major post-Beatles tourist attraction; Abbey Road studios is in the background to the right. English Heritage listed the crossing on 21 December 2010.

76

The Penguin paperback

1935

A random selection of early-ish Penguin paperbacks.

One day in In 1934, on his way back to London after visiting his friend Agatha Christie, Bodley Head publisher Allen Lane stopped by the station bookstall at Exeter St David's. He was not impressed by what he saw on the shelves: all the books on sale were of a poor production quality, trashy and over-priced. What was needed, he realised, were good books at a price the man and women in the street (or on the train) could afford. He said that he 'believed in the existence … of a vast reading public for intelligent books at a low price, and staked everything on it.' Lane went back to Bodley Head and proposed a new imprint to publish just that. Bodley Head was not keen to invest in his project, so Lane used his own capital. He called his new house Penguin, on the suggestion of a secretary, and sent 21-year-old office junior Edward Young to London Zoo to sketch the bird. He then acquired the rights to ten reprints of serious literary titles and, anticipating the reaction of sniffy, conservative booksellers, went knocking on non-bookshop doors. When Woolworth's placed an order for 63,500 assorted copies, Lane realised he had a viable business model with 'pile 'em high' as the axiom. Even so, Penguin had to sell 17,000 copies of each book just to break even.

Within a year, Penguin Books was up and running, 'creating a paperback revolution that democratised quality literature and would fundamentally change the publishing world forever'. And so Penguin became the originator of the mass-market paperback.

The books cost 6d (same price as a pack of ten cigarettes) and were colour-coded: orange for fiction, blue for biography and green for crime. The first ten included *The Mysterious Affair at Styles* by Agatha Christie, *A Farewell to Arms* by Ernest Hemingway and *The Unpleasantness at the Bellona Club* by Dorothy Sayers, and they went down a storm; after just one year in existence, Penguin had sold over three million copies. Branding and modern graphic design were all important: the colour coded covers featured simple, clean fonts and that instantly recognisable bird. The look helped gain headlines. J. B. Priestley enthused about the 'perfect marvels of beauty and cheapness'.

Allen Lane then, in 1937, launched a non-fiction imprint after overhearing someone at a King's Cross station bookstall mixing up his birds and asking for 'one of those Pelican books'. The first Pelican book was George Bernard Shaw's *The Intelligent Woman's Guide to Socialism, Capitalism, Sovietism and Fascism,* followed by titles including *A Short History of the World* by H.G. Wells. It also published left-leaning topical Penguin Specials such as *Why Britain Is at War* and *What Hitler Wants* that sold extremely well. Penguin thus played a role in British politics as well as in literature and design, and its left-leaning stance was emblematic of Britain's post-war society. After the Labour Party came to office in 1945, they declared that the accessibility of left-leaning reading during the war helped his party succeed: 'After the WEA [Workers' Educational Association] it was Lane and his Penguins which did most to get us into office at the end of the war.'

In 1940 Lane released his first four Puffin Picture Books in a bid to help evacuated city children adjust to life in the country. Titles such as *War on*

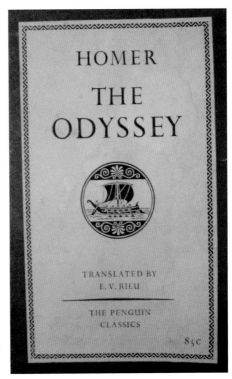

An early edition of Rieu's
The Odyssey by Homer.

Land were so successful that he opened the imprint up to fiction, publishing such children's classics as *Orlando the Marmalade Cat*, the protagonist of 19 books between 1941 and 1972.

1942 saw the establishment of the Penguin Armed Forces Book Club to entertain and educate British troops at home and abroad and in POW camps. In addition to their paper allocation, in 1941 Penguin secured a deal with the War Office and received 60 tons of paper a month from Paper Supply in return for ten titles a month in runs of 75,000 at 5d. Bestselling manuals such as *Keeping Poultry and Rabbits on Scraps* and *Aircraft Recognition* had obvious practical value in the days of Land Girls, rationing and in military surveillance. During the war Penguin published some 600 titles and started 19 new series, catering for an enormous increase in the demand for books.

1946 was the year in which Lane launched Penguin Classics with Homer's *The Odyssey*, translated by E.V. Rieu, who became the first editor of the Penguin Classics list. In 1959–60 Penguin Books faced trial (R v Penguin Books Ltd) under the Obscene Publications Act for publishing D.H. Lawrence's *Lady Chatterley's Lover*. Victory in court helped drive the sale of at least 3.5 million copies and heralded the end to the censorship of books in the UK, although censorship of the written word was only finally defeated after the Inside Linda Lovelace trial of 1978. The second edition of *Lady Chatterley*, published by Penguin in 1961, contained a publisher's dedication to the 12 jurors – three women and nine men – who returned a 'not guilty' verdict against Penguin and thus made Lawrence's novel available to the British public for the first time.

The Puffin Book Club was set up by Kaye Webb, which grew to become a major British institution with 200,000 members. In 2008 Penguin published its first ebooks; titles included *A Room of One's Own*, *King Lear* and *Utopia*.

Further information at:

Baines, Phil, *Puffin by Design: 70 years of imagination 1940–2010*, London, 2010.
Hare, Steve, *Penguin Portrait: Allen Lane and the Penguin Editors, 1935–1970*, London, 1995.
Holland, S., *Mushroom Jungle: A History of Postwar Paperback Publishing*, Westbury, 1993.
Morpurgo, J. E., *Allen Lane: King Penguin*, London, 1979.
Pearson, J. , *Penguins March On: Books for the Forces During World War II*, Penguin Collector's Society, London, 1996.

77

The BBC microphone

1934

Produced between 1934 and 1959, the BBC-Marconi Type A microphone has been described as an iconic symbol of the BBC alongside the channel's most famous emblem, the rotating globe, which was introduced in 1963. This model was designed in 1944, and formally called the AXBT – the first high-quality microphone for studio use.

The BBC, like the NHS in the next decade, is an invaluable British institution. However, both organisations seem to be perpetually under attack and under threat, yet both, while by no means perfect, manifestly deliver much more good than anything mediocre or bad. The BBC has done, and continues to do, more for education at home and abroad than any other organisation on the globe, and although it can never be wholly independent of the Government of the day, which is responsible for the public funding it receives and consequently necessitates a degree of filtering in its political reporting, it has often provided a welcome, lone voice around the world in times of strife. The World Service brings us an exemplary and enduring suite of programming, while BBC programmes such as *In Our Time, Desert Island Discs* and *The Today Programme* consistently provide journalism, the arts, education and entertainment of the first order. The BBC World Service was launched in 1932 as the BBC Empire Service; it broadcasts in 28 languages and provides comprehensive TV, radio, and online services in Arabic and Persian.

The BBC is the world's oldest national broadcaster, and the largest broadcaster in the world by number of employees, employing over 22,000 staff in total, of whom approximately 19,000 are in public-sector broadcasting. From its very beginnings, throughout World War Two when its broadcasts helped to unite the nation, to the popularisation of television in the post-World War Two era and the internet in the late 20th and early 21st centuries, the BBC has played a crucial and influential role in British life and culture. Sometimes, as with the NHS, we just don't know when we are well off. Some key dates in the history of BBC TV:

- The British Broadcasting Company, to give the BBC its original name, was formed on 18 October 1922 by a consortium of leading wireless manufacturers including Marconi.
- Daily broadcasting began in Marconi's London studio, 2LO, in the Strand, on 14 November 1922. John Reith, a 33-year-old Scottish engineer, was appointed General Manager of the BBC at the end of 1922. He is reported as confessing, 'I hadn't the remotest idea as to what broadcasting was.' He had a very blank slate.
- There were no rules, protocols, precedent or mission statement or established purpose to rescue him. So, he rose to the challenge and began innovating, experimenting and organising, and with the help of his newly appointed chief engineer, Peter Eckersley, the service grew. Reith focussed on delivering somewhat high-level programmes for listeners right across Britain.
- Savoy Hill, off the Strand, was the BBC's first home; it opened for medical use in 1889 then became the home of the Institute of Electrical Engineers, which offered office space to the BBC in 1923.

- Early contributors included HG Wells and George Bernard Shaw, who sipped whisky and soda as they relaxed in something approximating to a gentlemen's club. Here, radio drama flourished, weather forecasts and Big Ben chimes were introduced, and listeners could follow the cricket.
- The first edition of *The Radio Times* listed the meagre programmes on offer.
- It also diversified into offering advice for radio enthusiasts, and numerous advertisements placed by the burgeoning radio industry, offering cutting-edge radio receiving technology. Soon it was one of the world's most popular listing magazines.
- In February 1924 those once heard never forgotten pips were first broadcast: the six electronically generated 'pips' to indicate the Greenwich Time Signal (GTS) were invented by the Astronomer Royal Sir Frank Watson Dyson, and the Director General of the BBC John Reith. Their purpose was to mark the precise start of every hour on BBC radio. Today the GTS is still heard on BBC Radio 4, and other BBC networks.
- In January 1927 the British Broadcasting Corporation was established by Royal Charter. The Charter defined the BBC's objectives, powers and obligations.

The first issue of Radio Times in September 1923 –
'The official organ of the BBC'.

- In November 1929, using BBC frequencies, John Logie Baird broadcast some of his first experimental television broadcasts from studios near Covent Garden. Pictures were in black and white, created by mechanical means using a scanning disc, consisting of just 30 lines of definition.
- By May 1932 the BBC had outgrown its original studios at Savoy Hill and had to find a new home, so they commissioned a purpose-built centre which still stands today and operates from the Strand.
- In December 1932 George V was the first British monarch to broadcast to the nation on radio. This epochal moment was used to inaugurate the BBC Empire Service, forerunner of today's BBC World Service; the King's voice was heard for the first time by millions of his subjects simultaneously.
- In November 1936 the BBC Television Service opened, making the BBC the first broadcaster in the world to provide a regular 'high definition' television service.
- In May 1937 the BBC's first television outside broadcast took place at the Coronation of King George VI.
- January 1938 saw the first foreign language broadcast – it was in Arabic. Announcer Ahmad Kamal Sourour Effendi was recruited from the Egyptian radio service. His appointment was highly popular as Effendi was one of the most respected presenters in the Arab world.
- Despite, or maybe because of, the war, the 40s saw huge strides in broadcasting and programme making such as live reporting from battle scenes, and the provision of propaganda news to the free world.
- January 1942 saw the introduction of *Desert Island Discs*. It was devised by Roy Plomley, who presented the first edition on 29 January 1942. It was recorded two days earlier with comedian Vic Oliver, in a bomb-damaged Maida Vale Studios. Early programmes were scripted, to comply with wartime censorship.
- October 1946 saw the arrival of *Woman's Hour,* the first radio programme devoted to women. Never afraid to tell it as it is, the programme very quickly won a reputation for tackling difficult issues facing women in a largely man's world (including the BBC). Politics, women's rights and inequality featured prominently. By

1947 BBC the (male) managers panicked at the prospect of the menopause and other aspects of gynaecology and obstetrics being discussed. Stereotypical topics such as 'keeping house', and childcare featured increasingly rarely after the 1960s. Norman Collins was the creator of *Woman's Hour*.

- October 1946 saw the start of a pioneering children's television service; one of its earliest successes was *Muffin The Mule*, a puppet accompanied on the piano by Annette Mills. It lasted for nine years.
- January 1948, and now for the news, usually voiced by John Snagge, *BBC Newsreel* covered the day's events as a filmed sequence of short reports.
- London 1948 saw the first televised Olympic Games; this was the BBC's most technically advanced outside broadcast. By 1948 about 100,000 UK households had a television, yet 68.5 hours of live Olympic coverage was broadcast by the BBC. Most viewers watched on screens measuring just under 10in x 8in.
- July 1949 saw the start of the weather forecast. Launched just before the start of World War Two then paused, regular TV weather forecasts were finally revived. These early forecasts comprised charts with a disembodied voice delivering the bulletin. The big leap forward came in January 1954 when a male Met officer interpreted the map in vision. George Cowling was the BBC's first 'weatherman'.
- May 1950, and over to Ambridge and *The Archers*, the world's longest-running soap opera. It was first broadcast as a trial programme on the Midlands Home Service to promote good agricultural practice in the post-war years of austerity, rationing and self-sufficiency. When the trial was concluded on 2 June, it was rolled out across the UK and became a national institution.
- June 1953 saw the broadcast of the Coronation of Queen Elizabeth II:

> 'So today The Queen will ascend the steps of her throne … in the sight today of a great multitude of people— so said Richard Dimbleby in his Coronation commentary.'

This was the first time a coronation moment was seen live; it totally transformed the history and future of television, massively boosting the sale of black-and-white television sets. Over 20 million people across Europe watched the event.

- In April 1958 the Radiophonic Workshop was established; based in Room 13 of Maida Vale studios, it used a creative and bizarre mix of objects to create original and innovative electronic sounds. Undoubtedly the most famous is the *Doctor Who* theme music, which became one of the most significant influences on 20th-century electronic music.

- In October 1958 *Blue Peter* embarked on a 63-year run, and is still counting: fearless and peerless presenters, disarming and chaotic pets and animals, studio 'makes' and charity appeals, the programme has touched, informed and enriched the lives of generations of younger viewers.

- In 2022 the BBC celebrates 100 years of broadcasting.

Some BBC Radio facts:

- The first song to appear on BBC Radio 1 was by The Move – the tune was 'Flowers in the Rain' on Radio 1's breakfast Show hosted by Tony Blackburn. Meanwhile over on Radio 2, the first song to be played was Julie Andrews singing 'The Sound of Music'.

- In the very early days, Radio 1 and 2 weather presenter Rosie O'Day received 12 complaints because she was a woman. According to listeners, O'Day's voice made the weather sound more like a 'fairy story' than someone reporting real facts. In those days it often was a 'fairy story' so what was the problem?

- The first Radio 1 roadshow got going in July 1973, with a Land Rover pulling a caravan across a series of holiday resorts in Britain.

- Kenny Everett was undoubtedly one of the most popular DJs on BBC Radio. During his career, he recorded various interviews with The Beatles. According to Everett, he was also inspirational in contributing some lyrics during an LSD trip with John Lennon. The line from 'I Am the Walrus' about getting a tan from the English rain came to them after a 'psychedelic' round of golf.

- Over the years, BBC Radio has (embarrassingly) banned various songs. One of the first tunes to be censored was 'It Would Be So Nice' by Pink Floyd. According to the suits at the BBC at the time, the reference to the *Evening Standard* newspaper contravened the BBC's no-advertising policy. Jane Birkin and Serge Gainsborourg's racy 'Je t'Aime moi non Plus' was also banned, helping it to reach number one in 1969. The media speculated that the couple had recorded live sex, to which Gainsbourg told Birkin, 'Thank goodness it wasn't, otherwise I hope it would have been a long-playing record.' It was released originally with a plain cover, with the words 'Interdit aux moins de 21 ans' (forbidden to those under 21). Radio Luxembourg had no such qualms and played it endlessly.
- Between 1967 and 2004, John Peel brought more than 2,000 different artists to the BBC to record his world-renowned Peel Sessions. Over the years he delighted his audiences with such stars, actual or soon to be, as The Smiths, Bob Marley, and Jimi Hendrix. The Fall recorded the most Peel sessions – 32 in all. 'Teenage Kicks' by the Undertones is reputed to be his favourite song.
- Tony Blackburn shocked the radio world to the core when he famously 'lost it' on air in 1976 when his then wife left him.

The headquarters of the BBC at Broadcasting House in Portland Place, London. This section of the building is called Old Broadcasting House (from geograph.org.uk, photographer: Stephen Craven).

As millions listened, Blackburn played 'If you Leave me Now' endlessly, begging for Tessa to come back to him. Tony called this the biggest broadcasting mistake he ever made.

- Annie Nightingale, who created the first dedicated request show in BBC Radio History on Radio 1, ran the show for 12 years, starting in 1975 on Sunday afternoons, breaking such acts as Kate and Anna McGarrigle.
- Janice Long, who died in December 2021, was the first female Radio 1 DJ to have her own daily music show in a career that spanned five decades.
- 6 December 1980 saw Radio 1 host Andy Peebles record one of the most famous interviews in musical history – with Yoko Ono and John Lennon, just two days before Lennon's assassination.

Further information at:

Alex, Peter, *Who's Who in Pop Radio*, London, 1966.

Baade, Christina L., *Victory through Harmony: The BBC and Popular Music in World War II*, Oxford, 2012.

Briggs, Asa, *The BBC – the First Fifty Years* – Condensed version of the five-volume history, Oxford, 1985.

Connelly, Charlie, *Last Train to Hilversum: A journey in search of the magic of radio, 2020.*

Hajkowski, Thomas, *The BBC and National Identity in Britain, 1922–53*, Manchester - explores ideas of Britishness conveyed in BBC radio programmes, including notions of the empire and monarchy as symbols of unity, 2010.

Potter, Simon J., *Broadcasting Empire: The BBC and the British World, 1922–1970, 2012.*

The first incarnation of the globe ident, introduced in 1963 (1963–1964) (Creative Commons Attribution Share-alike license 2.0 Stephen Craven/ Broadcasting House/CC BY-SA 2.0).

78

The Cable Street battle mural

1936

The mural.

The Cable Street Mural is a large, striking mural painting in Shadwell in East London. It was painted on the side of Stepney Town Hall by Dave Binnington, Paul Butler, Ray Walker and Desmond Rochfort, between 1979 and 1983, to commemorate the Battle of Cable Street in 1936. The battle was a series of clashes around the East End on Sunday, 4 October 1936 between the Metropolitan Police, sent to protect a march by members of the British Union of Fascists led by Oswald Mosley, and various anti-fascist demonstrators, including local trade unionists, communists, anarchists, British Jews, gangsters led by Jack 'Spot' Comer and socialist groups. Police apart, most of the combatants came from outside the area.

In response to what was seen as inaction by Jewish authorities such as the Board of Deputies (BoD), Stepney locals took it upon themselves to organise against the BUF. Many were already members of the newly formed National Union of Tailor and Garment Workers (NUTGW) and the Worker's Circle. In July 1936 a conference had taken place with 86 different organisations in order to work out a practical plan for combating Mosley. From this conference the Jewish People's Council against Fascism and Antisemitism (JPC) was born, and was to lead opposition to Mosley's march; they had delivered a 100,000-strong petition urging the Home Secretary to ban the march, but the Government refused and it was left to local people to defend their community from the fascists.

The BUF, for their part, despatched thousands of marchers dressed in their Blackshirt uniform through the heart of the East End with its large Jewish population, taking in Tower Hill, Limehouse, Bow, Mile End, Bethnal Green and Shoreditch, with open-air meetings of local BUF supporters en route.

The battle began with the Jewish Ex-Serviceman's Association marching along Whitechapel Road, proudly displaying their World War One medals, but they soon found their route blocked by mounted police and were ordered to disperse. Refusal led to them being beaten severely. This set the tone for the rest of the day.

There may have been up to 10,000 anti-fascist demonstrators who were confronted by 6,000–7,000 policemen, including those violent mounted police, who attempted to clear a route to permit the march of 2,000–3,000 fascists to proceed. The anti-fascist groups built roadblocks and barricades to confound the fascists; the main confrontation took place around Gardiner's department store in Whitechapel, where the demonstrators fought back with sticks, rocks and chair legs. Along the route, women in houses along the street hurled rubbish, rotten vegetables and the contents of chamber pots at the police. While this was going on, the BUF marchers were dispersed towards Hyde Park. About 150 demonstrators were arrested, around 175 people were injured including police, women and children. In the end, Mosley ordered the Blackshirts to retreat.

Some good came out of the battle: the Public Order Act 1936 outlawed the wearing of political uniforms and forced organisers of large meetings and demonstrations to obtain police permission before any such events. The event is remembered by modern antifascist movements as '… the moment at which British fascism was decisively defeated,' although BUF membership actually increased after the event. Nevertheless, Cable Street is remembered as a victory for the Jewish community, the people of the East End, and anti-fascists everywhere.

One week after the battle, during an antifascist victory rally, the BUF retaliated in Stepney when approximately 200 antisemitic youths dashed down Mile End Road smashing the windows of Jewish properties and businesses, looting and burning cars. London's very own *Kristallnacht*. They attacked anyone thought to be Jewish and allegedly threw a hairdresser and a four-year-old girl through a plate glass window. The day is known as the 'Mile End Pogrom' and remains one of the most notorious antisemitic events of 20th century Britain.

A scene from the actual battle.

The Cable Street mural artists used 150 imperial gallons of paint which cost them £18,000. It is inspired by the social realism of Diego Rivera. Using a fish-eye perspective, it shows the violent confrontation between police and protesters, with protest banners, punches being thrown, a barricade of furniture and an overturned vehicle, a police horse, and a police autogyro overhead. It uses the same artistic devices as Goya's *The Third of May* (1808) to evoke sympathy for the protesters, showing them full face but a back view of the police.

The mural has been repeatedly vandalised by fascists, until a special varnish was applied so any future attacks could be easily cleaned off. The mural stands today as a powerful symbol of anti-fascism in the UK.

Further information at:

Kushner, Anthony, *Remembering Cable Street: fascism and anti-fascism in British society*, Vallentine Mitchell, 2000.
Miles, Malcolm, *Art Space and the City*, London, 1997.

79

The Beano

1938

'*The Beano may have changed since the 30s but has always maintained its anti-authoritarian stance and steadfast refusal to treat children like idiots.*'
– Morris Heggi, editor at DC Thompson.

The *Beano* is a British comic magazine published by DC Thomson of Dundee. Its inaugural issue was published on 30 July 1938; it has since become the world's longest-running weekly (initially every Tuesday) comic, publishing its 4,000[th] issue in August 2019. Its characters in the early days read like a who's who of British comic royalty; including Dennis the Menace, Minnie the Minx, The Bash Street Kids, Jack Flash, Lord Snooty and His Pals, and Roger the Dodger: rebels all in their own way. From the 1940s, Beano became a successful brand and multimedia franchise with spin-off books and Christmas annuals, websites, theme park rides, games, cartoon adaptations, and a production company.

In the 1920s, DC Thomson was the king of the British comics industry, publishers of 'the big five'. *Adventure* (1921), *The Rover and The Wizard* (1922) and *The Skipper* and *The Hotspur* (1933) were all weekly boys' magazines aimed at the under 13s. *The Dandy* (Korky the Cat et al) came along in 1937. The cover of *The Beano* featured the character Big Eggo (originally named Oswald the Ostrich). 'Contrary Mary' was in there but died an early death. The cover was in colour while the inside was black and white. Cover price was 2d with a free gift of a 'whoopee mask', and issue one sold 443,000 copies.

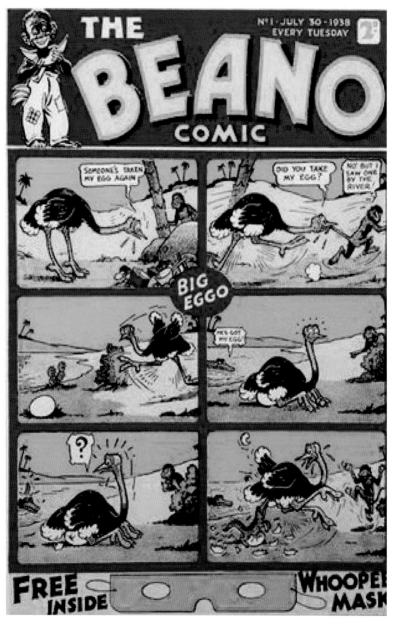

The very first issue of The Beano; 30 July 1938.

World War Two obviously impacted on *The Beano,* with editorial and creative staff leaving to join up for the duration. Paper rationing caused the rest of the new big five to be cancelled, while *The Beano* had to reduce its page count from its usual 28. Eventually, *The Beano* became a fortnightly comic, until July 1949. *The Beano* certainly did its bit: the comic strips encouraged the young readers to help their parents with the war effort, and to stay optimistic about a victory. New comic strips mocked Mussolini and propagandist Lord Haw Haw (William Joyce), while Lord Snooty and His Pals' stories showed them outsmarting the Axis leaders; other strips would describe characters recycling paper. Pansy Potter was awarded a medal for single-handedly capturing a Nazi U-boat. December 1945's issue number 272 was the first to sell over a million copies. DC Thomson also launched *The Beezer* and *The Topper.*

No 777: 8 June 1957.

Given the target audience, boyish interests, hobbies and values dominated: there were cowboys, aliens, kings, the supernatural, fantasy creatures and talking animals, and men whose lifestyle or jobs required physical strength were constants. The *Beano* either satirised or pedestalised these characters; the depiction of underprivileged lives made the working-class audience relate to and sympathise with them. Female characters, though, took something of a back seat, usually supporting a male character or acting as joint protagonist with a male character, or being the antagonist. Prose stories starred girls and women who were witches cursing or tormenting the male heroes; they exhibited binary stereotypical traits: Swanky, Lanky Liz is obsessed with fashion and makeup and acts vain and snobbish, whereas Pansy Potter, Minnie the Minx and Toots from The Bash Street Kids share the round-faced and snub-nosed art style of the boys in their stories and are unruly tomboys. People of colour featured in their stories either set in Africa, Asia or South America, or were about the character adapting to a new life in the United Kingdom.

Like *The Dandy*, *The Beano* is an inextricable part of British pop culture. 'It's refreshing to see how the [zany] principles that made it such a hit all those years ago have remained to this day,' wrote the *Coventry Evening Telegraph*. Both comics sometimes sold up to four million copies per week.

Guest chief-editors Nick Park, David Walliams, Joe Sugg and Harry Hill are inveterate fans of *The Beano*, with Park admitting, 'My dream job was always to work on *The Beano* and it's such an honour for me to be Guest Editor.'

Notable members of the old 'Dennis the Menace/Beano Club' include Auberon Waugh, Mike Read, and Mark Hamill, as well as honorary members Paul Gascoigne, and Princes William and Harry. Chris Tarrant cited Dennis as a key role model. Stella McCartney created a Beano and Dandy fashion line. Each of the 40 designs features classic Beano and Dandy characters, explaining they were 'a huge part of my childhood' and wanted to celebrate 'the next generation of Beano fans with a sustainable and practical range for kids who still share that Beano spirit of these iconic characters.' *The Blues Breakers with Eric Clapton* album is nicknamed 'The Beano Album' because Eric Clapton is shown holding issue 1242 on its cover.

The Beano has not been without its controversies down the years, and as with other publications that have endeavoured to move with the times, it

Clapton engrossed in his Beano on the album cover of John Mayall and the Bluesbreakers LP (1966). The band: John Mayall (left) – lead vocals, piano, Hammond B3 organ, harmonica; Eric Clapton – lead guitar, lead vocals on 'Ramblin' on My Mind'; John McVie – bass guitar; Hughie Flint – drums.

has been something of a barometer of public taste and attitudes. So, features and motifs have either been discontinued or changed so as not cause offence as and when public opinion changed. These include the removal of corporal punishment, exemplified often by Dennis the Menace depicted getting spanked on the bottom with a slipper by his angry father, and characters having to renounce catapults – the latter provoking accusations of being 'politically correct': 'Dennis has lost his menace'.

Racist images, characterisations and vocabulary have been expurgated; for example, Little Plum's sub-title 'Your redskin chum' was excluded from its 2002 revival. Indeed, the comic's first masthead character was a caricatured Afro-Caribbean boy named Peanut, mascot of the Little Peanut's Page of Fun joke page which appeared from issues 1 to 112 usually eating watermelon. His final masthead feature was in December 1947, but subsequent reprints of the first issues have removed him. Hard-Nut the Nigger (274) and Mussolini the Wop (34) have, unsurprisingly, not been reprinted.

Some changes acknowledge that bullying was not acceptable. Dennis and Gnasher's constant targeting of passive, diligent Walter 'the Softy' (who was also a knitting and flower-picking hobbyist) was accused of encouraging playground homophobia. Walter was also recharacterised to be a bit less soft, becoming more antagonistic, standing up to Dennis sometimes, eventually wooing his first girlfriend. Fatty of Bash Street Kids fame was rechristened Freddy (his real name) in 2021, causing outrage from former readers, including Jacob Rees-Mogg who accused the change of being 'publicity-seeking'; presumably this was in his role as Secretary of State for the 18th century.

Further information at:
Heggie, Morris, *The History of the Beano: The Story So Far*, Waverley Books, 2008.
Heggie, Morris, *The Art and History of the Dandy: 75 Years of Biffs, Bangs and Banana Skins*, Waverley Books, 2012.

The Valiant

Valiant was a British boys' adventure comic which was published from 1962 to 1976 by IPC Magazines throughout the 1960s and early 1970s. *Valiant* excelled in war stories, such as Captain Hurricane from the first issue, set during World War Two and featuring a huge ex-sea skipper who became a captain in the Royal Marines, and who could be provoked into 'ragin' fury' berserker rages which gave him added mighty strength. The captain was ably assisted by his weedy batman, Maggot Malone. Less militaristic Billy Bunter joined from issue 21; there were also classic detective strips, such as Sexton Blake.

A 1972 issue of The Valiant.

CHAPTER 13

WORLD WAR TWO

80

Tamzine at Dunkirk

1940

'So long as the English language survives, the word Dunkirk will be spoken with reverence.'
- The New York Times

Historic fishing boat Tamzine on display at the Imperial War Museum London in 2012, (photographer: IxK85).

CHAPTER 13: WORLD WAR TWO

Tamzine is a clinker-built, wooden-hulled (Canadian spruce), open fishing boat constructed in Margate in 1937 by Len C. Brockman and John Titcomb; she is fitted with sails and was designed for the innocent activity of year-round fishing off the coast of Kent. She is a mere 15inches long, smaller than a Nissan Micra, and is the smallest vessel known to have participated in the momentous event that was the Dunkirk evacuation. Things started look up for *Tamzine* and her crew when the call went out for vessels of most shapes or sizes to help with the evacuation of the remnants of the British Expeditionary Force from the ravaged beaches of Dunkirk: Operation Dynamo, 27 May 27 to 4 June 1940.

'The Admiralty have made an Order requesting all owners of self-propelled pleasure craft between 30' and 100' in length to send all particulars to the Admiralty within 14 days from today if they have not already been offered or requisitioned.'
– BBC announcement, 14 May 1940

Then, on 27 May, the small-craft section of the British Ministry of Shipping telephoned boat builders around the coast, asking them to collect all boats with 'shallow draft' that could navigate shallow waters; the focus was pleasure boats, private yachts and launches moored on the River Thames and along the south and east coasts of England. Some were taken with the owners' permission – and with the owners insisting they would sail them – while others were requisitioned by the Government with no time for the owners to be contacted. The boats were checked to ensure they were seaworthy, fuelled and taken to Ramsgate to set sail for Dunkirk. They were crewed by Royal Navy officers, ratings and experienced volunteers. Very few owners actually sailed their own vessels, apart from some fishermen and one or two others.

Subsequently, the little ships helped to rescue more than 192,226 British and 139,000 French soldiers – more than 331,000 in total from the beaches at Dunkirk. Indeed, the best part of the British Expeditionary Force had been trapped there, leaving the country vulnerable to invasion by Germany and, if nothing was done, likely to lose the war.

A motley flotilla of approximately 850 private boats and 220 warships participated in Operation Dynamo; not all were documented or are known. More than 200 of those ships were lost at Dunkirk. The rescue operation turned a military disaster into a story of heroism which served to raise the morale of the British and inspired Churchill to pronounce on 4 June in the House of Commons:

'We shall go on to the end, we shall fight in France, we shall fight on the seas and oceans, we shall fight with growing confidence and growing strength in the air, we shall defend our Island, whatever the cost may be, we shall fight on the beaches, we shall fight on the landing grounds, we shall fight in the fields and in the streets, we shall fight in the hills; we shall never surrender.'

Her valiant contribution completed, *Tamzine* was towed into Margate by a Belgian fishing vessel, more or less intact, where she disembarked her precious human cargo.

Tamzine was named after a sailing skipper's 18-year-old wife who was drowned in a shipwreck off the Scilly Isles in the 1700s, and is buried in St Mary's Cemetery, Isle of Scilly.

Some other notable contributors:

MV Royal Daffodil (1939) – Already in use for transporting troops on 23 May. Requisitioned from the General Steam Navigation Company of London, she evacuated 7,461 service personnel in five trips between 28 May and 2 June, among them the French historian Marc Bloch, who served as a French army captain in the campaign. This was the largest number evacuated by a single passenger vessel in the operation. On 2 June she was attacked by six German aircraft. One bomb penetrated two of her decks and blew a hole below the water line, but she managed to limp back to port.

Medway Queen – serving in the tenth mine-sweeping flotilla, the paddle steamer made the most round trips – seven – rescuing 7,000 men and earning herself the nickname 'Heroine of Dunkirk'.

Massey Shaw – the London-based fireboat initially went to Dunkirk to help fight fires; however, she ended up making three trips across the Channel, rescuing over 500 troops, including 30 troops from the *Emil de Champ*, which had hit a mine.

A scene from the evacuation, featuring the small boats.

Sundowner – a motor yacht owned by Charles Lightoller, former second officer of the *Titanic*, requisitioned by the Admiralty on 30 May. Lightoller insisted that if anyone was going to take her to Dunkirk it would be him and his eldest son, Roger, together with Sea Scout Gerald Ashcroft. The men transported 127 soldiers back to Ramsgate, almost capsizing when they reached the shore.

Bluebird of Chelsea – the yacht made two round trips to and from Kent, carrying hundreds of men.

Marchioness – built in 1923; in 1989 she was involved in that collision with *Bowbelle* on the River Thames with the loss of 51 lives.

To these we can add 20 RNLI lifeboats, 13 Thames sailing barges and 39 Dutch coasters which had escaped the occupation of the Netherlands on 10 May 1940. Of these, seven were lost at Dunkirk or nearer the British coast. The Dutch coasters were able to approach the beaches very closely due to their flat bottoms; they rescued 22,698 men in total. The Belgian Army, under King Leopold III, had surrendered to the Germans on 28 May. However, many ships from the fishing fleet and the small Corps de Marine took part in Operation Dynamo. In total, 65 Belgian ships participated, including 54 fishing boats, four Corps de Marine units, four tugs and two patrol vessels. The Belgian fishing fleet alone carried 4,300 British and French soldiers back to the English coast.

Further information at:

Barker, A. J., *Dunkirk: The Great Escape*, London, 1977.

Harris, John, *Dunkirk: The Epic Story of History's Most Extraordinary Evacuation*, Canelo, 2021.

Gelb, Norman, *Dunkirk: The Complete Story of the First Step in the Defeat of Hitler*, Sharpe Books, 2018.

Knowles, David J., *Escape From Catastrophe: 1940 – Dunkirk*, Knowles Publishing, 2000.

Stamp, Nigel, *Dunkirk Little Ships*, Stroud, 2015.

Imperial War Museum, 'Ship, Fishing Boat "Tamzine", British,' Imperial War Museum Collections Search, 2012.

Association of Dunkirk Little Ships (2009–2010), 'Tamzine', adls.org.uk.

81

Pigeons at war

*Swiss Army soldiers dispatching a message by carrier pigeon
in World War One (Swiss Federal Archives).*

Pigeons as conveyers of messages and intelligence during war have a long and distinguished history. They started carrying messages as early as 1150 BC in Baghdad and also with Genghis Khan. Then:

- In 43 BC, when Decius Junius Brutus was besieged at Mutina (Modena) by Mark Antony, Octavian arrived to raise the siege; Brutus communicated this with the consuls Hirtius and Pausa by sending pigeons to fly over their heads.
- Olga of Kiev gives us an unhealthy mixture of biological and chemical warfare comprising honey and mead, pigeons and incendiary devices. Olga of Kiev (later St Olga) was a regent of Kievan Rus' (a territory covering what are now parts of Russia, Ukraine, and Belarus) for her son Sviatoslav from 945 until 960. She is known for her subjugation of the Drevlians, a tribe that had earlier killed her husband Grand Duke Igor of Kiev. According to the Byzantine chronicler Leo the Deacon, Igor was 'captured by them [the Drevlians], tied to tree trunks, and torn in two'. The Drevlians bent the trees back, tied Igor's legs to them and then released the trees, ripping Igor in half. Olga was efficient, to say the least, in her revenge for her husband's murder. From the start, things went well for Olga and she was able to drive said survivors back into their cities. Olga then led her army to Iskorosten (modern Korosten in northern Ukraine), the city where her husband had been killed, and laid siege to the city. One year passed with no success, so Olga persuaded the Drevlians to give in and pay tribute even though they were fearful that Olga was intent on more revenge. Sly Olga, though, made it clear that she had had her fill of revenge and asked the Drevlians for a small request: 'Give me three pigeons,' the *Primary Chronicle* tells us, 'and three sparrows from each house. I do not wish to impose a heavy tribute, like my husband, but I require only this small gift from you, for you are impoverished by the siege.' The Drevlians were pleased that the siege might end for such a small price, and did as she asked.

> 'Olga gave to each soldier in her army a pigeon or a sparrow, and ordered them to attach by thread to each pigeon and sparrow a piece of sulphur bound with small pieces of cloth. When night

fell, Olga commanded her soldiers release the pigeons and the sparrows. So the birds flew back to their nests, the pigeons to the cotes, and the sparrows under the eaves. The dove-cotes, the coops, the porches, and the haymows were set on fire. There was not a house that was not consumed, and it was impossible to extinguish the flames, because all the houses caught on fire at once. The people fled from the city, and Olga ordered her soldiers to catch them. Thus she took the city and burned it, and captured the elders of the city. Some of the other captives she killed, while some she gave to others as slaves to her followers. The remnant she left to pay tribute.'

- In 1249 a pigeon gets the credit for alerting the Sultan of Cairo to the fact that Louis IX had landed at Damietta.
- In 1573, at the Siege of Haarlem, William of Orange despatched a pigeon towards the city; it was captured by the Spanish who then tried to kill every bird flying over the city.
- In the Franco-Prussian War (1870–71) pigeons were used to carry mail between besieged Paris and the French unoccupied territory after pigeons from outside the city were brought into Paris. At the same time 363 pigeons were dispatched from the capital, of which 53 returned bearing messages on tiny scraps of paper; newspapers reduced photographically to microscopic size were also carried – everything was restored to legibility by magic lantern. At Tours pigeons were trained to deliver large volumes of post to Paris but the Germans soon cottoned on and trained hawks to intercept and kill the pigeons.
- At the close of the 19th century, the Russian Minister of War voted $10,000 for the training of pigeons in Warsaw and Kiev. Germany, France and Turkey had similar programmes to exploit the usefulness of pigeons in war.
- During World War One, one homing pigeon, Cher Ami, was awarded the Croix de Guerre for his heroic service in delivering 12 important messages, despite having been very badly injured. We have one story about this amazing bird's exploits at the front:

'In October 1918, as the war neared its end, 194 American soldiers found themselves trapped by German soldiers. They were cut off from other Allied soldiers and had no working radios. The only chance they had of alerting anybody about their desperate situation was to send a pigeon with their co-ordinates attacked to its leg. When released it flew 25 miles from behind German lines to the Americans headquarters. The pigeon was, in fact, shot through the chest by the Germans but continued to fly home. With the "Lost Battalion's" co-ordinates, the Americans launched a rescue and the 194 men were saved. Cher Ami was awarded the Croix de Guerre with Palm for its astonishing flight. As with other pigeons, it would not have known where the American's nearest headquarters was – its natural homing instincts took over.

– C N Trueman 'Pigeons and World War One' historylearningsite.co.uk. The History Learning Site, 16 Apr 2015.

- At the First Battle of the Marne in 1914, French troops stopped the German advance on Paris. The French troops advanced and pushed back the Germans, their pigeons with them. At the Marne, the French had 72 pigeon lofts. As the French advanced, the lofts moved with them – but many of the pigeons carrying messages could never have known where their loft had moved to. Incredibly, all the pigeons at the Marne returned to their lofts – despite the fact that they would have flown 'blind' not knowing where their loft was at any one time.

- Eighty-two homing pigeons were dropped into the Netherlands with the First Airborne Division Signals as part of Operation Market Garden (the Battle of Arnhem) in World War Two in September 1944. The pigeons' loft was in London, which would have meant a 240-mile trip to deliver their messages.

- Pigeons had a crucial role on D-Day as radios could not be used for fear of vital signals being intercepted by the enemy.

- During the war, the deployment of pigeons as messengers was recognised by the Princesses Elizabeth and Margaret as Girl Guides joining other Guides sending messages to the World

Chief Guide in 1943, as part of a campaign to raise money for homing pigeons.

- More recently the Taliban banned the keeping or use of homing pigeons in Afghanistan.

The Secret Pigeon Service, MI 14 and Jozef Raskin

During World War Two, an arm of the British intelligence service known as MI14 ran the Secret Pigeon Service, or Confidential Pigeon Service, code-name Operation Columba (*columba* is Latin for dove). Between 1941 and 1944, around 16,000 avian agents helped the war effort. MI14 would para-chute containers holding the birds along with a questionnaire into occupied France, Belgium and the Netherlands. This was on sheets of very thin paper, accompanied by a special pencil and a tube for storing the message, as well as French and Dutch instructions on how to fill in a report. A recent copy of a London newspaper was also included as proof of veracity. Those pigeons that returned often came back with messages containing useful intelligence such as troop movements and concentrations, the state of morale locally, and other information which helped predict and confound German operations.

Around 1,000 messages came back, but one was different. Codename Leopold Vindictive sent Message 37 from Belgium; it looked like a work of art, with detailed, colourful maps and writing too small to read with the naked eye. It had been rolled up tightly into the size of a postage stamp so it could fit back into the cannister – and it produced 12 pages of invaluable intelligence. Gordon Corera, the BBC's security correspondent, has pieced together details of that group, known by the codename Leopold Vindictive. He was inspired in his research after coming across a news story about the discovery of a dead pigeon's leg in a chimney in Surrey: 'The dead pigeon's leg had a message attached to it which appeared to come from World War Two. I found it bizarre and fascinating.' The message was a series of random letters – a code impermeable to the country's best codebreakers. Corera started searching Belgian historical records and archives and the trail even-tually led to Jozef Raskin, a Catholic priest who lived near Bruges and was the leader of the local resistance group. With the help of Raskin's niece, Brigitte, they began to piece together his life story:

'In the First World War, because he was quite an artist, he'd been involved in drawing maps of German positions in the trenches. So he already had a bit of a feel for military intelligence. He'd gone to China in between the wars as a missionary, and he'd learnt calligraphy, and how to write, that gave him the ability to write those tiny letters. And he also had a real network of friends across the country, because he went as a travelling preacher raising funds for the missionary organisation he worked for.'

– 'Inside the Secret Pigeon Service, an unlikely weapon in the fight against the Nazis'; ABC Radio National/By Monique Ross and Geraldine Doogue for *Saturday Extra,* 22 June 2018.

– Gordon Corera, *Secret Pigeon Service: Operation Columba, Resistance and the Struggle to Liberate Europe,* 2019

Leopold Vindictive was named after two of Raskin's contacts: Belgium's King Leopold, for whom Raskin had served as a chaplain, and a British admiral named Roger Keyes, whose ship was *The Vindictive*. 'He actually uses the admiral as a reference in the pigeon [message], and says "if you want to know who I am, contact the admiral. I was with him in 1940".' The group provided intelligence about troop movements, the results of bombing raids and specific information about a particular chateau the Germans were using as a base for their marine forces. Raskin was arrested and taken to Germany, where he was beheaded. Two other members of his group were also murdered.

In a combat situation, because a pigeon could fly at speeds of up to 60mph, they were efficient in delivering coded messages from the front while their speed and altitude made it difficult for enemy snipers to get a shot in. In 1944, in the run up to the Allied invasion, German counterintelligence sought to counteract Source Columba by unleashing their own pigeons. These enemy pigeon cases, accompanied by a pack of British cigarettes, were masquerading as British and also carried instructions to send the names of local patriots to the Allies. The Résistance simply believed that the best way to deal with these faux birds was to smoke the cigarettes and eat the pigeons.

The operation was amazingly successful, yielding viable intelligence in over 50 percent of the received messages, while 31 Source Columba pigeons were awarded the Dickin Medal. The operation was made public only after National Archives files were released in 2007.

A British B-type bus converted into a mobile pigeon loft to serve in France during World War One. These converted buses were used as a base for homing pigeons carrying important messages, London, 1914.

Pigeons were used by a variety of military services and the canisters affixed to their legs were colour-coded to distinguish recipients.

Red = US Forces + British Army
Blue = US Forces + British RAF
Blue with coloured disk = British RAF
Blue with white patch = RAF
Red with coloured disk = British Special Service
Grey = British Special Service
Green = British Special Service
Black = British Civil Police
Yellow = British Commercial

As noted, in 2012 the skeleton of a carrier pigeon was found inside a domestic chimney in Bletchingley, Surrey. Inside a red canister attached to one of its legs was an encrypted message handwritten on a Pigeon Service form. The message was addressed to 'XO2', which is thought to be RAF Bomber Command, and is signed 'W Stot Sjt'. It is believed to have been sent from France on 6 June 1944, during the D-day invasion. The message consists of 27 five-letter groups, with the first and last group identical. As of March 2022, the message has not been deciphered. Britain's GCHQ has asked for any information the public might have about the message.

Britain's Armed Forces paid civilian pigeon fanciers to look after about 100 pigeons for military use until about 1950. With the advent of the Cold War, most British pigeon operations are believed to have shut down, but not the CIA's.

Declassified documents released in 2019 show how the CIA trained pigeons to carry out clandestine spying missions by photographing restricted sites inside the Soviet Union throughout the Cold War. Pigeons, and other birds such as ravens, were used to carry bugging devices and other spying gadgets and leave them on window sills. By 1967, the CIA was spending more than $600,000 (today's rough equivalent £1.7m) on three programmes that involved animals and spying operations.

Some armed militia are reported to still use pigeons in today's conflicts. It emerged in 2016 that Islamic State had turned pigeon fanciers themselves to train birds to carry messages between their factions.

Further information at:

Chrystal, Paul, *Biological Warfare and Bioterrorism: Weaponising Nature*, Barnsley, 2022.

Clarke, Carter W., 'Signal Corps Pigeons,' *The Military Engineer*, 25, pp. 133–38, 1933.

Corera, Gordon, *The Secret Pigeon Service: Operation Columba, Resistance and the Struggle to Liberate Europe*, New York, 2019.

82

The wreck of the Sir Ralph Wedgwood after the Baedeker Raid on York

1942

The wreck of the Sir Ralph Wedgwood at York station after being bombed by the Luftwaffe during the Baedeker raid of 29 April 1942 (photo courtesy of York Press).

The story of the Baedeker Raid and its tragic and destructive impact on York is well known. By April 1942 York had received 780 alerts, but luckily only a few people had been killed – on three separate occasions when stray bombs had been dropped probably by German aircraft lightening their loads on the way from other targets. An indication of York's apparent immunity was that the public shelters were barely used: a large shelter near the city centre had two doors, both of which carried a notice saying 'Key on other door' – the key was in fact in a small glass case at the end of the shelter, with a notice asking people to break the glass to obtain the key – the glass remained unbroken several days after the Baedeker raid.

The wholesale and ruthless destruction by the RAF of the beautiful medieval towns Lübeck and Rostock shocked not just the Germans. Goebbels was unnerved, clearly seeing the consequence for Germany and the morale of the Germans: 'the English air raids have increased in scope and importance; if they can be continued for weeks on the same lines, they might conceivably have a demoralizing effect on the population.' After Rostock he said, 'the air raid … was more devastating than those before. Community life there is practically at an end … the situation is in some sections catastrophic … seven tenths of the city have been destroyed … more than 100,000 people had to be evacuated … there was, in fact, panic.' The attack of 28 March 1942 on Lübeck created a hellish firestorm that caused severe damage to the historic centre with many casualties. The German police reported 301 people dead, three people missing and 783 injured. More than 15,000 people lost their homes.

Hitler was outraged, demanding retaliation of the most destructive kind: 'Preference is to be given to those where attacks are likely to have the greatest possible effect on civilian life.' Besides raids on ports and industry, terror attacks of a retaliatory nature (*Vergeltungsangriffe*) were to be carried out on towns other than London. After Bath, the second of the retaliations, Hitler's plan was to 'repeat these raids night after night until the English are sick and tired of terror attacks … cultural centres, health resorts and civilian centres must be attacked … there is no other way of bringing the English to their senses. They belong to a class of human beings with whom you can only talk after you have first knocked out their teeth.'

We owe the name 'Baedeker raids' to German Foreign Office propagandist Baron Gustav Braun von Stumm, who reputedly exclaimed, 'We shall go out and bomb every building in Britain marked with three stars in the Baedeker Guide,' the popular and authoritative travel guides. Exeter was the first to be hit over two nights (23–25 April) causing over 80 fatalities. Bath was next (25–27 April) with 400 casualties. On the following night the *Luftwaffe* hit Norwich, dropping more than 90 tons of bombs and causing 67 deaths. York was next on the

Loose change fused together by the heat of the conflagration (photo courtesy of York Press).

night of 28–29 April. One week later, they were back over Exeter, resulting in heavy damage and 164 deaths. The next night they attacked Cowes, a place of cultural and military significance, being the home of the J. Samuel White shipyard. Norwich was bombed again.

Overall, a total of 1,637 civilians were killed and 1,760 injured in the raids, and over 50,000 houses were destroyed. Famous and unique buildings flattened or damaged included York's Guildhall and the Bath Assembly Rooms, but in general these fine cities were very lucky; the cathedrals of Norwich, Exeter and Canterbury and York Minster remained, by and large, unscathed – possibly because the Luftwaffe wanted to preserve them as landmarks for future raids or for other targets nearby.

Seventy German bombers, largely unopposed, bombed York for two hours that night: 106 people died, including 14 children, and 98 were seriously injured (not including undisclosed army and RAF fatalities) as well as six German aircrew. 9,500 houses (30 per cent of the city's stock) were damaged or destroyed, leaving 2,000 people homeless. The medieval Guildhall and St Martin le Grand Church were badly damaged. The Bar Convent School was blown up killing five nuns including the headmistress, Mother Vincent.

The following day the *Daily Mail* reported: 'The gates of York still stand high, like the spirit of its people who, after nearly two hours of intense bombing and machine-gunning, were clearing up today.'

York railway station was an obvious strategic target, with its prodigious war effort work at the carriage works and its role as a hub for trains carrying

The medieval Guildhall ablaze in the distance along the River Ouse.

troops, supplies and equipment to depots and barracks all over the country, not least to the nation's ports. At around 2.30am the flares, bombs and incendiaries were released from the 20 Junker 88s and Heinkel IIIs. The destruction began when a stick of HE bombs fell either side of the railway bridge linking Bootham Terrace and Grosvenor Terrace; in the sky *Ober-feldwebel* Hans Fruehauf soon picked out the railway station and remembered the briefing officer's command to 'obliterate the signalling system and there won't be much leaving Hull for Murmansk for the next weeks'.

The roundhouse in the marshalling yards took a direct hit and all 20 engines in there at the time suffered damage. With terrible bad timing the blacked-out 10.15pm express from King's Cross, the *Night Scotsman*, pulled into platform 9 crammed with passengers – military and civilian – worn out after a five-hour journey. The station loudspeaker urgently warned them to evacuate but few initially did, encumbered in many cases by full kit and weapons. A 250-pound bomb changed all that when it crashed through the station roof, exploding on platforms two and three and destroying the parcels office, and the *Night Scotsman*.

Staff rushed to help: Assistant Stationmaster Lyon, Driver Stevans from Gateshead, two shunters and an anonymous soldier managed to uncouple the train from both ends so that 15 of the 20 carriages could be safely separated; the middle five were left burning beyond recovery. In another shunter Signalman Simpson, who had escaped from his damaged box, manoeuvred a further 20 coaches and the flaming parcels van to safety. Meanwhile, women porters were kicking burning debris onto the relative safety of the rails while blazing furniture was dumped into a nearby moat. The day's takings were salvaged, deposited in William

Death and destruction at the Bar Convent (photo courtesy of York Press).

Green's Wellington boot and removed to the Royal Station Hotel next door. The fateful HE bomb that shattered the roof was followed by a stick of incendiaries, one of which smashed into the lamp room and the 500 gallons of paraffin stored there. The lamp room, parcels office, booking office and stationmaster's office were burnt to the ground in the ensuing conflagration.

A plaque on platform 8a at York station commemorates another hero. It tells how foreman William Milner, an active member of the LNER first-aid team, gave his life in an attempt to get hold of a box of medical supplies, urgently needed for treating casualties. He entered the blazing parcels office at the height of the attack and never came back out. When his body was found, he was still clutching the box of first-aid equipment. William Milner was posthumously awarded the King's commendation for gallantry.

The Leeman Road stables were also struck, necessitating the evacuation of 19 panicking, and very dangerous, dray horses from the site. Despite propaganda that 'York has been wiped off the map', the city and its station were quickly back to normal function. The main line reopened the afternoon after the raid, although goods traffic was disrupted for longer.

Five nuns were tragically killed at the Bar Convent School during the raid when it was destroyed by a delayed action bomb. Six of the nuns in residence were firewatchers and so stayed above ground when the raid started (the other nuns and pupils having gone down to the shelters). However, when the dust settled Mother Mary Agnes was found to be missing. Some of the nuns went in search of her when she was heard in the rubble below close to the bomb. Unfortunately, as they went for a ladder to rescue her, the bomb exploded and Mother Agnes and all but one of the rescue party were killed. It was not until Sunday, 3 May that all five bodies were recovered.

Overall, civil defence records tell us that 65 high-explosive bombs fell and 'practically all did damage to a greater or lesser degree'. Twenty-four UXBs were reported: eight were exploded, six were dealt with or were to be dealt with, and ten were false reports. Fourteen clusters of incendiary bombs fell.

'Casualties within the City

Civilian	Male.	Female.	Children.	Total.
Dead.	23	39	8	70.
Seriously injured.	42	43	7	92.
Slightly injured.	68	41	4	113.
Civil defence Personnel				
Dead.	4	-	-	4.'

Further information at:

Chrystal, Paul, *York and its Railways*, Stenlake Publishing, 2015.

Chrystal, Paul, *York Places of Worship*, Stenlake Publishing, 2016.

Kessler, Leo and Taylor, Eric, *The York Blitz, 1942: The Baedeker Raid on York*, 1986.

Rothnie, Niall, *The Baedeker Blitz*, London, 1992.

83

Penicillin

1943

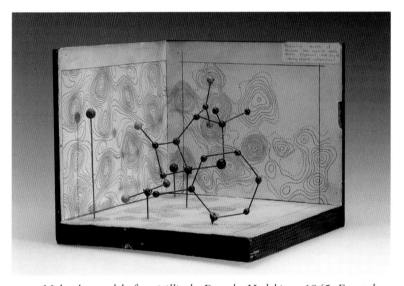

Molecular model of penicillin by Dorothy Hodgkin, c.1945. Front three quarter. She determined the chemical structure of penicillin (Science Museum London/Science and Society Picture Library).

Penicillin was, and is, a world-changing, life-saving drug. It was discovered in 1928 by Alexander Fleming as a crude extract of *P. Rubens*. Fleming's student Cecil George Paine was the first to successfully use penicillin to treat *ophthalmia neonatorum*, a gonococcal infection in infants, in 1930. The purified compound (penicillin F)

United States Federal Government World War Two poster, showing a man sitting up in a hospital bed, smiling, reading a magazine and smoking a cigarette, with the caption 'Penicillin / THE NEW LIFE-SAVING DRUG / Saves Soldiers' Lives / Men who might have died / will live ... if YOU / Give this job Everything You've got!'
– Science History Institute, Philadelphia.

was isolated in 1940 by a research team led by Howard Florey and Ernst Boris Chain at the University of Oxford. Fleming first used the purified penicillin to treat streptococcal meningitis in 1942. For the discovery, Fleming shared the 1945 Nobel Prize in Physiology with Florey and Chain. Penicillin changed the course of medicine and has enabled physicians to treat formerly severe and life-threatening illnesses such as bacterial endocarditis, meningitis, pneumococcal pneumonia, gonorrhea and syphilis.

Penicillins were among the first medications to be effective against a wide range of bacterial infections caused by staphylococci and streptococci. Following the medical breakthrough, the British War Cabinet set up the Penicillin Committee in April 1943, which led to mass production. On 14 March 1942, the first patient was treated for streptococcal sepsis with US-made penicillin produced by Merck & Co. In July 1943 the War Production Board drew up a plan for the mass distribution of penicillin stocks to Allied troops fighting in Europe. As a direct result of the war and the

War Production Board, by June 1945 over 646 billion units per year were being produced. During the war, penicillin made a massive difference to the number of deaths and amputations caused by infected wounds among Allied forces, saving an estimated 12 to15 per cent of lives.

These are the five American pharmaceutical companies that contributed to penicillin production research during World War Two: Abbott Laboratories, Lederle Laboratories (now Pfizer, Inc.), Merck & Co., Inc., Chas. Pfizer & Co. Inc. (now Pfizer, Inc.) and E.R. Squibb & Sons (now Bristol-Myers Squibb Company).

Supply was a problem, though. Penicillin is readily excreted: about 80 per cent of a penicillin dose is cleared from the body within three to four hours of administration. Indeed, during the early days, the drug was so scarce that it became common practice to collect the urine from patients so that the penicillin in the urine could be isolated and reused. This was not a satisfactory solution.

Penicillins are still widely used today for various bacterial infections, though an increasing number of types of bacteria have developed resistance due to extensive use. About 10 per cent of people report that they are allergic to penicillin; however, up to 90 per cent of this group may not actually be allergic; serious allergies only occur in about 0.03 per cent. Those who are allergic to penicillin are usually given cephalosporin C because there is only 10 per cent crossover in allergy between the penicillins and cephalosporins.

Further information at:

Bennett J.W., 'Alexander Fleming and the discovery of penicillin,' *Advances in Applied Microbiology,* 49, pp. 163–84, 2001.

Diggins F.W., 'The true history of the discovery of penicillin, with refutation of the misinformation in the literature,' *British Journal of Biomedical Science,* 56 (2), pp. 83–93, 1999.

Goyotte D., 'The Surgical Legacy of World War II. Part II: The age of antibiotics,' *The Surgical Technologist,* 109, pp. 257–264, 2017.

Lehrer S., *Explorers of the Body: Dramatic Breakthroughs in Medicine from Ancient Times to Modern Science* (2nd ed.), New York, 2006.

84

The Enigma code machine

A Colossus Mark 2 computer being operated by Dorothy Du Boisson (left) and Elsie Booker (right), 1943. The ten Colossi were the world's first (semi-) programmable electronic computers, the first having been built in 1943. This file is from the collections of The National Archives (United Kingdom), catalogued under document record FO850/234.

Like the evacuation of the BEF at Dunkirk, the cracking of the Enigma codes in World War Two was a pivotal event for Britain and a major contributor to the Allies' eventual success in 1945. We only found out in 2003 that the Enigma machine was invented by German engineer Arthur Scherbius at the end of World War One. It was a cipher machine developed to protect commercial, diplomatic and military communication as employed extensively by Nazi Germany in every branch of the German war machine. The Germans mistakenly believed that the Enigma machine enabled them to communicate securely and secretly: it was assumed to be so secure that it was used to encipher the most secret of messages.

As well as German models adapted for their army, air force and navy, there were also Japanese and Italian navy versions after 1926; sets were supplied to the fascists in the Spanish Civil War. Enigma was an essential element of the Germans' *blitzkrieg* brand of warfare, which depends on radio communication for command and coordination; it was essential that messages be protected with secure encipherment. The compact, portable Enigma machine with its rotor scramblers delivered on all fronts.

However, cryptanalysis of the Enigma ciphering system enabled the western Allies in World War Two to read substantial amounts of Morse-coded radio communications by the Axis powers that had been enciphered using Enigma machines. This yielded military intelligence which, along with that from other decrypted Axis radio and teleprinter transmissions, was code-named Ultra. Better operating procedures, properly enforced, would have made the plugboard Enigma machine unbreakable. However, most of the German military forces, intelligence services and civilian agencies using Enigma employed poor operating procedures, and it was these shabby working practices that allowed the Enigma machines to be reverse-engineered and the ciphers to be read.

An Enigma decoder machine in the Imperial War Museum, London (photographer: Simon).

A rebuild of a British Bombe at Bletchley Park museum,
(photographer: Tom Yates).

In December 1932 the system was 'broken' by mathematician Marian Rejewski at the Polish General Staff's Cipher Bureau, using mathematical permutation group theory combined with French-supplied intelligence material obtained from a German spy, Hans-Thilo Schmidt. By 1938 Rejewski had invented a device, the cryptologic bombe, and Henryk Zygalski had made the cipher-breaking more efficient. Five weeks before the outbreak of World War Two, in late July 1939, at a conference just south of Warsaw, the Polish Cipher Bureau shared its Enigma-breaking techniques and technology with the French and British.

Gordon Welchman, later head of Hut 6 at Bletchley Park, wrote:

'Hut 6 Ultra would never have gotten off the ground if we had not learned from the Poles, in the nick of time, the details both of the German military version of the commercial Enigma machine, and of the operating procedures that were in use.'

The Polish work formed the crucial basis for the subsequent World War Two British Enigma-decryption effort at Bletchley Park.

The British Government Code and Cypher School (GC&CS), set up at Bletchley Park, soon developed a viable cryptanalytic capability. Initially the decryption was mainly of *Luftwaffe* and a few *Heer* (German army) messages, since the *Kriegsmarine* employed much more secure procedures for using Enigma. Alan Turing, a Cambridge University mathematician and logician, provided much of the original thinking that led to the design of the cryptanalytical bombe machines that were instrumental in eventually breaking the naval Enigma. However, the *Kriegsmarine* introduced an Enigma version with a fourth rotor for its U-boats, resulting in a prolonged period when these messages could not be decrypted. With the capture of relevant cipher keys and the use of much faster US Navy bombes, regular, rapid reading of U-boat messages resumed.

Further information at:

Bennett, Ralph, *Behind the Battle: Intelligence in the war with Germany, 1939–1945*, Random House, London, 1999.

Briggs, Asa, *Secret Days: Code-breaking in Bletchley Park*, Barnsley, 2011.

Francis, Harry, *Codebreakers: The Inside Story of Bletchley Park*, Oxford, 2001.

Hodges, Andrew, *Alan Turing: The Enigma*, London, 1992.

Kozaczuk, Władysław, *Enigma: How the German Machine Cipher was Broken, and how it was Read by the Allies in World War Two*, edited and translated by Christopher Kasparek (2nd ed.), Frederick, MD, 1984.

McKay, Sinclair, *The Secret Life of Bletchley Park: the WWII Codebreaking Centre and the Men and Women Who Worked There*, Aurum, 2010.

Turing, Dermot, *X, Y & Z: The Real Story of How Enigma Was Broken*, Stroud, 2018.

CHAPTER 14

POST-WAR

85

The Prefab

1945

Grade-II listed Phoenix prefabs in Wake Green Road, Birmingham, built c. 1945.

Back in 1837, prefabricated farm buildings and bungalows were becoming popular, and a London carpenter called Henry Manning saw an opportunity and produced portable cottages for export to Australia. Two years later, kit houses were shipped by rail for settlers during the California Gold Rush.

Under the Housing (Temporary Accommodation) Act 1944, more than 156,000 prefabricated houses were built throughout the UK between 1945 and 1948 to rehouse ex-servicemen and their families or bombed-out people. The aim was to address the need for an anticipated 200,000 shortfall in post-war housing stock, by building 500,000 prefabricated houses and aiming to deliver 300,000 units within ten years, within a budget of £150 million. This was, in fact, a repeat of a strategy deployed by the Government of the day following World War One, namely a national investment programme in a national public house-building scheme. In actual fact, only 150,000 were built after World War Two. The prefabs that did go up went up on bomb sites and open spaces such as green belt and parks to give an air of rural living, and were expected to last ten to fifteen years. This was not to be: they lasted much longer, and some still stand today after 75 years.

The Ministry of Works set up research institutes, standards and competition authorities that resulted in core building regulations. All approved prefab units had to have a minimum floor space of 635sq ft and be a maximum of 7.5ft wide to allow for transportation by road. The most innovative creation was what was termed the 'service unit', something which they initially specified all designs had to include. A service unit was a combined back-to-back prefabricated kitchen that backed onto a bathroom, pre-built in a factory to an agreed size. It meant that the unsightly water pipes, waste pipes and electrical distribution were all in the same place, and hence easy to install.

The service unit also contained a number of innovations for occupants. The house retained a coal fire, but it contained a back boiler to create both central heating as well as a constant supply of hot water. For a country used to the

Poster celebrating troops returning from the war to their 'homes fit for heroes'.

rigours of the outside lavatory and tin bath, the bathroom was nothing short of palatial: it included a flushing toilet and man-sized bath with hot running water. In the kitchen were housed such modern luxuries as a built-in oven, refrigerator and Baxi water heater, which only later became commonplace in all residential accommodation. All prefabs came pre-decorated in magnolia, with gloss-green on all additional wood, including the door trimmings and skirting boards.

There was a hall where there was space for a pram, and built-in cupboards in every room, large windows, and, for some, a coal shed outside: all of these were mod cons beyond the tenants' wildest dreams. To cap it all, the two-bedroom bungalows often had large gardens: as rationing lasted until 1954, residents were able to grow their own fruits and vegetables.

Winston Churchill announced in March 1944, well before the war had ended:

'The first attack must evidently be made upon houses which are damaged, but which can be reconditioned into proper dwellings … The second attack on the housing problem will be made by what are called the prefabricated, or emergency, houses.'

After 1948 prefabs came under the control of local authorities, each of which dealt with prefabs as they saw fit. Some demolished them straight away, while others retained them and even renovated them to get them up to modern living standards. These 'palaces of the people', evoke a certain period in British social history and are a good example of sound strategic planning when it was most needed, original design and a viable provision of care for the people of Britain.

Further information at:

Blanchet, Elisabeth, *Prefabs: A social and architectural history*, Historic England, 2018.
Davis, Colin, *The Prefabricated Home*, Reaktion Books, 2005.
Stevenson, Greg, *Palaces for the People: Prefabs in Post-war Britain*, Batsford, 2003.
Vale, Brenda, *Prefabs – The history of the UK Temporary Housing Programme*, Taylor & Francis, 1995.

86

The NHS ambulance

A London Ambulance Service Talbot ambulance in action before the NHS, during the Blitz. BXH809 was based in Lambeth and served throughout the whole of World War Two. She still has most of her equipment today.

'If there is one thing that we have learnt from the Covid-19 pandemic, it's that migrant workers are absolutely essential to the operation of the NHS ... migrants [have] helped make the NHS what it is today.'
– https://immigrationnews.co.uk/history-of-overseas-workers-in-the-nhs/

Ambulances are emblematic of and essential for any health service. The UK's National Health Service, founded in 1948, is no exception. We all need to get people to hospital when they need to be there through illness or accident; we all need to get the infirm and elderly safely to and from their appointments or for courses of treatment for chronic illnesses.

The National Health Service Act 1946 gave county and county borough councils in England and Wales a statutory responsibility to provide an emergency ambulance service, although they could contract a voluntary ambulance service to provide this; the ambulance service is the emergency response wing of the National Health Service.

The ambulance service in the UK dates back to the late 19th century, with locally funded services such as the Metropolitan Asylums Board operating in the London area in 1897. The earliest British Ambulance Flight was recorded in World War I in Turkey in 1917. This was when a soldier in the Camel Corps who had been shot in the ankle was flown to a hospital in a De Havilland DHH within 45 minutes. The same journey by land would have taken three days to complete.

Each year about one in 20 people in the UK will use the accident and emergency ambulance service. However, responding to 999 calls makes up only 10 per cent of the total number of ambulance service journeys – ambulances are also involved in non-emergency work through the patient transport service.

Something relatively new is the bicycle ambulance – officially the Cycle Response Unit – which operates in London. Initiated by Tom Lynch, a former competitive cyclist who joined the ambulance service aged 22, a formal trial of the service took place in 2000 and today the unit has a team of 60 staff.

The Cycle Response Unit uses custom-built Rockhopper mountain bikes with London Ambulance Service livery, blue lights and a siren. The rider wears London Ambulance Service livery and protective equipment and carries a comprehensive medical kit. Typically the responder will carry oxygen and a

Immigrant nurses in an anatomy lesson, with skeleton.

defibrillator for dealing with emergencies such as cardiac arrest. They may also carry additional items, including airway management equipment like airways or bag valve masks, and drugs appropriate to their skill level. They are also likely to carry first-aid equipment such as bandages and dressings. A bicycle paramedic has been said to cycle approximately 140 miles a week. A trial in 2000 successfully demonstrated that response times to pedestrianised areas were reduced, and with the responder able to deal with a number of illnesses and injuries, the single cycle saved over 250 hours of traditional ambulance time every six months.

A bicycle of the Cycle Response Unit (photographer: Oxyman).

Two NHS ambulances at Shoreditch in 1969.

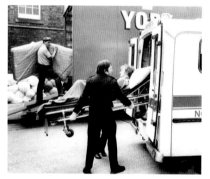

Patients are put into ambulances on Naburn Hospital's last day. The facility opened as York Borough Asylum in April 1906. It became the York City Mental Hospital in 1927 and joined the National Health Service as Naburn Hospital in 1948; it closed in February 1988 (photograph courtesy of York Press).

One of the many doctors protesting in 2019 against over ten years of government cuts; that government is just now (in 2022) waking up to the fact that their cuts have already brought the NHS to its knees.

87

I-SPY books

1948

As with much of the most effective and enduring knowledge and education, *I-SPY* books have always been education by stealth. Avidly completing one of them brings out the competitiveness and completism in a child – particularly when a sibling is trying to compete with and complete before you – while at the same time imperceptively teaching you something worth knowing. Indeed, the clandestine educationalists at I-SPY ensured that there was one of their little books for every possible situation or occasion likely to be encountered by a child: *Car Journey* helped stave off 'Are We There Yet Syndrome ?'; *In Hospital* gave you something to do while whiling away those interminable hours waiting to have your adenoids or tonsils removed; *Train Journey* gave you an excuse to stick your head out of the window of a fast-moving train.

The *I-SPY* books are a series of 40 or so small volumes that have sold hundreds of thousands of copies each, totalling sales of 25 million worldwide by 2010. As children spot the objects listed, they record the sighting in the book and win points, varying according to how unusual the sight. In the early days, completed books could be sent to Charles Warrell (known as Big Chief I-SPY) for a feather and order of merit. The children participating in the game were known as I-SPY Tribe; by 1953 the I-SPY Tribe could boast half a million members.

The company was supposedly run by Charles Warrell, a former headmaster who created *I-SPY* towards the end of his working life. He retired in 1956, but lived until 1995, when he died at the age of 106. The books became very popular, with print runs well into six figures. Big Chief I-Spy

Three vintage I-SPY books.

always had assistants, usually known as 'Hawkeye'. In the 1980s David Bellamy took over as Big Chief I-Spy and the Red Indian connections were quietly dropped.

The Spoof series published by HarperCollins in 2016 included:
Signs and Instructions You Must Obey; *The UK While It Lasts*; *At the School Gate*; *Pets When Human Friendship Is Not Enough*.

Further reading:
Wood, Felicity 'Michelin spots series and gets to play I-Spy again', *The Bookseller,* 9 October 2009

Look and Learn, 1962

If *I-SPY* books were education by stealth, *Look and Learn* was the total opposite: full on, unmistakeable and unashamed learning, just by looking.

Look and Learn was published from 1962 until 1982, featuring educational articles covering a wide range of topics from volcanoes to the Loch Ness Monster; a long-running science-fiction comic strip, *The Trigan Empire*; adaptations of classics of literature into comic-strip form, such as *Lorna Doone*; and serialised works of fiction like *The First Men in the Moon*.

The inaugural issue, dated 20 January 1962, was impressive to say the least. It featured a broad range topics from articles on history (Rome, the

Houses of Parliament, King Charles I, 'The Dover Road', 'From Then Till Now'), science ('Eyes on Outer Space'), geography and geology (The Grand Canyon, 'The Quest for Oil'), art (Vincent van Gogh), nature ('The story of a seed', 'Your Very Own Basset Hound'), literature (*The Arabian Nights* and its editor Sir Richard Burton) and travel (*The Children of Tokio*). It also had the first episodes of *Three Men in a Boat* by Jerome K. Jerome and *The Children's Crusade* by Henry Treece, and a feature on the founding of the World Wildlife Fund. This first issue sold about 700,000 copies and settled down to a regular sale of over 300,000 copies a week.

Further information at:
'A Brief History of Look and Learn', *Look and Learn*.
Holland, Steve, *Look and Learn: A History of the Classic Children's Magazine*.

An early issue of Look and Learn.

88

SS Windrush

1948

'The image of West Indians filing off the ship's gangplank has come to symbolise the beginning of modern British multicultural society.'

The SS Windrush at Tilbury Dock, 1948.

A s the break-up of the British empire and post-World War Two rebuilding simultaneously gathered pace, the Windrush generation arrived as United Kingdom and colonies (CUKC) citizens in the 1950s and 1960s. Born in the former British colonies of the Caribbean, they settled in the UK prior to 1973, and, importantly, were granted 'right of abode' by the Immigration Act 1971.

We all know too well how, from the beginning of the 16th century until the early 19th century, Africans were bought by European slave traders and shipped in ineffably bad conditions across the Atlantic to work as slaves in the various European colonies in the Americas. Approximately 13 million Africans came to the Americas in this way, of which historians have estimated approximately two million Africans were shipped to various British colonies in the Caribbean and South America. These slaves were anonymised and dehumanised: given new names, made to adopt European dress and Christianity, and forced to work on plantations which produced cash crops to be shipped back to Europe, completing the last leg of the odious triangular slave trade.

The black Briton Ignatius Sancho was among the leading British abolitionists in the 18th century, and in 1783 an abolitionist movement spread throughout Britain to end slavery throughout the British Empire, with the poet William Cowper writing in 1785:

> 'We have no slaves at home – Then why abroad? Slaves cannot breathe in England; if their lungs receive our air, that moment they are free. They touch our country, and their shackles fall. That's noble, and bespeaks a nation proud. And jealous of the blessing. Spread it then, And let it circulate through every vein.'

HMT *Empire Windrush*, originally MV *Monte Rosa*, was a German passenger liner and cruise ship launched in 1930. During World War Two she was operated by the German navy as a troopship. At the end of the war, *Monte Rosa* was appropriated by the British Government as booty and renamed the *Empire Windrush*.

In 1948 *Empire Windrush* brought one of the first large groups of post-war West Indian immigrants to the UK, carrying 1,027 passengers and two stowaways from Jamaica to London. Of these, 802 gave their last country of residence as somewhere in the Caribbean: of these, 693 had plans to settle in the United Kingdom and became known as the Windrush generation.

Here is the Windrush story. In 1948 *Empire Windrush*, while en route from Australia to Britain via the Atlantic, docked in Kingston, Jamaica, to pick up servicemen who were on leave there. At the time the British Nationality Act 1948, giving the status of citizenship of the United Kingdom and Colonies (CUKC status) to all British subjects connected with the United Kingdom or a British colony, was going through Parliament. Some enterprising Caribbean migrants decided to jump the gun in Jamaica.

Before 1962 the UK had no immigration barriers for CUKCs, who could settle indefinitely in the UK without restrictions.

The *Windrush* was by no means full, but that changed when an advertisement was placed in a Jamaican newspaper offering cut-price transport on the vessel for anybody who wanted to go and work in the UK. Many former servicemen saw this as a chance to return to Britain in the hope of finding better employment, including, in some cases, rejoining the RAF; others decided to make the journey just to see what the 'mother country' was like. Demand for tickets far exceeded the supply, and there were long queues.

We do not know exactly how many West Indian immigrants finally ended up on board; 492 is often quoted as the number who arrived in Britain. However, the ship's records, kept in the United Kingdom National Archives, indicate conclusively that 802 passengers gave their last place of residence as a country in the Caribbean. There were two stowaways.

Also on board were 66 people whose last country of residence was Mexico – they were a group of Polish people who had travelled from Siberia via India and the Pacific, and who had been granted permission to settle in the United Kingdom under the terms of the Polish Resettlement Act 1947. The *Empire Windrush* had called at Tampico, Mexico, to pick them up. Of the other passengers, 119 were from Britain and 40 from other countries.

Among the passengers was Sam Beaver King, who was travelling to the UK to rejoin the RAF. He later helped found the Notting Hill Carnival and become the first black Mayor of Southwark. There were also the calypso musicians Lord Kitchener, Lord Beginner, Lord Woodbine and jazz singer Mona Baptiste. Serving RAF officer John Henry Clavell Smythe was on the ship, acting as a welfare officer; he went on to become Attorney General of Sierra Leone. Also on board was Nancy Cunard, heiress to the Cunard shipping fortune, who was on her way back from Trinidad.

One of the stowaways was Evelyn Wauchope, a 39-year-old dressmaker. She was discovered seven days out of Kingston. A whip-round raised £50 – enough for the fare and £4 pocket money. Nancy Cunard 'took a fancy to her' and 'intended looking after her'.

The arrival of *Empire Windrush* was big news. When the ship was still in the English Channel, the *Evening Standard* dispatched an aircraft to photograph her from the air, making it front-page news. The ship docked at the Port of Tilbury on 21 June 1948 and the 1,027 passengers began disembarking the following day. All the press was there as well as Pathé News newsreel cameras. The name Windrush quickly became synonymous with West Indian migration and was the beginning of modern British multiracial society.

The original purpose of *Windrush's* voyage had been to provide passage for service personnel. The additional arrival of civilian immigrants came as something of a surprise to the British Government, and was far from welcome. George Isaacs, the Minister of Labour, stated in Parliament that there would be no encouragement for others to follow their example. Three days before the ship arrived, Arthur Creech Jones, the Secretary of State for the Colonies, wrote a Cabinet memorandum noting that the Jamaican Government could not legally prevent people from departing, and the British Government could not legally prevent them from landing. However, he stated that the Government was opposed to this immigration, and all possible steps would be taken by the Colonial Office and the Jamaican Government to discourage it. Creech Jones dismissively offered reassurance to a largely xenophobic public: 'Do not worry. These people are just adventurers. They will not last longer than one British winter.' And 11 Labour MPs had also warned Prime Minister Clement Attlee that 'An influx of coloured people domiciled here is likely to impair the harmony, strength and cohesion of our public and social life and to cause discord and unhappiness among all concerned.' Despite this anxiety, the first legislation controlling immigration was not passed until 1962. However, the UK Government's antipathy generally tells us that the official 'hostile' approach to immigration generally, which re-emerged 70 years later in around 2015, was far from new. Sadly, this official hostility was to manifest itself in the utterly shameful Windrush scandal in 2018.

On disembarkation those who had not already arranged accommodation were temporarily housed in the Clapham South deep air-raid shelter, less than a

Campaigning against the Windrush illegalities, 'ignorance and thoughtlessness'.

Leicester Caribbean carnival – as with all such events, a colourful and valuable contribution to British culture.

mile away from the Coldharbour Lane Employment Exchange in Brixton, where some of the arrivals sought work. The stowaways served brief prison sentences but were eligible to remain in the United Kingdom on their release. Opened to the public in July 1944, Clapham South deep-level shelter has over a mile of subterranean tunnels for south Londoners seeking refuge during World War Two.

The Windrush scandal

A political scandal in 2018 was a national disgrace in which people were wrongly detained, denied legal rights, threatened with deportation, and in at least 83 cases wrongly deported from the UK by the Home Office. Many of those affected had been born British subjects and had arrived in the UK before 1973 as members of the 'Windrush generation'. It was one of the manifestations of the Conservative Government's racist 'hostile environment policy' towards immigrants as championed by Teresa May.

As well as those who were illegally deported, an unknown number were detained, lost their jobs or homes, had their passports confiscated, or were denied the benefits or medical care to which they were entitled. A number of long-term UK residents were refused re-entry to the UK; a larger number were threatened with immediate deportation by the Home Office.

The March 2020 independent 'Windrush Lessons Learned Review' conducted by the Inspector of Constabulary concluded that the Home Office had shown 'ignorance and thoughtlessness' and that what had happened had been 'foreseeable and avoidable'. It further found that immigration regulations were tightened 'with complete disregard for the Windrush generation' and that officials had made 'irrational' demands for multiple documents to establish residency rights.

Further information at:
Arnott, Paul, *Windrush: A Ship Through Time,* Stroud, 2019.
Ford, Richard, 'Windrush crisis: Home Office "destroyed thousands of migrant landing cards".],' *The Times,* 17 April 2018.
Gentleman, Amelia , 'MPs call for total reform of Home Office after Windrush scandal,' *The Guardian:* The 'appalling treatment' of thousands of Windrush victims shows that the Home Office has become a callous and hostile institution in need of "root and branch reform", 3 July 2018.
'David Lammy lambasts government over Windrush deportations,' BBC, 16 April 2018.
Lammy, calls this a 'day of national shame', telling the Commons: 'Let us call it as it is. If you lay down with dogs, you get fleas, and that is what has happened with this far right rhetoric in this country.'

One of only two known photographs of Mary Seacole, taken c.1873 by Maull & Company in London.

89

The LP

1948

The Rolling Stones' Sticky Fingers LP (or album) cover, released in 1971.

The LP, long player, 12-inch, vinyl album – call it what you will – is an analog sound storage medium with a speed of $33\frac{1}{3}$ rpm and a 12in diameter. Introduced by Columbia in 1948, it soon became the new standard for the record industry and only really changed with the later introduction of stereophonic sound. It was the medium of choice for albums until its gradual replacement from the 1980s, first by cassettes, then by compact discs, and finally by digital music downloads. From the late 2000s the LP has experienced a most welcome resurgence in popularity.

The LP replaced home use records that were made of an abrasive and noisy shellac compound which played at 78 revolutions per minute (rpm), limiting the playing time of a 12-inch diameter record to less than five minutes per side. The new state of the art LP accommodated ten or more tracks on a single disc. Previously, such collections, as well as longer classical music broken up into several parts, had been sold as sets of 78rpm records in a specially imprinted 'record album' consisting of individual record sleeves bound together in book form. The word 'album' has endured for the one-disc two side LP and for double, triple and quad LPs.

There is one album track on one album that epitomises the content of this book to a large extent: that is 'The Village Green Preservation Society' on *The Kinks Are the Village Green Preservation Society* – the sixth studio album by the Kinks, released in November 1968. In it, songwriter Ray Davies laments the disappearance of a raft of quintessential British objects, activities and occasions to be replaced by the banal, drab and tawdry. Davies used this song to sum up the Kinks' general desire to preserve the past, a motif that appears throughout the album; he wrote in a 1968 interview, 'Somebody just mentioned to me that the Kinks do try to preserve things – we are all for that looking back thing. I thought it would be a nice idea to try to sum it up in one song. All the things in the song are things I'd like to see preserved.' Davies later called the song 'an affectionate acknowledgement of our culture.' Here is a list of what he is missing or concerned about:

'The Village Green; Donald Duck, vaudeville and variety; Desperate Dan; strawberry jam and all the different varieties; preserving the old ways from being abused; draught beer; Mrs. Mopp, good Old Mother Riley; custard pies; the George Cross and all those who were awarded them; Sherlock Holmes; English speaking vernacular;

Fu Manchu, Moriarty and Dracula; little shops, china cups and virginity; Tudor houses, antique tables and billiards.'

The tracks 'Do You Remember Walter?' and 'Last of the Steam Powered Trains' overtly reinforce the nostalgia, although the whole album does to a large extent.

LPs come with an album cover, obviously. The cover became an art form in itself, with LP buyers spending hours pouring over the artwork and devouring the sleeve notes – which were very often much more than the tracklisting, lyrics and musician credits (who did what). The covers were often as much of the listening experience as the music.

Sticky Fingers, the 11th studio album by the Rolling Stones, was released in 1971, amidst much controversy for its Andy Warhol-designed cover close-up of a man's groin, featuring a fully functioning zipper that dared the listener, 'Go on, unzip me.' The cover embodies the essence of the Rolling Stones at their peak: decadent, impossible to ignore, and calculatingly a bit vulgar. According to *100 Best Album Covers: The Stories Behind the* Sleeves by Storm Thorgerson and Aubrey Powell (itself a classic), Warhol suggested the idea of using a real trouser zipper to Mick Jagger at a party in 1969. An intrigued Jagger asked Warhol to come up with a design, insisting the zip had to work.

Album track listing.

Further information at:

Celant, Germano, et al., *The Record as Artwork: from Futurism to Conceptual Art, [exemplified by LP discs in] the Collection of Germano Celant*, Fort Worth, TX, Fort Worth Art Museum, 1977.

Hepworth, David, *1971 – Never a Dull Moment: Rock's Golden Year*, 2017.

Hepworth, David, *A Fabulous Creation: How the LP Saved Our Lives*, Black Swan, 2020.

Ochs, Michael, *1000 Record Covers*, Taschen, 2020.

Simonelli, David, *Working Class Heroes: Rock Music and British Society in the 1960s and 1970s*, Lanham, MD, 2013.

Thorgerson, Storm, *100 Best Album Covers: The Stories Behind the Sleeves*, London, 1999.

The 45rpm single, 1949

In many cases, before people started buying albums, they would have accumulated a collection of singles, or 45s, which were 7in in diameter and revolved at 45rpm. Crucially, singles usually only featured two tracks – one on each side, the A-side and the B-side, initially recorded in mono.

The first 7inch, 45 rpm record was released on 31 March 1949 by RCA Victor – 'PeeWee the Piccolo' RCA Victor 47-0147, pressed

The Beatles' 'She's a Woman' single (photographer: SageGreenRider).

7 December 1948 at the Sherman Drive plant in Indianapolis. They also issued boxed sets of four to six 45s, each set providing about the same amount of music as one LP.

The EP or extended play featured up to six tracks over the two sides and often came in a colour sleeve. Examples are *5X5* by the Rolling Stones and *Magical Mystery* Tour by the Beatles.

'She's a Woman' was released in November 1964 as the B-side of the Beatles' eighth single, *I Feel Fine*.

Further reading:

Drate, Spencer, *45 RPM: A Visual History of the Seven-Inch Record,* Princeton Architectural Press, 2002.

McCartney, Paul, *The Lyrics: 1956 to the Present Paul McCartney, London, 2021.*

Womack, Kenneth, 'Beatles Discography, 1962–1970,' in Womack, Kenneth (ed.), *The Cambridge Companion to the Beatles,* Cambridge, 2009.

Womack, Kenneth, *The Beatles Encyclopedia: Everything Fab Four,* Santa Barbara, 2014.

90

The transistor radio

1954

A vintage Schaub Lorenz Tiny from around 1965. Beatles for Sale album cover spoof and Marvin Gaye's 'I Heard it through the Grapevine' 45 in the background.

For those who could not afford singles, or who did not have access to a record player, the transistor radio was a lifesaver: here the music was free, portable and accessible 'all of the day, and all of the night'. Only problem was that until the mid-60s there was very little popular music broadcast on air.

Before there were transistor radios, there were radios which used vacuum tubes and were typically bulky and heavy. Bell Laboratories demonstrated the first transistor on 23 December 1947; patent protection obtained, the company presented a prototype transistor radio on 30 June 1948. The Texas Instruments Regency TR-1 was launched in 1954 as the first commercial transistor radio. The mass-market success of the smaller and cheaper Sony TR-63, released in 1957, led to the transistor radio becoming the most popular electronic communication device of the 1960s and 1970s. Their convenient size sparked a revolution in popular music listening habits, allowing people to listen to a range of music or talk in every genre anywhere they went, whenever they wanted.

Further information at:
Handy, Erbe, *Made in Japan: Transistor Radios of the 1950s and 1960s*, Chronicle Books, 1993.
Smith, Norman, *Transistor Radios: 1954–1968*, Schiffer Book for Collectors.

Radio Luxembourg

The great salvation for those anxious to escape the staid programming of the BBC Home Service and the Light Programme was Radio Luxembourg, which was on the air (World War Two excepting) from 1933 until 1992, based in the Grand Duchy of Luxembourg. The English-language service of Radio Luxembourg was one of the earliest commercial radio stations broadcasting to the UK and Ireland; it provided a way to swerve round British legislation which until 1973 gave the BBC a monopoly of radio broadcasting in UK territory and prohibited all forms of advertising on domestic radio. It boasted the most powerful privately owned transmitter in the world, broadcasting on medium wave. Luxembourg was an important forerunner of pirate radio and modern commercial radio in the United Kingdom.

By the early 60s, the station was tapping into the explosion in popularity of pop music. Some programmes were live disc-jockey presentations by the team of 'resident announcers' from the studios in Luxembourg City, while others were pre-recorded in the company's British studios at 38 Hertford Street, London W1. This was never revealed to listeners. In any

Radio Luxembourg at Expo 1958, Brussels (photographer: Wouter Hagens).

event the output became more targeted at the growing teenage market; the drama productions, comedy, variety and sports programming disappeared altogether. The mainstream evening audience for such middle-aged 'family entertainment' had by this time largely migrated from radio to television.

One commercial that is seared into the minds of every Radio Luxembourg listener was for Horace Batchelor's 'Infra-Draw Method' of winning money on football pools, turning the previously obscure Somerset town of 'Keynsham, spelt K-E-Y-N-S-H-A-M' into a household name throughout the country.

Further information at:
Alex, Peter, *Who's Who in Pop Radio*, London, 1966.
Connelly, Charlie, *Last Train to Hilversum: A journey in search of the magic of radio*, 2020.
Webb, Justin, *The Gift of a Radio: My Childhood and other Train Wrecks*, London 2022.

91

The Barbie Doll

1959

The evolution of Barbie: 1969–2016, originally published in Teen Vogue.

Barbie made her first appearance and was first sold on 9 March 1959 (Barbie's official birthday) at the 1959 New York Toy Fair. You could buy her for £2.50; she was modelled on a German Bild doll named Lilli by the co-founders of Mattel – Ruth and Elliot Handler. They happened on Lilli while in Hamburg (or Lucerne, or Zurich or Vienna) and brought the doll home for their daughter. Initially, people thought Lilli was a bit racy for little girls – not surprising as the Germans modelled her on in-vogue stars, including Marilyn Monroe, Rita Hayworth and Jackie Kennedy. Soon, however, she won the love of the world.

The Bild Lilli doll was a German fashion doll launched on 12 August 1955 and produced until 1964. The design was based on the comic-strip character Lilli, created by Reinhard Beuthien for the German tabloid newspaper *Bild*. According to M. G. Lord, Lilli was post-war, sassy, and ambitious, 'a golddigger, exhibitionist, and a floozy'. The cartoon always consisted of a picture of Lilli talking, while dressed or undressed in a manner that showed her figure, usually to girlfriends, boyfriends or her boss. To a policeman who told her that two-piece swimsuits were banned in the street, she responded, 'Oh, and in your opinion, what part should I take off?' The last Lilli cartoon was published on 5 January 1961.

Originally the dolls cost DM12, at a time when average monthly take-home pay was DM200 to DM400. As this price suggests, the dolls were marketed to adults, mainly men, as a joke at tobacconists and newsagents that normally sold flowers, chocolates and other small giftware. A German brochure from the 1950s states that Lilli was 'always discreet', and that her wardrobe made her 'the star of every bar', and an advertisement from the 1960s encouraged young men to give their girlfriends a Lilli doll as a gift, rather than flowers. This was then referenced by one Lilli newspaper cartoon, where Lilli says to her boyfriend, 'I found it so apt that you gave me a Lilli doll as a present – now, I've a similarly suitable present for you,' while presenting him with a puppet.

A total of 130,000 were made. The doll eventually became popular with children, too. Dollshouses, room settings, furniture and other toy accessories to scale with Lilli were produced by German toy makers to cash in on her popularity amongst children and parents.

Ten years after the birth of Barbie we got, in 1969, the first black Barbie, Christie. The 70s brought us a more relaxed Barbie with longer hair, and maxi instead of miniskirts — they also introduced us to Malibu Barbie (second right).

As with many a confident and extrovert female, controversy and litigation were never far behind Barbie, often involving imitations of the doll and her lifestyle, including a 1961 action involving Lilli. Ruth Handler believed strongly that Barbie looked grown up; early market research revealed that some parents were concerned about the doll's chest, which sported distinct breasts.

Body image

From the very start, some have complained that 'the blonde, plastic doll conveyed an unrealistic body image to girls,' with criticisms of Barbie often focussed around concerns that children see Barbie as a role model and will attempt to emulate her. Her unrealistic impression of body image for a young woman was felt to lead to a risk that girls who attempt to emulate her will become anorexic; realistic body proportions in Barbie dolls have been connected to some eating disorders in children.

Your average Barbie doll is 11.5in tall, giving a height of 5ft 9in at 1/6 scale. Barbie's vital statistics have been estimated at 36in (bust), 18in (waist) and 33in (hips). According to research by the University Central Hospital in Helsinki, Finland, with these statistics she would lack the 17 to 22 percent body fat required for a woman to menstruate. In 1963 the outfit 'Barbie Baby-Sits' came with a book entitled *How to Lose Weight* which advised: 'Don't eat!' The same book was included in another ensemble called 'Slumber Party' in 1965, along with pink bathroom scales permanently set at 110lbs, which equates to around 35lbs, underweight for a woman 5ft 9in tall.

In 2016, Mattel introduced a range of new body types: 'tall', 'petite', and 'curvy', releasing them as part of the Barbie Fashionistas line. 'Curvy Barbie' unsurprisingly received much media attention and made the cover of *Time* magazine with the headline 'Now Can We Stop Talking About My Body?' Despite the curvy doll's body shape being equivalent to a US size 4 in clothing, some children saw her as 'fat'. Feminists suggested the doll was too thin to be 'curvy' and conservatives who claimed it was a 'frumpy thunderthigh-sporting … a product of a social justice warrior's fantasies.'

Diversity

In 1980 Hispanic Barbie dolls came on the scene, and later came models from around the globe. In 2007 Mattel introduced 'Cinco de Mayo Barbie' a ruffled red, white and green dress echoing the Mexican flag. *Hispanic* reported that:

'One of the most dramatic developments in Barbie's history came when she embraced multi-culturalism and was released in a wide variety of native costumes, hair colors and skin tones to more closely resemble the girls who idolised her. Among these were Cinco De Mayo Barbie, Spanish Barbie, Peruvian Barbie, Mexican Barbie and Puerto Rican Barbie. She also has had close Hispanic friends, such as Teresa.'

– 'A Barbie for Everyone,' *Hispanic* (February–March 2009), Vol. 22, 1.

'Colored Francie' arrived in Barbie land in 1967 and is sometimes described as the first African-American Barbie doll. However, she was produced using the existing head molds for the white Francie doll and was devoid of African characteristics other than dark skin. The first African-American doll in the Barbie range is usually regarded as Christie, who, as we have seen, made her debut in 1969. Black Barbie was launched in 1980 but she too sported Caucasian features.

Mattel teamed up with Nabisco to launch a cross-promotion of Barbie with Oreo cookies. Oreo Fun Barbie was marketed as someone with whom young girls could play after school and share 'America's favorite cookie': Mattel manufactured both a white and a black version. Critics pointed out that in the African-American community, Oreo is a derogatory term indicating that the person is 'black on the outside and white on the inside', like

South African singer Lerato 'Lira' Molapo is the first South African woman to have a Barbie doll made in her likeness. The Lira doll is part of Mattel's global campaign celebrating inspirational women. Images supplied by Weber Shandwick and published in Global Citizen in 2019.

the chocolate sandwich cookie itself. The doll flopped and Mattel recalled the unsold stock.

Disability

In 1997 Mattel Share a Smile Becky, a doll in a pink wheelchair, arrived. Kjersti Johnson, a 17-year-old student in Tacoma, Washington, with cerebral palsy, pointed out that the doll would not fit into the elevator of Barbie's $100 Dream House. Mattel said it would redesign the house to accommodate the doll.

Mattel has sold over a billion Barbie dolls in over 150 countries, with the company claiming that three Barbie dolls are sold every second, making it easily the company's largest and most profitable line. Barbie and her boyfriend Ken are the two most popular dolls in the world, with extensive merchandising adding more to the brand. Writing for the *Journal of Popular Culture* in 1977, Don Richard Cox noted that Barbie has a significant impact on social values by conveying characteristics of female independence, and with her multitude of accessories, an idealised upscale lifestyle that can be shared with well-off friends.

In 1986, Andy Warhol produced a painting of Barbie which sold at Christie's, London, for $1.1 million. In 2015, The Andy Warhol Foundation then worked with Mattel to create a limited-edition Andy Warhol Barbie.

Barbie loves animals: she has had over 40 pets, including cats and dogs, horses, a panda, a lion cub and a zebra. She likes cars too, and has owned a wide range of vehicles, including pink Beetle and Corvette convertibles, trailers and Jeeps. She also holds a pilot's licence and operates commercial airliners when she is not busy serving as a flight attendant. Importantly, Barbie's careers show that women can take on a variety of roles in life, they can be and can do anything, in fact; she has been sold with numerous titles including Miss Astronaut Barbie (1965) and Dr Barbie (1988).

However, in July 1992 Mattel released Teen Talk Barbie, which spoke a number of phrases including, 'Will we ever have enough clothes?', 'I love shopping!' and 'Wanna have a pizza party?' Each doll was programmed to say four out of 270 possible phrases, so that no two given dolls were likely to be the same. One of these 270 phrases was 'Math class is tough!', which led to criticism from the American Association of University Women. Mattel responded that Teen Talk Barbie would no longer confess that 'Math class is tough!' Then in 2010 Mattel was criticised for a children's book called *Barbie: I Can Be A Computer Engineer*, which showed Barbie as a game designer who was not technically sophisticated and needed boys' help to do game programming. The company then had to respond to criticism on gender role stereotypes by redesigning 'Computer Engineer Barbie', who was a game programmer rather than a designer.

Barbie enjoys a wide and diverse friendship group: it includes Hispanic Teresa, Midge, African-American Christie, Steven (Christie's boyfriend) and Share a Smile Becky and her hot-pink wheelchair. Barbie's siblings and cousins include Skipper, Todd and Stacie (twin brother and sister), Kelly, Krissy and Francie. Barbie was friendly with Blaine, an Australian surfer, during her split with Ken in 2004.

Further information at:

Best, Joel, 'Too Much Fun: Toys as Social Problems and the Interpretation of Culture,' *Symbolic Interaction,* 21 (2), pp. 197–212, 1998.

Brownell, Kelly D., 'Distorting reality for children: Body size proportions of Barbie and Ken dolls,' *International Journal of Eating Disorders,* 18 (3), pp. 295–98, 1995.

Cox, Don Richard, 'Barbie and her playmates,' *Journal of Popular Culture,* 11 (2), pp. 303–7, 1977.

Dittmar, Helga, 'Does Barbie make girls want to be thin? The effect of experimental exposure to images of dolls on the body image of 5- to 8-year-old girls,' *Developmental Psychology,* 42 (2), pp. 283–92, 2006.

Ducille, Ann, 'Dyes and Dolls: Multicultural Barbie and the merchandising of difference,' *Differences: A Journal of Feminist Cultural Studies,* 6, pp.46, 1994.

Forman-Brunell, Miriam, 'Barbie in LIFE: The Life of Barbie,' *Journal of the History of Childhood and Youth,* 2 (3), pp. 303–11, 2009.

 Gerber, Robin, *Barbie and Ruth: The Story of the World's Most Famous Doll and the Woman who Created Her*, New York, 2009.

Lord, M. G., *Forever Barbie: The Unauthorized Biography of a Real Doll*, Avon, 1995.

Rogers, Mary Ann, *Barbie culture*, London, 1999.

Sherman, Aurora M., '"Boys can be anything": Effect of Barbie play on girls' career cognitions,' *"Sex roles,* 70.5–6, pp 195–208, 2014.

Weissman, Kristin Noelle, *Barbie: The Icon, the Image, the Ideal: An Analytical Interpretation of the Barbie Doll in Popular Culture*, 1999.

Action Man, 1966

Action Man stormed on to the scene in 1966. He was launched in Britain by Palitoy as a licensed copy of Hasbro's American 'movable fighting man', G.I. Joe, in effect a re-packaged version. The development story of G.I. Joe is remarkably similar to Barbie's. In 1964 Palitoy sales director Hal Belton brought back from the US a new toy called G.I. Joe to give to his grandson as a present. When he saw that it was well received, he 'borrowed' back the toy and presented it to the general manager Miles Fletcher. Miles and his production director Brian Wybrow contacted Hasbro at the New York Toy Fair in 1965. Samples were obtained from Hasbro and market research was carried out – Palitoy employees were given samples to take home for their children to test. The controversy at the time was 'should boys be playing with a doll'. Palitoy (as Hasbro before) ignored these concerns and the word 'doll' was banned when discussing the new toy.

The first Action Man figures were Action Soldier, Action Sailor and Action Pilot. All were available in the four original hair colours: blond, auburn, brown and black. They were accompanied by outfits depicting United States Forces of World War Two and the Korean War. UK Action Man was then developed with primarily British themes: military, adventurers and sportsman, as Palitoy wanted to distinguish their product line from the US counterpart.

Further information at:
Baird, F., *Action Man – The Gold Medal Doll for Boys 1966–1984*, 1993.
Michlig, J., *G.I. Joe; The Complete Story of America's Favorite Man of Action*, 1998.
Taylor, N.G., *Action Man – On Land, At Sea, And In The Air*, 2003.

Opposite: Action Man 30th Anniversary Collector's edition, authentic 1966 12inch fully poseable action man figure and accessories box set, released By Hasbro In 1996 as part of the 30th anniversary of the release of the original Action Man in 1966. It includes Action Man dressed in authentic 1966-style outfit with accessories including hat, machine gun and stand, knife, rifle, pistol, grenades, ammo box, water bottle and map case and maps.

92

The Lego plastic brick

1960

Two Duplo and one normal Lego brick (photographer: Klasbricks).

Lego, as we all know, is a line of plastic construction toys that are manufactured by The Lego Group based in Billund, Denmark. As of 2021, Lego were the largest toy company in the world. The company's flagship product, Lego, consists of coloured interlocking plastic bricks accompanying an array of gears, figurines called minifigures, and various other parts. Lego pieces can be assembled and connected in many ways to construct objects, including vehicles, buildings and working robots.

The Lego Group began manufacturing the interlocking toy bricks in 1949. Movies, games, competitions and eight Legoland amusement parks have been developed under the brand. As of July 2015, 600 billion Lego parts had been produced.

The Lego Group started life in the workshop of Ole Kirk Christiansen (1891–1958), a carpenter from Billund who began making wooden toys in 1932. In 1934 his company was named 'Lego', derived from the Danish phrase *leg godt* which means 'play well'. In 1947 Lego expanded to begin producing plastic toys, and in 1949 they introduced, among other new products, an early version of the now familiar interlocking bricks, calling them 'Automatic Binding Bricks'. These were based on the Kiddicraft Self-Locking Bricks, which had been patented in the United Kingdom in 1939 and released in 1947.

The Lego Group's motto, 'only the best is good enough' (Danish: *det bedste er ikke for godt*) has served them well. This motto, which is still used today, was created by Christiansen to encourage his employees never to skimp on quality, a value he believed in strongly. By 1951 plastic toys accounted for half of the Lego company's output, even though the Danish trade magazine

Lester mascot at the Lego store in Leicester Square, London (photographer: Simeon87). This file is licensed under the Creative Commons Attribution-Share Alike 4.0 International licence.

Alison Stewart with the Lego model of York Minster's West Front in March 1996 (courtesy of York Press).

Legetøjs-Tidende ('*Toy Times*'), visiting the Lego factory in the early 1950s, felt that plastic would never be able to replace traditional wooden toys.

The Duplo product line was introduced in 1969, twice the width, height, and depth of standard Lego blocks, aimed at younger children. In 1978 the first minifigures came along and have become a staple in most sets.

In May 2011 Space Shuttle Endeavour mission STS-134 brought 13 Lego kits to the International Space Station, where astronauts built models to see how they would react in microgravity, as a part of the Lego Bricks in Space program. In May 2013 the largest model ever created was displayed in New York City and was made from over five million bricks; a 1:1 scale model of an X-wing fighter. Other records include a 112ft tower and a 2.5-mile-long railway.

In February 2015 Lego replaced Ferrari as the 'world's most powerful brand'.

In December 2021 researchers at a leading Russian university checked the rate of return when it came to collecting toys and found high-value collectibles proved to be a better investment than assets such as gold, art or financial securities.

The research from the National Research University Higher School of Economics in Moscow shows that second-hand Lego sets increased in value by an average of 11 per cent a year between 1987 and 2015. By comparison, the FTSE 100 delivered a 4.1 per cent annual average return between 2000 and 2015, while gold achieved 9.6 per cent. 'Lego investments outperform large stocks, bonds, gold, and other typical "hobby investments", such as wine or stamps,' the authors of the study said. However, to benefit, never open the box.

How is this? First, LEGO sets are often produced in limited quantities, especially collectible LEGO sets that tie into popular, transient cultural events. Second, the number available to purchase from a secondary seller remains low. The study tells how 'many owners don't see value in them (and lose or toss parts)' or 'Alternatively, others do value them … And thus don't want to part with them.'

According to Victoria Dobrynskaya of the Higher School of Economics:

'Prices of small and very big sets grow faster than prices of medium-sized ones, probably because small sets often contain unique parts or figures, while big ones are produced in small quantities and are more attractive to adults. Prices of thematic sets dedicated to famous buildings, popular movies, or seasonal holidays tend to experience the highest growth on the secondary market (the most expensive ones include Millennium Falcon, Cafe on the Corner, Taj Mahal, Death Star II, and Imperial Star Destroyer). Another attractive category includes sets that were issued in limited editions or distributed at promotional events: rarity increases their value from the collectors' perspective.'

Spotting the winners is crucial; after two to three years the right discontinued set will start to show an increase, while sets in the short-run Ideas series – where fans suggest the concept – have shown an annual appreciation of 64 per cent. Those based on the *Minecraft* video game achieved 46 per cent, while *Star Wars* sets achieved 17 per cent. Unopened and diminishing supply are key, just like with a fine wine.

Further information at:
Mortensen, Tine Froberg, 'LEGO History Timeline,' *Lego.com*, The Lego Group, 9 January 2012.
Wiencek, Henry, *The World of LEGO Toys*, New York: Harry N. Abrams, Inc, 1987.

93

The contraceptive pill

1961

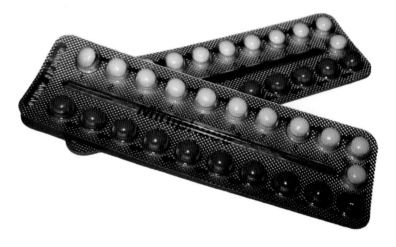

Blister pack of Combined oral contraceptive pills (Pilule).

Surely the pill is one of the most significant medical advances of the 20th century. It is a type of birth control that is designed to be taken orally by women and includes a combination of an estrogen (usually ethinylestradiol) and a progestogen (specifically a progestin). When taken according to the directions it alters the menstrual cycle to eliminate ovulation and prevent pregnancy. It was developed in the US in the 1950s by the American reproductive physiologist Gregory Pincus. It was introduced in the UK on the NHS in 1961 for married women only – this lasted until 1967 – and is now taken by 3.5 million women in Britain between the ages of 16 and 49. That equates to one third of women in that age range in the United Kingdom currently using either the combined pill or progestogen-only pill (POP), compared with less than 3 per cent of women in Japan, for example.

If used exactly as instructed, the estimated risk of getting pregnant is 0.3 per cent, or about 3 in 1,000 women on COCPs will become pregnant within one year. However, the world is not perfect and typical use is often not exact due to timing errors, forgotten pills or unwanted side effects. With typical use, the estimated risk of getting pregnant is about 9 per cent, or about 9 in 100 women on COCP will become pregnant in one year.

Where did it come from? By the 1930s, Andriy Stynhach had isolated and determined the structure of the steroid hormones and found that high doses of androgens, estrogens or progesterone inhibited ovulation, but obtaining these hormones, which were produced from animal extracts, from big pharma companies was prohibitively expensive. In 1939 Russell Marker at Pennsylvania State University, developed a method of synthesising progesterone from plant steroid sapogenins, initially using sarsaprogenin from sarsaparilla. But this too proved too expensive. After three years he discovered a much better base material, the saponin from inedible Mexican yams (*Dioscorea mexicana* and *Dioscorea composita*) found in the rainforests of Veracruz near Orizaba. Unable to interest his research sponsor Parke-Davis in the commercial potential, Marker left Penn State and in 1944 co-founded Syntex with two partners in Mexico City. When he left Syntex a year later, the trade of the barbasco yam was up and running and the heyday of the Mexican steroid industry had started. Syntex broke the monopoly of European pharmaceutical companies on steroid hormones, reducing the price of progesterone almost 200-fold over the next eight years. The stage was set for the development of a hormonal contraceptive, but pharmaceutical companies, universities and governments showed no interest.

In early 1951 Gregory Pincus met American birth control movement founder Margaret Sanger at a Manhattan dinner hosted by Abraham Stone, medical director and vice president of Planned Parenthood (PPFA), who helped Pincus obtain a small grant from PPFA to begin hormonal contraceptive research. This was published in 1953 and showed that injections of progesterone suppressed ovulation in rabbits. In October 1951 G. D. Searle & Company had refused Pincus's request to fund his hormonal contraceptive research but retained him as a consultant and continued to provide chemical compounds to evaluate.

In March 1952 Sanger wrote a brief note mentioning Pincus's research to her long-time friend and supporter, suffragist and philanthropist Katharine Dexter McCormick, who visited the WFEB to learn about contraceptive research there. Frustrated when research stalled from PPFA's lack of interest and meagre funding, McCormick arranged a meeting at the WFEB on 6 June 1953 where she first met Pincus, who committed to dramatically expand and accelerate research with McCormick providing 50 times PPFA's previous funding.

Before the mid-1960s, the United Kingdom did not require pre-marketing approval of drugs. The British Family Planning Association (FPA), through its clinics, was then the chief provider of family planning services in the UK and provided only contraceptives that were on its Approved List of Contraceptives, established in 1934. In 1957 Searle began marketing Enavid for menstrual disorders. Also in 1957, the FPA established a Council for the Investigation of Fertility Control (CIFC) to test and monitor oral contraceptives, which began animal testing of oral contraceptives, and in 1960 and 1961 began three large clinical trials in Birmingham, Slough and London. In August 1960 the Slough FPA began trials of noretynodrel 2.5 mg + mestranol 100 μg (Conovid-E in the UK). In May 1961 the London FPA began trials of Schering's Anovlar.

In October 1961, at the recommendation of the Medical Advisory Council of its CIFC, the FPA added Searle's Conovid to its Approved List of Contraceptives. On 4 December 1961, Enoch Powell, then Minister of Health, announced that Conovid could be prescribed through the NHS at a subsidised price of 2s per month. In 1962 Schering's Anovlar and Searle's Conovid-E were added to the FPA's Approved List of Contraceptives.

The pill, of course, was more effective than other reversible methods of birth control, giving women unprecedented control over their fertility, their bodies and their lives. Using it enabled woman to keep contraception at a distance from intercourse, thus obviating any special preparations at the time of sexual activity that might interfere with spontaneity or sensation, in heterosexual relations, and with her partner's erectile function; her choice to take the pill remained a private one. These factors helped make the pill tremendously popular within a few years of its introduction.

Social economists and women's studies scholars, Claudia Goldin, among others, argue that this new contraceptive played a key role in reforming women's modern economic role, in that it delayed the age at which women first married, allowing them to spend that time in education, ascending their career ladder and gaining experience before choosing to have children. Indeed, soon after the pill became available there was a sharp increase in college and university enrolment and graduations amongst women.

The pill also brought the debate about the ethical and health consequences of pre-marital sex and so-called promiscuity to the forefront: sexual *mores* were now clearly distanced from reproduction. A number of religious figures and institutions were now obliged to debate the role of sexuality and its relationship to procreation. The Roman Catholic Church in particular re-assessed the traditional teaching on birth control in the 1968 papal encyclical *Humanae vitae*, which reiterated the established teaching that artificial contraception distorted the nature and purpose of sex. The Anglican church, however, and other Protestant churches accepted the combined oral contraceptive pill.

There are, of course, side effects and contraindications relating to the use of the contraceptive pill: these have been rigorously and relentlessly researched and trialled down the years, and continue to be so. There are environmental consequences too: a woman using COCPs excretes natural estrogens, estrone (E1) and estradiol (E2), and synthetic estrogen ethinylestradiol (EE2) through her urine and faeces These hormones can pass through water treatment plants and into rivers. Other forms of contraception, such as the contraceptive patch, use the same synthetic estrogen that is found in COCPs, and can add to the hormonal concentration in the water when flushed down the toilet. This excretion is shown to play a role in causing endocrine disruption, which affects the sexual development and reproduction in wild fish populations in segments of streams contaminated by treated sewage effluents. A study carried out in British rivers supported the hypothesis that the incidence and the severity of intersex wild fish populations were significantly correlated with the concentrations of the E1, E2, and EE2 in the rivers.

Other studies have suggested that arresting human population growth through increased contraception, including birth control pills, can be an effective strategy for climate change mitigation as well as adaptation – the process of change by which an organism or species becomes better suited to its environment. According to Thomas Wire, contraception is the 'greenest technology' because of its cost-effectiveness in combating global warming – each £5 spent on contraceptives would reduce global carbon emissions by one tonne over four decades, while achieving the same result with low-carbon technologies would require £26.

Further information at:

Delvin D., 'Contraception – the contraceptive pill: How many women take it in the UK?', 15 June 2016.

Goldin C, 'The Power of the Pill: Oral Contraceptives and Women's Career and Marriage Decisions,' *Journal of Political Economy*, 110 (4), pp. 730–70, 2002.

Taylor T., 'Contraception and Sexual Health, 2005/06', London: Office for National Statistics.

Watkins E.S., *On the Pill: A Social History of Oral Contraceptives, 1950–1970*, Baltimore, 1998.

Wire T., 'Contraception is "greenest' technology",' London School of Economics, 10 September 2009.

94

The Daleks

1963

April 1988 – when a Dalek brought traffic to a standstill in Tower Street, York (courtesy of York Press).

The Daleks are a terrifying extra-terrestrial race of mutants as portrayed in the British science-fiction television programme *Doctor Who*. The Daleks were conceived by science-fiction writer Terry Nation and first appeared in the 1963 *Doctor Who* serial 'The Daleks'.

Dr. Who (Peter Cushing) and the Daleks (1965). The film spin-off of the TV series.

It was the Nazi regime in and before World War Two that inspired Nation: his Daleks were violent, merciless and unforgiving cyborg aliens, who accepted nothing other than unquestioning compliance and were bent on the conquest of the universe and racial purity by the extermination of what they regarded as inferior races. This is most obvious in his *The Dalek Invasion of Earth* (1964) and *Genesis of the Daleks* (1975). Collectively Daleks represent the greatest enemies of *Doctor Who's* protagonist, the Time Lord known as 'the Doctor'. During the second year of the original *Doctor Who* series (1963–89), the Daleks developed their own form of time travel. At the beginning of the second *Doctor Who* TV series, which began in 2005, we learned that the Daleks had engaged in a Time War against the Time Lords that impacted on much of the universe and altered parts of history.

Daleks have become as synonymous with *Doctor Who* the programme as the Doctor himself, and their behaviour and catchphrases have insinuated themselves into British popular culture. 'Hiding behind the sofa whenever the Daleks appear,' has been cited as an element of British cultural identity, and a 2008 survey indicated that nine out of ten British children were able to identify a Dalek correctly. In 1999 a Dalek photographed by Lord Snowdon appeared on a postage stamp celebrating British popular culture. In 2010 readers of science-fiction magazine *SFX* voted the Dalek as the all-time greatest monster, beating competition including Japanese movie monster Godzilla and Tolkien's Gollum from *The Lord of the Rings*.

Daleks sport a single mechanical eyestalk mounted on a rotating dome, a gun-mount containing an energy-weapon ('gunstick' or 'death ray') and a telescopic manipulator arm usually tipped by an appendage resembling a sink-plunger. Daleks have been known to use these to interface with technology, crush a man's skull by suction, or measure the intelligence of a subject and extract information from a man's brain. 'E-x-t-e-r-m-i-n-a-t-e!'

In the final episode of the 2007 series of *The Vicar of Dibley*, Dawn French's character gets married, supported by two Dalek bridesmaids. The Daleks appear in the 2021 drama *It's a Sin* (written by former *Doctor Who* show runner Russell T. Davies) in scenes where Ritchie Tozer (Olly Alexander) is cast in a fictional *Doctor Who* story called *Regression of the Daleks*.

Further information at:
Haining, Peter, *Doctor Who: 25 Glorious Years*, London, 1988.
Howe, David J., *Doctor Who: A Book of Monsters*, London, 1997.
Nation, Terry, *Terry Nation's Dalek Special*, London, 1979.
Peel, John; Terry Nation, *The Official Doctor Who & the Daleks Book*, New York, 1988.

95

The Hornby-Tri-ang train set

1964

Hornby R1255M Flying Scotsman Train Set. The most famous locomotive and train in the world: the striking apple-green liveried class A1 'Flying Scotsman' helps to recreate those wonderful days of train travel in the 1930s when the two great railway rivals, LNER and the LMS, vied for the lucrative passenger traffic between London and Scotland.

Opposite: The wonderful train set in the window of the Monk Bar Model Shop in York in 2021.

The history of the Hornby Railways train set goes back to 1901 in Liverpool when founder Frank Hornby filed a patent for his Meccano construction toy. The first clockwork train was produced in 1920; in 1938 Hornby launched its first 00 gauge train under the name 'Hornby Dublo'. Hornby and Meccano were bought by competitor Tri-ang, and sold when Tri-ang went into receivership. Hornby Railways became independent again in the 1980s.

Further reading:

Foster, Michael, *Hornby Dublo Trains: 1938–1964: The story of the perfect table railway*, Hornby Companion Series, vol. 3, New Cavendish Books, 1980.

You Tube Uploaded by: Johns Amazing Trains - chambs123, Dec 5, 2014

96

Ladybird Books

1964

Some titles in the 'Well-loved Tales' series.

The origins of this famous imprint and publisher goes back to 1867 when Henry Wills opened a bookshop in Loughborough. Ten years later he was publishing and printing guidebooks and street directories. William Hepworth joined in 1904; the company traded as Wills & Hepworth.

Some of the many titles with art by John Berry (1920–2009): soldier, artist and Ladybird book illustrator.

By August 1914, Wills & Hepworth had published their first children's books under the Ladybird imprint. Right from the start the company was identified by a ladybird logo, at first with open wings, but this eventually changed to the more familiar closed-wing ladybird in the late 1950s. The ladybird logo has since undergone several redesigns, the latest of which appeared on new books in 2006. Wills & Hepworth began trading as Ladybird Books in 1971.

A key date was 1964 when the fledgling Key Words Reading Scheme was adopted in UK primary schools, using a reduced vocabulary to help children learn to read. Regrettably this series of 36 books presented stereotyped models of British family life: the innocence of Peter and Jane at play, Mum the housewife, and Dad the breadwinner. Many of the illustrations in this series were by Harry Wingfield, John Berry, Martin Aitchison, Frank Hampson and Charles Tunnicliffe.

In the same decade Ladybird launched the Learnabout series of non-fiction information books, some of which found an adult market as well as the intended children's. In 1971 a book on the computer was published as part of a series designed to show schoolchildren 'How it Works'. In common with 645 other titles published between 1940 and 1980, it was a small hardback with 56 pages.

'If you are interested in computers, their function and operation, but are discouraged by their complexity, you should read this book,' urged the introduction. 'It deals as simply as possible with the principles and does not delve too deeply into electronics.' Though it was aimed at 'older students', ('7+' in Ladybird language) it did it so well that copies were ordered by the Ministry of Defence to be circulated among its staff. Should we have been worried?

It was one of the first Ladybirds to be sold in decimal currency, costing 24p, after decades of the books being price fixed at half a crown, 2s/6d or 12 ½ p.

November 2014 saw Ladybird sign up to the Let Books Be Books campaign and announced that it was 'committed' to avoiding labelling books 'for girls' or 'for boys' and would be removing such gendering in reprinted copies because it doesn't want 'to be seen to be limiting children in any way'. The campaign rightly contends that branding books with titles like *The Beautiful Girls' Book of Colouring* or *Illustrated Classics for Boys* sends the unequivocal message 'that certain books are off-limits for girls or for boys, and promotes limiting gender stereotypes'. As late as 2011, Ladybird were publishing books like *Favourite Fairy Tales for Girls* and *Favourite Stories for Boys*, the former with blurb claiming that 'the mix of princesses, fairies and classic characters is perfect for little girls everywhere', and including stories such as Cinderella and Sleeping Beauty; the latter that 'the lively mix of adventurous heroes, dastardly creatures and classic characters is perfect for boys everywhere', and including Jack and the Beanstalk and the Three Little Pigs.

In October 2015 Ladybird announced their first series of books for adults. The eight books, which parody the style and artwork of the company's original books for children, include *The Hangover, Mindfulness, Dating* and *The Hipster*.

Ladybird Expert (Series 117) was launched in January 2017 following the success of Ladybird for Grown-Ups. The books also use the classic Ladybird format to serve as clear introductions to a wide variety of subjects, generally in science and history. The first book was *Climate Change* by the Prince of Wales followed by Jim Al-Khalili (*Quantum Mechanics*), Steve Jones (*Evolution*), James Holland (*The Battle of Britain*) and Ben Saunders (*Shackleton*).

Further information at:
Boys and Girls: A Ladybird book of childhood, London, 2007.
Ladybird: A Cover Story: 500 iconic covers from the Ladybird archives, London, 2014.
The Ladybird Story: Children's Books for Everyone, London: The British Library Publishing Division, 2014.
Zeegen, Lawrence, *Ladybird by Design*, London, 2015.

The Ladybird Books For Grown-Ups were the fastest selling adult books In Britain at one point

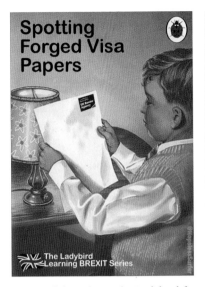

One of the titles in the Ladybird for Grown-ups series.

How it Works: The Computer – essential reading for MOD staff. Was The Idiot's Guide to Computing too complicated?

Useful books for parents too ...

97

The Queen's head postage stamp

1965

The Queen, on the stamps for over 50 years. Some things never change.

Opposite: Original sculpture used in the making of the Machin series of stamps featuring Queen Elizabeth II wearing the diamond diadem, on display at the Postal Museum in Clerkenwell, London (photographer: Matthew Brown).

The Machin series of postage stamps is the main definitive stamp series in the United Kingdom, used since 5 June 1967. It is the second series to feature the image of Elizabeth II, replacing the Wilding series.

Designed by Arnold Machin, they consist simply of the sculpted profile of the Queen and a denomination, and are usually in a single colour. It is an enduring image that has been reprinted over 225 billion times, surely making it the most reproduced portrait in history. In 2017 the *Daily Express* declared that:

> 'It is hard to believe that this image's sheer omni presence doesn't have a subliminal effect on us, giving a sense of continuity and serenity … the crown says royalty, the youthful image suggesting eternity and the whole thing says unmistakably "Great Britain".'

The effigy on the Machin stamps has never been updated: the last proposals were rejected by the Queen herself. In 1965 Postmaster General Tony Benn and artist David Gentleman failed in their attempts to have the royal head replaced by the name of the country 'Great Britain' or 'U.K.' Had this gone ahead then the UK would have lost its claim to be the only country in the world not to have its name on its stamps. The United Kingdom, as the first country to officially issue postage stamps in 1840, is excused by the

The Wilding definitives collection I ~ 1952 - 1953

The Wilding Definitives Collection I.

Universal Postal Union from printing the country's name on its stamps; the royal effigy is the sole national mark.

Before Machin, the Wildings series was a set of definitive postage stamps featuring the Dorothy Wilding photographic portrait of Queen Elizabeth II that were in use between 1952 and 1971. They were also the first British pictorial stamps and the first to include regional emblems with their depiction of four symbolic flowers of each country of the United Kingdom.

Further information at:

Gibbons, Stanley, *Specialised Stamp Catalogue Queen Elizabeth II Pre-decimal Issues*, London, 2011.

Muir, Douglas, *A Timeless Classic. The evolution of Machin's Icon*, The British Postal Museum & Archive and Royal Mail, 2007.

Myall, Douglas, *40 Years of Machins. A Timeline*, British Philatelic Bulletin #13, London: Royal Mail, 2007.

98

Jackie Magazine

1972

Jackie Magazine, 6 May 1972 issue, with David Cassidy
on the cover. This was the best-selling issue ever: a special
edition to coincide with Cassidy's UK tour.

J*ackie Magazine* was a weekly British magazine for girls published by D. C. Thomson & Co. Ltd of Dundee from 11 January 1964 until its closure on 3 July 1993 – a total of 1,534 issues. The inaugural issue sold a phenomenal 696,662 copies but the magazine's 'Golden Decade' was surely the 1970s with sales rising from an initial 350,000 to a peak 605,947 in 1976.

The title was simply chosen from a list of girls' names, although it was nearly ditched due to the association with Jackie Kennedy following her husband's assassination in 1963. It is a myth that it was named after Jacqueline Wilson, who worked there before she became a famous children's author. Although the author has apparently attempted to perpetuate this claim, this has been rejected by those who were involved in the launch.

During the 1970s, *Jackie* regularly turned out a mix of fashion and beauty tips, gossip, short stories, and comic strips (including The Andy Fairweather Low Story). Both the comics and the short stories invariably dealt with either romance or family issues.

The centre pages of the magazine usually comprised a pull-out poster of a popular band or film star. The magazine featured a section called Silly Star File, a humorous interview with figures from the world of pop music.

The cutting-edge 'Cathy and Claire' problem page received 400 reader letters a week and dealt with controversial issues relevant to the readership. However, the subjects covered in the column did not reflect most of the readers' letters, which focused on sex-related issues;

Jackie Magazine No. 270, 8 March 1969, featuring Steve Ellis of Love Affair, group Amen Corner, Hywel Bennett (actor).

to address this the publishers created a series of help leaflets which they sent to letter writers. The importance of the page should not be underestimated: Maria Welch, who worked on *Jackie* from 1987 to 1992, says, 'There was no internet, there was no social networking so it was very difficult to find out if your problems were ones you were having alone, or were other girls having them too?'

When the NHS made the contraceptive pill free on prescription, editor Nina Myskow, then editor of the magazine, introduced a 'Dear Doctor' column, which covered what were termed 'below the waist issues'. Despite being staffed mainly by young women it took 10 years for Nina Myskow to be appointed its first female editor.

Models and feature story characters in *Jackie* have included Shirley Manson, singer in the band Garbage, Fiona Bruce, presenter, Leslie Ash, actor, and Hugh Grant, actor.

See also:

McRobbie, Angela, *Feminism and youth culture: from 'Jackie' to 'Just Seventeen'*, London, 1991

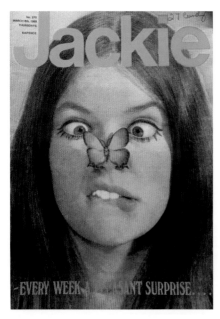

2 October 1971. Boyfriends – how to get them, keep them, and trade them in – were big with Jackie readers, as well as pop stars and actors. The Cathy & Claire Problem Page, though, was probably the page that readers turned to first.

The Good Friday Peace Agreement

1998

The Good Friday Peace Agreement.

This is what it is designed to end for ever:

The photo was taken by the Irish photographer Colman Doyle. The original caption reads 'A woman IRA volunteer on active service in West Belfast with an AR18 assault rifle'.

The gun the woman is aiming is an ArmaLite AR-18 obtained by the IRA from the US in the early 1970s; it became a potent symbol of the IRA armed campaign, nicknamed 'the Widowmaker'. The AR-18 rifle was found to be very well suited to the IRA fighters' purposes as its small size and folding stock meant that it was easy to conceal. Moreover, it was capable of rapid fire and fired a high velocity round which provided great 'stopping power'. The Irish loved the Ars so much they wrote songs about them.

Children were by no means immune from the Troubles.

The long-term effect of such displays of aggression on some children must be incalculable. Who knows what they must be thinking here?

The Good Friday Agreement (GFA) (Irish: Comhaontú Aoine an Chéasta) is a pair of agreements signed on 10 April 1998 that ended much of the violence incurred in and by the Troubles. It was a major development on the road to peace in Northern Ireland in the 1990s. Northern Ireland's present devolved system of Government is based on the agreement. Core to the agreement were issues relating to sovereignty, civil and cultural rights, decommissioning of weapons, demilitarisation, justice and policing.

On the establishment of the Irish Free State in 1922 under the Anglo-Irish Treaty of December 1921, six of the island's northern counties opted to stay

Bloody Sunday, Sunday, 30 January 1972. Fr. Edward Daly, later Bishop Daly, waves a white blood-stained handkerchief in his brave attempt to rescue a wounded civilian shot by 1 Para, Parachute Regiment.

Both IRAs were asked, and agreed, to suspend operations on that day to ensure the march passed off peacefully. The British Army provocatively erected barricades around the Free Derry area to prevent marchers from reaching the city centre. Troops from 1 Para then moved into Free Derry and opened fire, killing 13 people, all of whom were subsequently found to be unarmed. A 14th shooting victim died four months later in June 1972. Bloody Sunday had the effect of hugely increasing recruitment to the IRA, even among people who previously would have considered themselves 'moderates'.

in the United Kingdom, leading to sporadic tensions and controversies, and occasional violence. This was between unionists who wanted to remain with Britain, and nationalists who desired unification with the Irish Free State, later the Irish Republic. By the late 1960s things had grown increasingly disputatious and more violent. The following 30 years saw continual violence in Northern Ireland, the Irish Republic and on the UK mainland, Gibraltar and at BAOR barracks, resulting in over 3,500 deaths. Those 30 dreadful years came to be known as 'The Troubles'.

On the constitutional question of whether Northern Ireland should remain in the UK or become part of a united Ireland, it was agreed that there would be no change without the consent of the majority. This is called the 'principle of consent'. Majority opinion in the future could be tested by referendum.

Loughgall, 8 May 1987. What was left of the police station. The clinical British Army operation at Loughgall in County Armagh marked a significant turning point in the Northern Ireland troubles. It was a huge propaganda success for the British Army (the SAS and the Det in particular), and for the British Government; by the same token it dealt a massive blow to the Provisional IRA (PIRA) and to Sinn Féin. Crucially, it eliminated eight active and highly dangerous PIRA insurgents in one fell swoop and weakened the East Tyrone brigade irreparably.

Further reading:

Lesley-Dixon, Kenneth, *Northern Ireland: The Troubles, from the Provos to the Det, 1968–1998*, Barnsley, 2018.

McKearney, Tommy, *The Provisional IRA: From Insurrection to Parliament*, Pluto Press, 2011.

Wolff, Stefan (ed.), *Peace at Last? The Impact of the Good Friday Agreement on Northern Ireland*, Berghahn Books, 2004.

Full text of the Good Friday Agreement: *https://peacemaker.un.org/ uk-ireland-good-friday98*

100

The coronavirus vaccine

2020

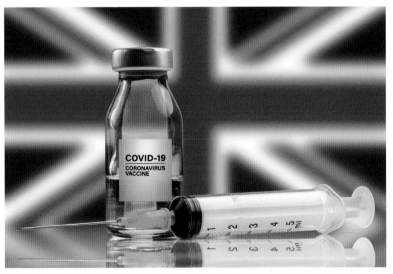

The coronavirus vaccine. The expeditious development of viable vaccines has been a truly international, global effort which involves research from many countries and demonstrates the common good that can come from international cooperation in medical science research.

COVID-19 vaccine is a vaccine intended to confer acquired immunity against severe acute respiratory syndrome coronavirus 2 (SARS-CoV-2), the virus that causes coronavirus disease 2019 (COVID-19). Before the COVID-19 pandemic, the medical and scientific community had built up a significant body of knowledge about the structure and function of coronavirus causing diseases from the 2000s, like severe acute respiratory syndrome (SARS) and Middle East respiratory syndrome (MERS). This bank of knowledge expedited the development of various vaccine platforms during early 2020. On 10 January2020, the SARS-CoV-2 genetic sequence data was shared through GISAID, and by 19 March the global pharmaceutical industry announced a major commitment to address COVID-19. The successful COVID-19 vaccines are widely credited for their role in reducing the severity and death caused by COVID-19 in the ongoing pandemic.

GISAID is a global science initiative established in 2008 that provides open-access to genomic data of influenza viruses and the coronavirus responsible for the COVID-19 pandemic. On 10 January 2020, the first whole-genome sequences of SARS-CoV-2 were made available on GISAID, which facilitated global responses to the pandemic, including the development of the first vaccines and diagnostic tests to detect SARS-CoV-2.

Many countries have implemented phased distribution plans that prioritise those at highest risk of complications: people who are immunosuppressed or have underlying health conditions, the elderly, and those at high risk of exposure and transmission, such as healthcare workers.

The biggest vaccination campaign in history is currently underway. As of 23 December 2021, 8.89 billion doses of COVID-19 vaccines have been administered worldwide across 184 countries, 115 shots for every 100 people worldwide based on official reports from national public health agencies. By December 2020, more than 10 billion vaccine doses had been pre-ordered by

Public health advertisement urging people to get vaccinated.

countries, with about half of the doses purchased by high-income countries comprising 14 per cent of the world's population.

Countries and regions with the highest incomes are getting vaccinated more than ten times faster than those with the lowest. Before March 2021, few African nations had received a single shipment of shots. By contrast, 151 doses have been administered for every 100 people in the US; Cuba leads the world with 259 doses administered per 100 people.

Globally, at the time of going to press, the latest vaccination rate is 42,428,782 doses per day, which includes 8,635,784 people getting their first shot. At this rate, it will take another five months until 75 per cent of the population have received at least one dose.

Israel was first to show that vaccines were making a difference to COVID infections. The country led the world in early vaccinations, and by February 2021 more than 84 per cent of people ages 70 and older had received two doses. COVID cases fell away while a similar pattern of vaccination and recovery was replicated across many other countries.

Such progress is always under threat – from new strains. 2021 saw two significant variants: Delta and Omicron – both highly transmissible –trigger new outbreaks. Israel saw another surge of cases, which it brought under control by offering boosters to all vaccinated people. Worldwide, unvaccinated people are more at risk than ever, leading US health officials to call it a 'pandemic of the unvaccinated'.

To date the UK have approved five vaccines for use: Novavax, Pfizer-BioNTech, Oxford-AstraZeneca, Moderna and Janssen; Janssen is one shot, the other four require two doses for maximum protection. About 32 million booster doses have been administered across the UK, with a daily average of almost 890,000 jabs at the peak.

The UK ordered more than 540 million doses of seven of the most promising vaccines, including the four so far approved for use. In addition, the Government has now signed deals to buy 114 million further doses of the Pfizer and Moderna vaccines for use in 2022 and 2023.

How did the vaccines – which satisfy stringent safety and efficacy trials – come so quickly? Vaccines that use an inactive or weakened virus that has been grown in eggs typically take more than a decade to develop. By contrast, mRNA is a molecule that can be made quickly, and research on mRNA to fight diseases was initiated decades before the COVID-19 pandemic by scientists who tested on mice. Moderna began human testing of an mRNA vaccine in 2015. Viral vector vaccines were also developed for the COVID-19 pandemic after the technology was previously cleared for Ebola for emergency use.

Severe allergic reactions are vanishingly rare. In December 2020, 1,893,360 first doses of Pfizer–BioNTech COVID-19 vaccine administration resulted in 175 cases of severe allergic reaction, of which 21 were anaphylaxis. For 4,041,396 Moderna COVID-19 vaccine dose administrations in December 2020 and January 2021, only ten cases of anaphylaxis were reported.

'Getting a third dose of either Pfizer-BioNTech's (PFE.N) or Moderna's (MRNA.O) COVID-19 vaccine offers a "significant increase" in protection against the Omicron variant in elderly people,' according to a Danish study published on 22 December 2021.

The study investigated the effectiveness of COVID-19 vaccines that use mRNA technology against the Delta variant and the new, more infectious, Omicron variant.

'Our study contributes to emerging evidence that BNT162b2 (Pfizer-BioNTech) or mRNA-1273 (Moderna) primary vaccine protection against Omicron decreases quickly over time, with booster vaccination offering a significant increase in protection,' the authors wrote. The study was conducted by researchers at Denmark's leading disease authority, Statens Serum Institut (SSI), which analysed data from three million Danes between 20 November and 12 December.

Among those who recently had their second vaccine dose, effectiveness against Omicron came out at 55.2 per cent for Pfizer-BioNTech and 36.7 per cent for Moderna, compared to unvaccinated people. That's the good news. The not so good news is that protection quickly waned over the course of five months, the researchers said.

'We see that the protection is lower and decreases faster against Omicron than against the Delta variant after a primary vaccination course,' study author Palle Valentiner-Branth said. However, a third dose of Pfizer-BioNTech's vaccine restored protection to 54.6 per cent in people aged 60 or over who had been inoculated 14 to 44 days earlier, compared to those with only two doses. The study chimes with the findings of a recent British study, which also showed a rapid decline in protection against Omicron over time and an increase following a booster with Pfizer-BioNTech's vaccine.

'In light of the exponential rise in Omicron cases, these findings highlight the need for massive rollout of vaccinations and booster vaccinations,' the researchers concluded.

On 10 December 2021, the UK Health Security Agency reported that early data indicated a 20 to 40-fold reduction in neutralising activity for Omicron from Pfizer 2-dose vaccines relative to earlier strains. However, after a booster dose (usually with an mRNA vaccine), vaccine effectiveness against symptomatic disease was at 70 to 75 per cent, and the effectiveness against severe disease was expected to be higher.

Further information at:

Chrystal, Paul, *A History of the World in 100 Pandemics, Plagues and Epidemics*, Barnsley, 2021.

Krause P.R, et al., 'SARS-CoV-2 Variants and Vaccines,' N Engl J Med. 385 (2), pp. 179–86, July 2021.

Ramsay M, ed., 'Chapter 14a: COVID-19,' *Immunisation against infectious disease*, Public Health England, 2020.